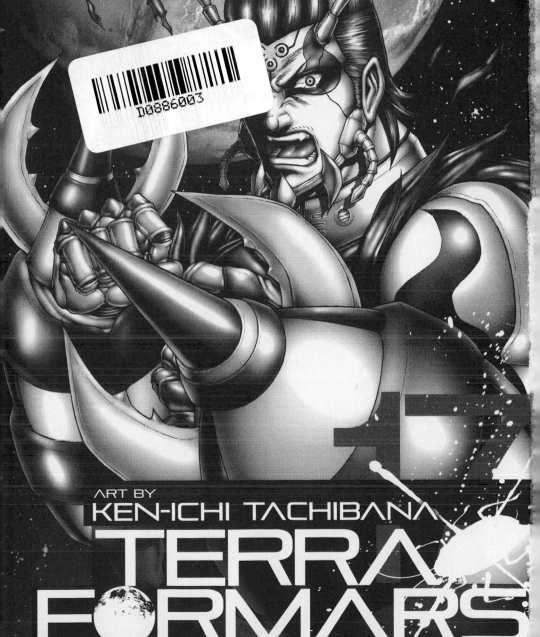

ART BY
KEN-ICHI TACHIBANA

TERRA FORMARS

STORY BY
YU SASUGA

TERRA FORMARS 17

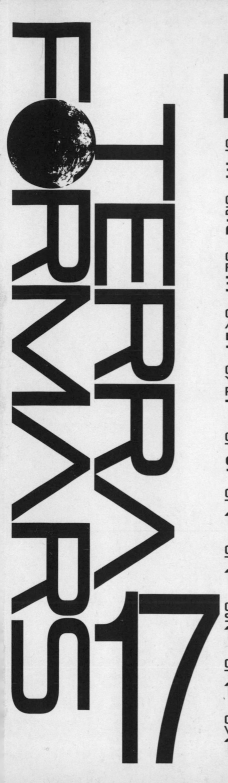

CONTENTS

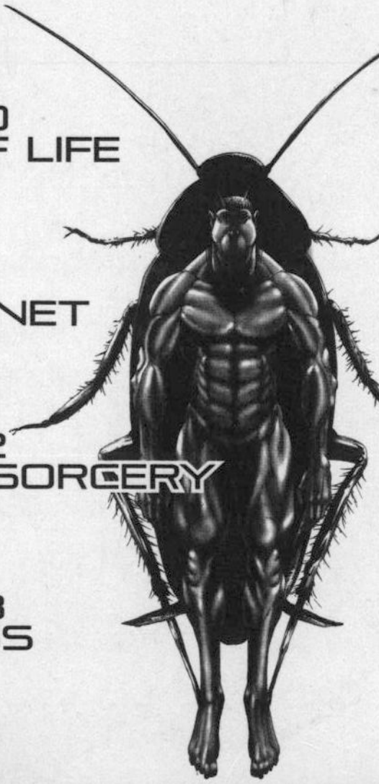

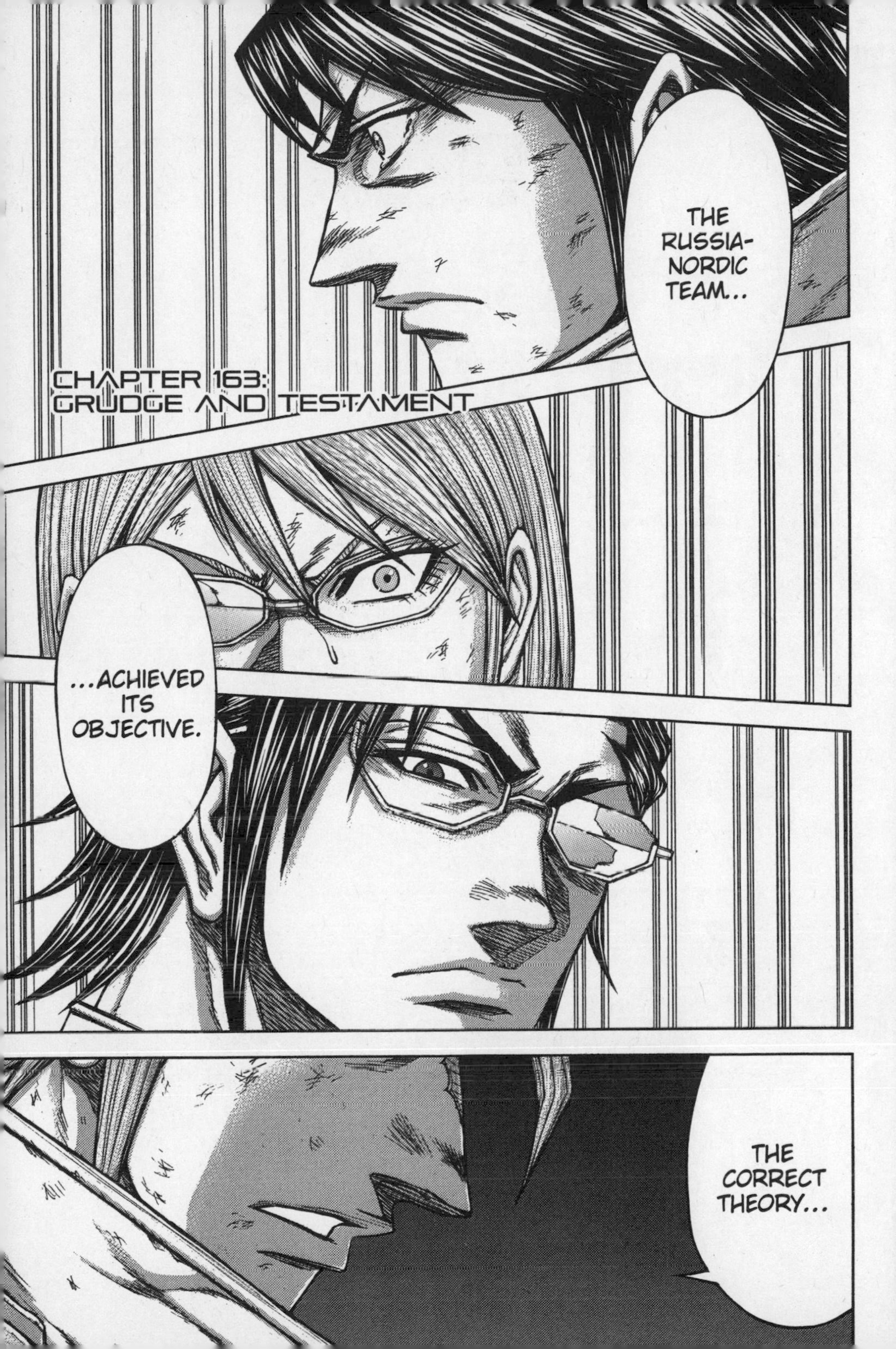
THE RUSSIA-NORDIC TEAM...
CHAPTER 163: GRUDGE AND TESTAMENT
...ACHIEVED ITS OBJECTIVE.
THE CORRECT THEORY...

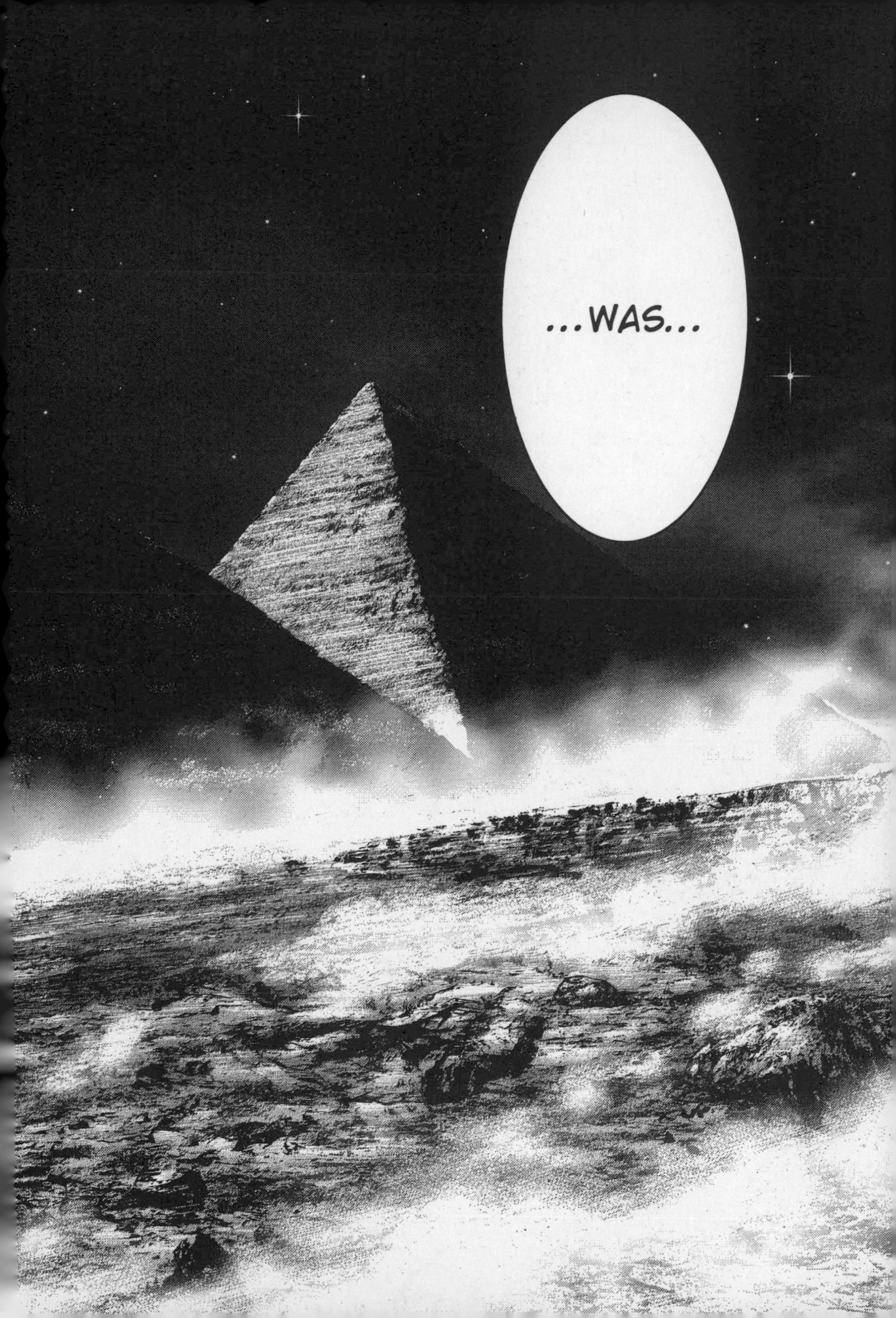
...WAS...

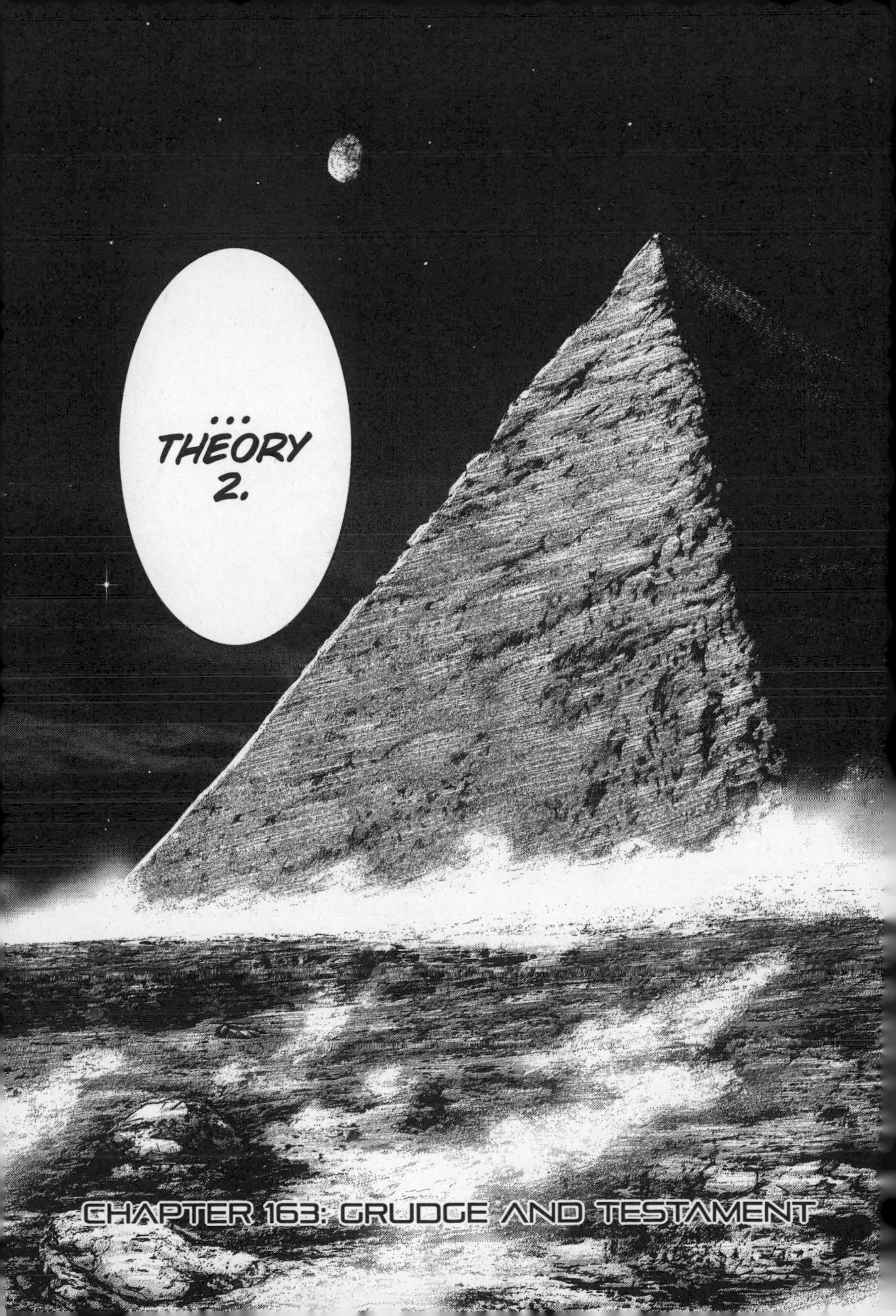
...THEORY 2.
CHAPTER 163: GRUDGE AND TESTAMENT

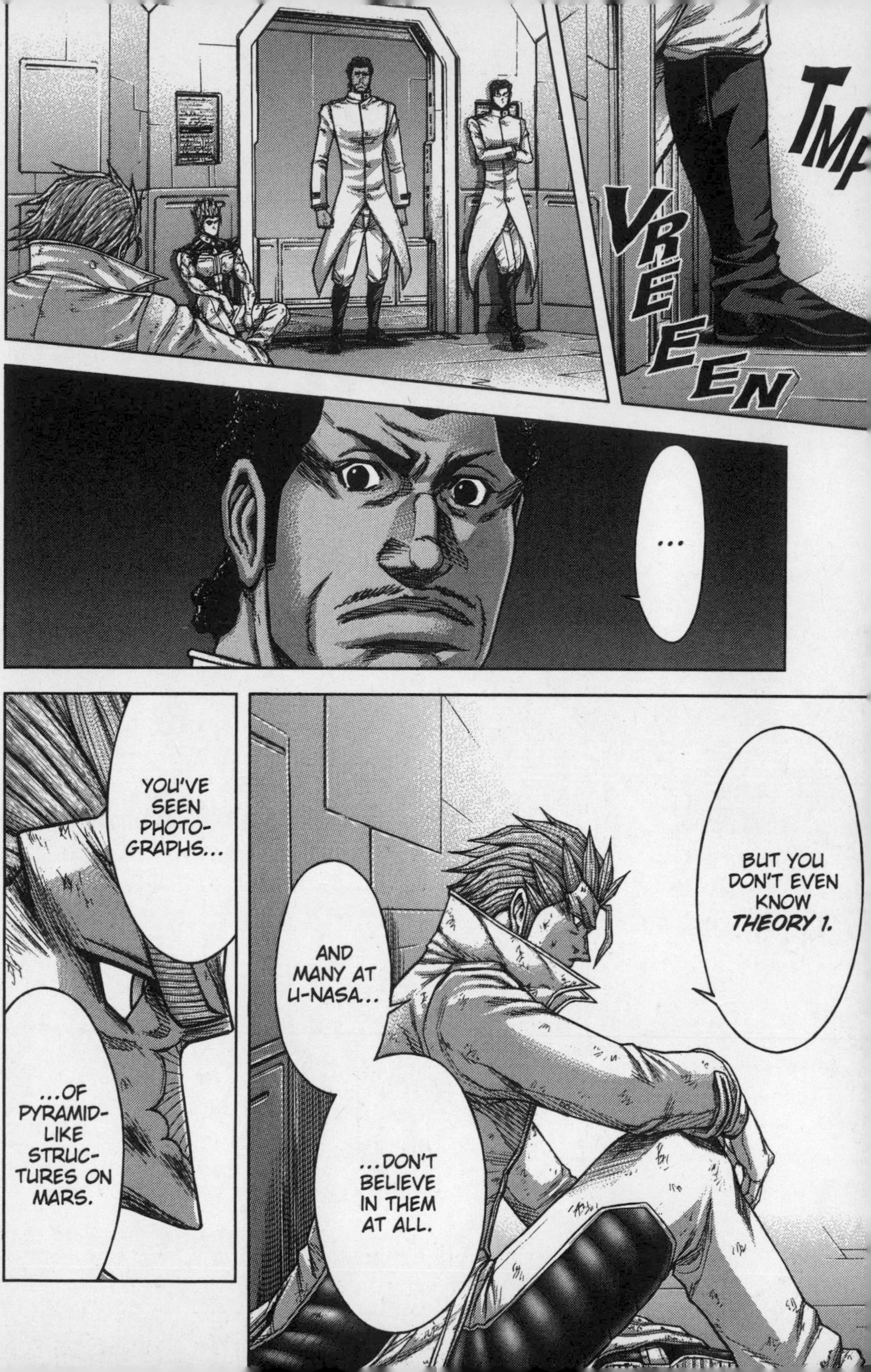
TM
VREEEEN
...
BUT YOU DON'T EVEN KNOW *THEORY 1.*
AND MANY AT U-NASA...
...DON'T BELIEVE IN THEM AT ALL.
YOU'VE SEEN PHOTO-GRAPHS...
...OF PYRAMID-LIKE STRUC-TURES ON MARS.

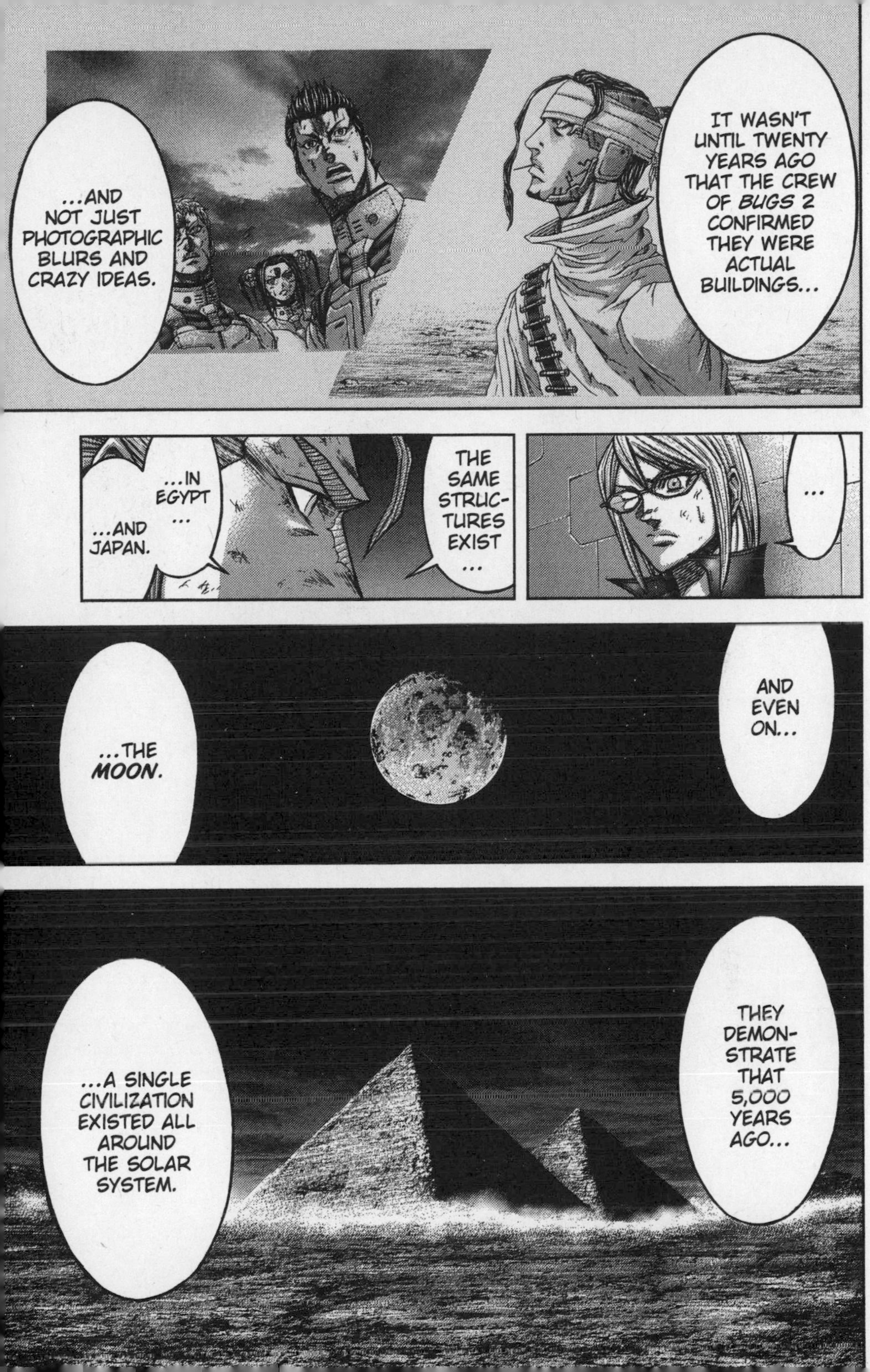
IT WASN'T UNTIL TWENTY YEARS AGO THAT THE CREW OF *BUGS 2* CONFIRMED THEY WERE ACTUAL BUILDINGS...
...AND NOT JUST PHOTOGRAPHIC BLURS AND CRAZY IDEAS.
...
THE SAME STRUCTURES EXIST...
...IN EGYPT...
...AND JAPAN.
AND EVEN ON...
...THE ***MOON***.
THEY DEMONSTRATE THAT 5,000 YEARS AGO...
...A SINGLE CIVILIZATION EXISTED ALL AROUND THE SOLAR SYSTEM.

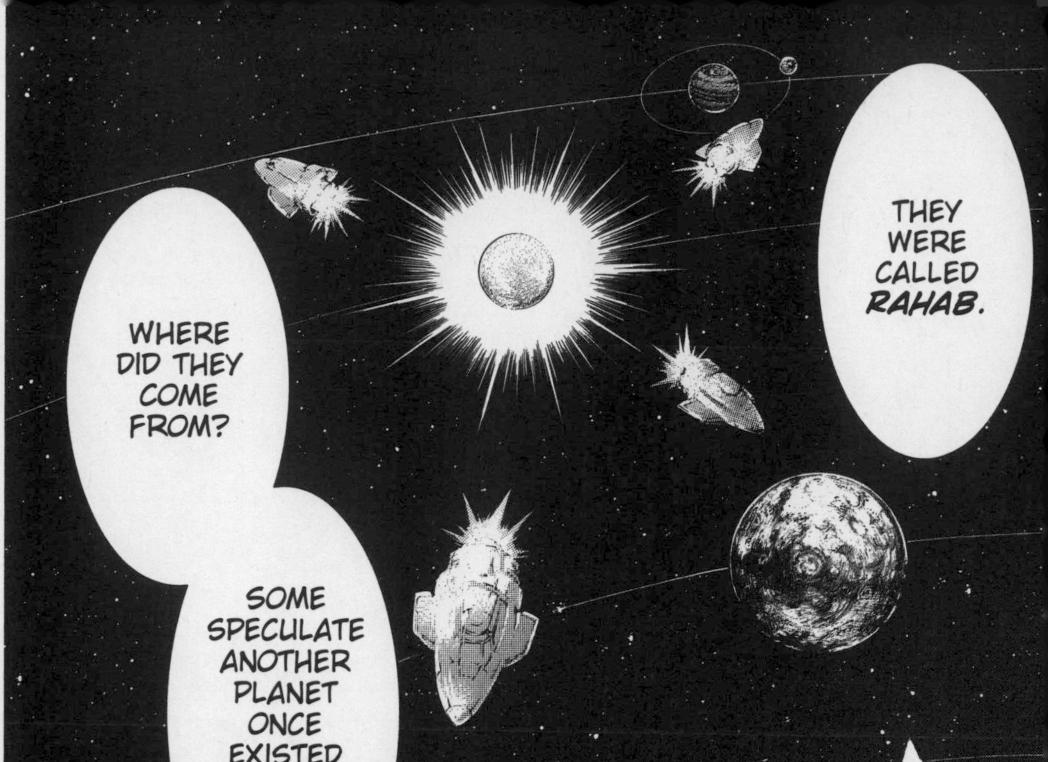
THEY WERE CALLED RAHAB.
WHERE DID THEY COME FROM?
SOME SPECULATE ANOTHER PLANET ONCE EXISTED BETWEEN MARS AND JUPITER.
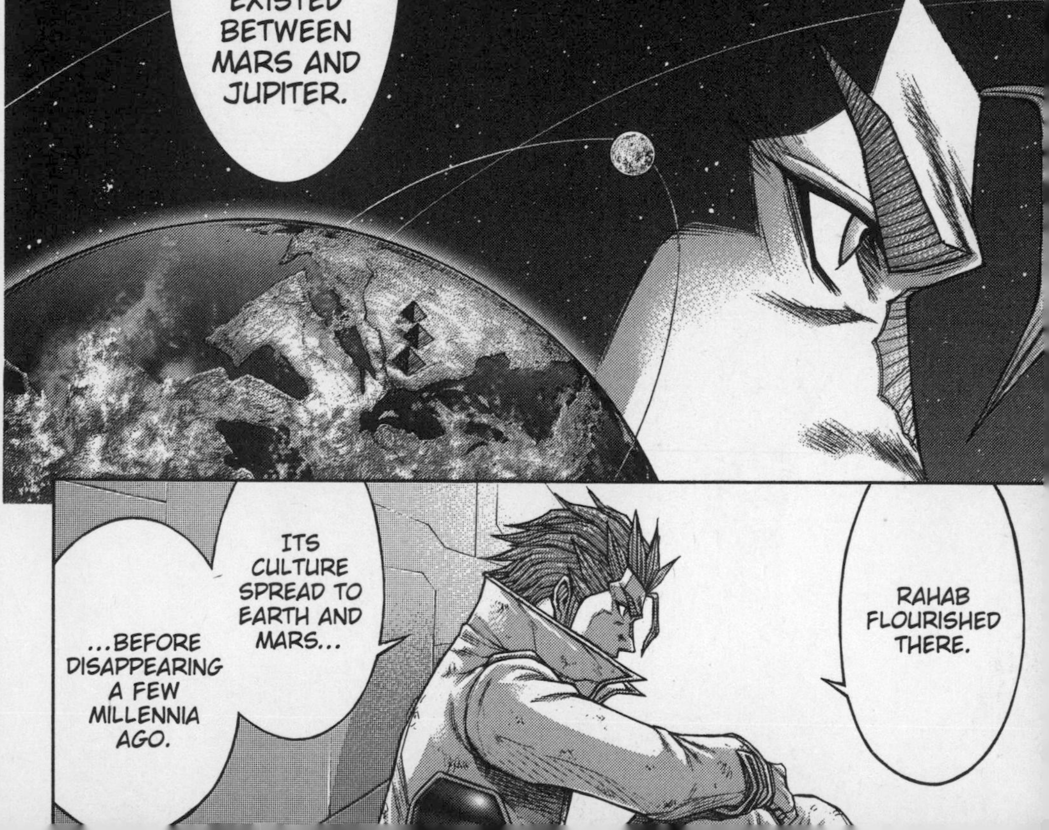
RAHAB FLOURISHED THERE.
ITS CULTURE SPREAD TO EARTH AND MARS...
...BEFORE DISAPPEARING A FEW MILLENNIA AGO.

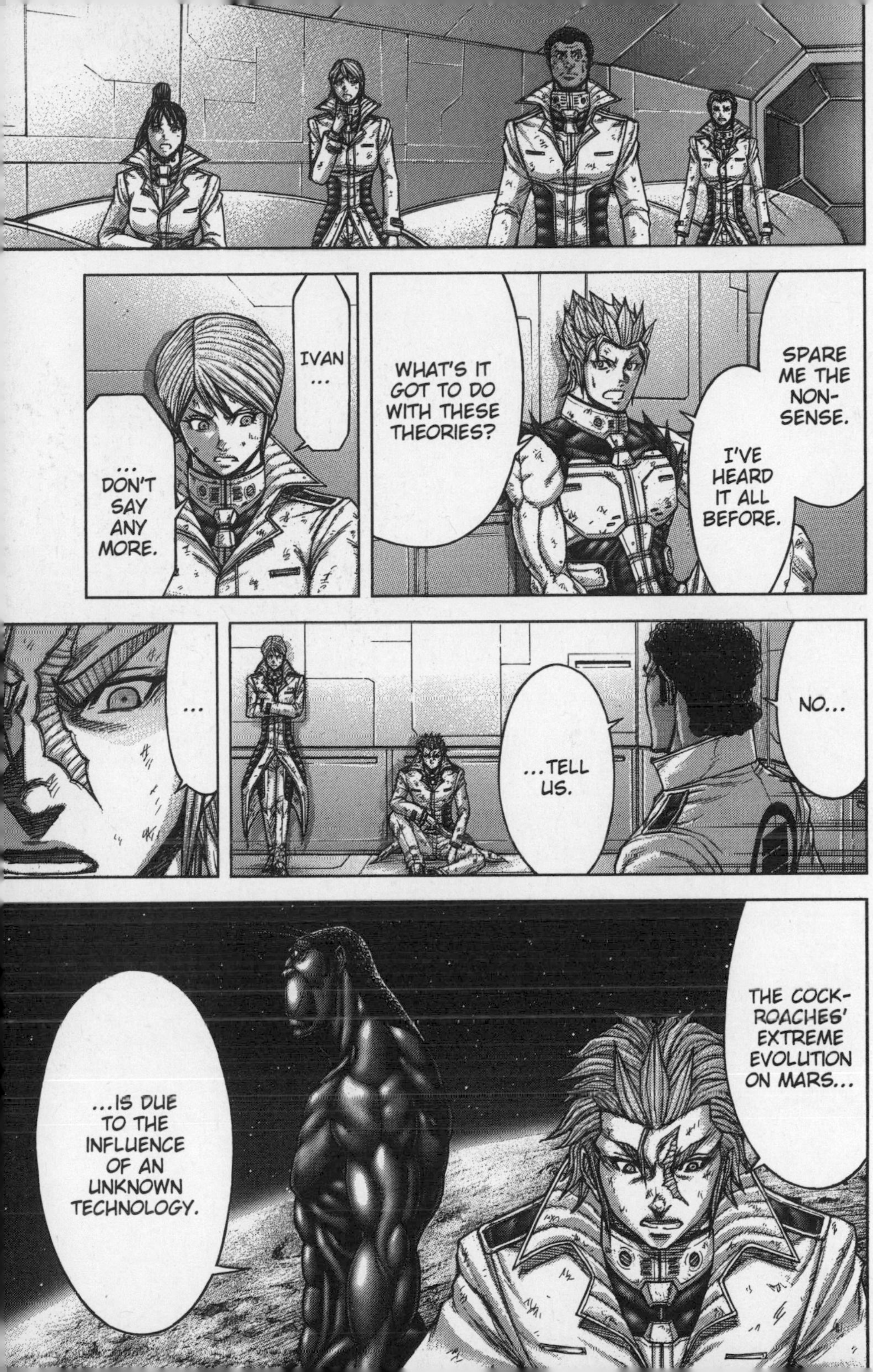
SPARE ME THE NON-SENSE. I'VE HEARD IT ALL BEFORE.
WHAT'S IT GOT TO DO WITH THESE THEORIES?
IVAN...
...DON'T SAY ANY MORE.
NO...
...TELL US.
...
THE COCK-ROACHES' EXTREME EVOLUTION ON MARS...
...IS DUE TO THE INFLUENCE OF AN UNKNOWN TECHNOLOGY.

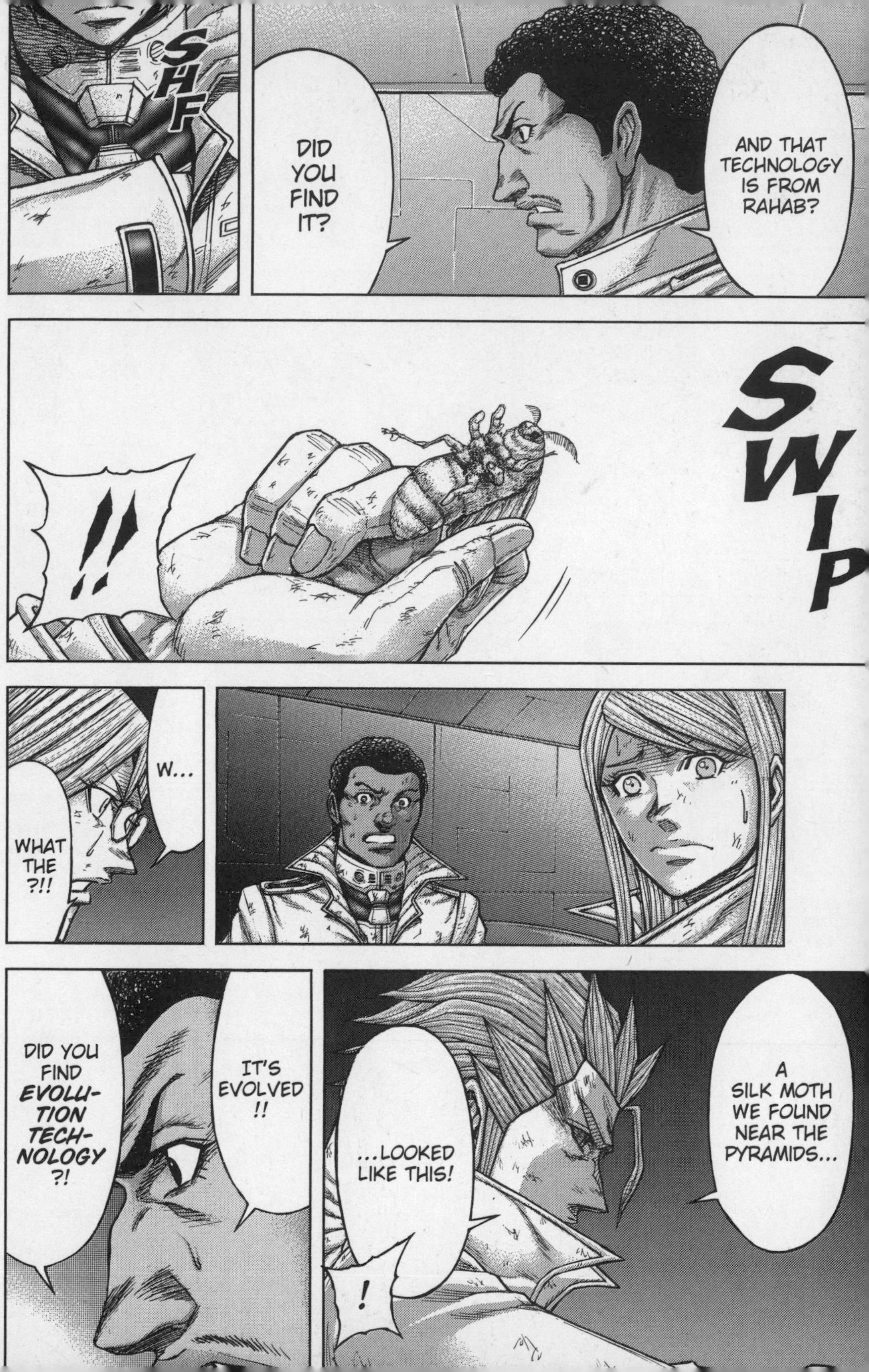
AND THAT TECHNOLOGY IS FROM RAHAB?
DID YOU FIND IT?
SHF
SWIP
!!
W...
WHAT THE ?!!
A SILK MOTH WE FOUND NEAR THE PYRAMIDS...
...LOOKED LIKE THIS!
!
IT'S EVOLVED !!
DID YOU FIND *EVOLUTION TECHNOLOGY* ?!

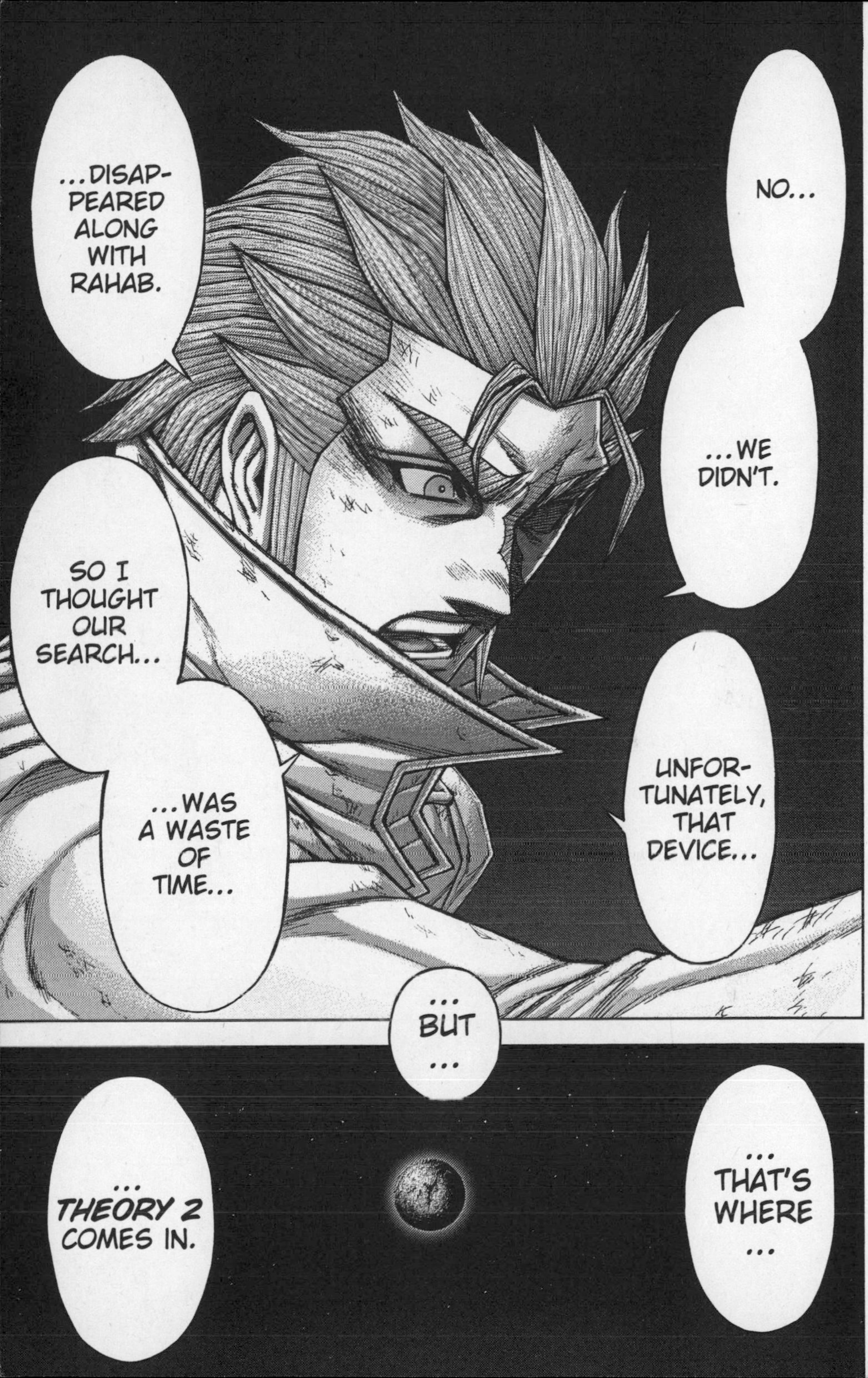
NO...
...WE DIDN'T.
UNFOR-TUNATELY, THAT DEVICE...
...DISAP-PEARED ALONG WITH RAHAB.
SO I THOUGHT OUR SEARCH...
...WAS A WASTE OF TIME...
... BUT ...
... THAT'S WHERE ...
... *THEORY 2* COMES IN.

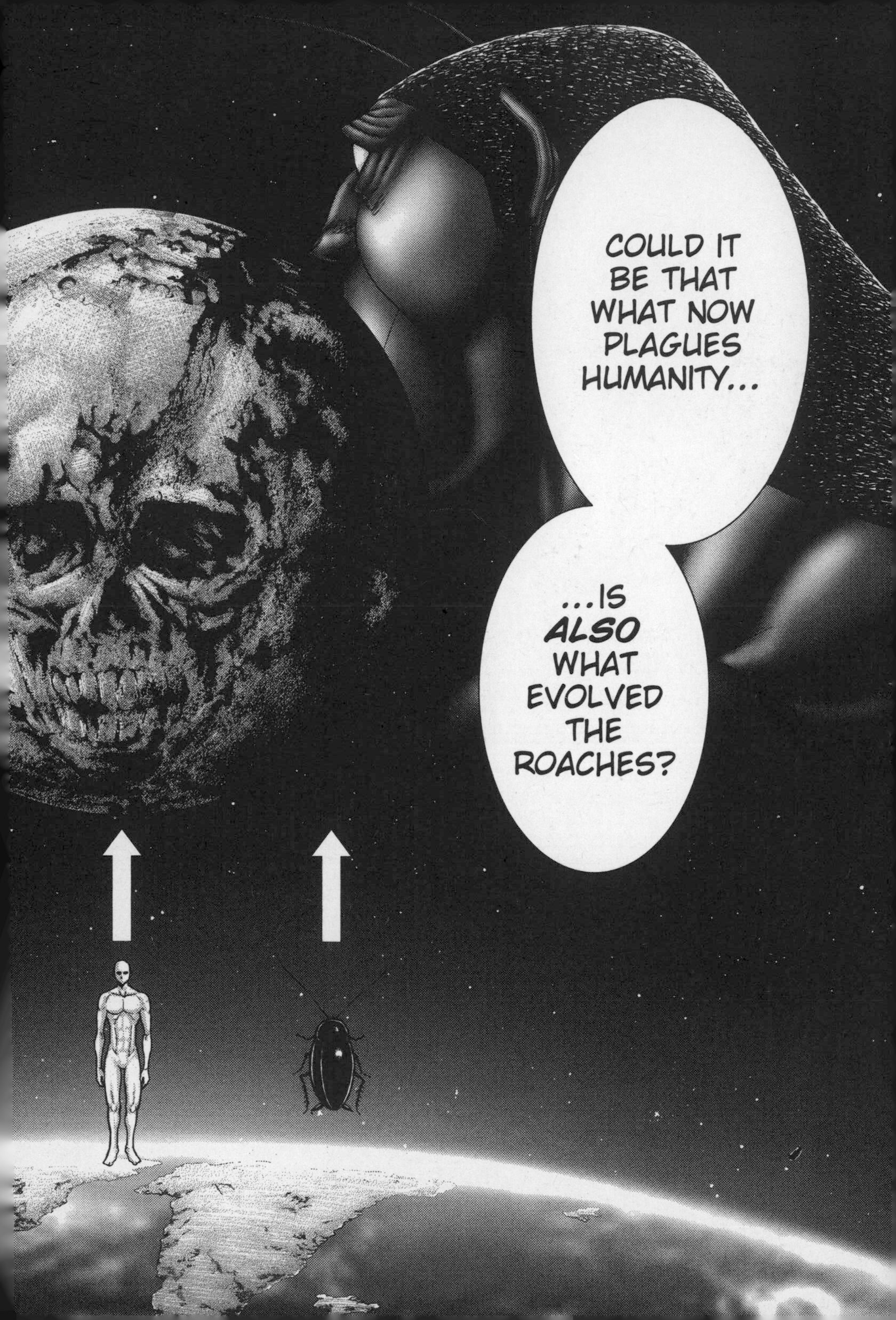
COULD IT BE THAT WHAT NOW PLAGUES HUMANITY...
...IS ALSO WHAT EVOLVED THE ROACHES?

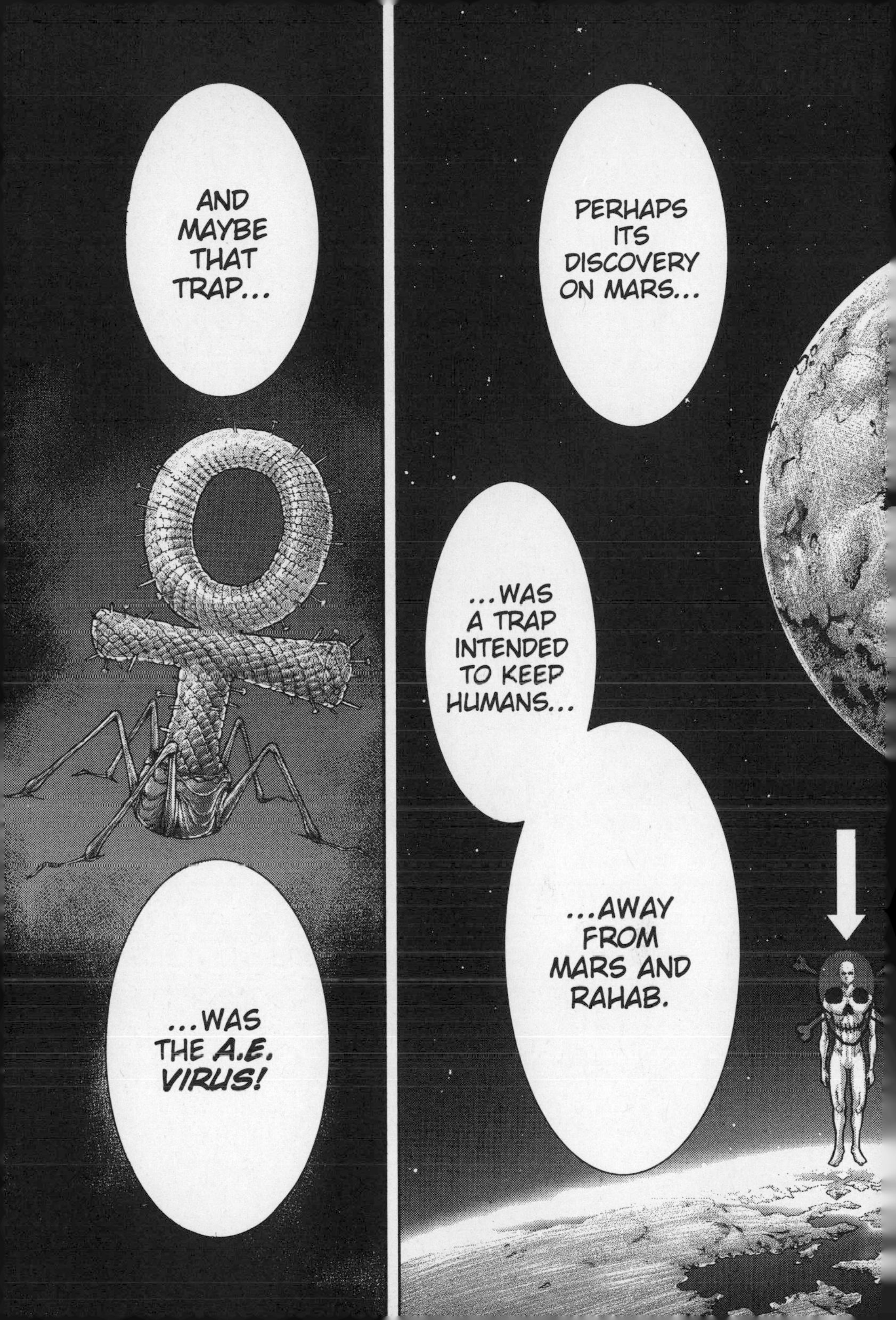
PERHAPS ITS DISCOVERY ON MARS...
...WAS A TRAP INTENDED TO KEEP HUMANS...
...AWAY FROM MARS AND RAHAB.
AND MAYBE THAT TRAP...
...WAS THE *A.E. VIRUS!*

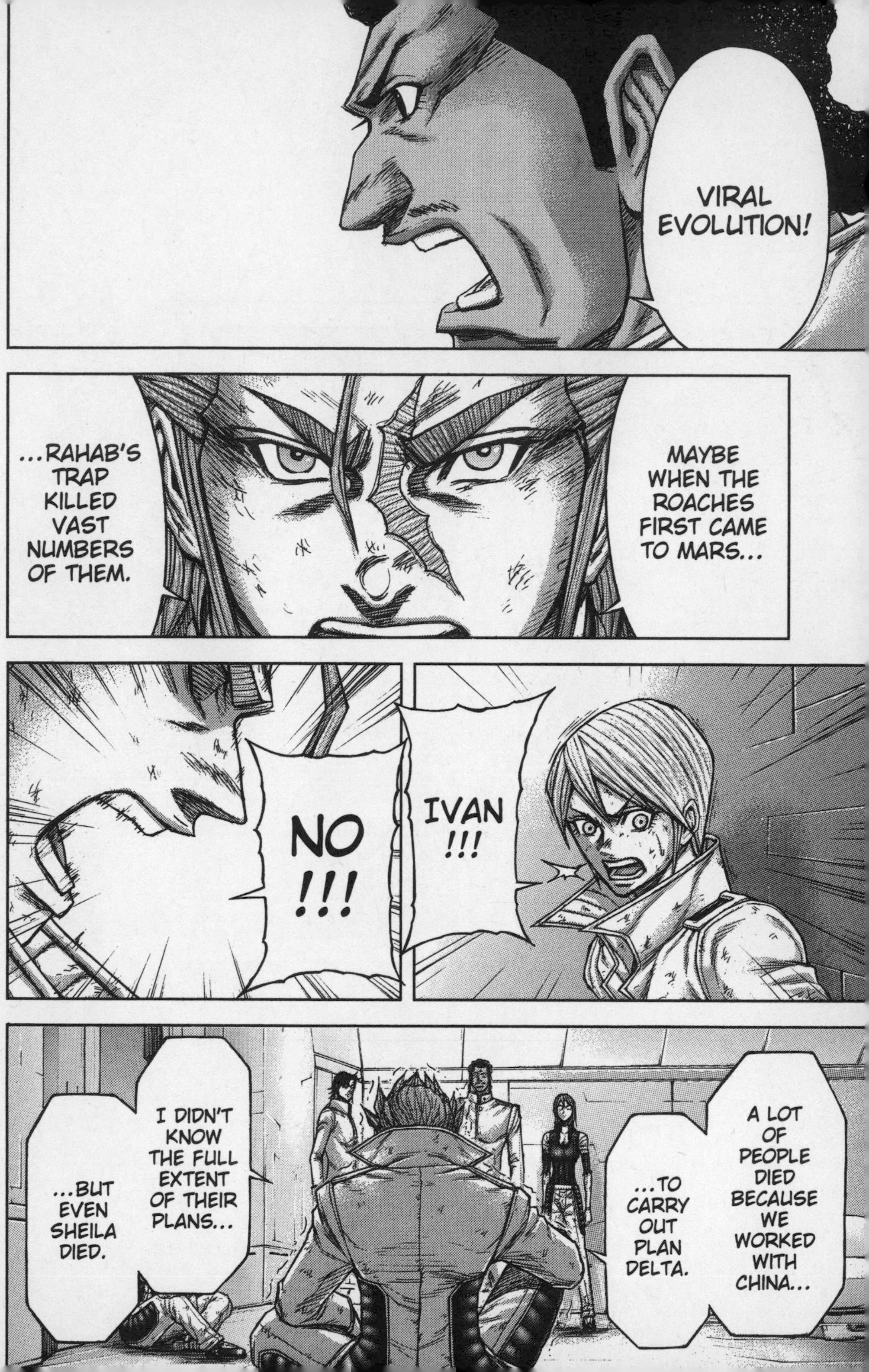
VIRAL EVOLUTION!
MAYBE WHEN THE ROACHES FIRST CAME TO MARS...
...RAHAB'S TRAP KILLED VAST NUMBERS OF THEM.
IVAN!!!
NO!!!
A LOT OF PEOPLE DIED BECAUSE WE WORKED WITH CHINA...
...TO CARRY OUT PLAN DELTA.
I DIDN'T KNOW THE FULL EXTENT OF THEIR PLANS...
...BUT EVEN SHEILA DIED.

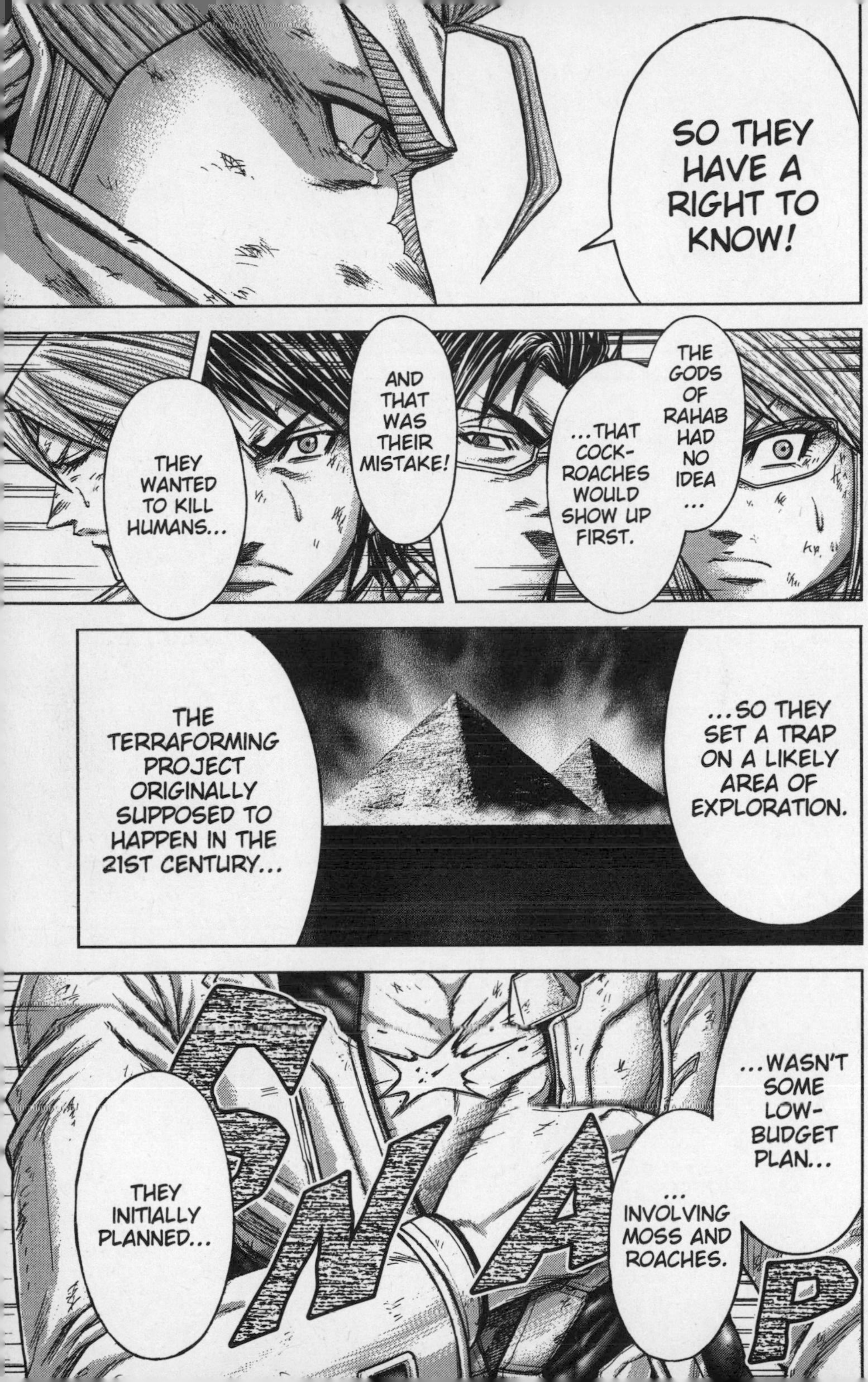
SO THEY HAVE A RIGHT TO KNOW!
THE GODS OF RAHAB HAD NO IDEA ...
...THAT COCK-ROACHES WOULD SHOW UP FIRST.
AND THAT WAS THEIR MISTAKE!
THEY WANTED TO KILL HUMANS...
...SO THEY SET A TRAP ON A LIKELY AREA OF EXPLORATION.
THE TERRAFORMING PROJECT ORIGINALLY SUPPOSED TO HAPPEN IN THE 21ST CENTURY...
...WASN'T SOME LOW-BUDGET PLAN...
...INVOLVING MOSS AND ROACHES.
SNAP
THEY INITIALLY PLANNED...

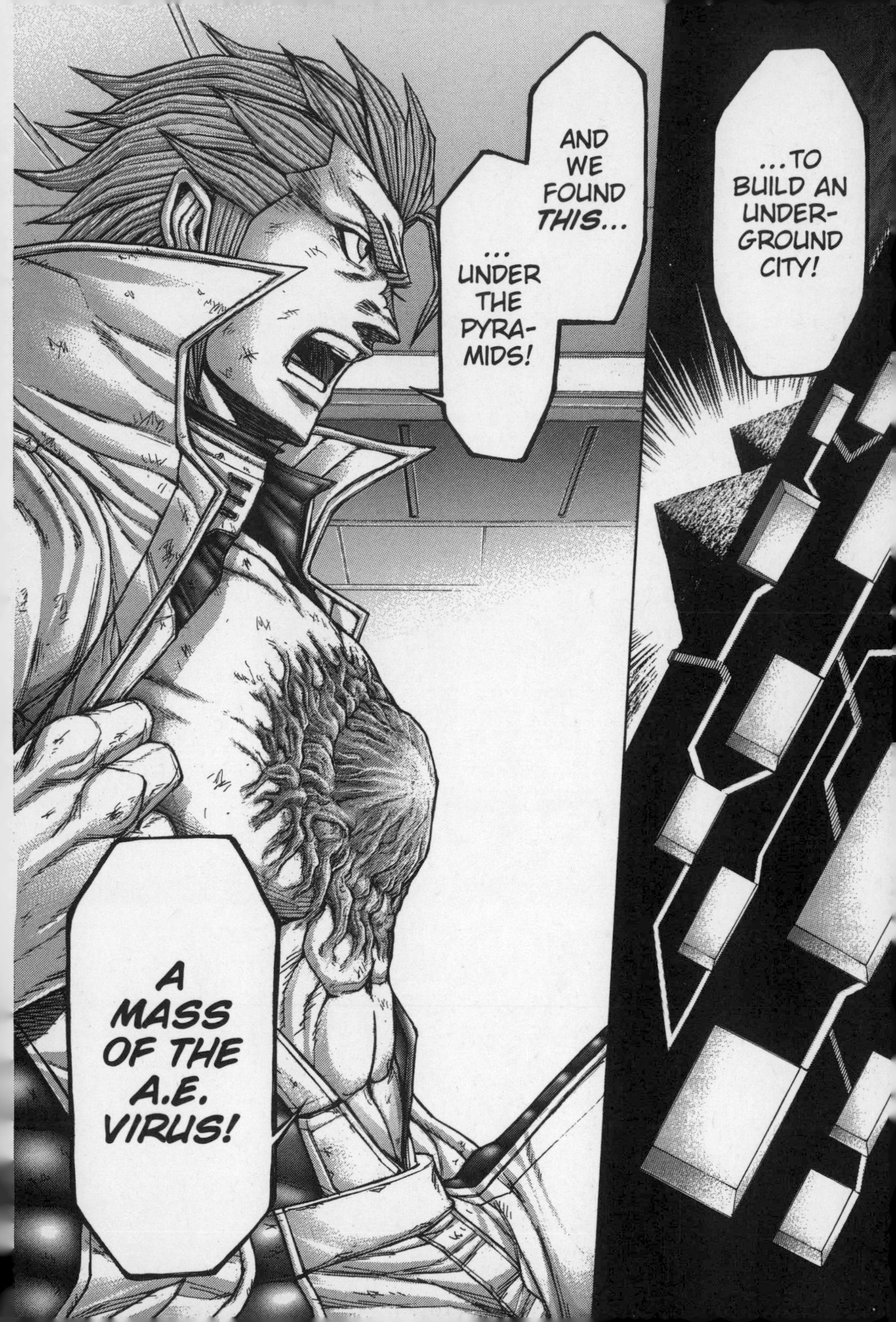
...TO BUILD AN UNDER-GROUND CITY!
AND WE FOUND THIS...
...UNDER THE PYRA-MIDS!
A MASS OF THE A.E. VIRUS!

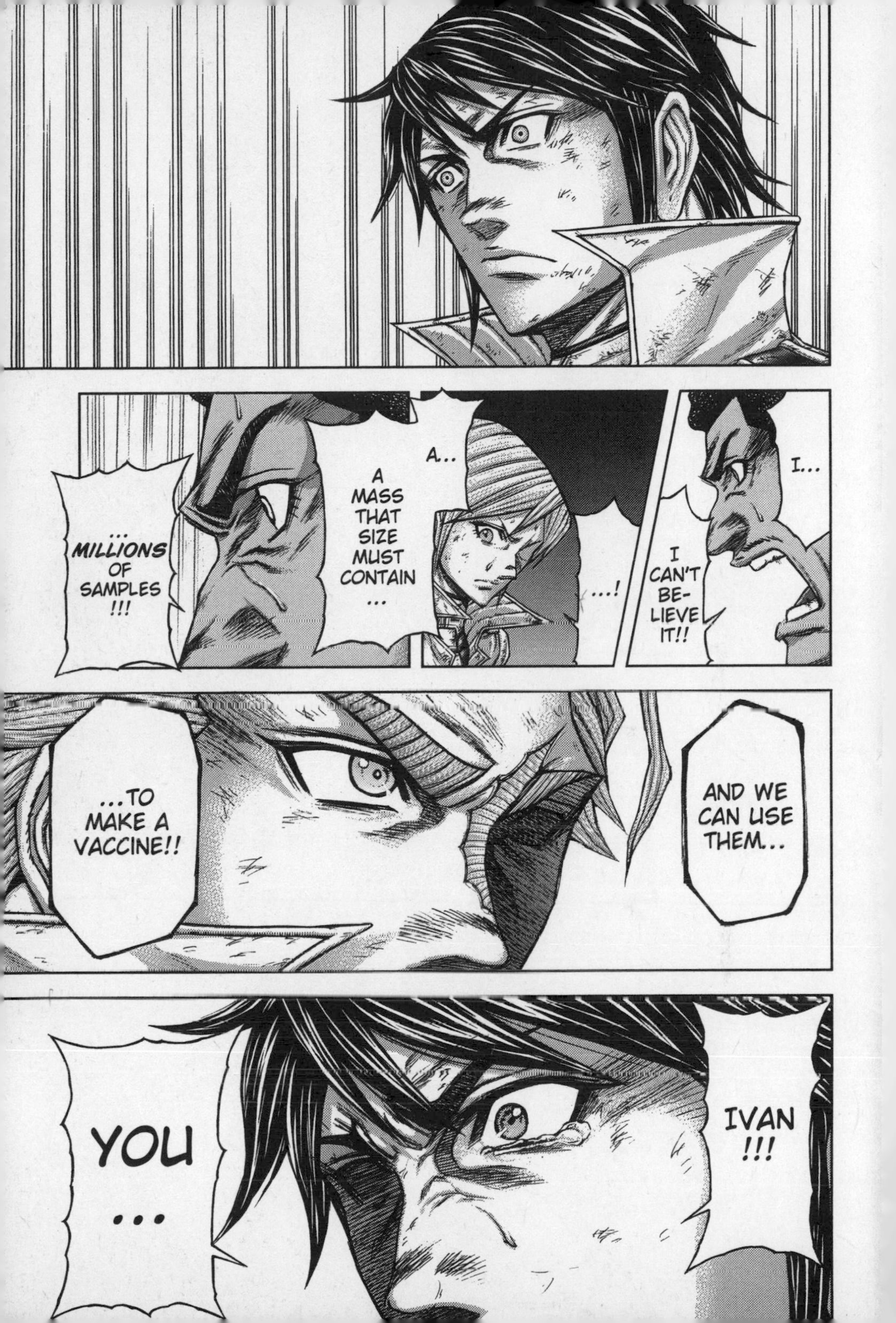
I...
I CAN'T BE-LIEVE IT!!
A...
A MASS THAT SIZE MUST CONTAIN...
...!
...MILLIONS OF SAMPLES!!!
AND WE CAN USE THEM...
...TO MAKE A VACCINE!!
IVAN!!!
YOU...

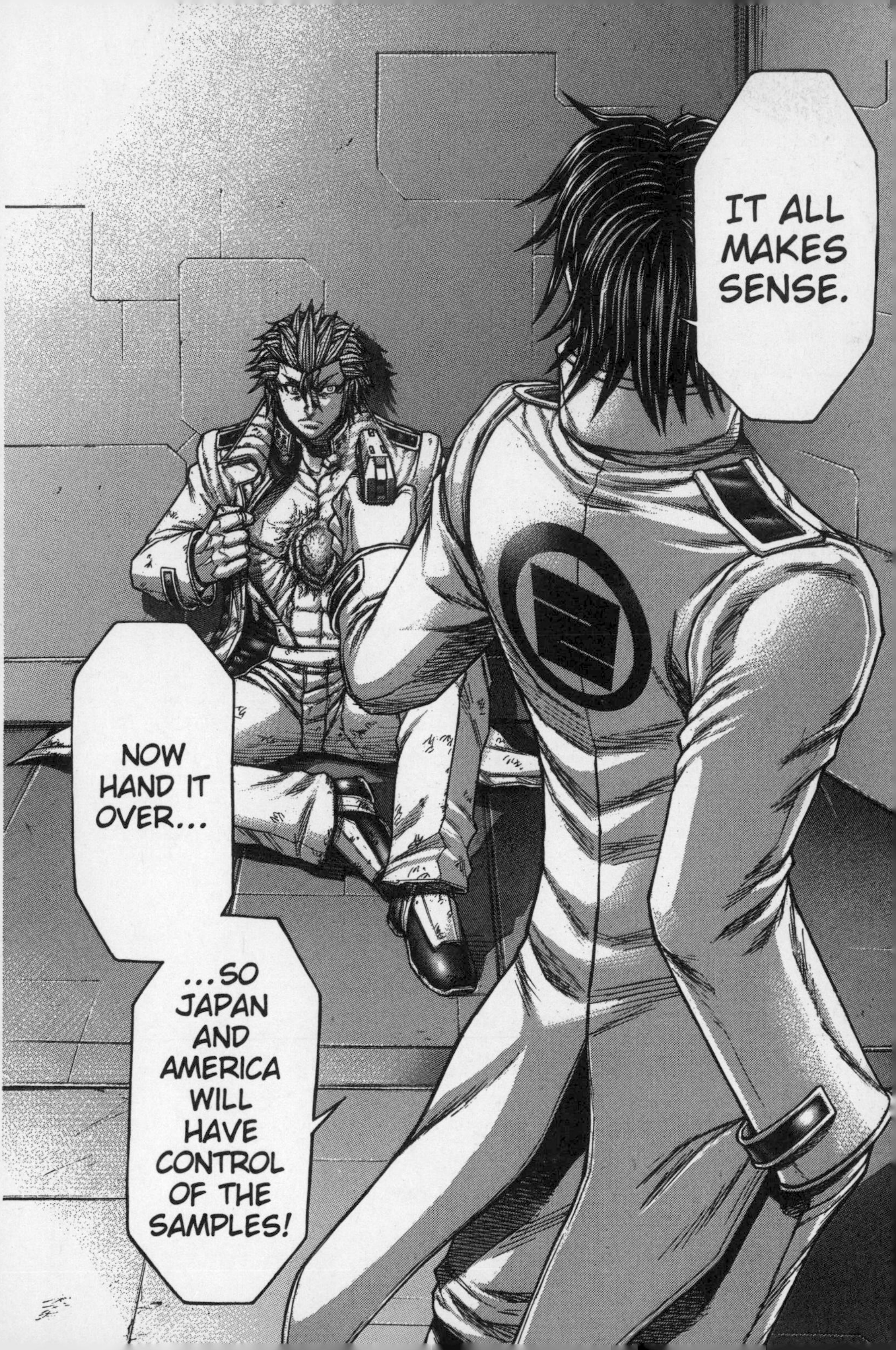
IT ALL MAKES SENSE.
NOW HAND IT OVER...
...SO JAPAN AND AMERICA WILL HAVE CONTROL OF THE SAMPLES!

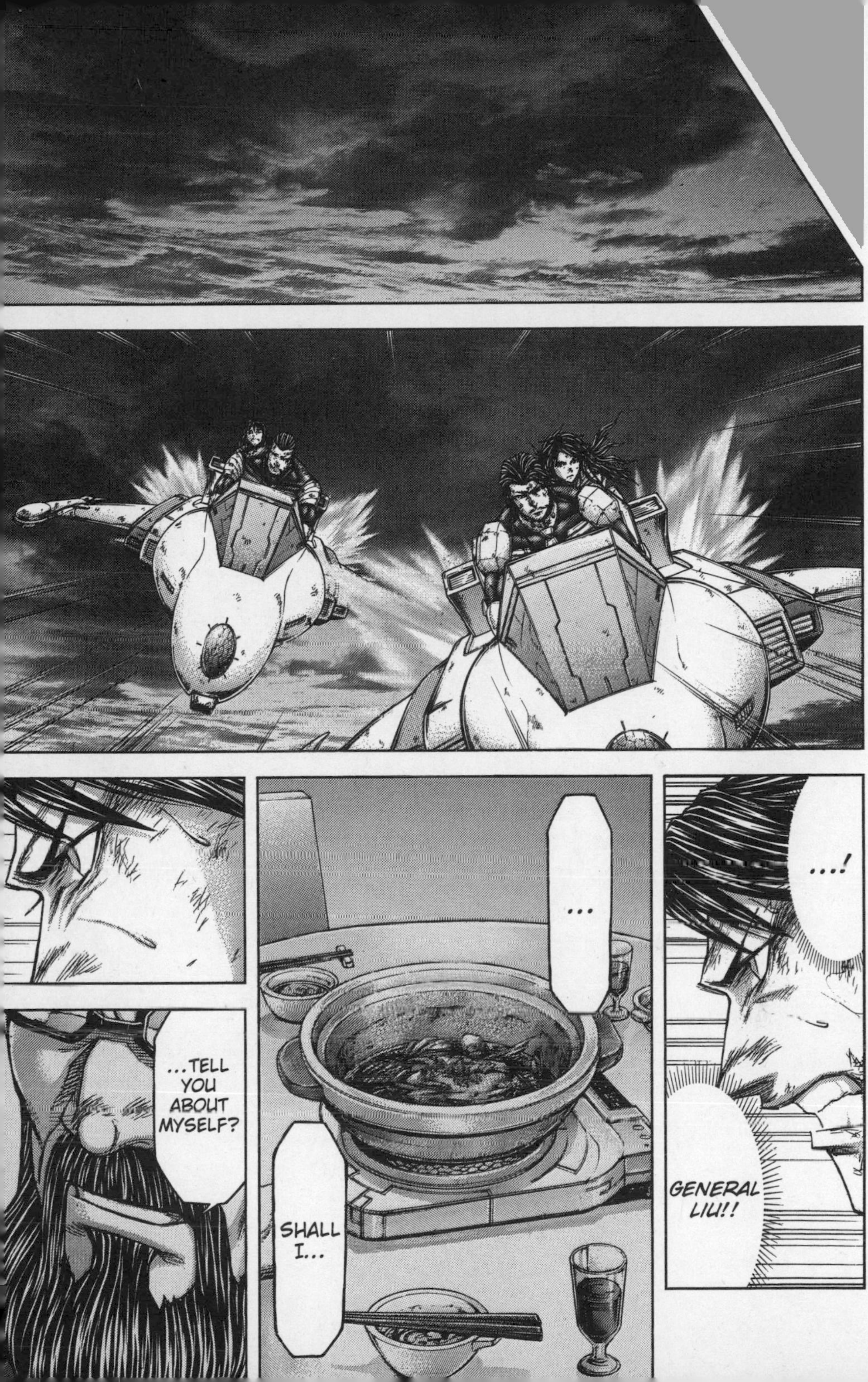
...!
GENERAL LIU!!
...
SHALL I...
...TELL YOU ABOUT MYSELF?

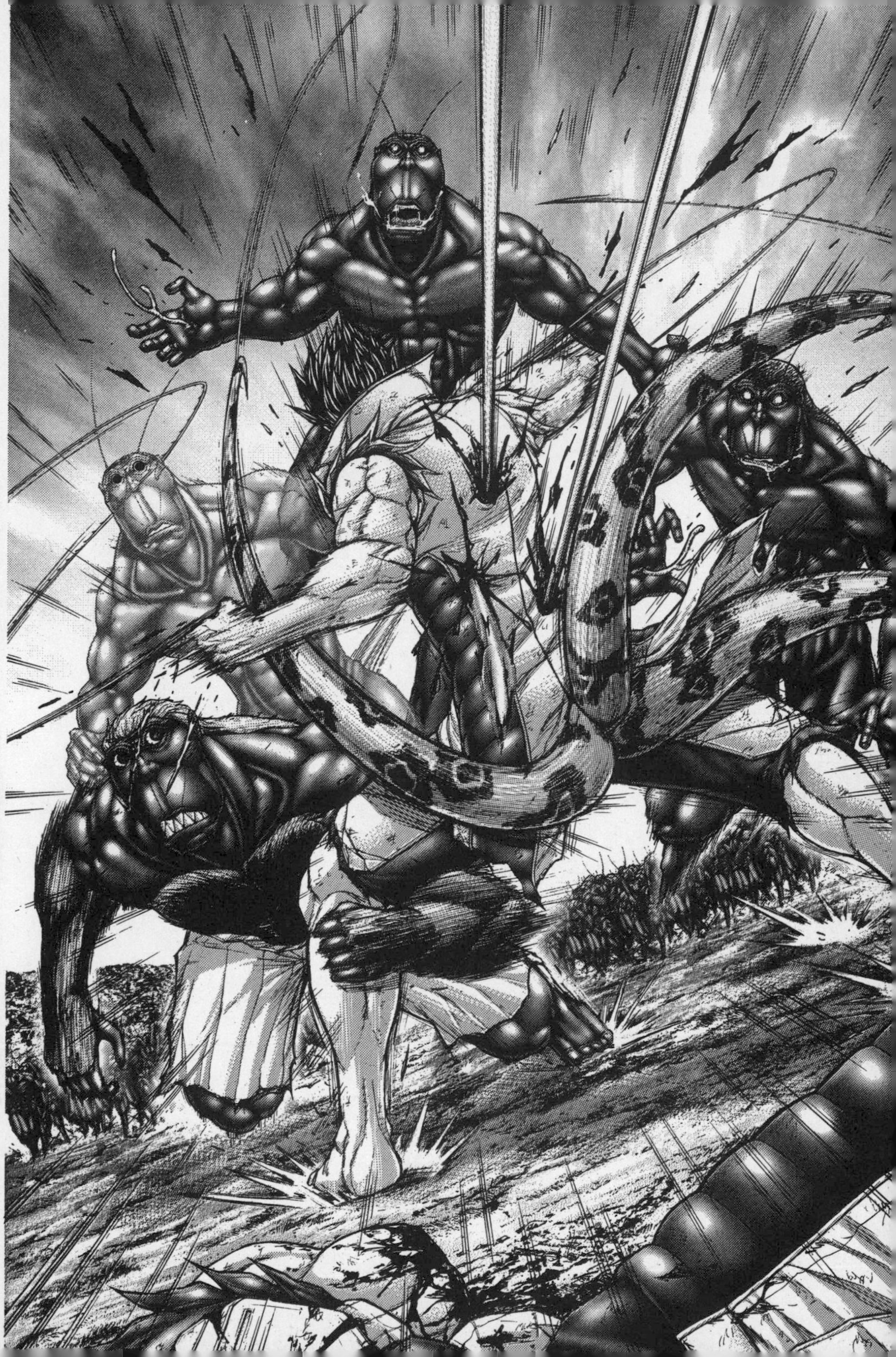

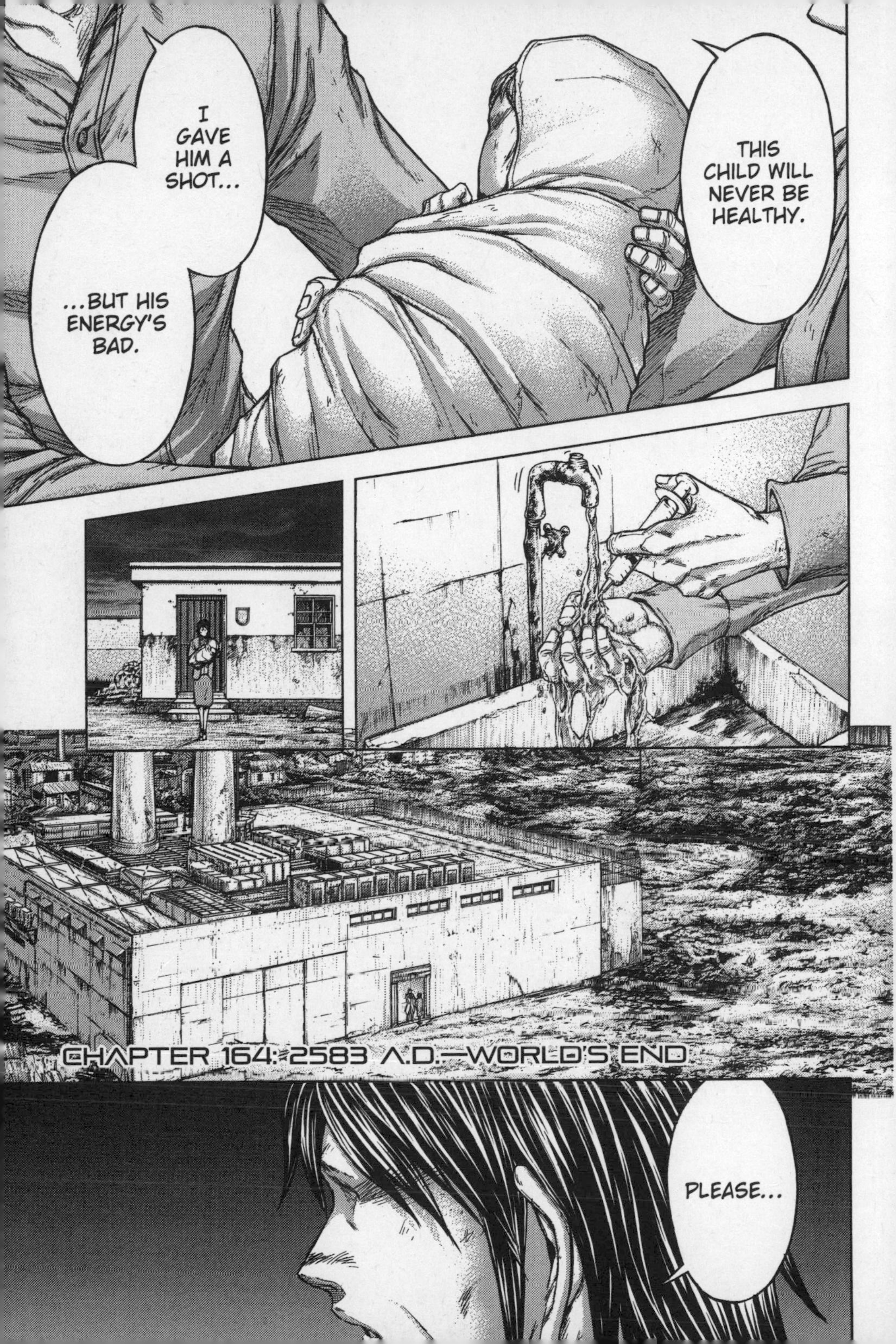
THIS CHILD WILL NEVER BE HEALTHY.
I GAVE HIM A SHOT...
...BUT HIS ENERGY'S BAD.
CHAPTER 164: 2583 A.D.—WORLD'S END
PLEASE...

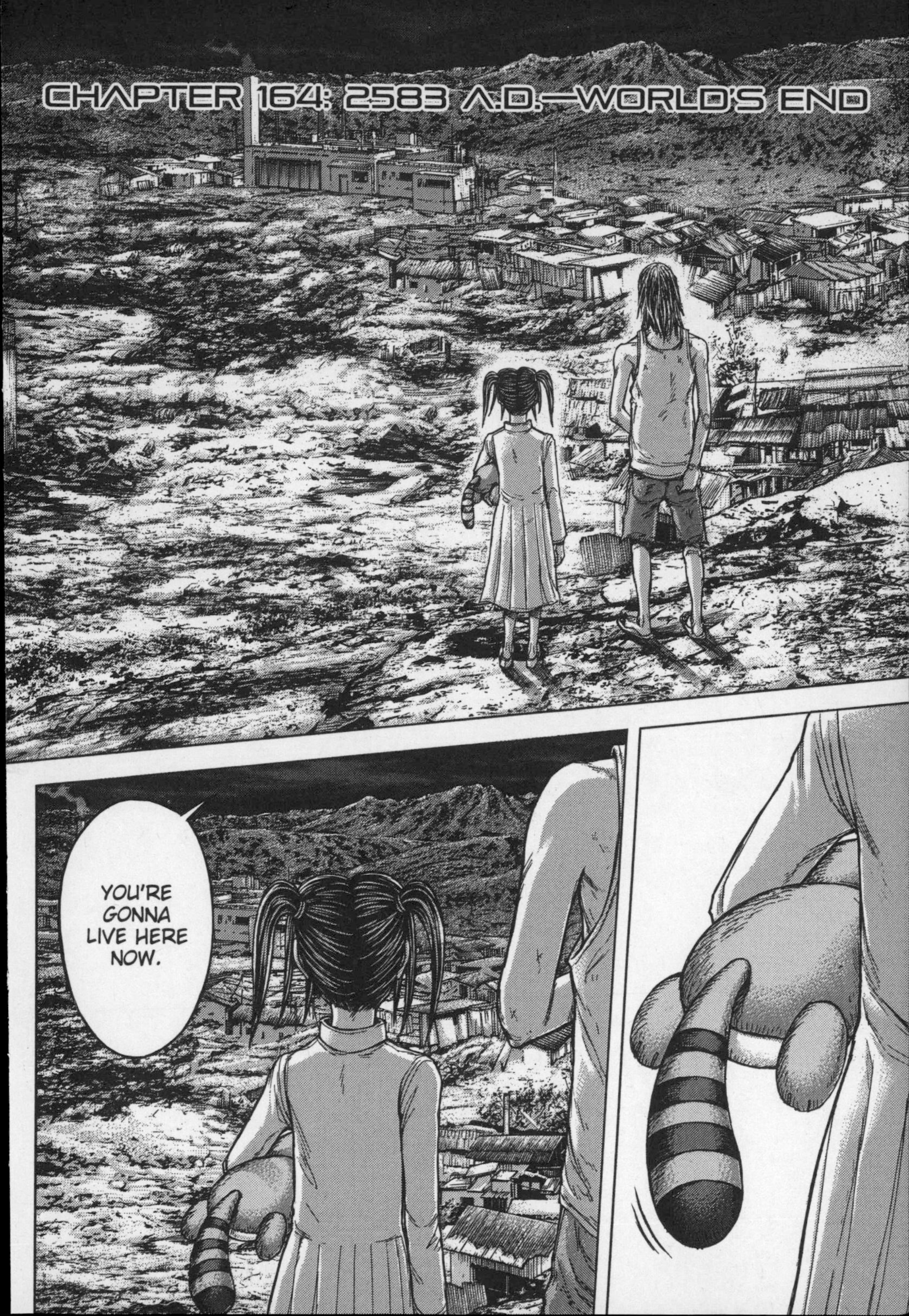
CHAPTER 164: 2583 A.D.—WORLD'S END
YOU'RE GONNA LIVE HERE NOW.

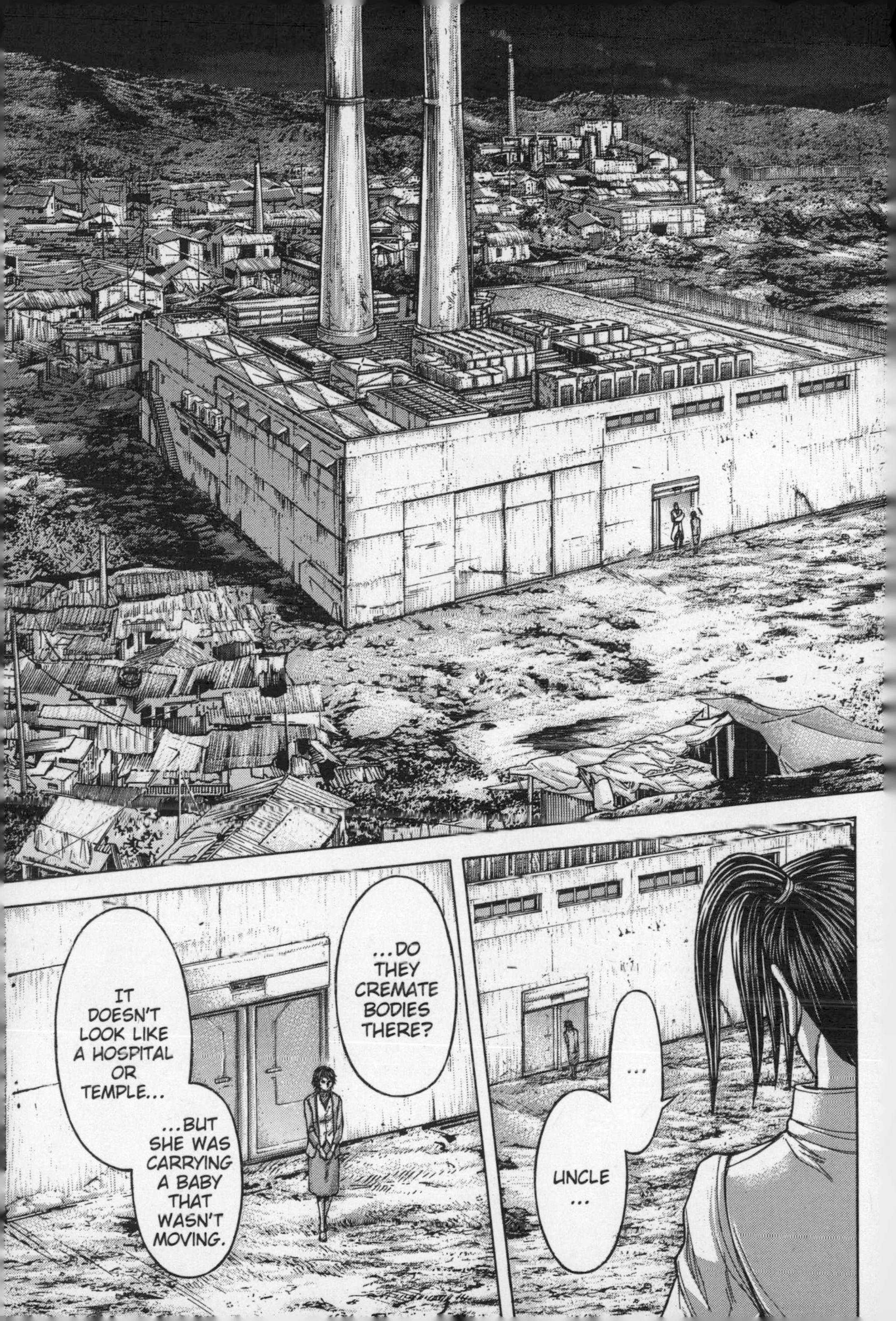
...
UNCLE ...
...DO THEY CREMATE BODIES THERE?
IT DOESN'T LOOK LIKE A HOSPITAL OR TEMPLE...
...BUT SHE WAS CARRYING A BABY THAT WASN'T MOVING.

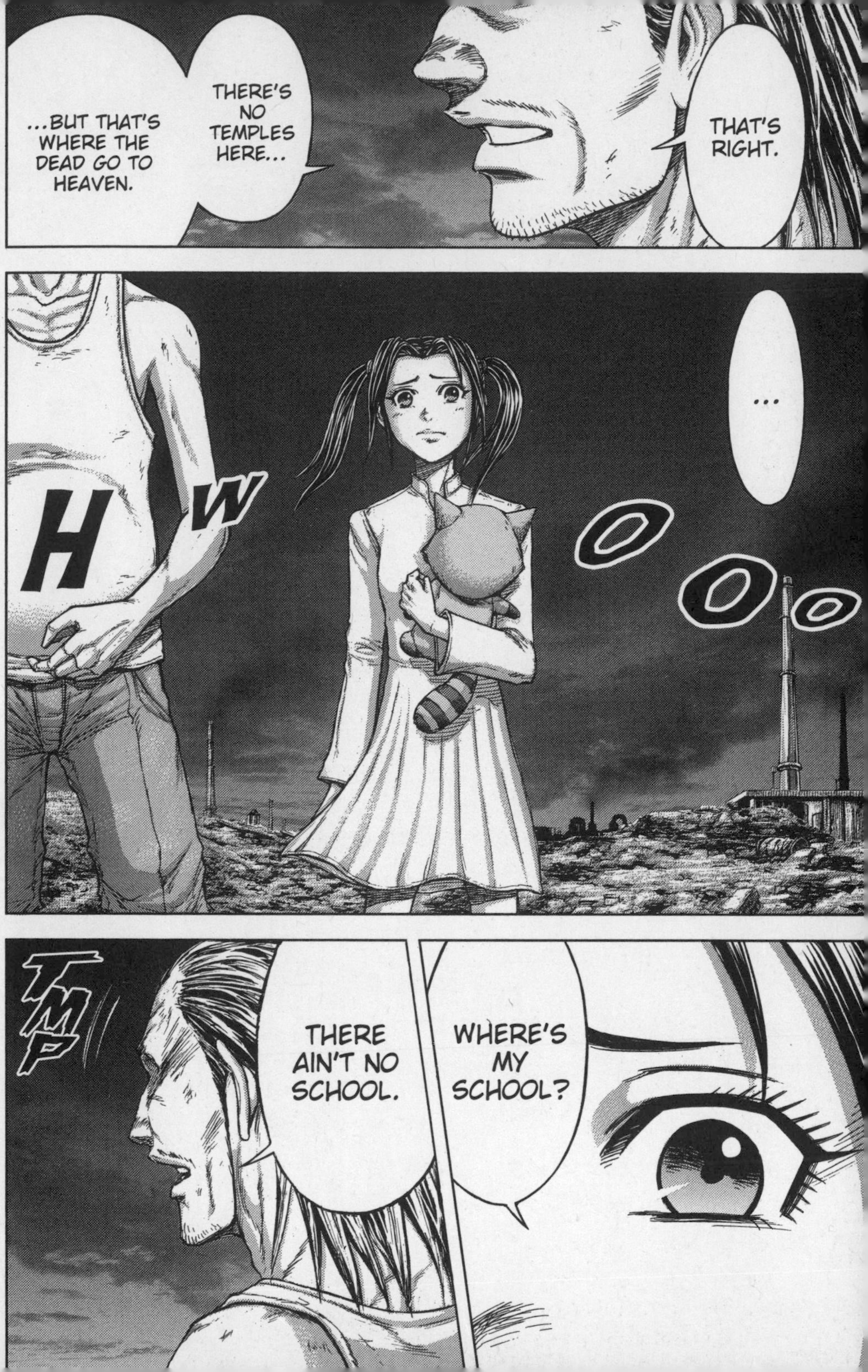
THAT'S RIGHT.
THERE'S NO TEMPLES HERE...
...BUT THAT'S WHERE THE DEAD GO TO HEAVEN.
...
HWOOO
WHERE'S MY SCHOOL?
THERE AIN'T NO SCHOOL.
TMP

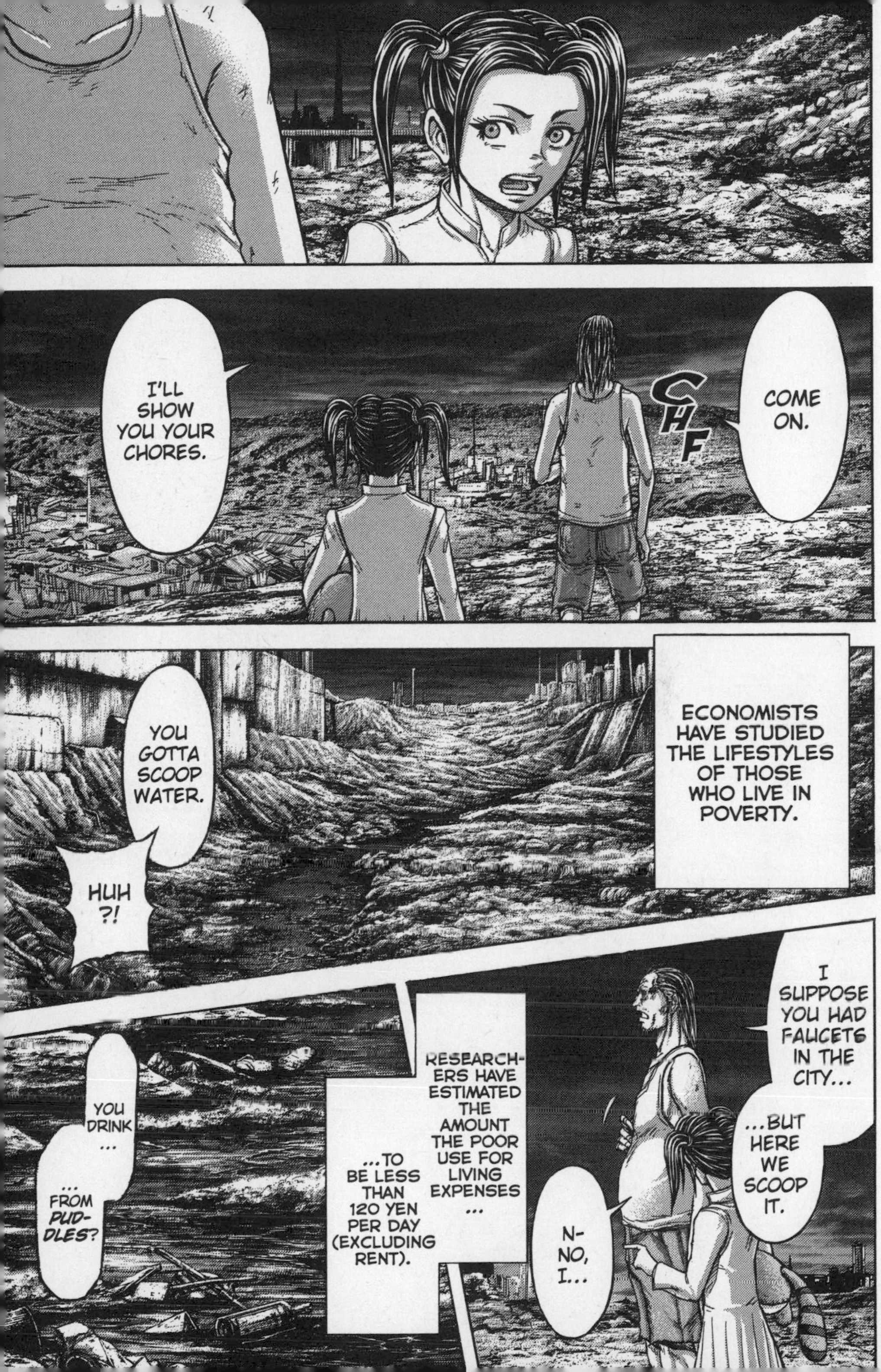
COME ON.
CHF
I'LL SHOW YOU YOUR CHORES.
ECONOMISTS HAVE STUDIED THE LIFESTYLES OF THOSE WHO LIVE IN POVERTY.
YOU GOTTA SCOOP WATER.
HUH?!
I SUPPOSE YOU HAD FAUCETS IN THE CITY...
...BUT HERE WE SCOOP IT.
N-NO, I...
RESEARCHERS HAVE ESTIMATED THE AMOUNT THE POOR USE FOR LIVING EXPENSES...
...TO BE LESS THAN 120 YEN PER DAY (EXCLUDING RENT).
YOU DRINK...
...FROM PUDDLES?

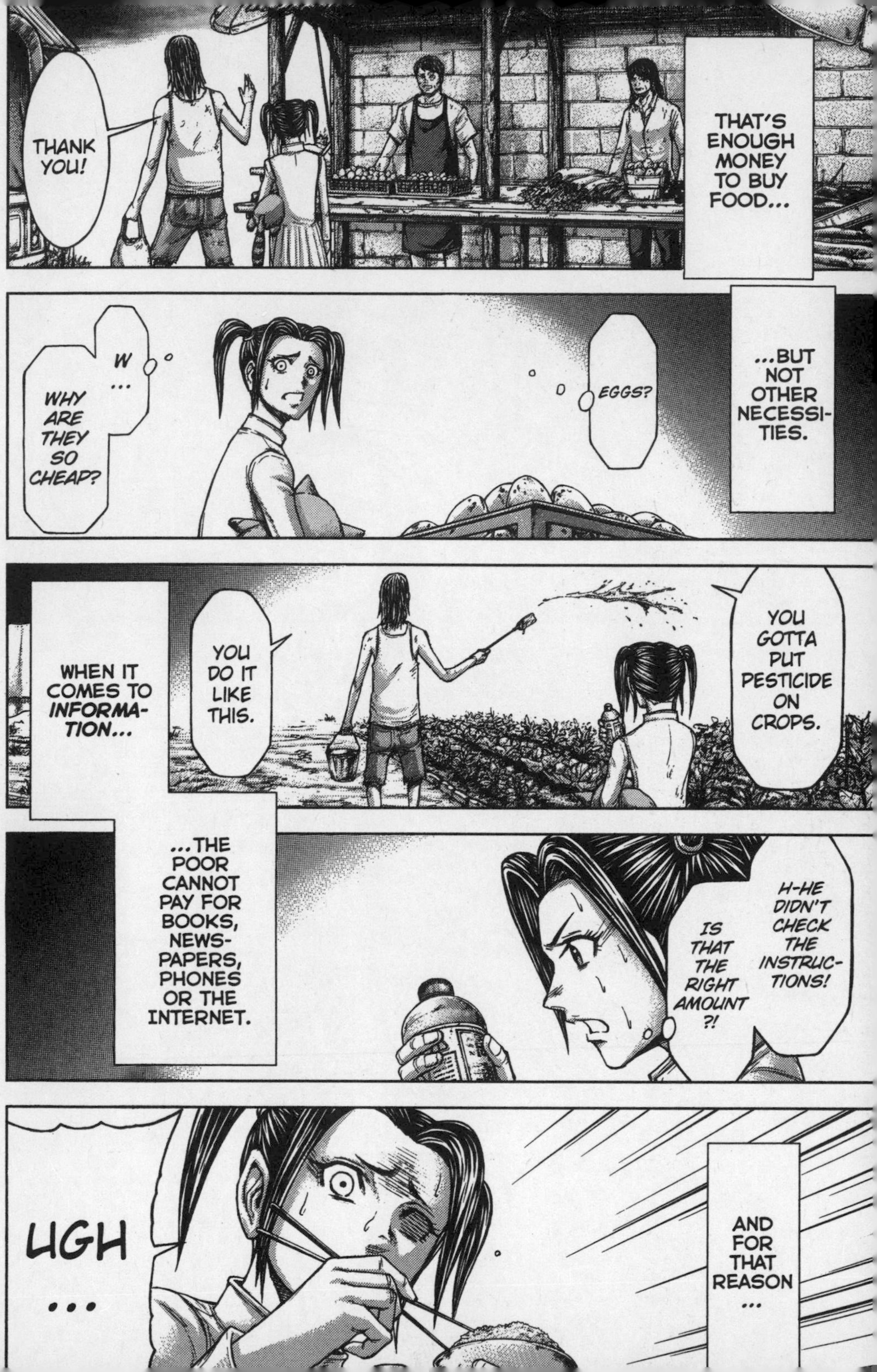
THAT'S ENOUGH MONEY TO BUY FOOD...
THANK YOU!
...BUT NOT OTHER NECESSITIES.
EGGS?
W... WHY ARE THEY SO CHEAP?
YOU GOTTA PUT PESTICIDE ON CROPS.
YOU DO IT LIKE THIS.
WHEN IT COMES TO INFORMATION...
H-HE DIDN'T CHECK THE INSTRUCTIONS!
IS THAT THE RIGHT AMOUNT?!
...THE POOR CANNOT PAY FOR BOOKS, NEWSPAPERS, PHONES OR THE INTERNET.
AND FOR THAT REASON...
UGH...

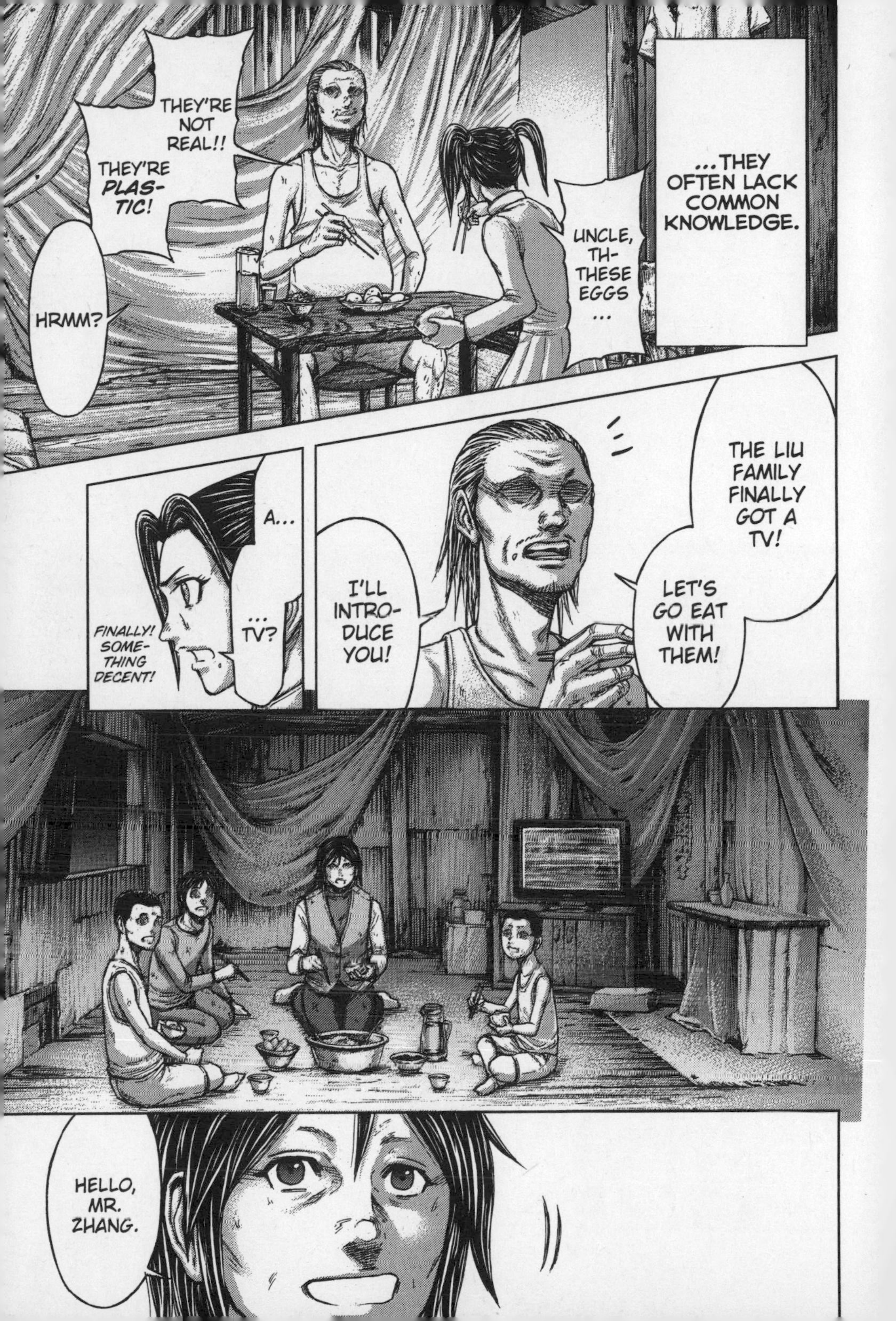
...THEY OFTEN LACK COMMON KNOWLEDGE.
UNCLE, TH- THESE EGGS...
HRMM?
THEY'RE NOT REAL!!
THEY'RE *PLASTIC!*
THE LIU FAMILY FINALLY GOT A TV!
LET'S GO EAT WITH THEM!
I'LL INTRODUCE YOU!
A...
...TV?
FINALLY! SOMETHING DECENT!
HELLO, MR. ZHANG.

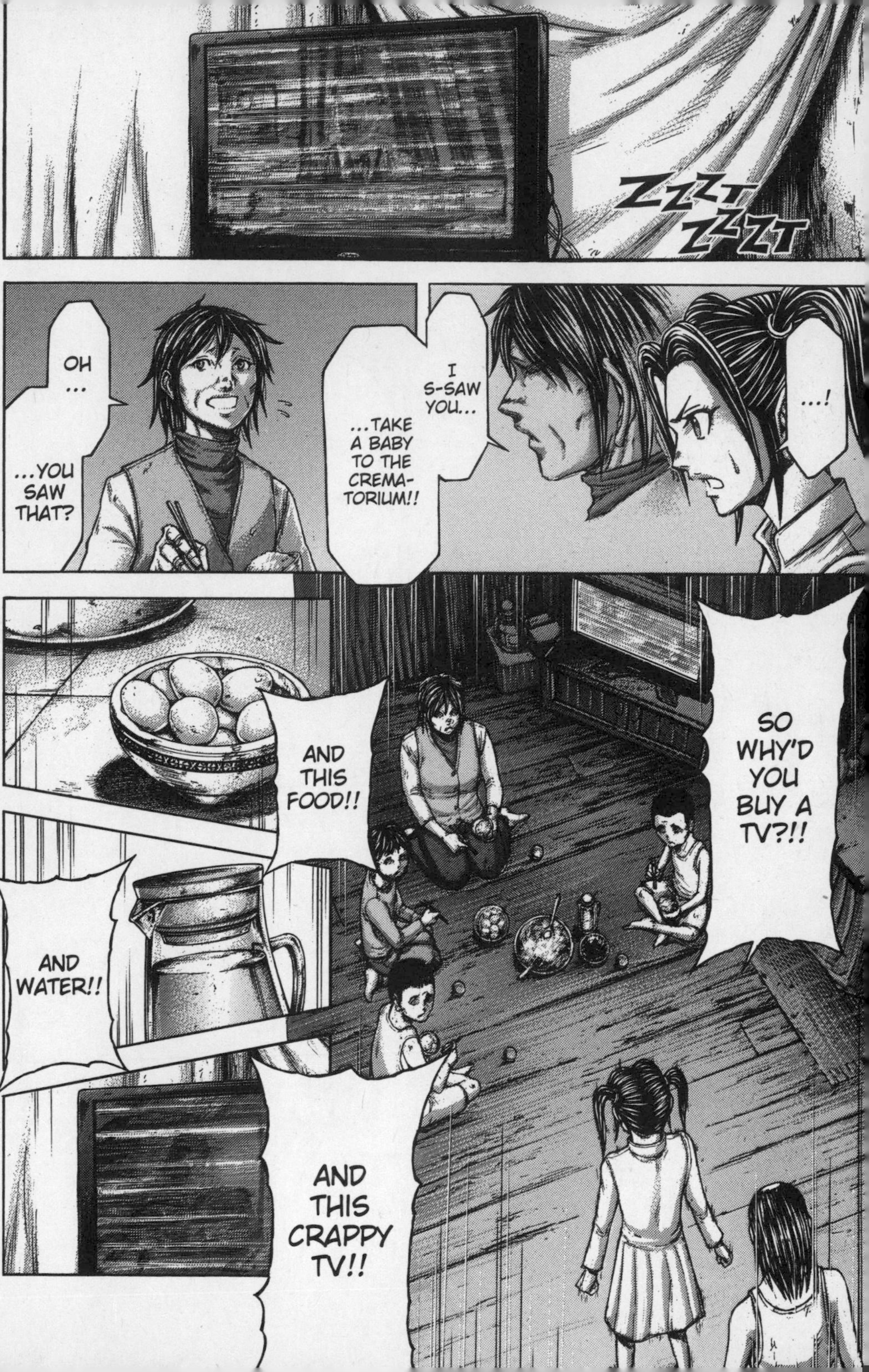
ZZZT ZZZT
...!
I S-SAW YOU...
...TAKE A BABY TO THE CREMATORIUM!!
OH ...
...YOU SAW THAT?
SO WHY'D YOU BUY A TV?!!
AND THIS FOOD!!
AND WATER!!
AND THIS CRAPPY TV!!

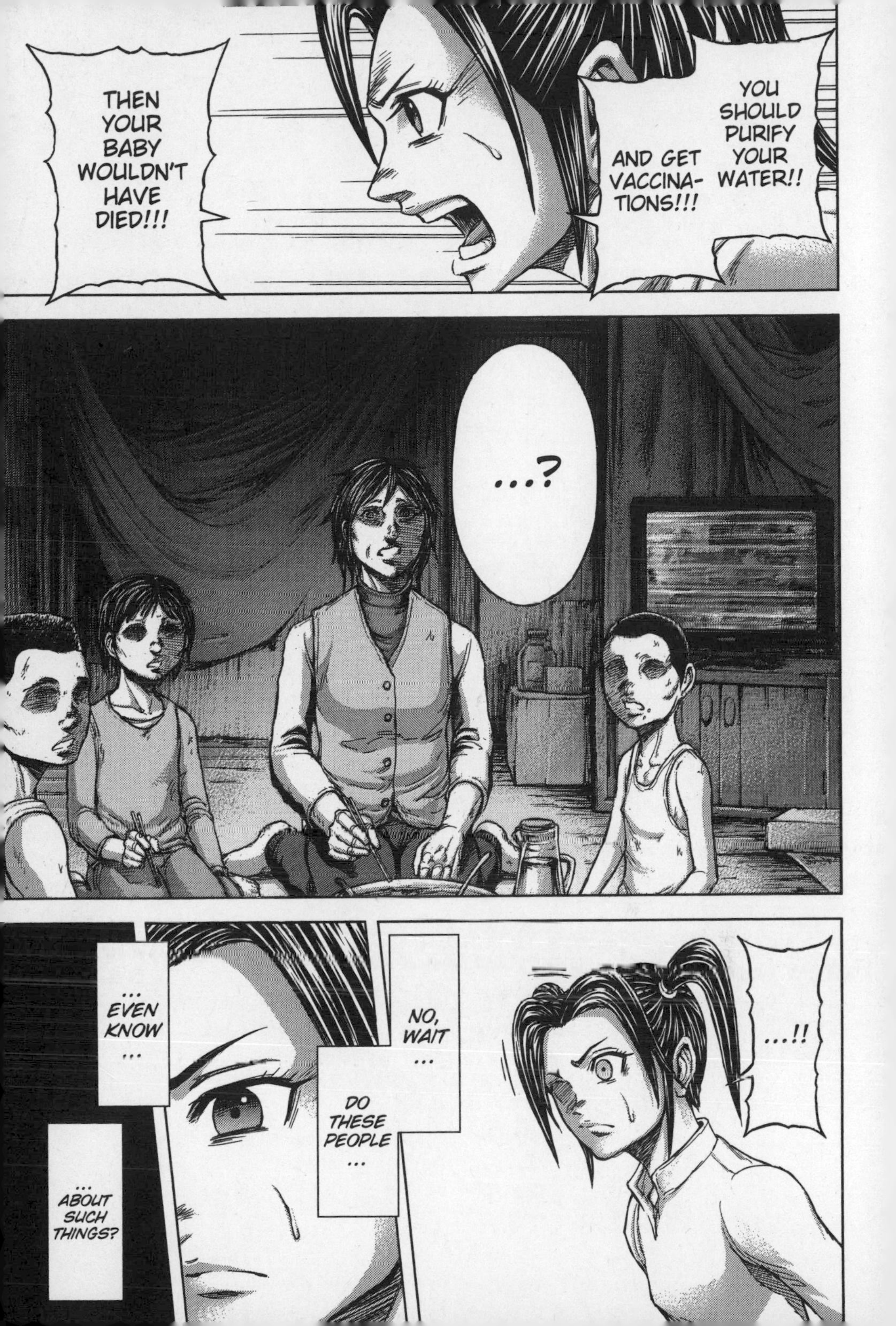
YOU SHOULD PURIFY YOUR WATER!!
AND GET VACCINATIONS!!!
THEN YOUR BABY WOULDN'T HAVE DIED!!!
...?
...!!
NO, WAIT ...
DO THESE PEOPLE ...
... EVEN KNOW ...
... ABOUT SUCH THINGS?

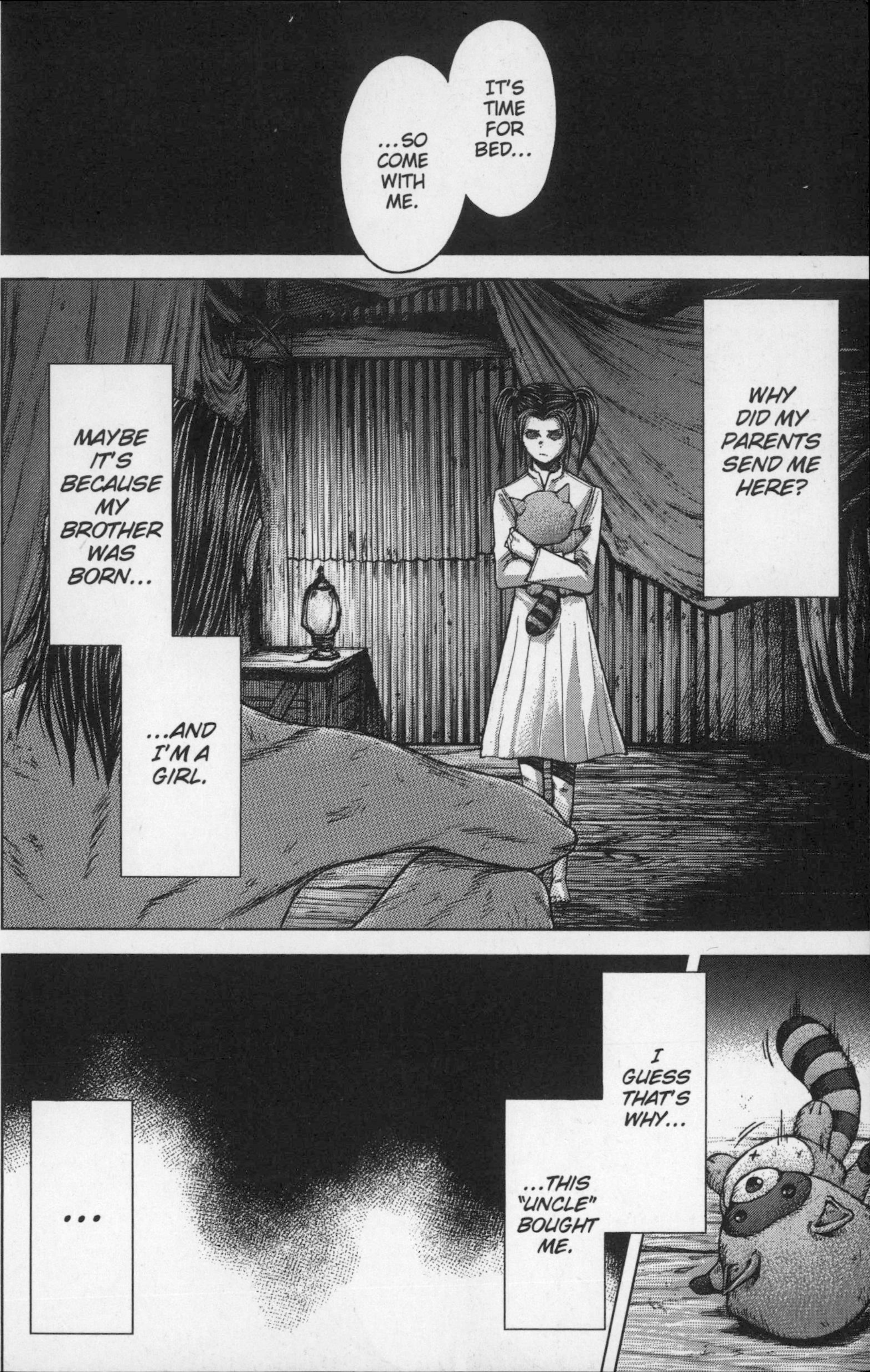
IT'S TIME FOR BED...
...SO COME WITH ME.
WHY DID MY PARENTS SEND ME HERE?
MAYBE IT'S BECAUSE MY BROTHER WAS BORN...
...AND I'M A GIRL.
I GUESS THAT'S WHY...
...THIS "UNCLE" BOUGHT ME.
...

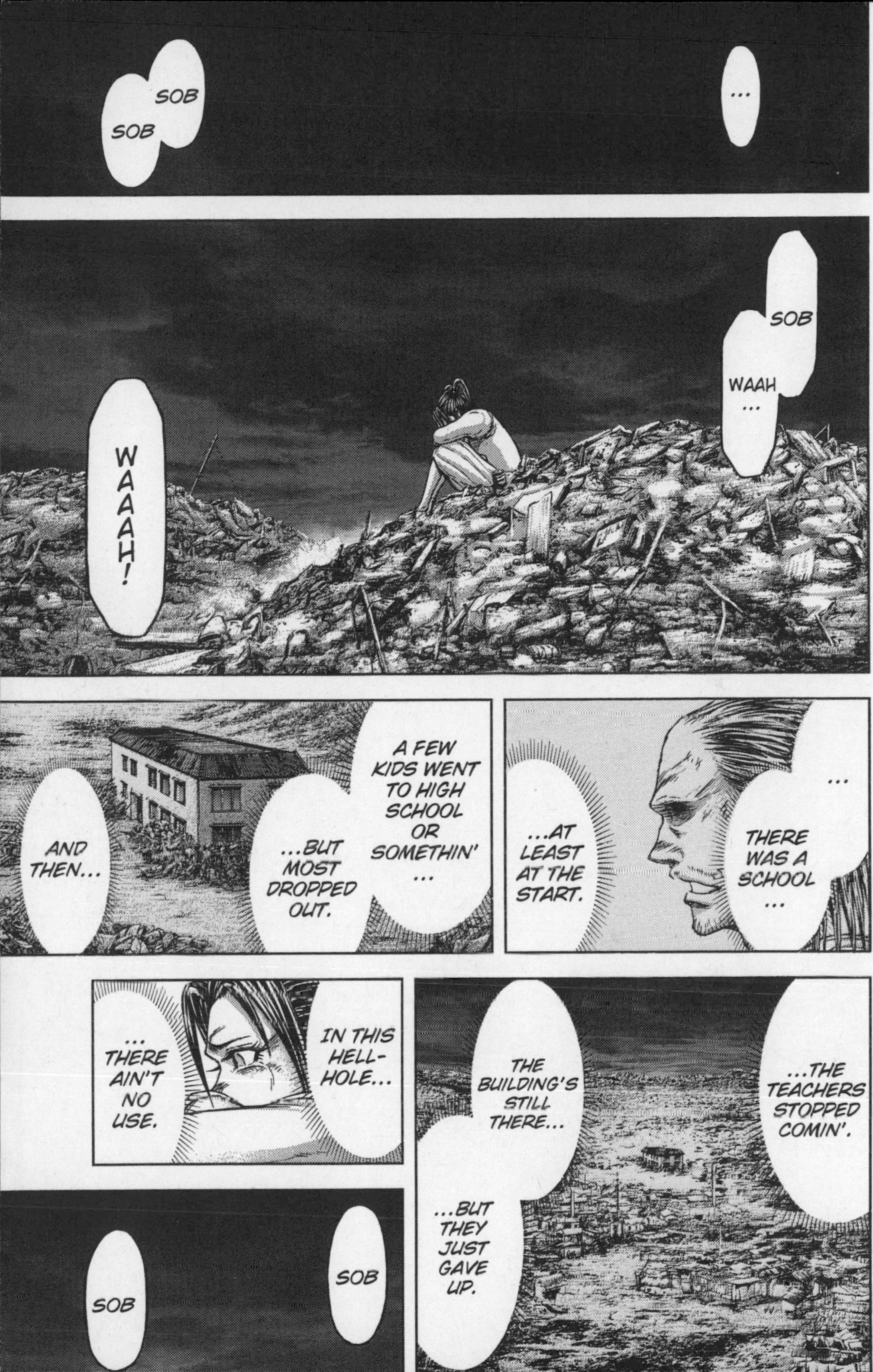
...
SOB SOB
SOB WAAH...
WAAAAH!
... THERE WAS A SCHOOL ...
...AT LEAST AT THE START.
A FEW KIDS WENT TO HIGH SCHOOL OR SOMETHIN' ...
...BUT MOST DROPPED OUT.
AND THEN...
...THE TEACHERS STOPPED COMIN'.
THE BUILDING'S STILL THERE...
...BUT THEY JUST GAVE UP.
IN THIS HELL-HOLE...
... THERE AIN'T NO USE.
SOB
SOB

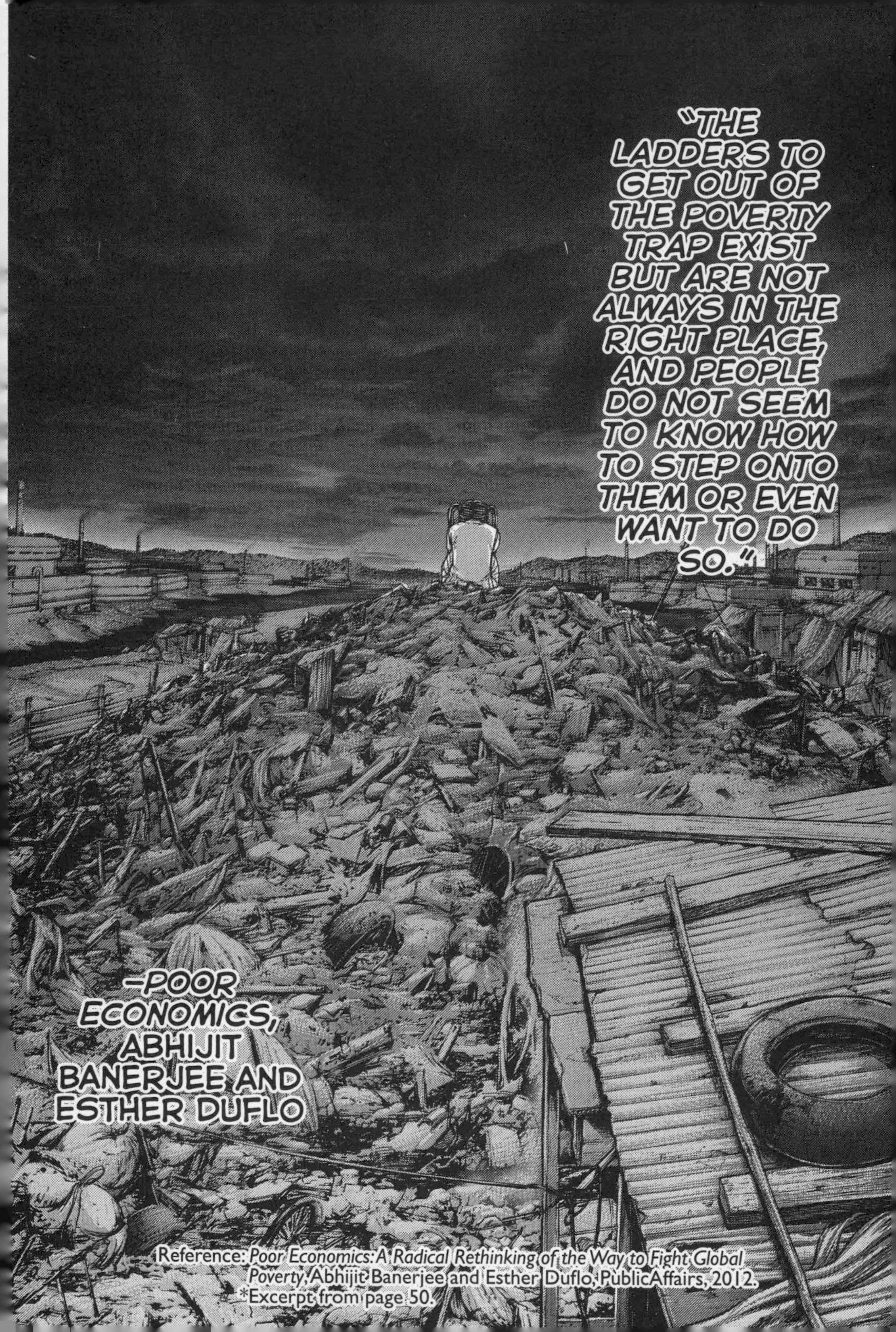
"THE LADDERS TO GET OUT OF THE POVERTY TRAP EXIST BUT ARE NOT ALWAYS IN THE RIGHT PLACE, AND PEOPLE DO NOT SEEM TO KNOW HOW TO STEP ONTO THEM OR EVEN WANT TO DO SO."
–POOR ECONOMICS, ABHIJIT BANERJEE AND ESTHER DUFLO
Reference: *Poor Economics: A Radical Rethinking of the Way to Fight Global Poverty*, Abhijit Banerjee and Esther Duflo, PublicAffairs, 2012.
*Excerpt from page 50.

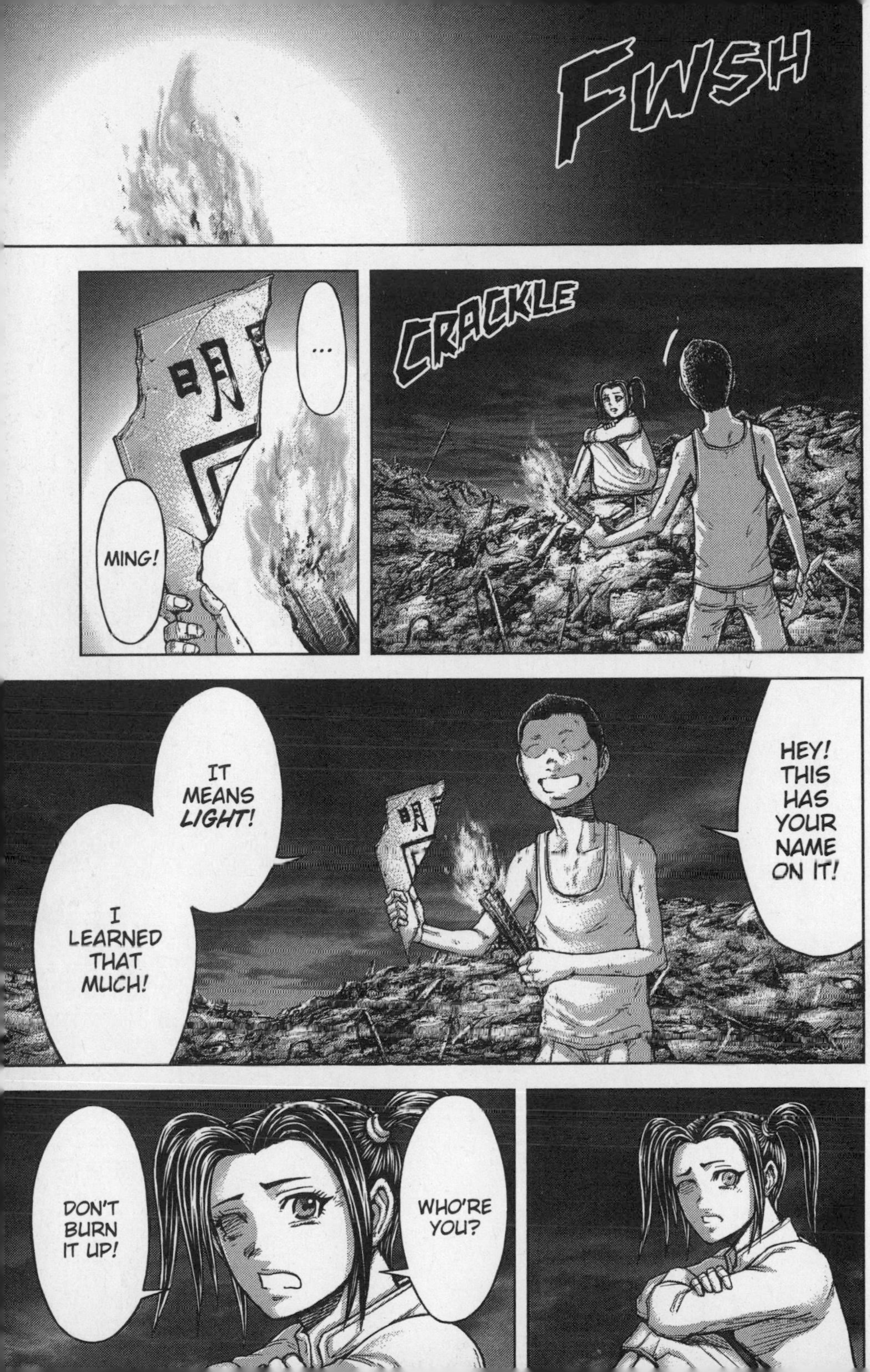
FWSH
CRACKLE
明
...
MING!
HEY! THIS HAS YOUR NAME ON IT!
IT MEANS LIGHT!
I LEARNED THAT MUCH!
WHO'RE YOU?
DON'T BURN IT UP!

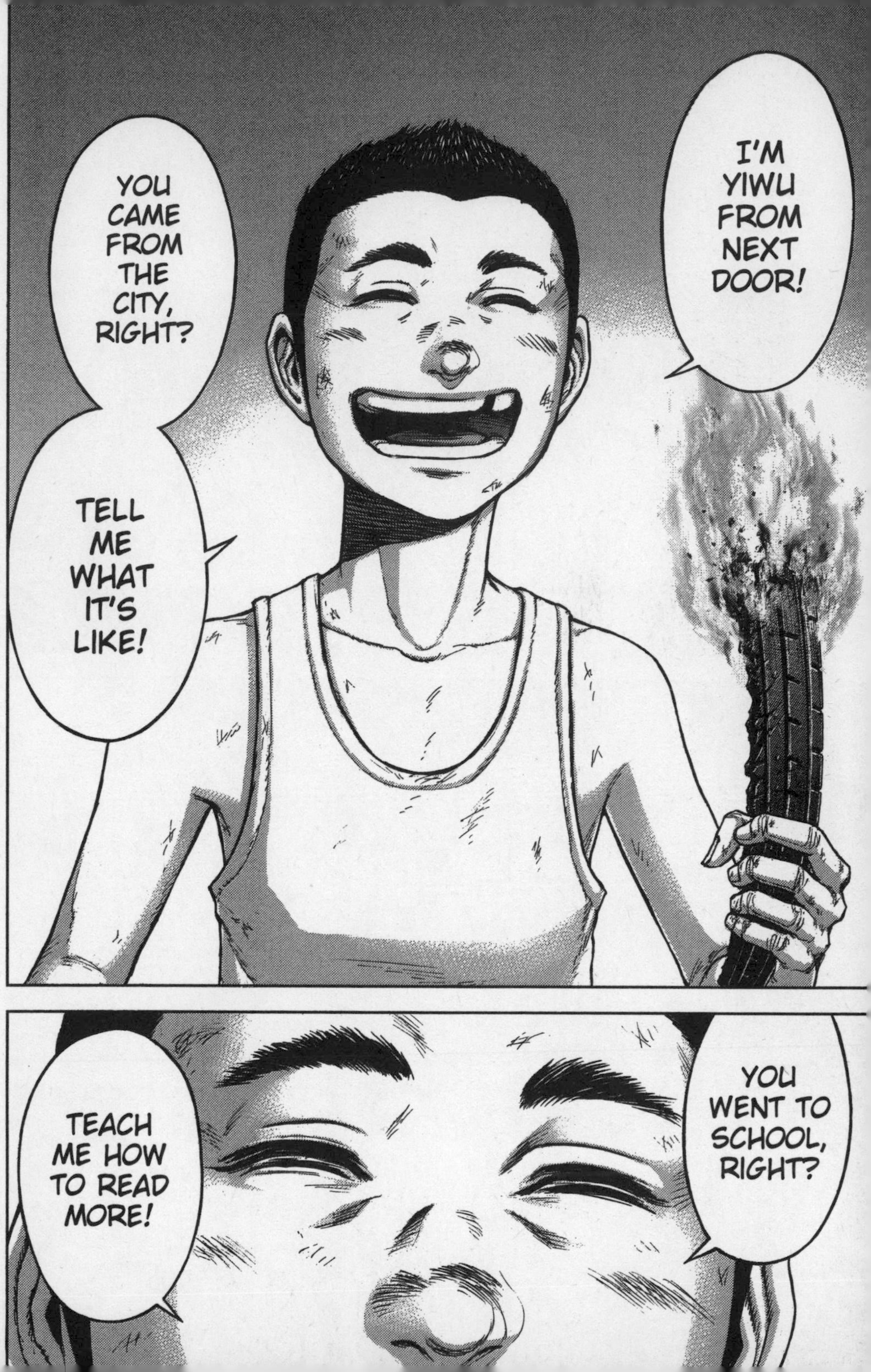
I'M YIWU FROM NEXT DOOR!
YOU CAME FROM THE CITY, RIGHT?
TELL ME WHAT IT'S LIKE!
YOU WENT TO SCHOOL, RIGHT?
TEACH ME HOW TO READ MORE!

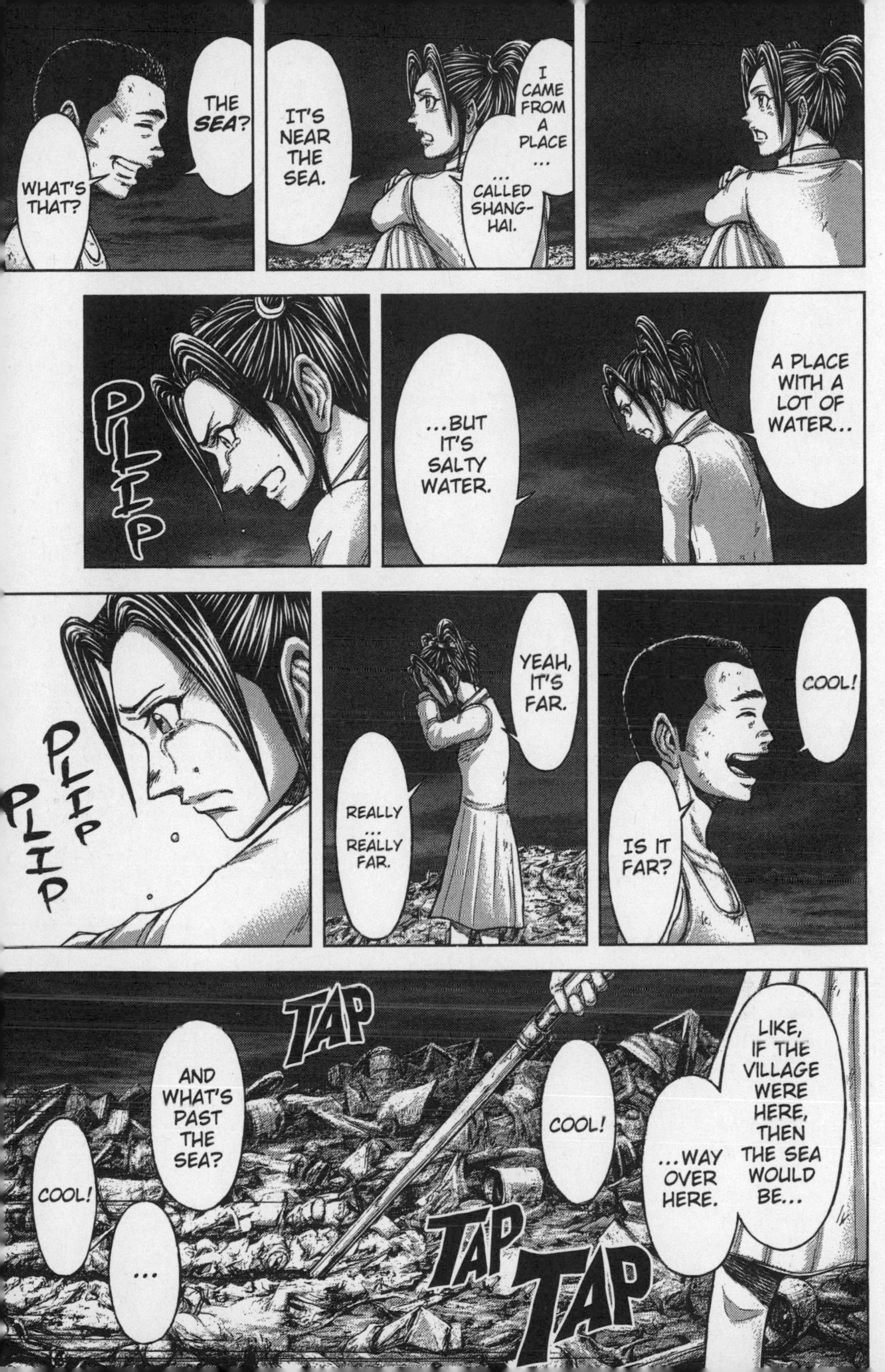
I CAME FROM A PLACE...
...CALLED SHANG-HAI.
IT'S NEAR THE SEA.
THE SEA?
WHAT'S THAT?
A PLACE WITH A LOT OF WATER...
...BUT IT'S SALTY WATER.
PLIP
COOL!
IS IT FAR?
YEAH, IT'S FAR.
REALLY... REALLY FAR.
PLIP
PLIP
LIKE, IF THE VILLAGE WERE HERE, THEN THE SEA WOULD BE...
...WAY OVER HERE.
TAP
TAP
COOL!
TAP
AND WHAT'S PAST THE SEA?
COOL!
...

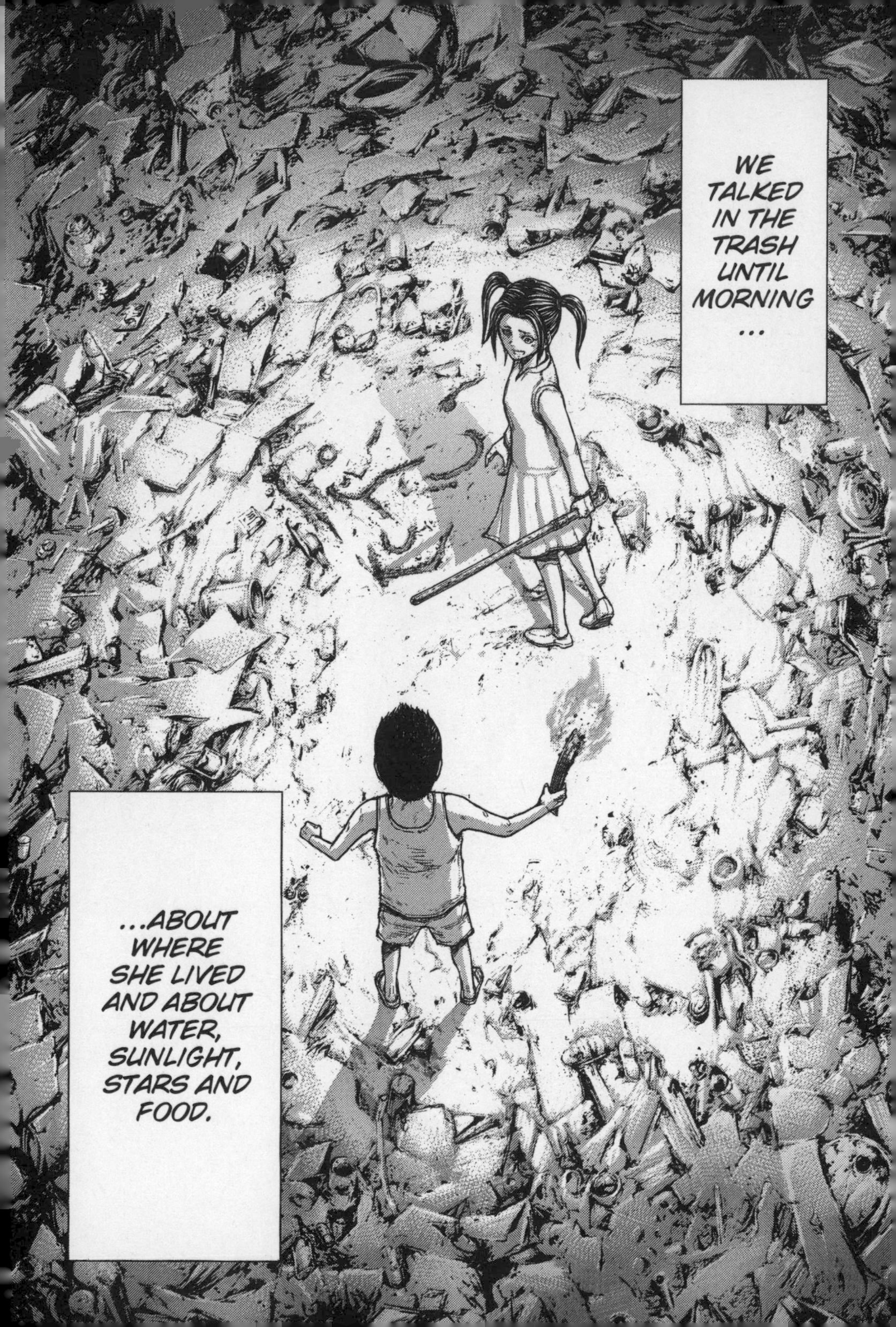
WE TALKED IN THE TRASH UNTIL MORNING ...
...ABOUT WHERE SHE LIVED AND ABOUT WATER, SUNLIGHT, STARS AND FOOD.

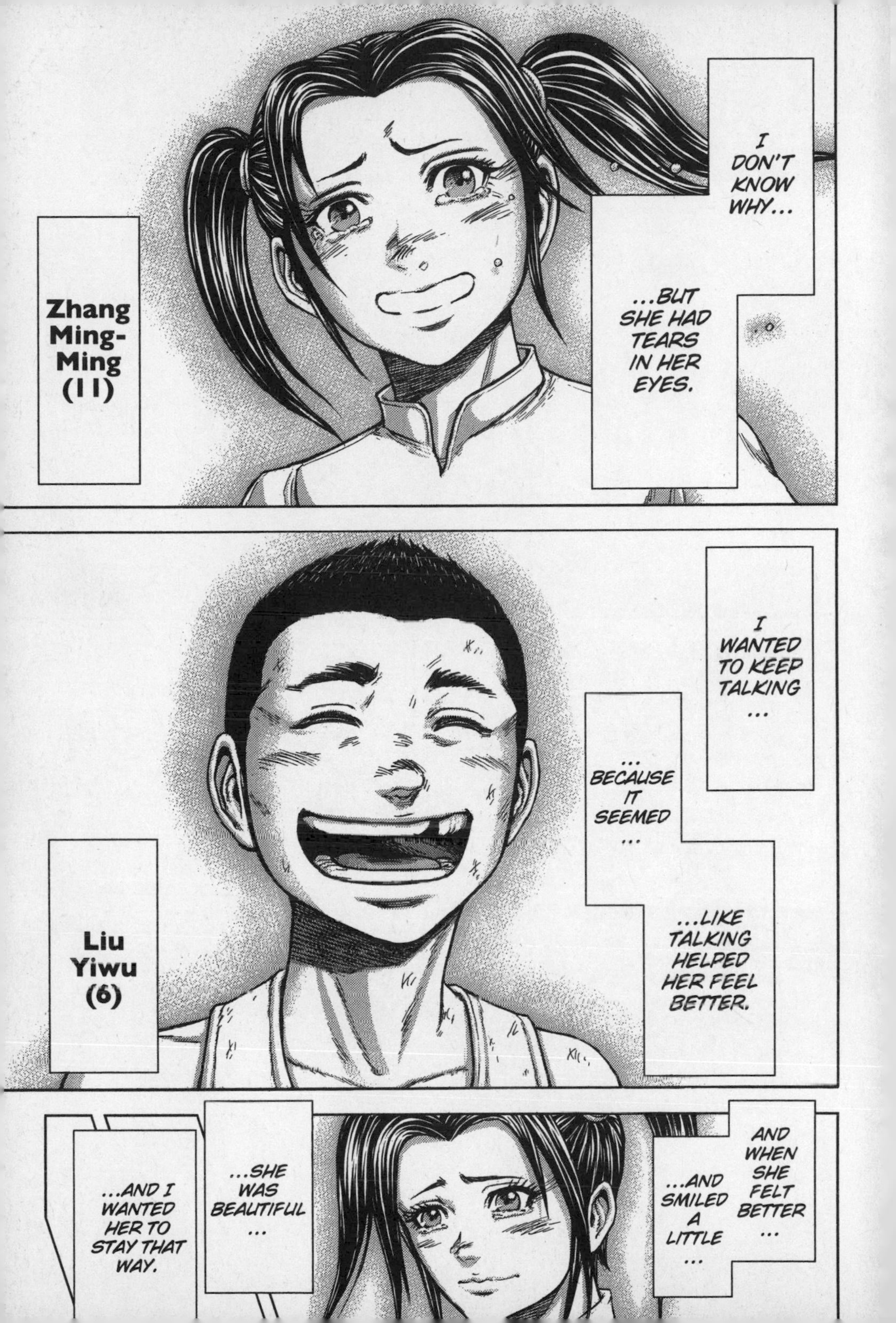
I DON'T KNOW WHY...
...BUT SHE HAD TEARS IN HER EYES.
Zhang Ming-Ming (11)
I WANTED TO KEEP TALKING ...
... BECAUSE IT SEEMED ...
...LIKE TALKING HELPED HER FEEL BETTER.
Liu Yiwu (6)
AND WHEN SHE FELT BETTER ...
...AND SMILED A LITTLE ...
...SHE WAS BEAUTIFUL ...
...AND I WANTED HER TO STAY THAT WAY.

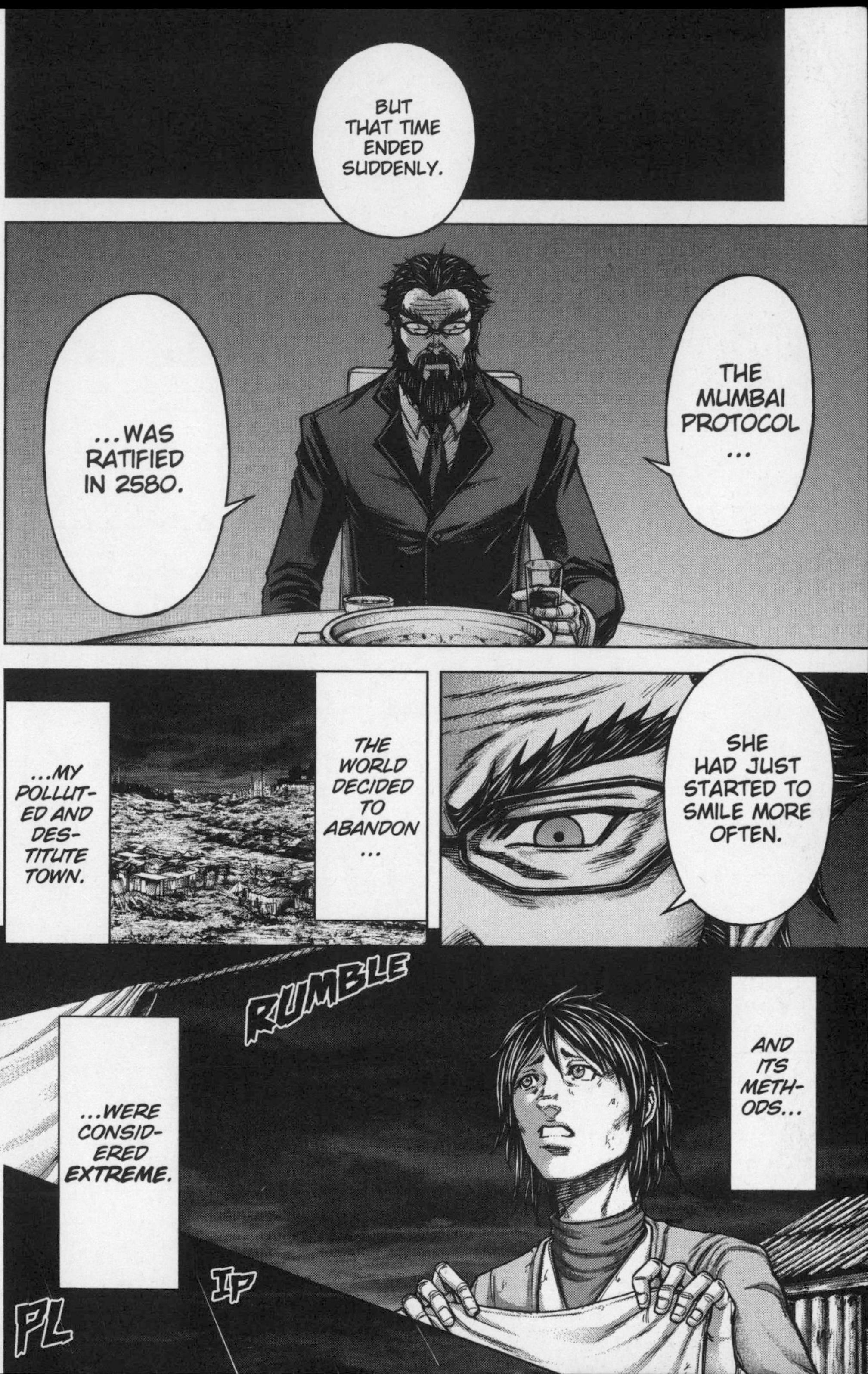
BUT THAT TIME ENDED SUDDENLY.
THE MUMBAI PROTOCOL ...
...WAS RATIFIED IN 2580.
SHE HAD JUST STARTED TO SMILE MORE OFTEN.
THE WORLD DECIDED TO ABANDON ...
...MY POLLUT-ED AND DES-TITUTE TOWN.
AND ITS METH-ODS...
RUMBLE
...WERE CONSID-ERED EXTREME.
IP
PL

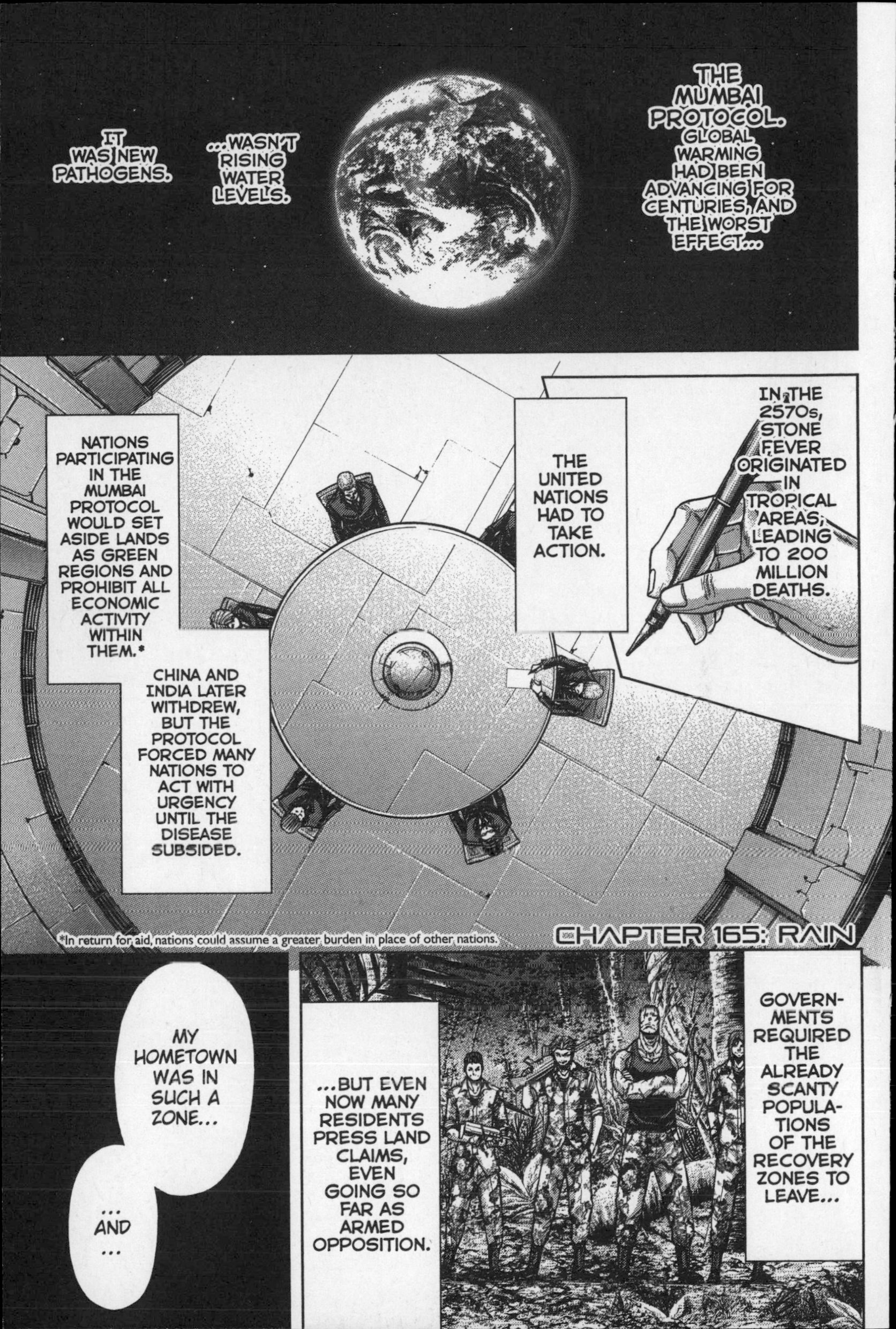
THE MUMBAI PROTOCOL. GLOBAL WARMING HAD BEEN ADVANCING FOR CENTURIES, AND THE WORST EFFECT...
...WASN'T RISING WATER LEVELS.
IT WAS NEW PATHOGENS.
IN THE 2570s, STONE FEVER ORIGINATED IN TROPICAL AREAS, LEADING TO 200 MILLION DEATHS.
THE UNITED NATIONS HAD TO TAKE ACTION.
NATIONS PARTICIPATING IN THE MUMBAI PROTOCOL WOULD SET ASIDE LANDS AS GREEN REGIONS AND PROHIBIT ALL ECONOMIC ACTIVITY WITHIN THEM.*
CHINA AND INDIA LATER WITHDREW, BUT THE PROTOCOL FORCED MANY NATIONS TO ACT WITH URGENCY UNTIL THE DISEASE SUBSIDED.
*In return for aid, nations could assume a greater burden in place of other nations.
CHAPTER 165: RAIN
GOVERN-MENTS REQUIRED THE ALREADY SCANTY POPULA-TIONS OF THE RECOVERY ZONES TO LEAVE...
...BUT EVEN NOW MANY RESIDENTS PRESS LAND CLAIMS, EVEN GOING SO FAR AS ARMED OPPOSITION.
MY HOMETOWN WAS IN SUCH A ZONE...
... AND ...

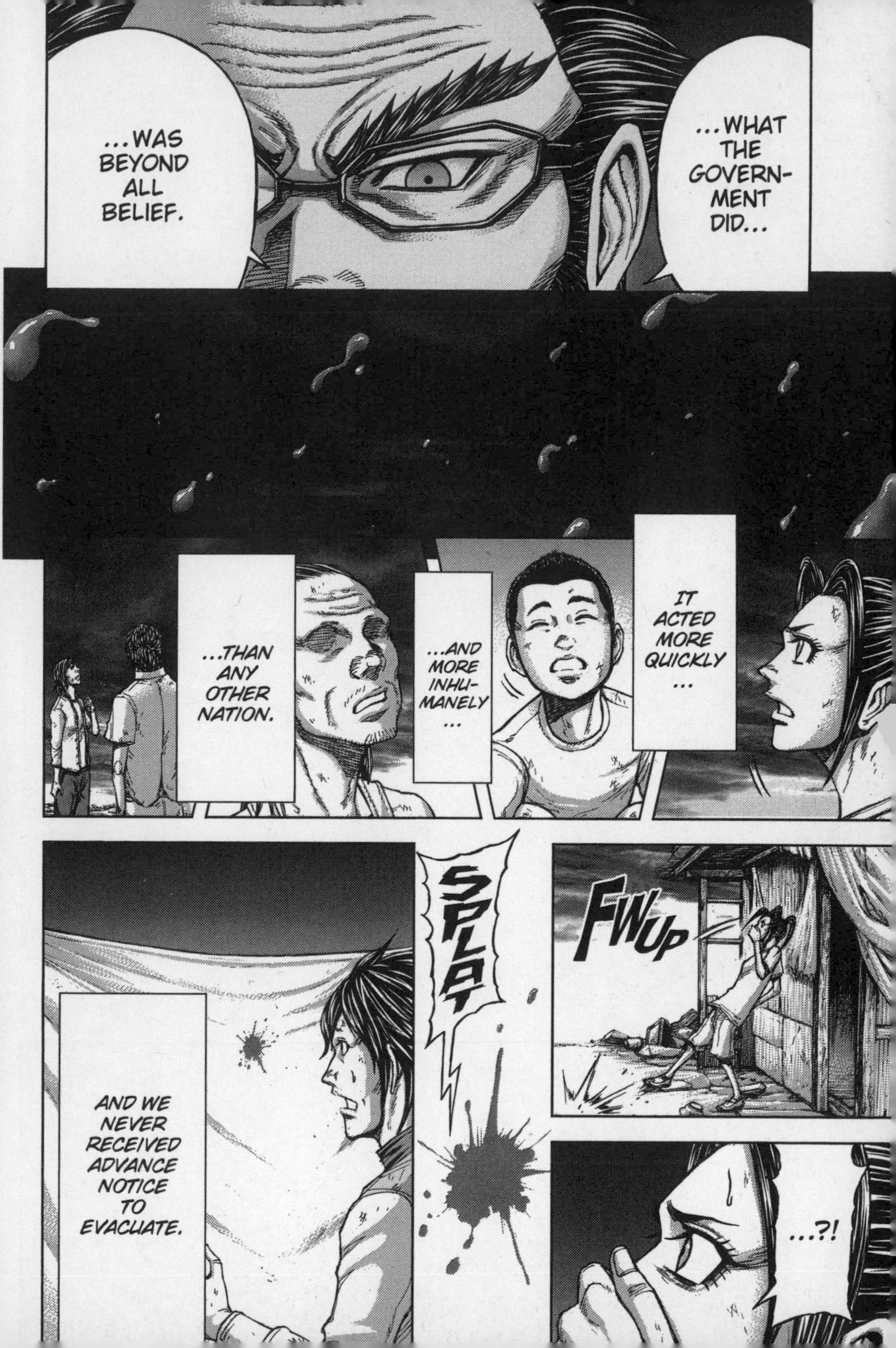
...WHAT THE GOVERNMENT DID...
...WAS BEYOND ALL BELIEF.
IT ACTED MORE QUICKLY...
...AND MORE INHUMANELY...
...THAN ANY OTHER NATION.
FWUP
...?!
SPLAT
AND WE NEVER RECEIVED ADVANCE NOTICE TO EVACUATE.

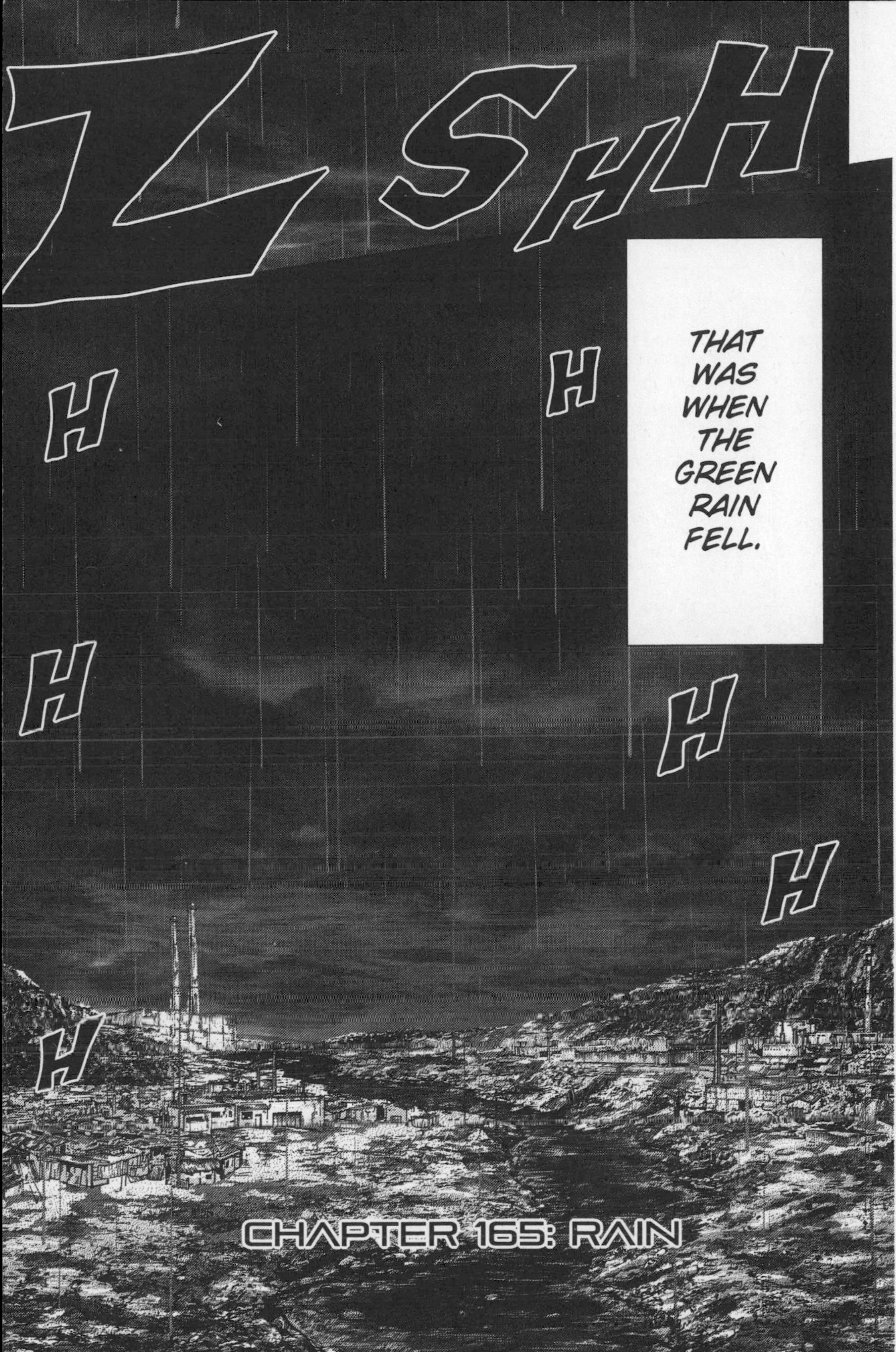
ZSHH
THAT WAS WHEN THE GREEN RAIN FELL.
H
H
H
H
H
H
CHAPTER 165: RAIN

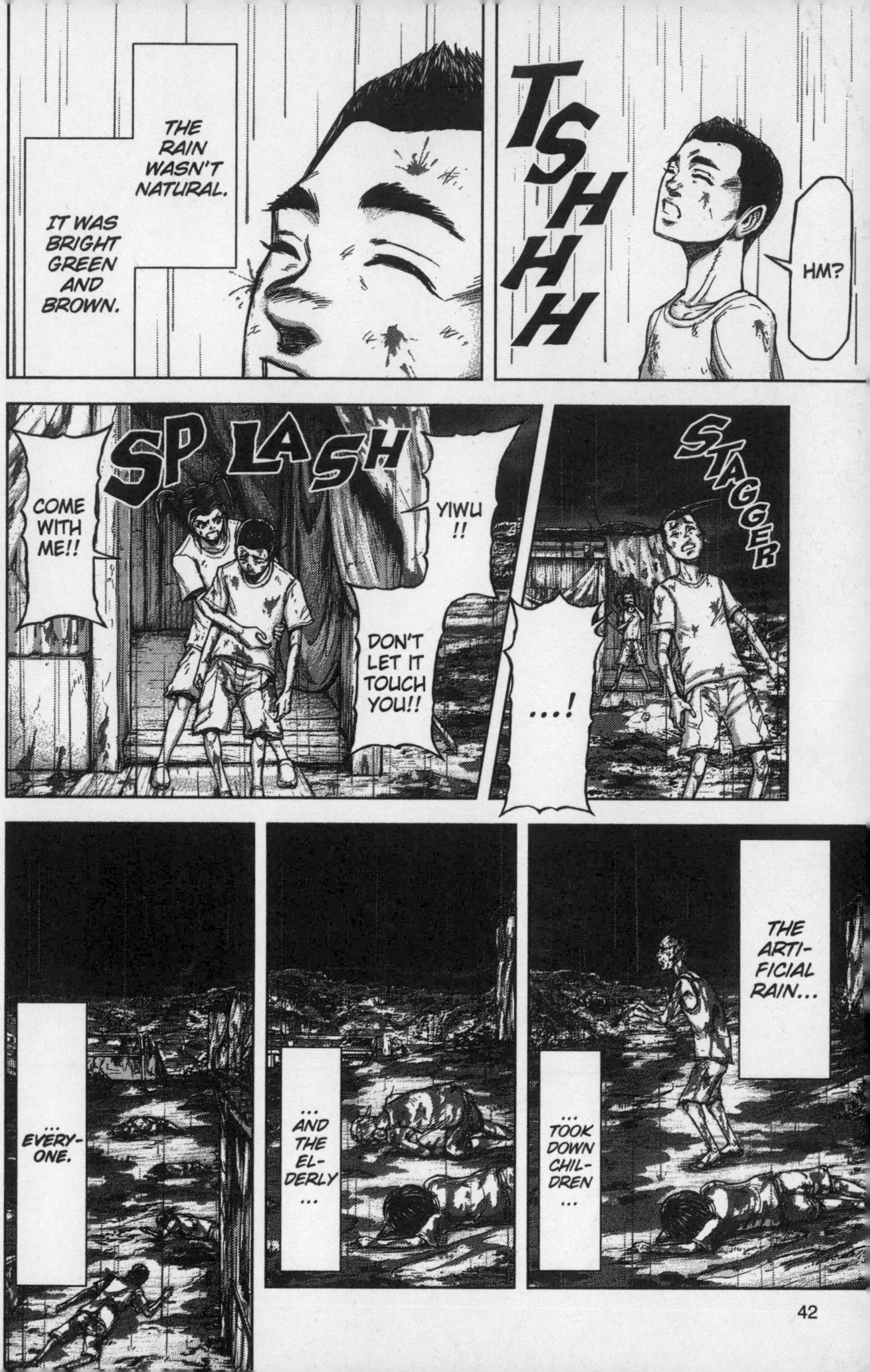
TSHHH
HM?
THE RAIN WASN'T NATURAL.
IT WAS BRIGHT GREEN AND BROWN.
STAGGER
...!
SPLASH
YIWU!!
DON'T LET IT TOUCH YOU!!
COME WITH ME!!
THE ARTI-FICIAL RAIN...
...TOOK DOWN CHIL-DREN...
...AND THE EL-DERLY...
...EVERY-ONE.

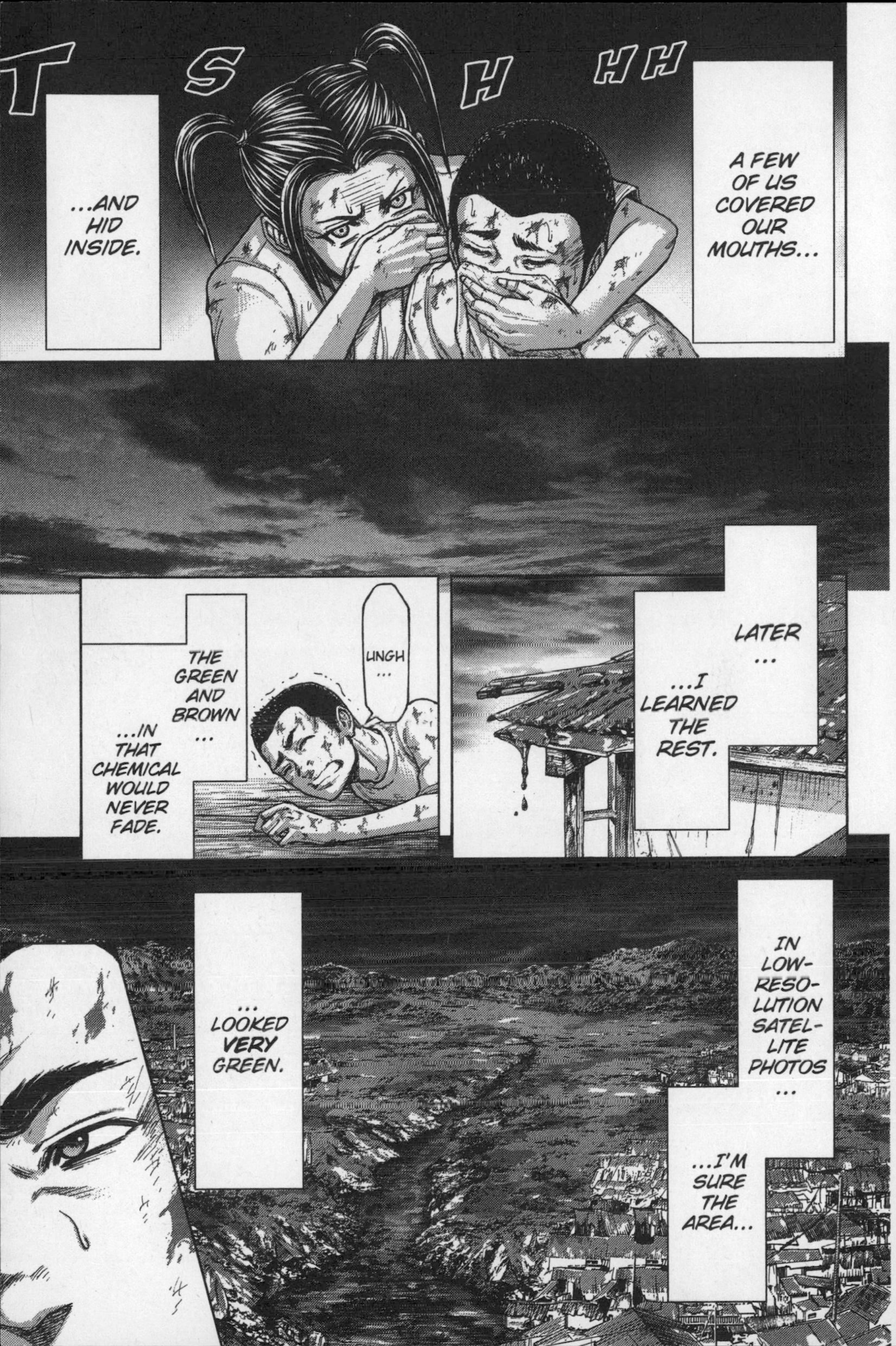
TSHHH
A FEW OF US COVERED OUR MOUTHS...
...AND HID INSIDE.
LATER...
...I LEARNED THE REST.
UNGH...
THE GREEN AND BROWN...
...IN THAT CHEMICAL WOULD NEVER FADE.
IN LOW-RESOLUTION SATELLITE PHOTOS...
...I'M SURE THE AREA...
...LOOKED **VERY** GREEN.

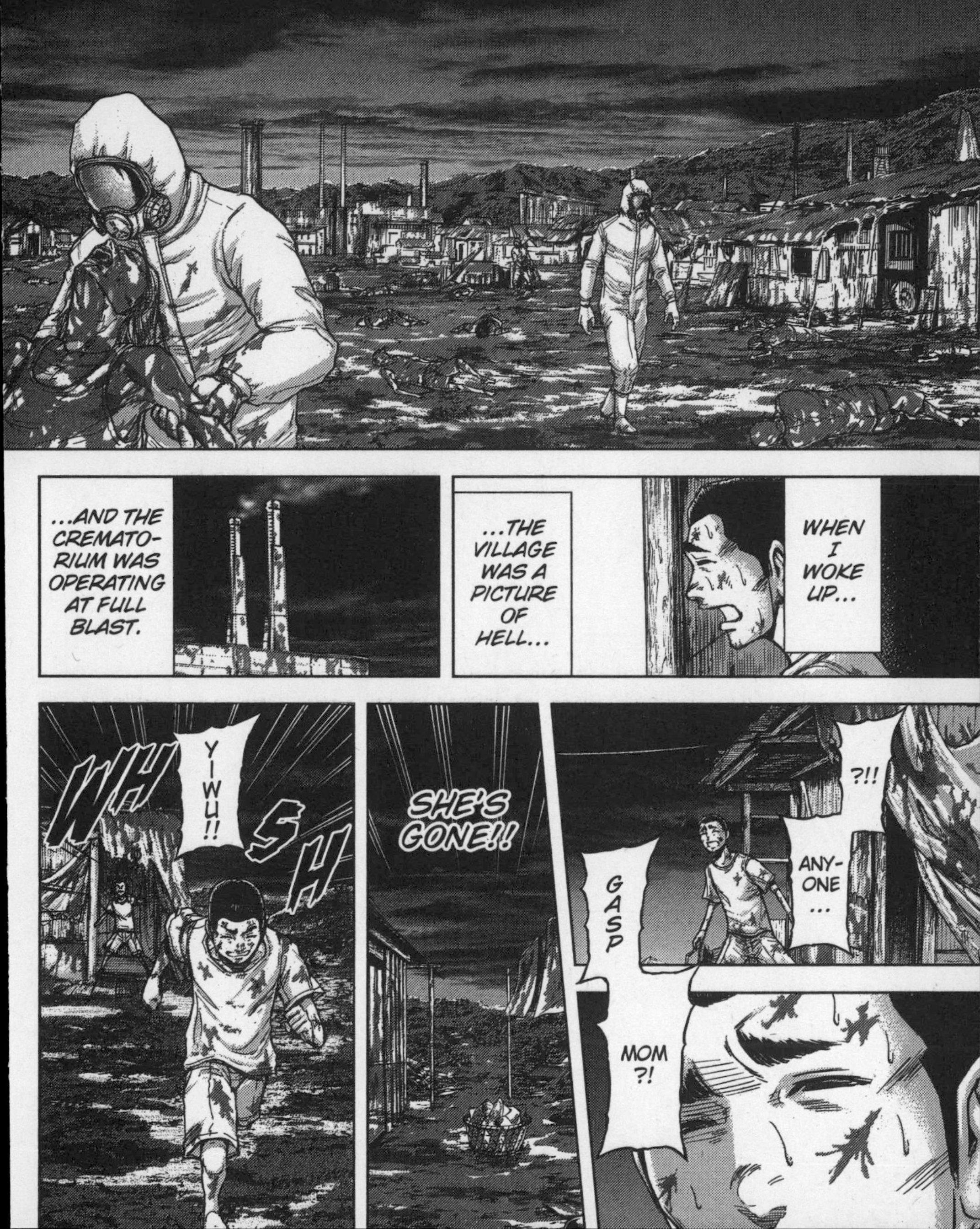
WHEN I WOKE UP...
...THE VILLAGE WAS A PICTURE OF HELL...
...AND THE CREMATO-RIUM WAS OPERATING AT FULL BLAST.
?!!
ANY-ONE ...
GASP
MOM ?!
SHE'S GONE!!
YIWU!!
WHSH

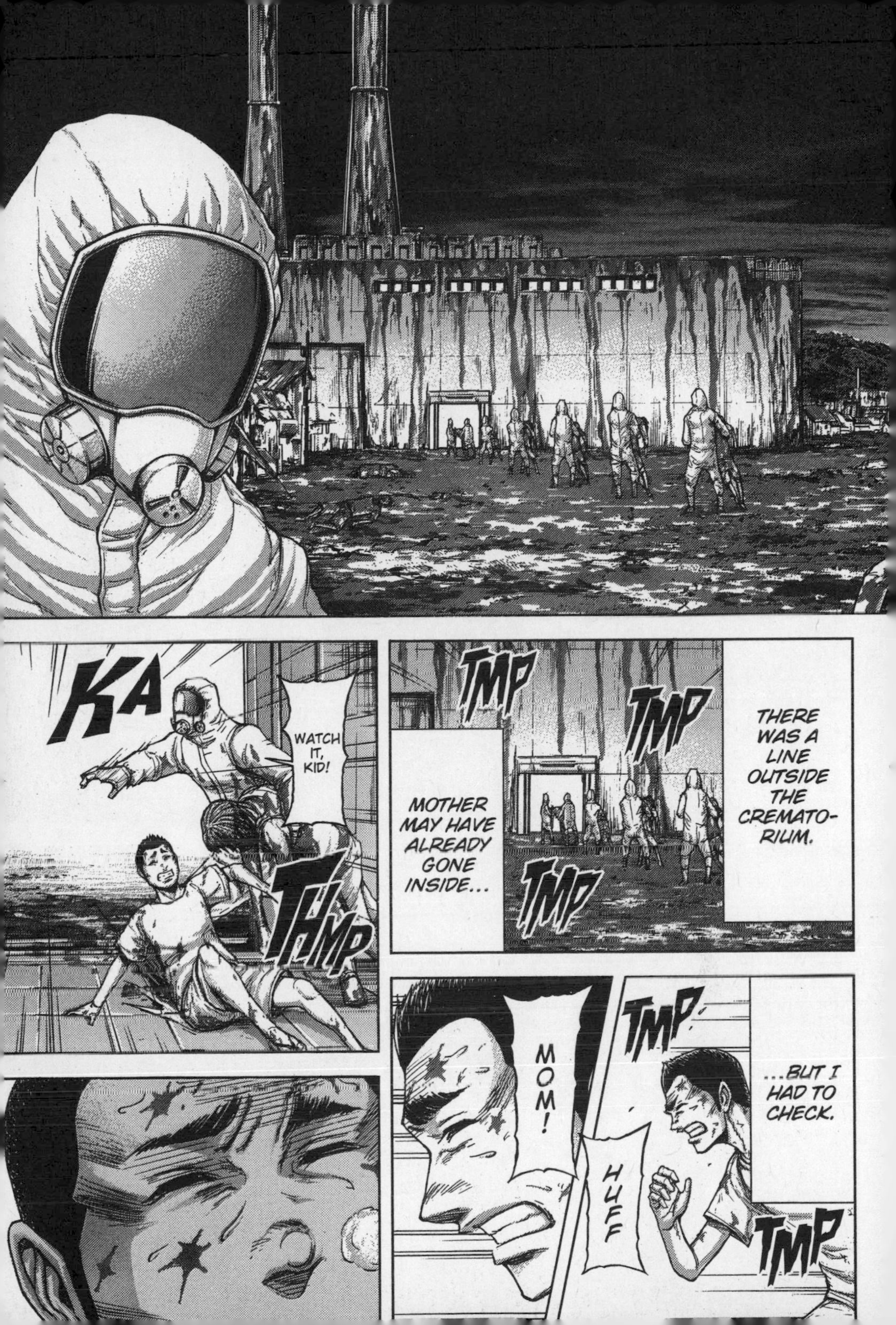
THERE WAS A LINE OUTSIDE THE CREMATO-RIUM.
TMP
TMP
MOTHER MAY HAVE ALREADY GONE INSIDE...
TMP
KA
WATCH IT, KID!
THMP
TMP
...BUT I HAD TO CHECK.
HUFF
TMP
MOM!

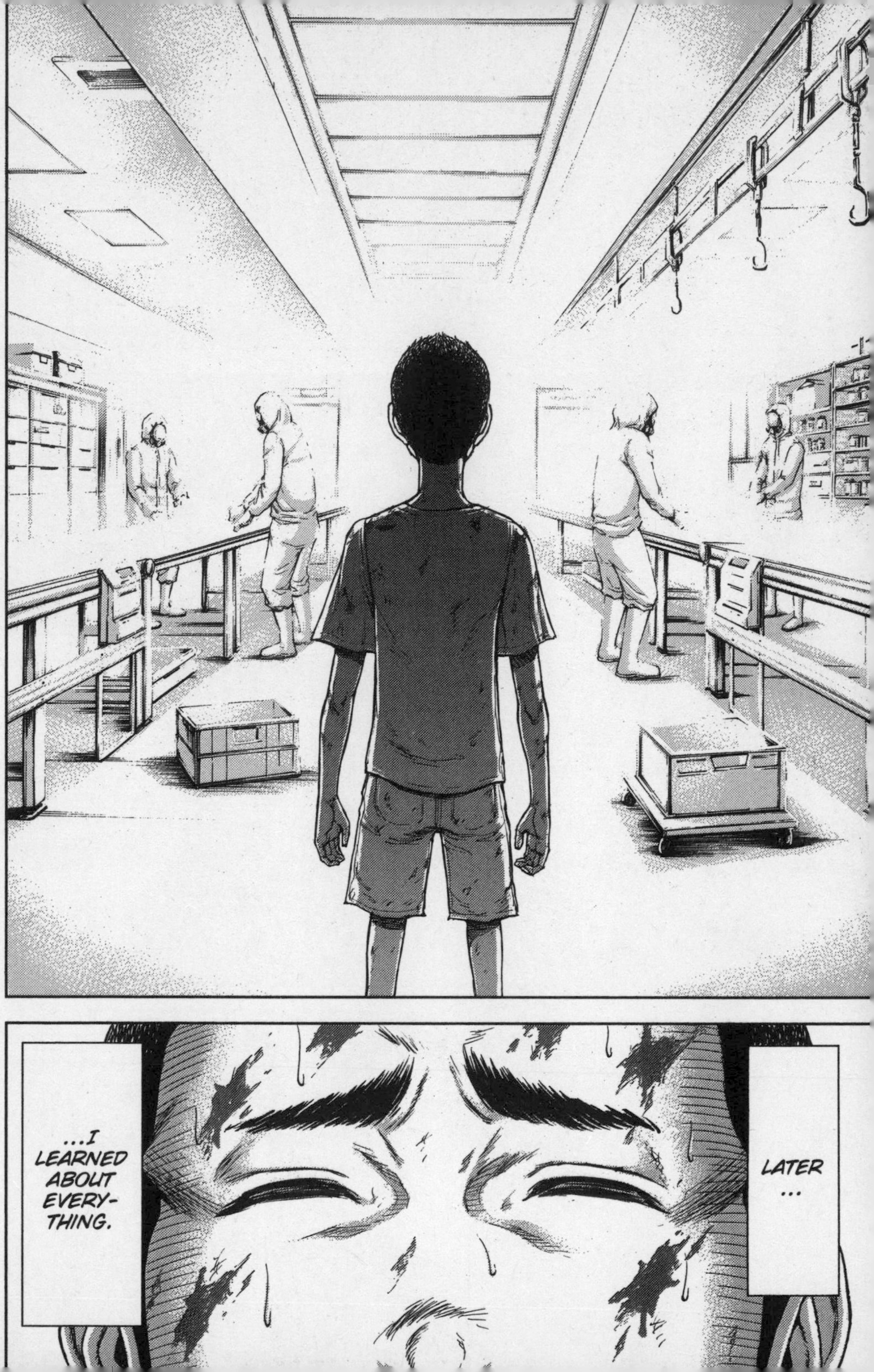
LATER ...
...I LEARNED ABOUT EVERY-THING.

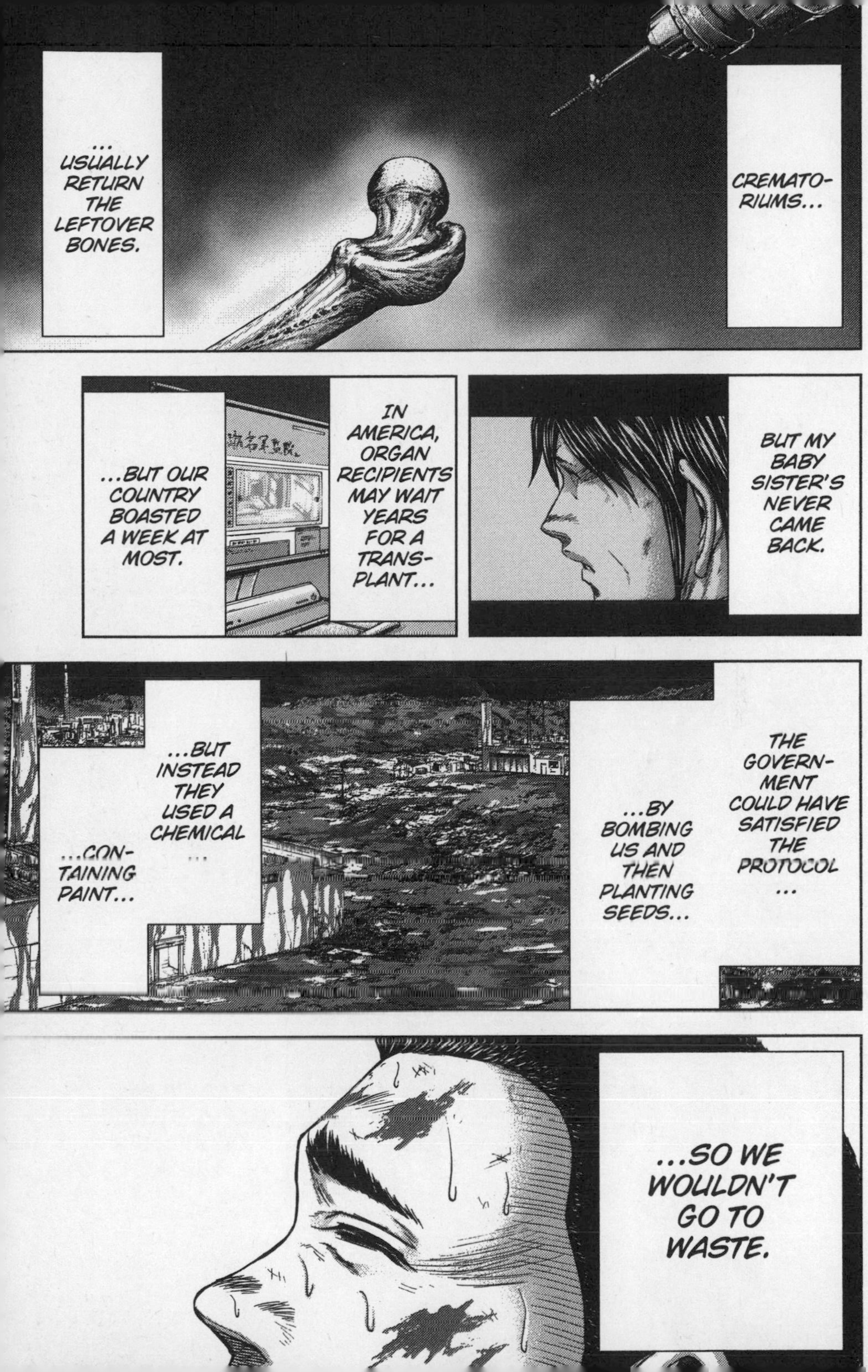
CREMATO-RIUMS...
...USUALLY RETURN THE LEFTOVER BONES.
BUT MY BABY SISTER'S NEVER CAME BACK.
IN AMERICA, ORGAN RECIPIENTS MAY WAIT YEARS FOR A TRANS-PLANT...
...BUT OUR COUNTRY BOASTED A WEEK AT MOST.
THE GOVERN-MENT COULD HAVE SATISFIED THE PROTOCOL...
...BY BOMBING US AND THEN PLANTING SEEDS...
...BUT INSTEAD THEY USED A CHEMICAL...
...CON-TAINING PAINT...
...SO WE WOULDN'T GO TO WASTE.

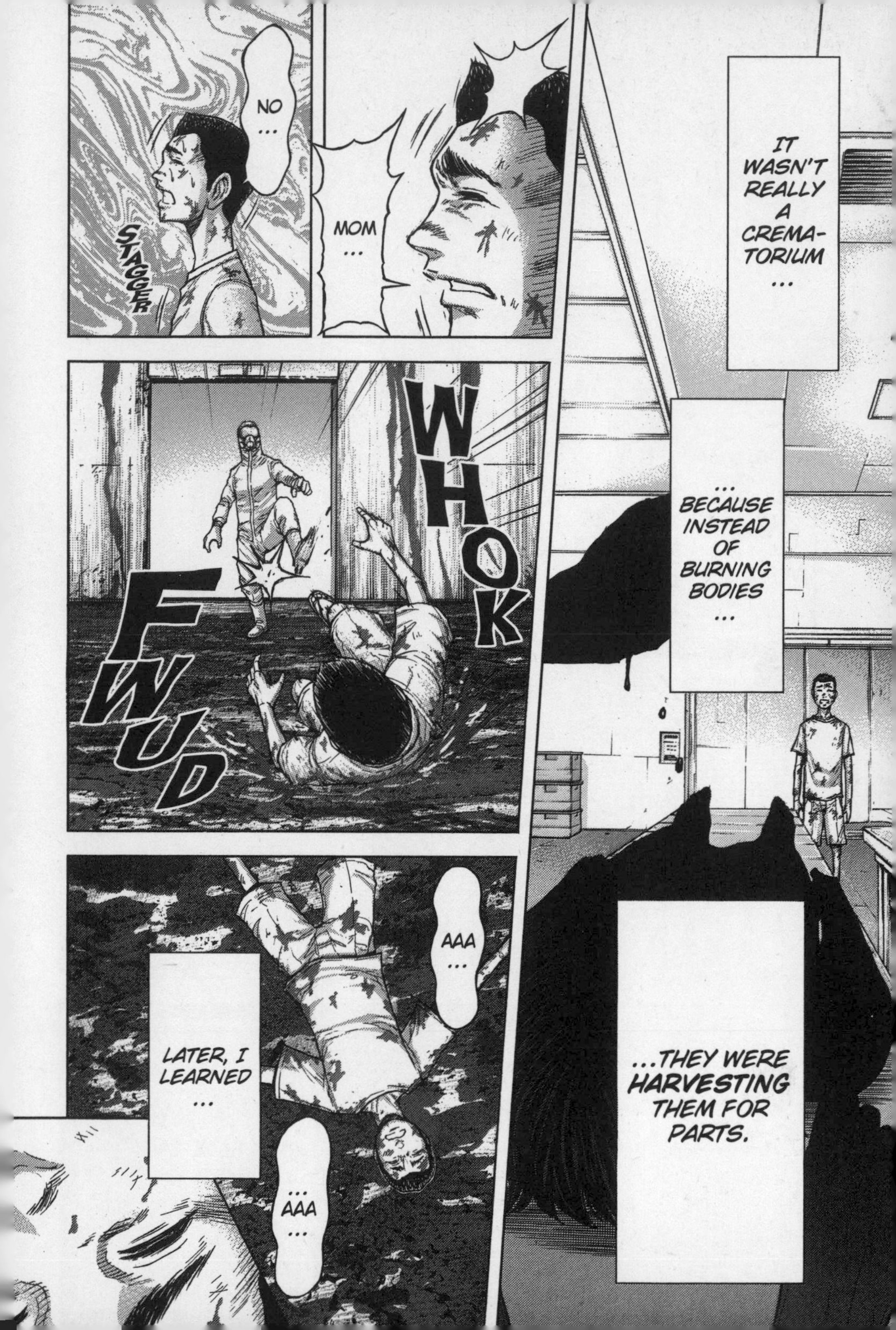
MOM
...
NO
...
STAGGER
WHOK
FWUD
AAA
...
LATER, I LEARNED
...
...
AAA
...
IT WASN'T REALLY A CREMATORIUM
...
...BECAUSE INSTEAD OF BURNING BODIES
...
...THEY WERE HARVESTING THEM FOR PARTS.

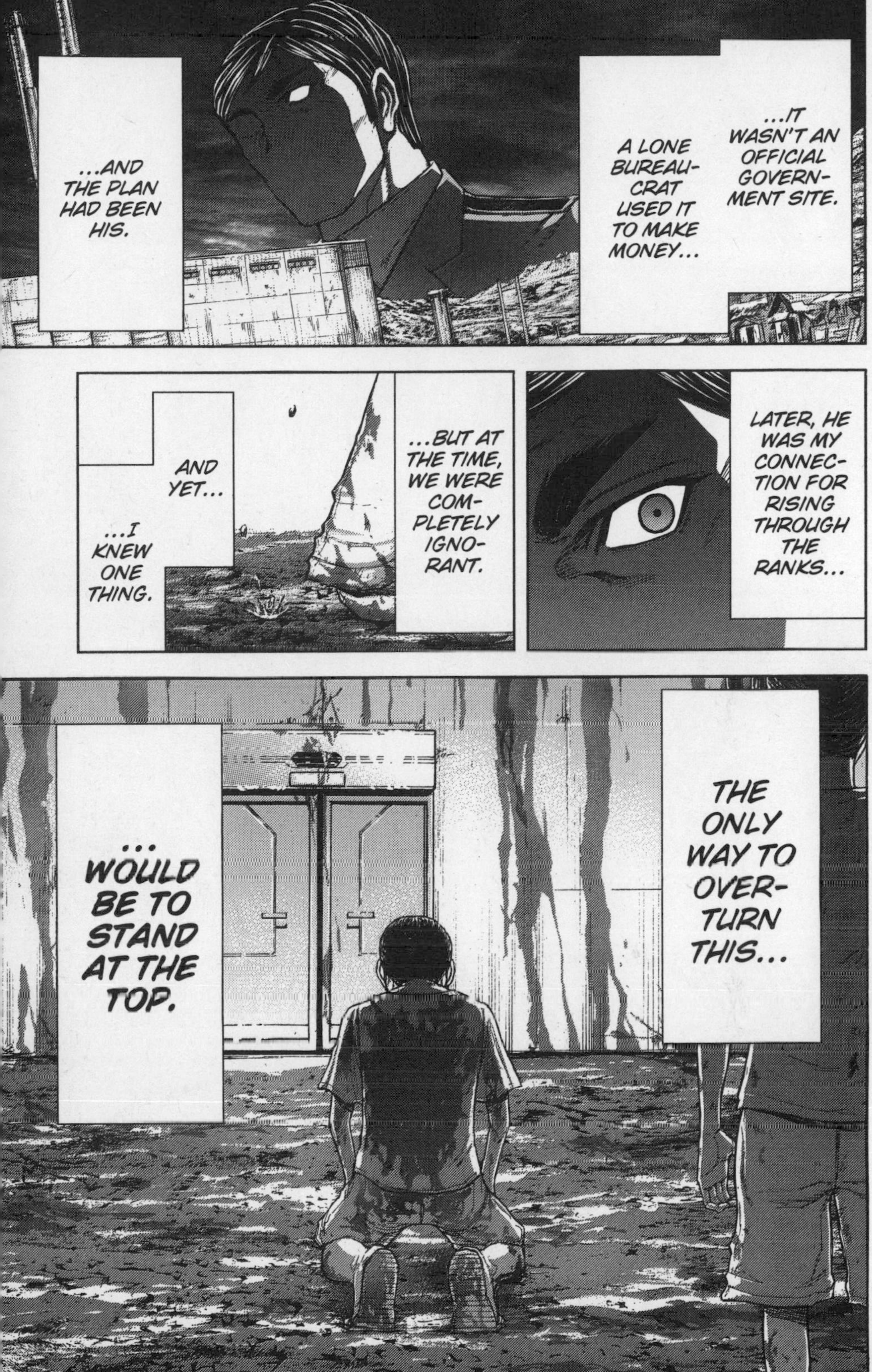
...IT WASN'T AN OFFICIAL GOVERN-MENT SITE.
A LONE BUREAU-CRAT USED IT TO MAKE MONEY...
...AND THE PLAN HAD BEEN HIS.
LATER, HE WAS MY CONNEC-TION FOR RISING THROUGH THE RANKS...
...BUT AT THE TIME, WE WERE COM-PLETELY IGNO-RANT.
AND YET...
...I KNEW ONE THING.
THE ONLY WAY TO OVER-TURN THIS...
...WOULD BE TO STAND AT THE TOP.

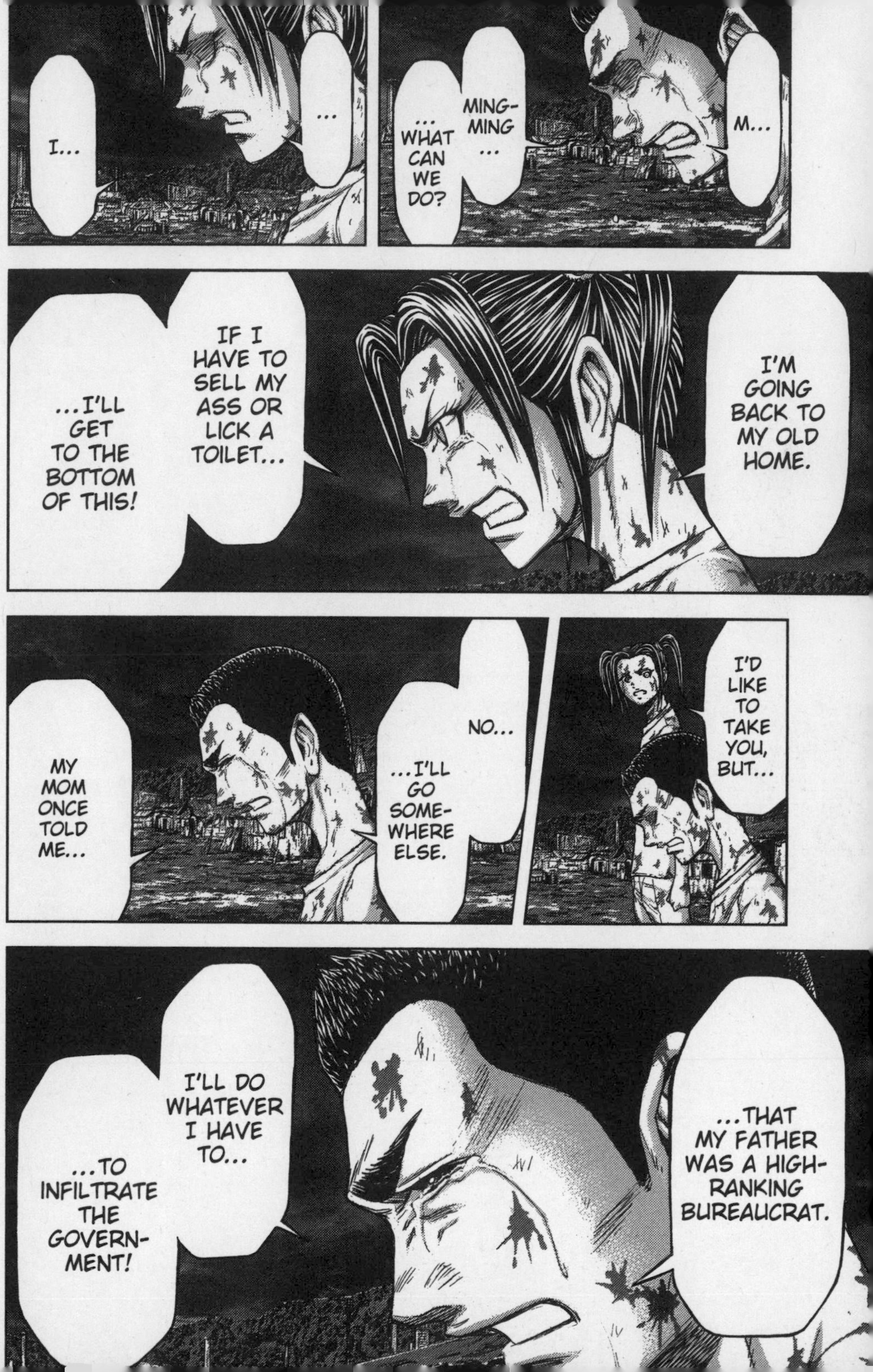
M...
MING-MING...
...WHAT CAN WE DO?
...
I...
I'M GOING BACK TO MY OLD HOME.
IF I HAVE TO SELL MY ASS OR LICK A TOILET...
...I'LL GET TO THE BOTTOM OF THIS!
I'D LIKE TO TAKE YOU, BUT...
NO...
...I'LL GO SOMEWHERE ELSE.
MY MOM ONCE TOLD ME...
...THAT MY FATHER WAS A HIGH-RANKING BUREAUCRAT.
I'LL DO WHATEVER I HAVE TO...
...TO INFILTRATE THE GOVERNMENT!

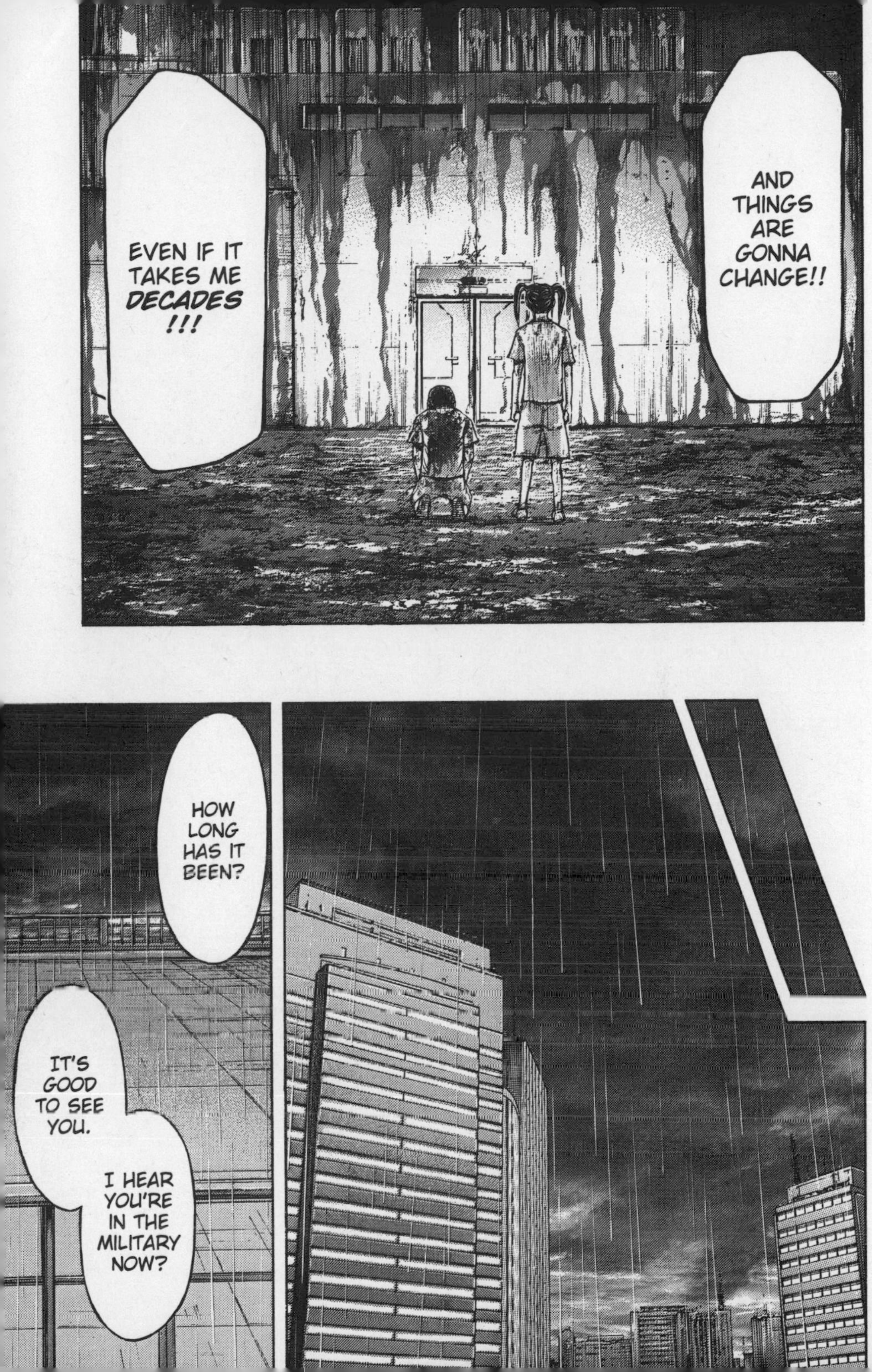
AND THINGS ARE GONNA CHANGE!!
EVEN IF IT TAKES ME *DECADES* !!!
HOW LONG HAS IT BEEN?
IT'S GOOD TO SEE YOU.
I HEAR YOU'RE IN THE MILITARY NOW?

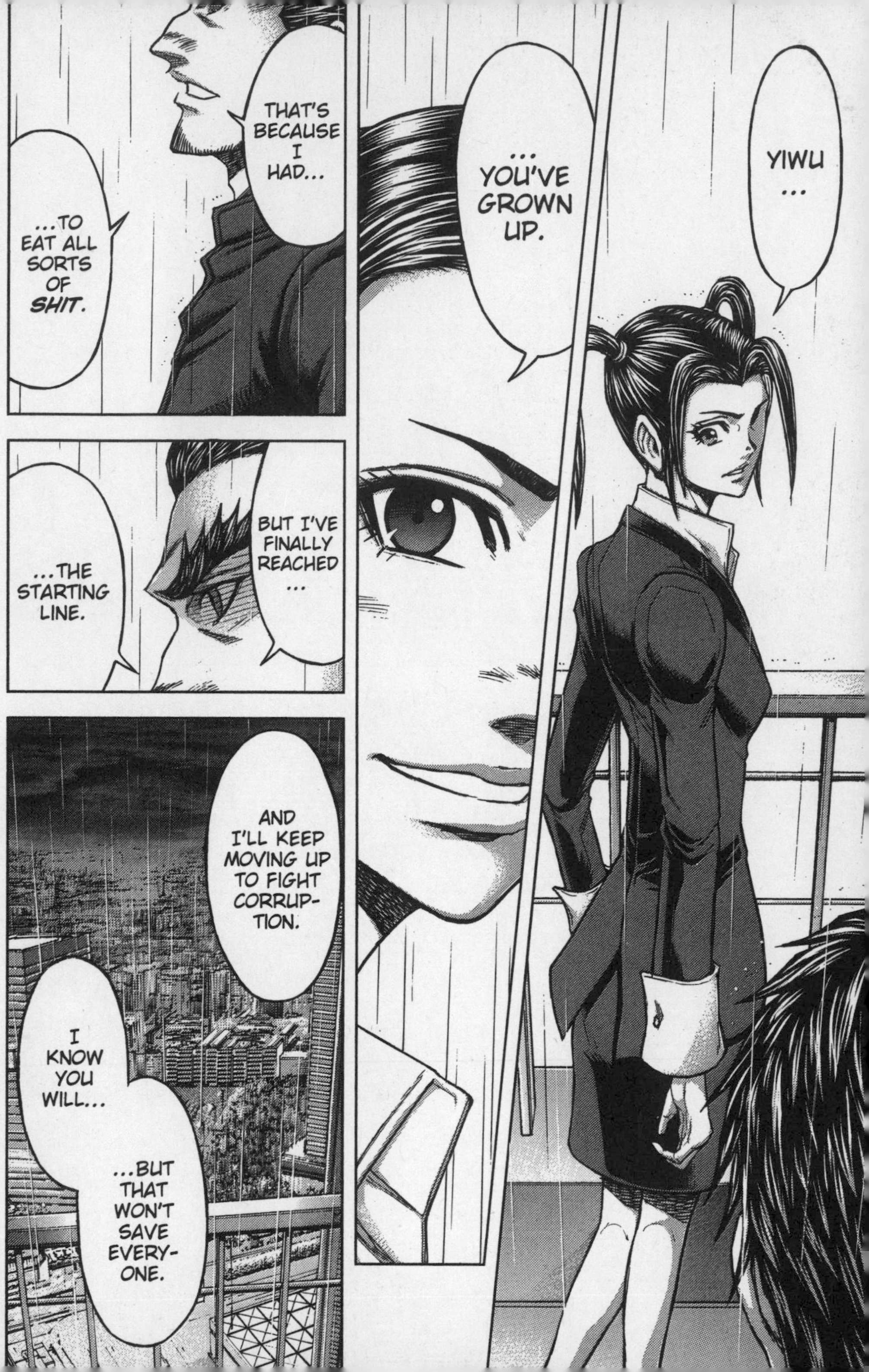
YIWU ...
... YOU'VE GROWN UP.
THAT'S BECAUSE I HAD...
...TO EAT ALL SORTS OF *SHIT*.
BUT I'VE FINALLY REACHED ...
...THE STARTING LINE.
AND I'LL KEEP MOVING UP TO FIGHT CORRUP-TION.
I KNOW YOU WILL...
...BUT THAT WON'T SAVE EVERY-ONE.

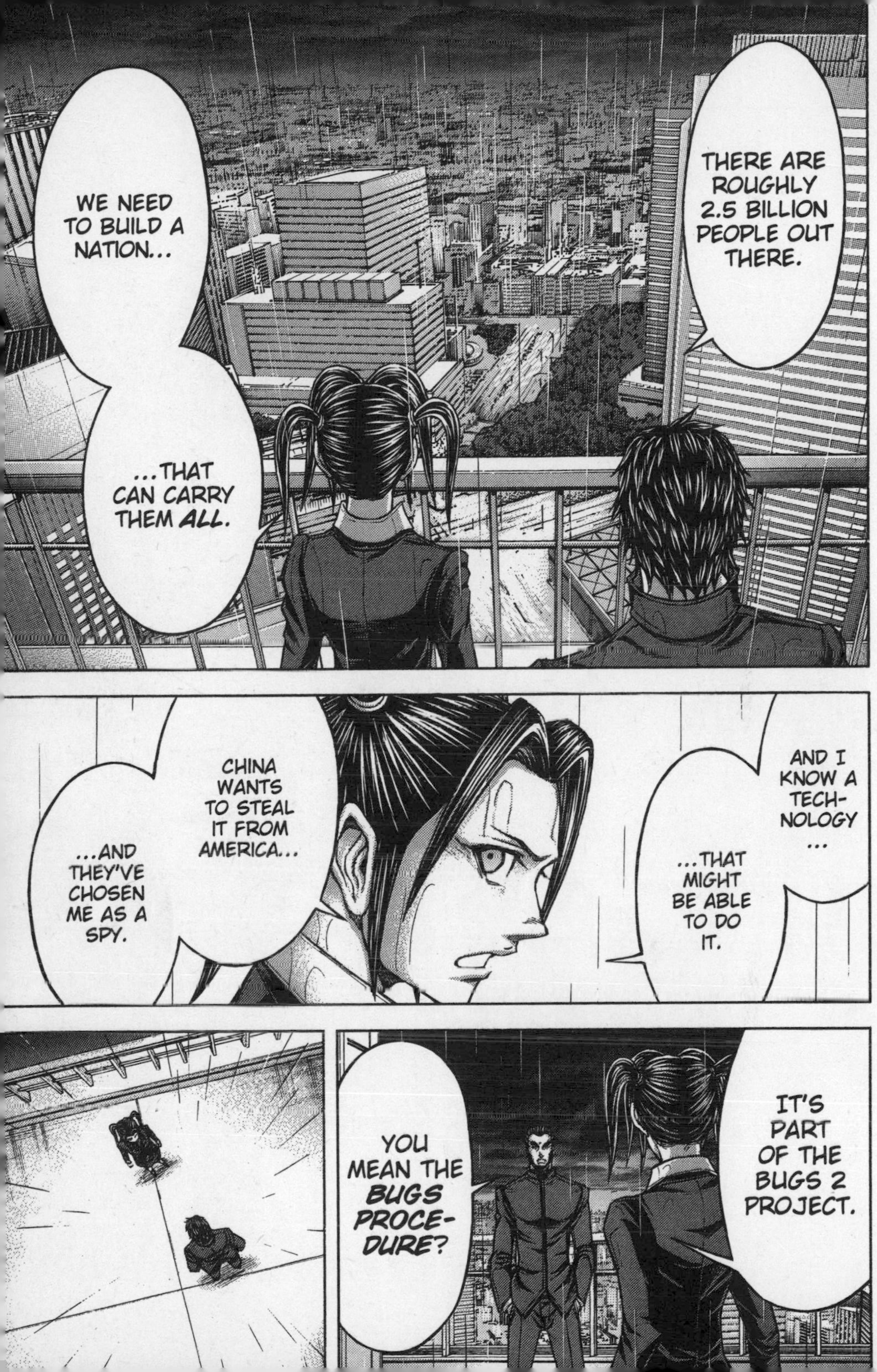
THERE ARE ROUGHLY 2.5 BILLION PEOPLE OUT THERE.
WE NEED TO BUILD A NATION...
...THAT CAN CARRY THEM *ALL*.
AND I KNOW A TECHNOLOGY...
...THAT MIGHT BE ABLE TO DO IT.
CHINA WANTS TO STEAL IT FROM AMERICA...
...AND THEY'VE CHOSEN ME AS A SPY.
IT'S PART OF THE BUGS 2 PROJECT.
YOU MEAN THE *BUGS PROCEDURE*?

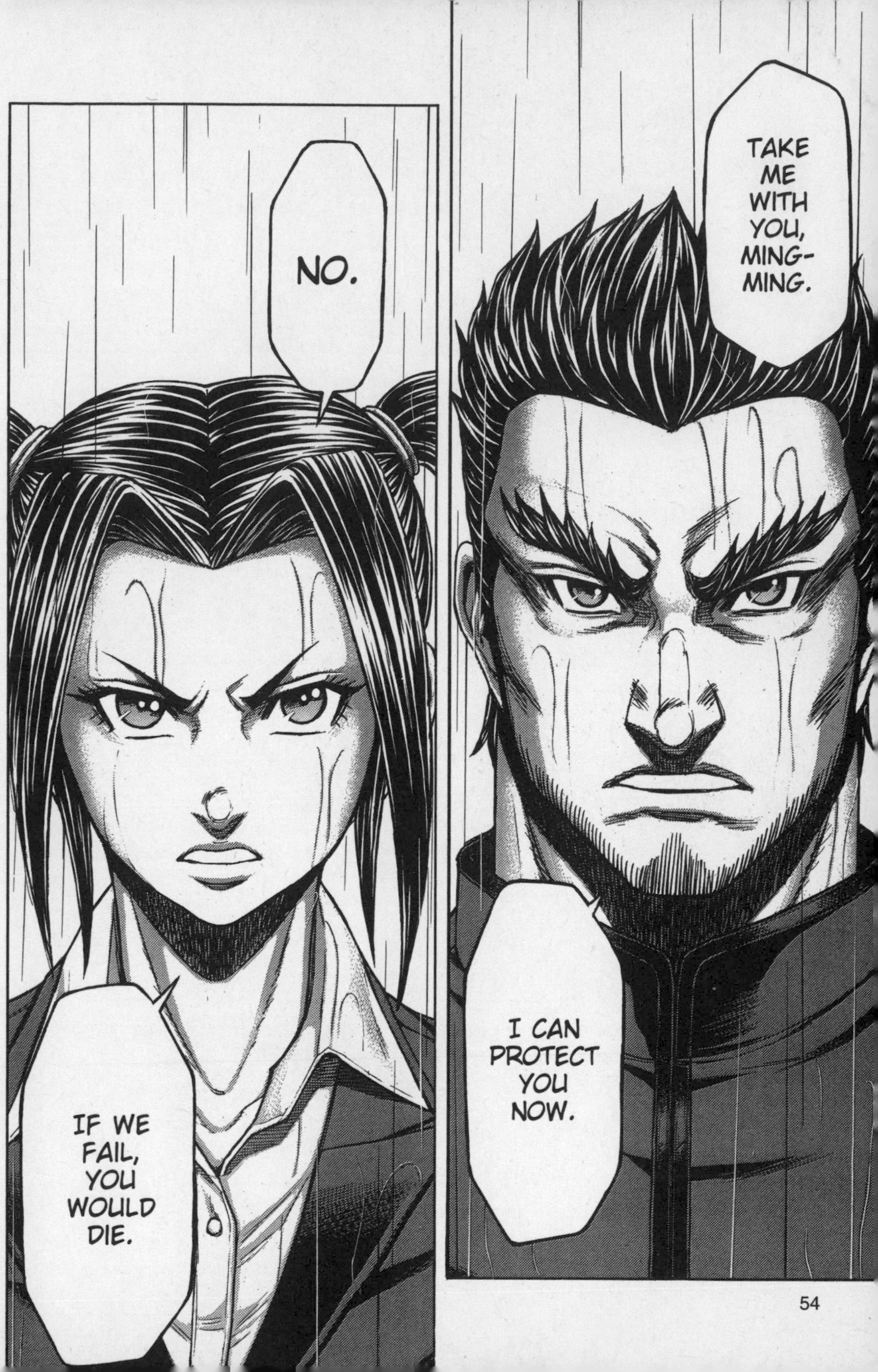
TAKE ME WITH YOU, MING-MING.
I CAN PROTECT YOU NOW.
NO.
IF WE FAIL, YOU WOULD DIE.

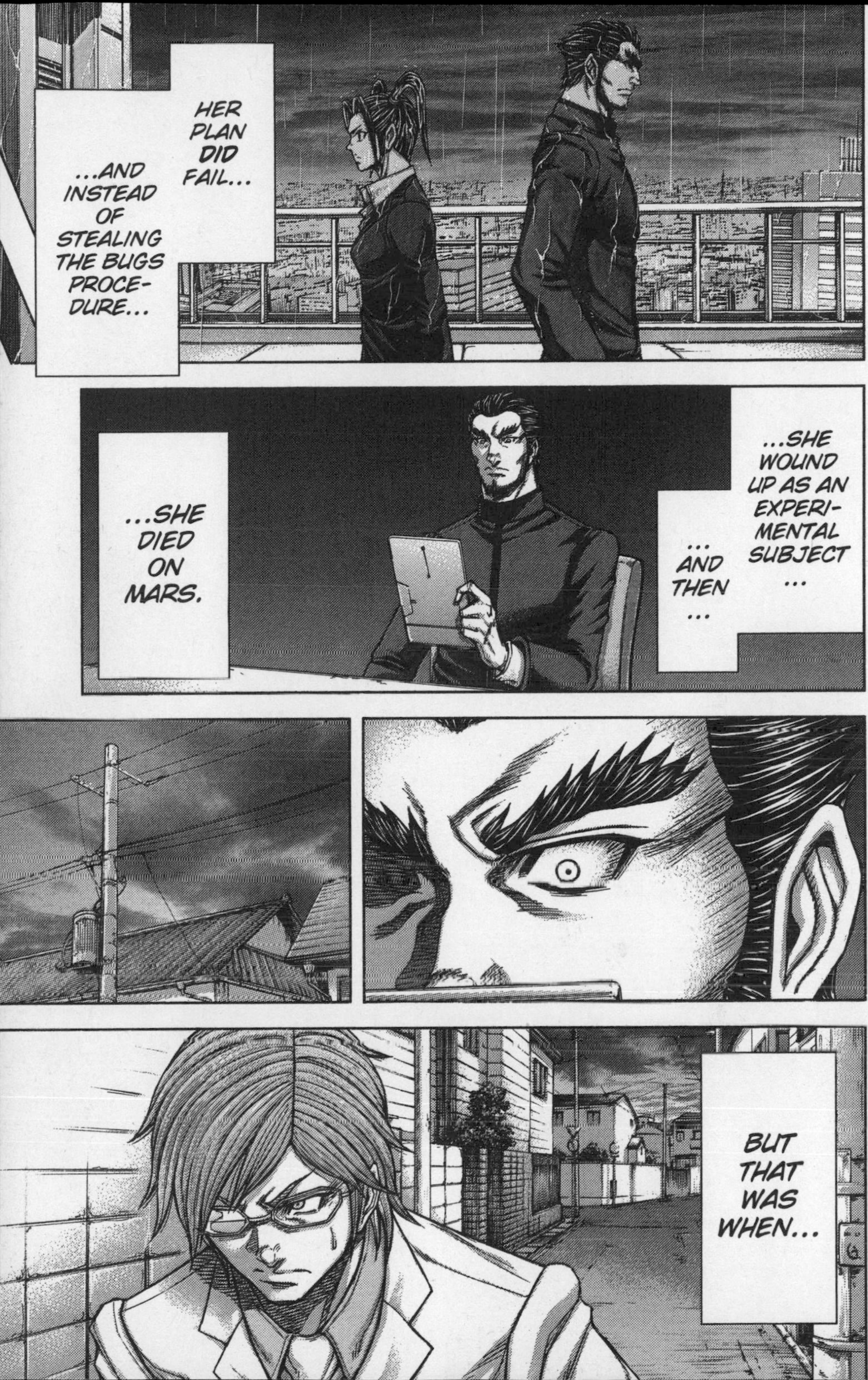
HER PLAN DID FAIL...
...AND INSTEAD OF STEALING THE BUGS PROCE-DURE...
...SHE WOUND UP AS AN EXPERI-MENTAL SUBJECT...
...AND THEN...
...SHE DIED ON MARS.
BUT THAT WAS WHEN...

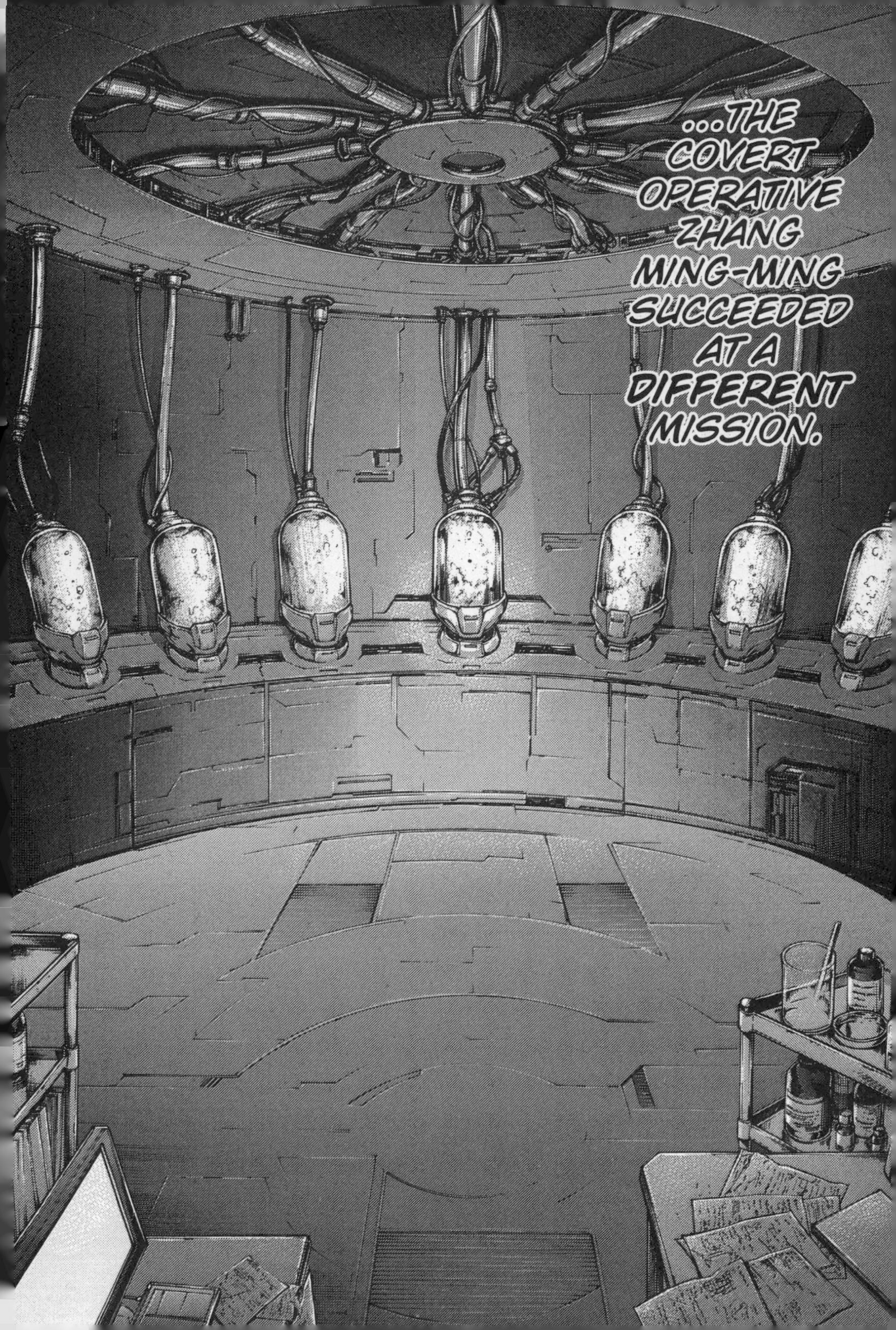
...THE COVERT OPERATIVE ZHANG MING-MING SUCCEEDED AT A DIFFERENT MISSION.

CHAPTER 166: AMARANTH

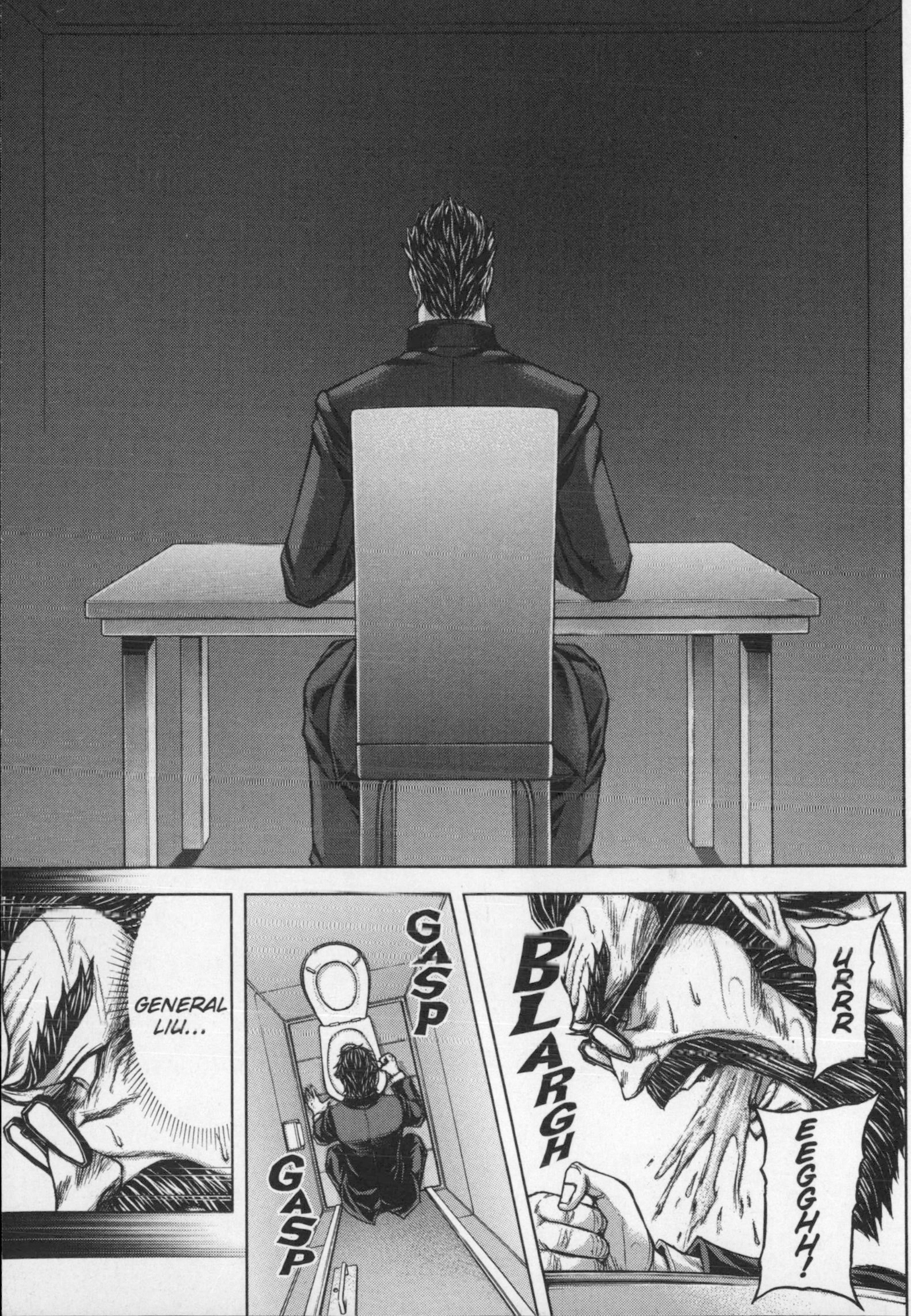
BLARGH
URRR
EEGGHH!
GASP
GASP
GENERAL LIU...

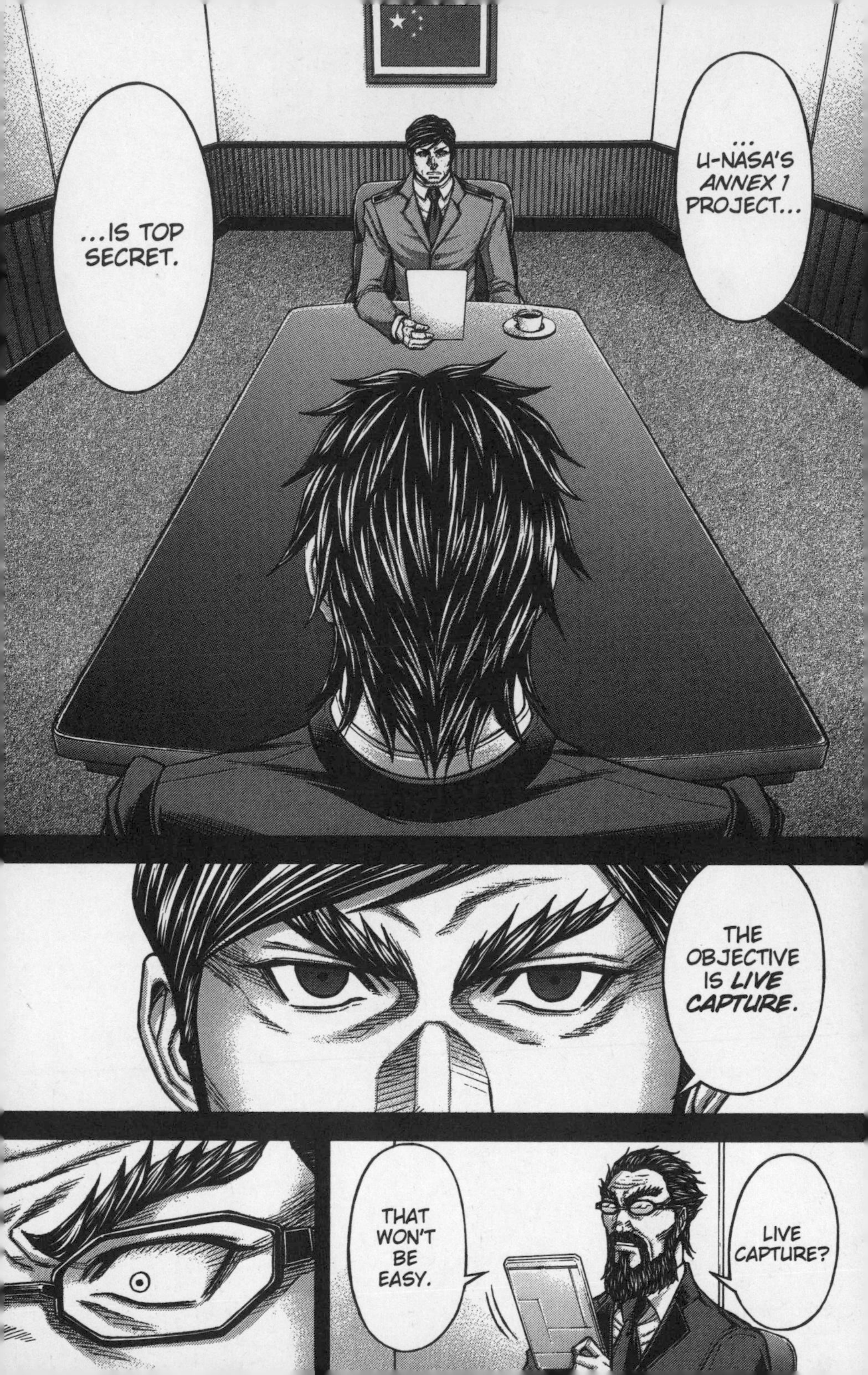
...U-NASA'S ANNEX 1 PROJECT...
...IS TOP SECRET.
THE OBJECTIVE IS LIVE CAPTURE.
LIVE CAPTURE?
THAT WON'T BE EASY.

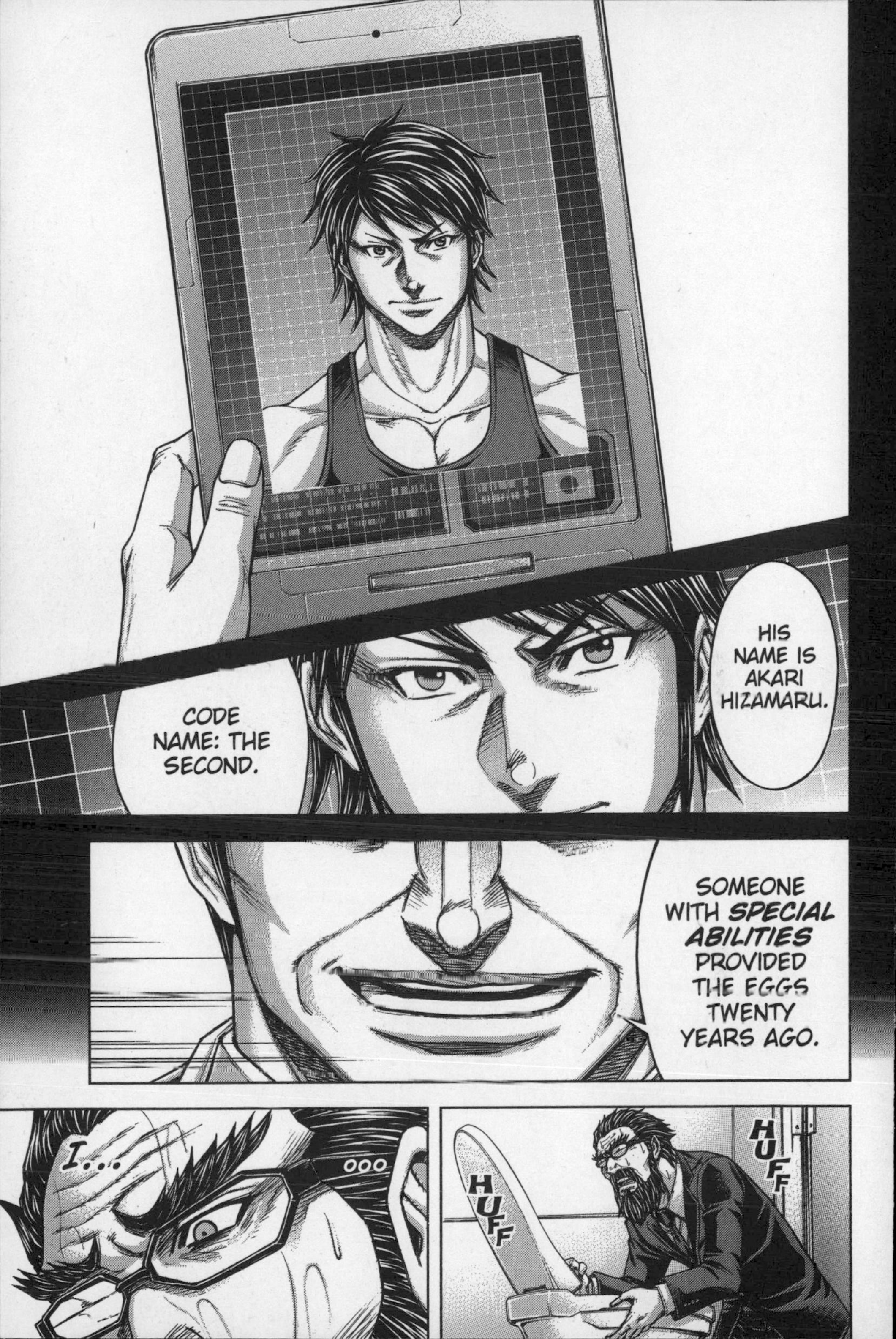
HIS NAME IS AKARI HIZAMARU.
CODE NAME: THE SECOND.
SOMEONE WITH ***SPECIAL ABILITIES*** PROVIDED THE EGGS TWENTY YEARS AGO.
HUFF
HUFF
I...
ooo

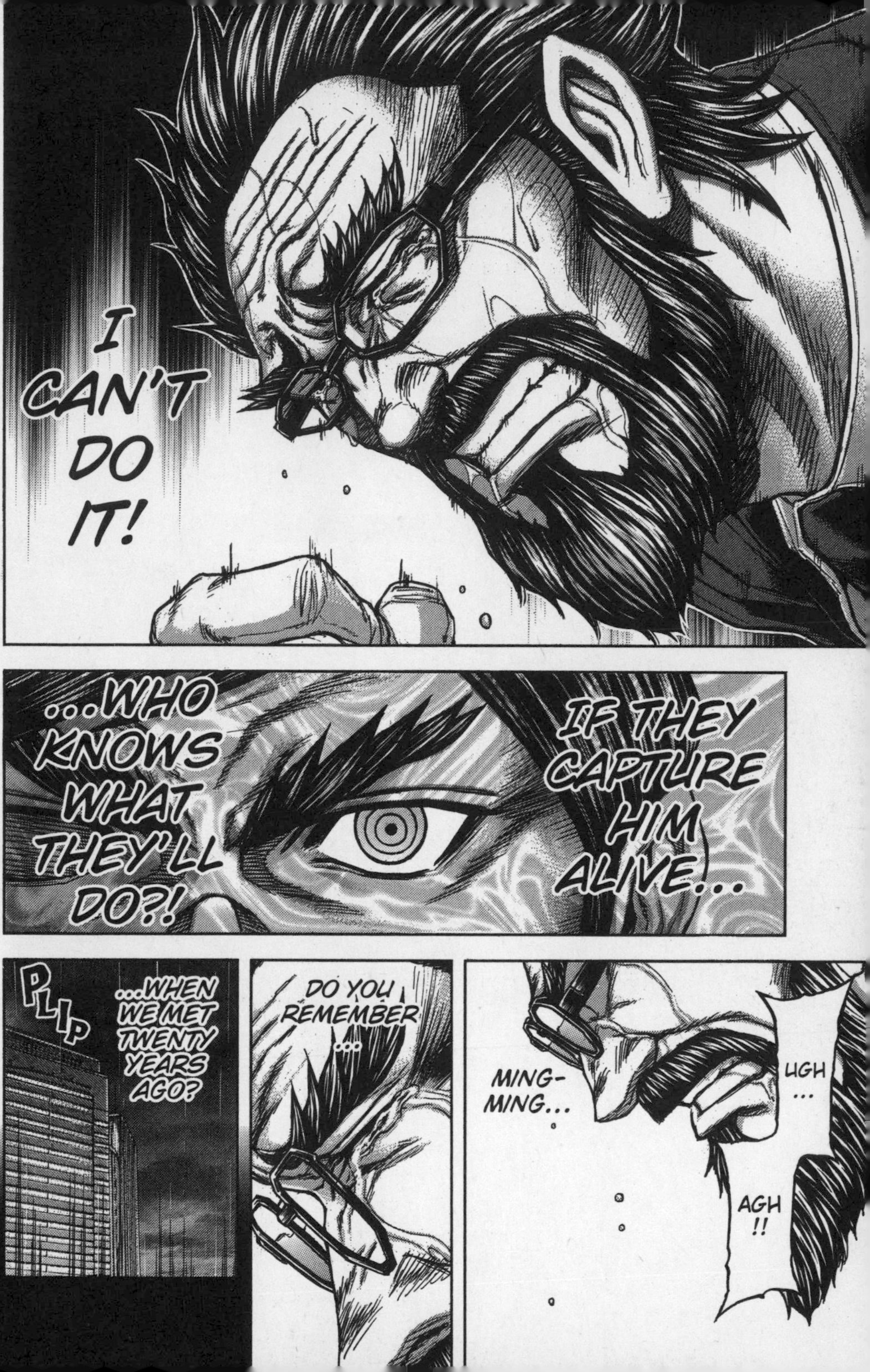
I CAN'T DO IT!
IF THEY CAPTURE HIM ALIVE...
...WHO KNOWS WHAT THEY'LL DO?!
UGH...
MING-MING...
AGH!!
DO YOU REMEMBER...
PLIP
...WHEN WE MET TWENTY YEARS AGO?

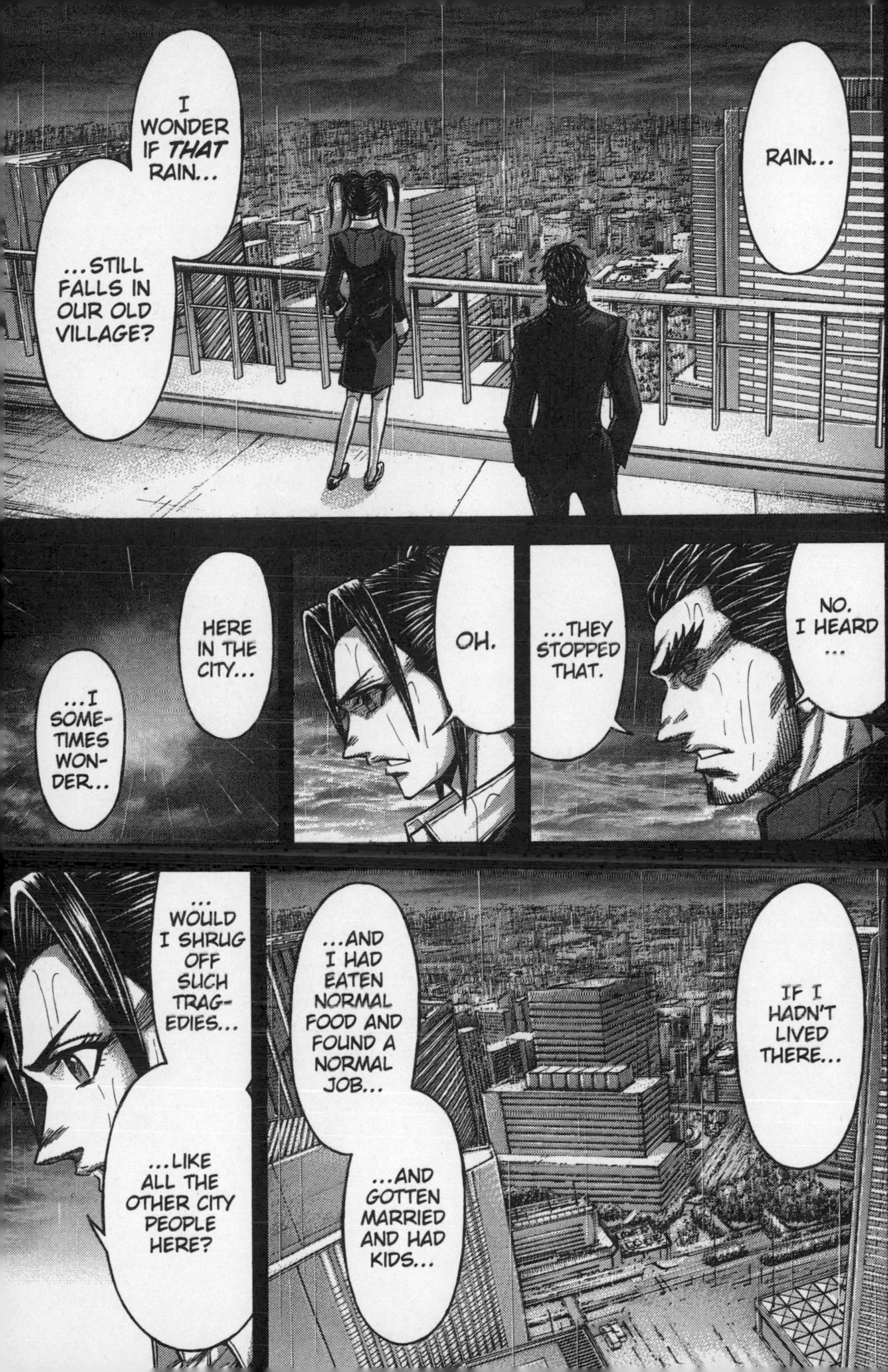
RAIN...
I WONDER IF *THAT* RAIN...
...STILL FALLS IN OUR OLD VILLAGE?
NO. I HEARD ...
...THEY STOPPED THAT.
OH.
HERE IN THE CITY...
...I SOMETIMES WONDER...
IF I HADN'T LIVED THERE...
...AND I HAD EATEN NORMAL FOOD AND FOUND A NORMAL JOB...
...AND GOTTEN MARRIED AND HAD KIDS...
...WOULD I SHRUG OFF SUCH TRAGEDIES...
...LIKE ALL THE OTHER CITY PEOPLE HERE?

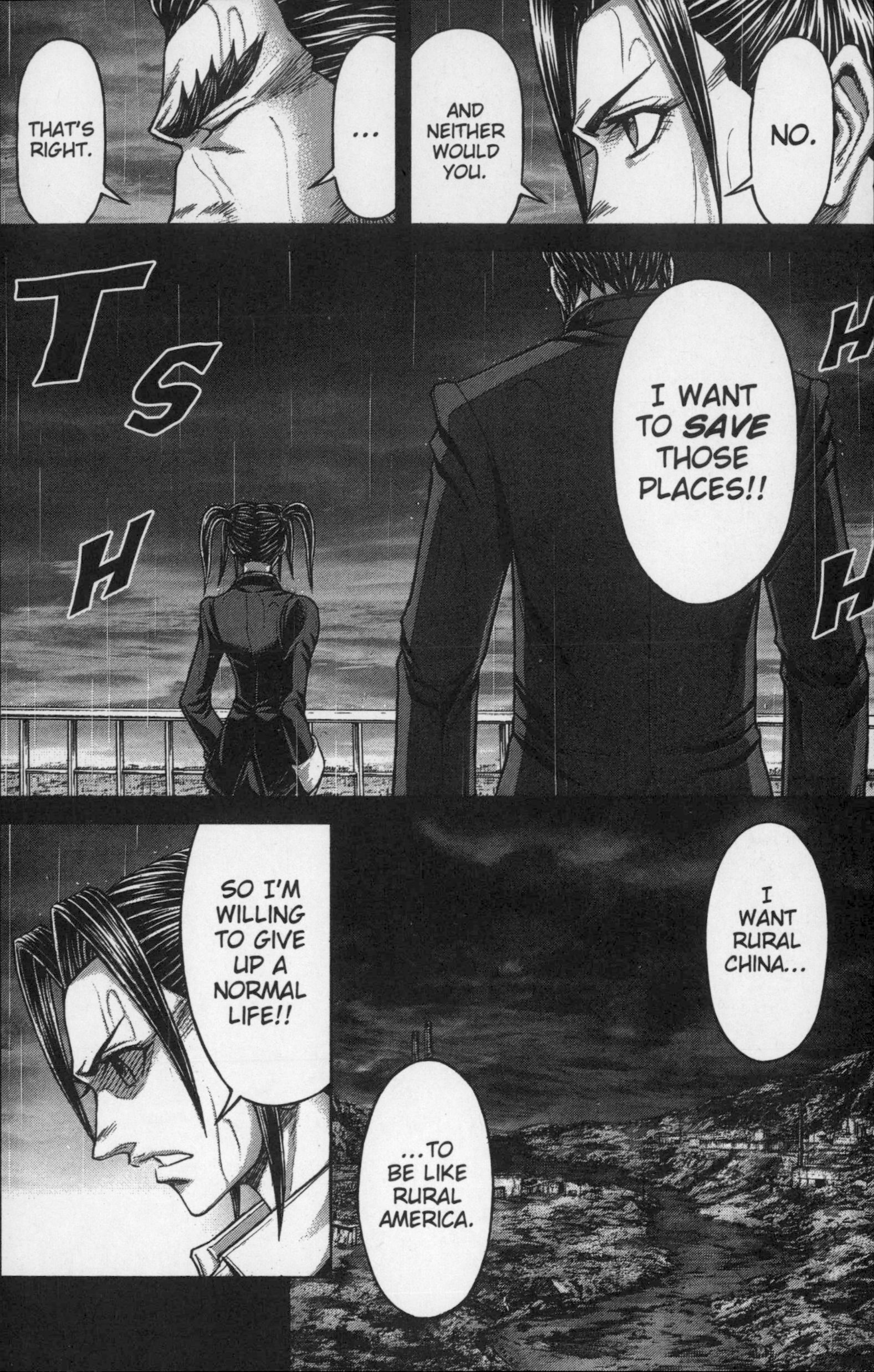
NO.
AND NEITHER WOULD YOU.
...
THAT'S RIGHT.
I WANT TO **SAVE** THOSE PLACES!!
TSH
I WANT RURAL CHINA...
...TO BE LIKE RURAL AMERICA.
SO I'M WILLING TO GIVE UP A NORMAL LIFE!!

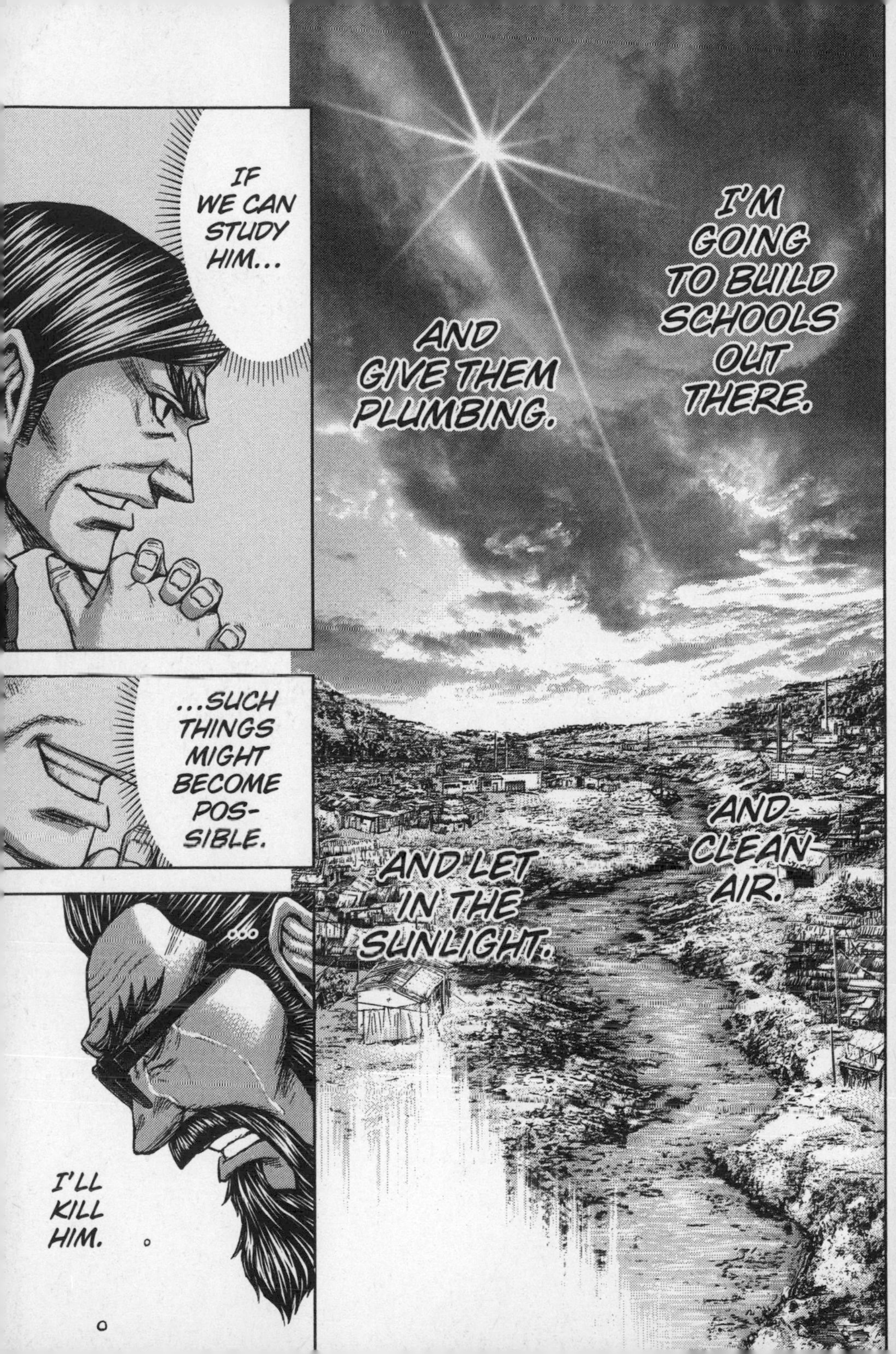
I'M GOING TO BUILD SCHOOLS OUT THERE.
AND GIVE THEM PLUMBING.
AND CLEAN AIR.
AND LET IN THE SUNLIGHT.
IF WE CAN STUDY HIM...
...SUCH THINGS MIGHT BECOME POS-SIBLE.
...
I'LL KILL HIM.

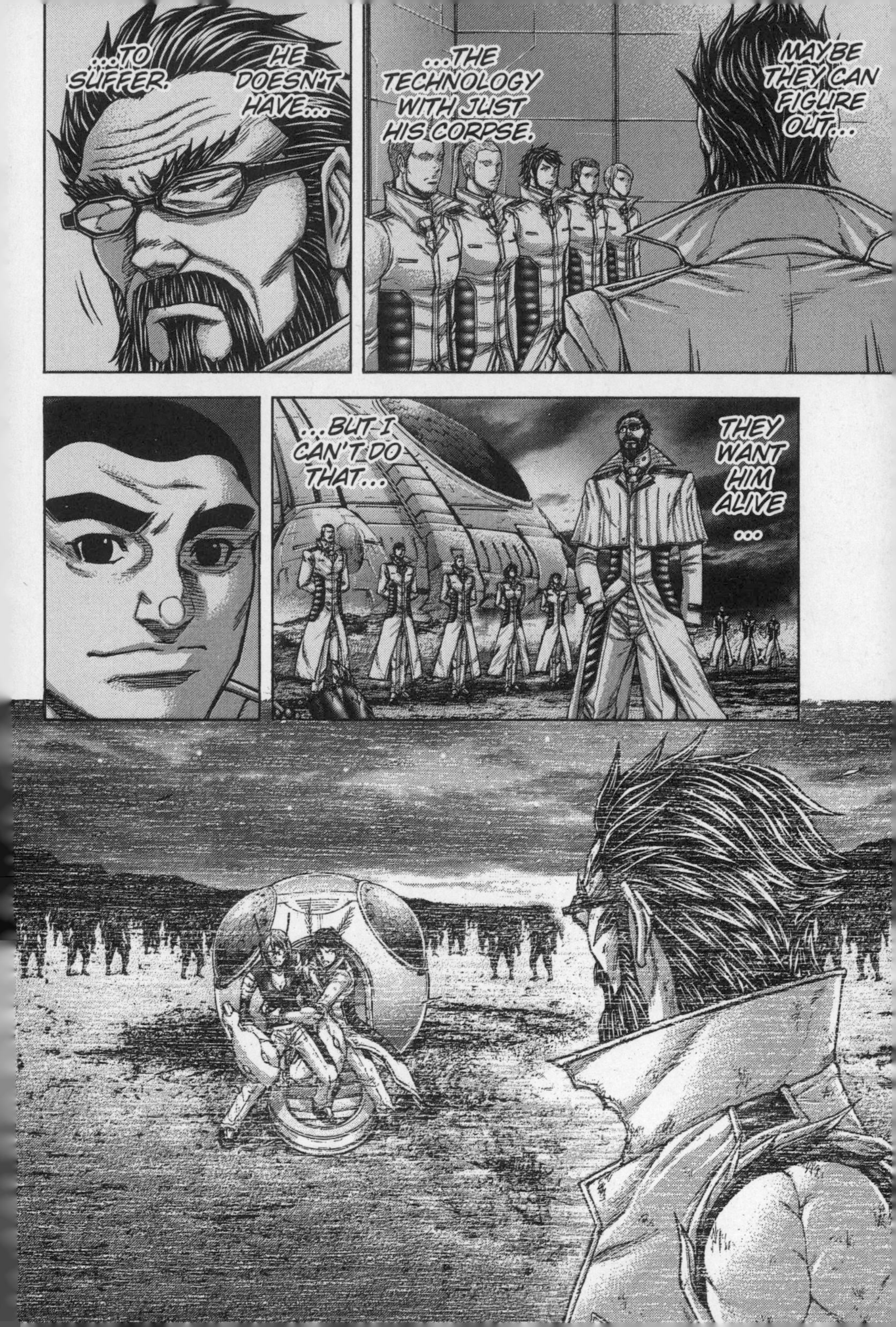
MAYBE THEY CAN FIGURE OUT...
...THE TECHNOLOGY WITH JUST HIS CORPSE.
HE DOESN'T HAVE...
...TO SUFFER.
THEY WANT HIM ALIVE...
...BUT I CAN'T DO THAT...

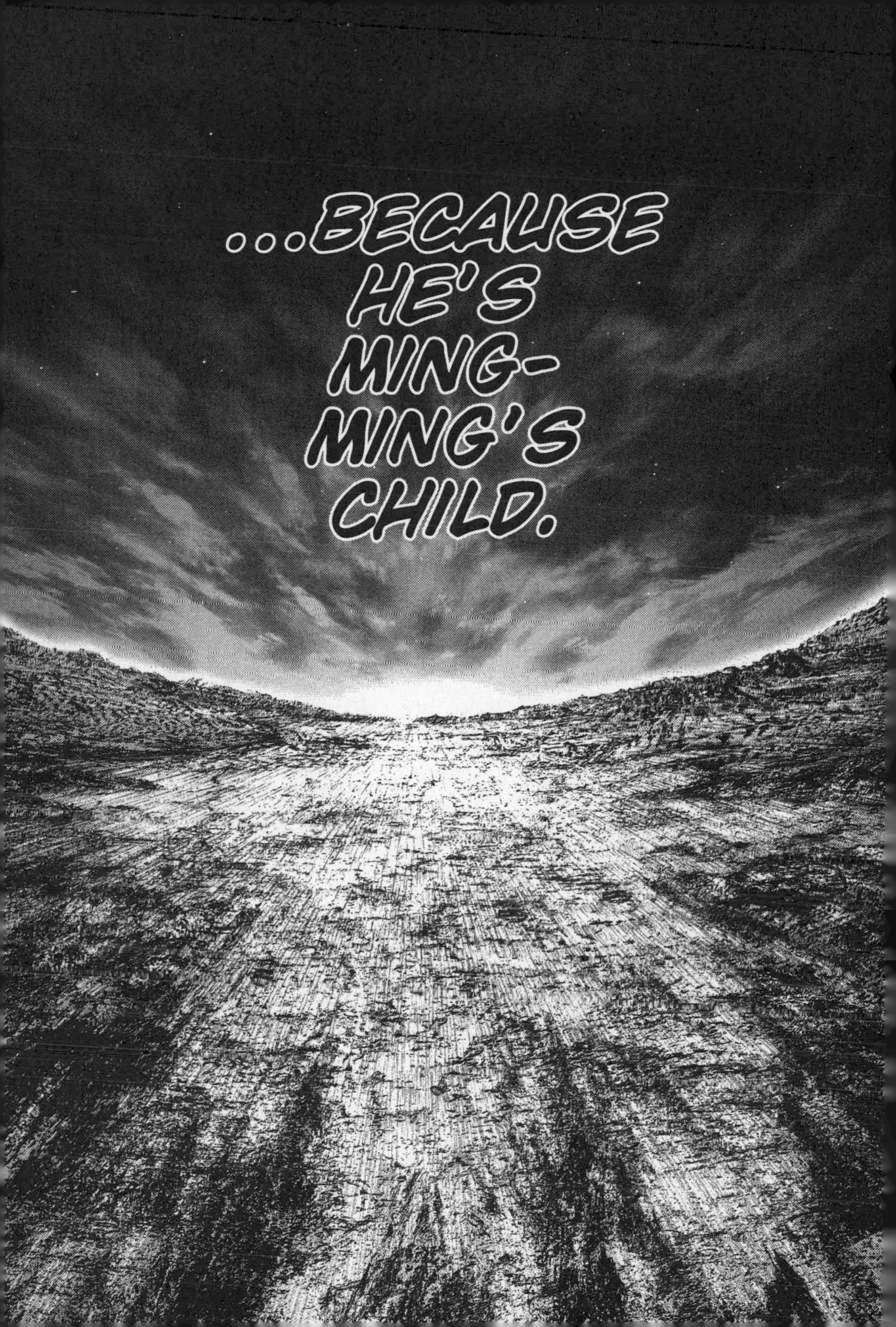
...BECAUSE HE'S MING-MING'S CHILD.

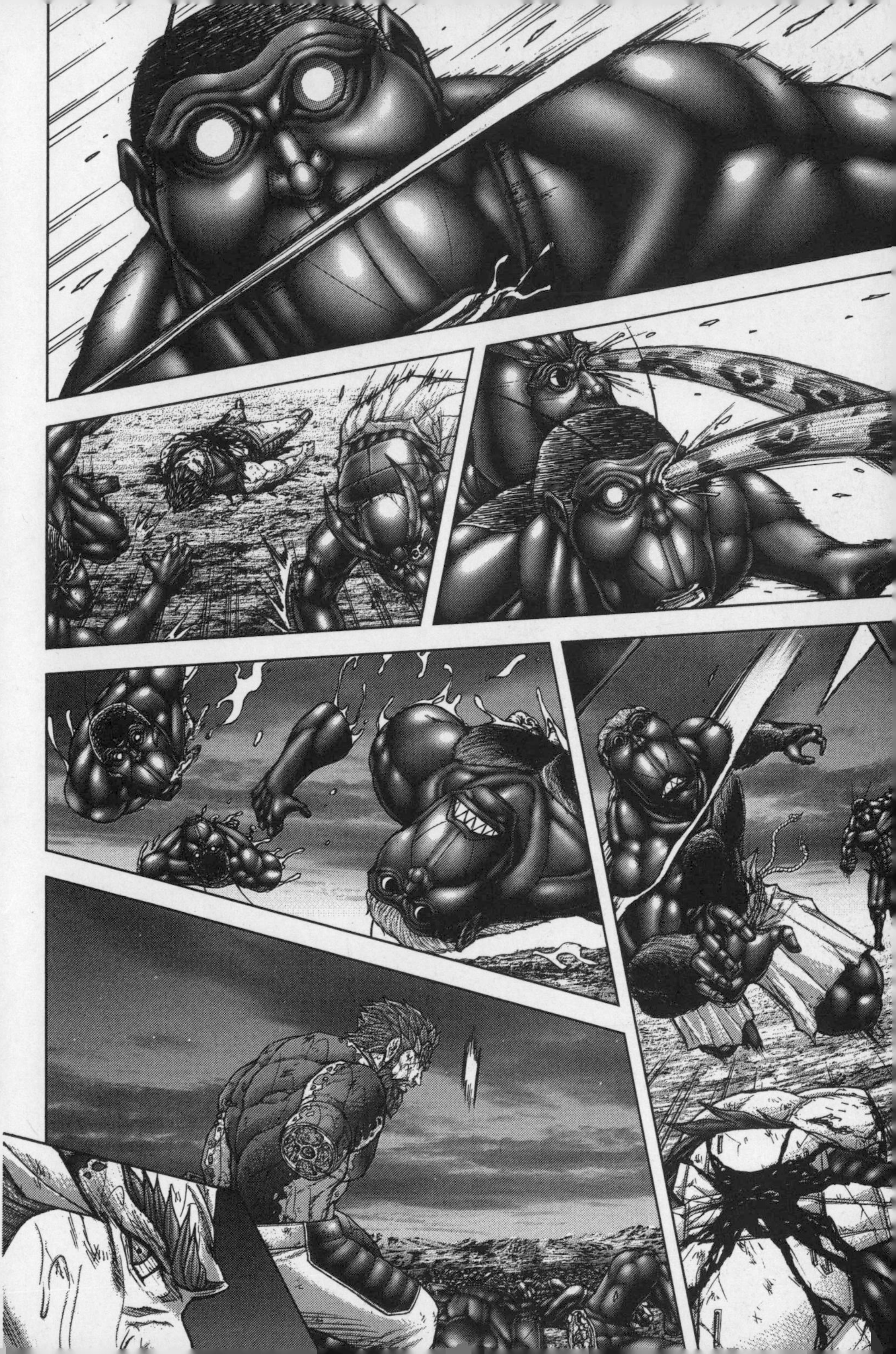

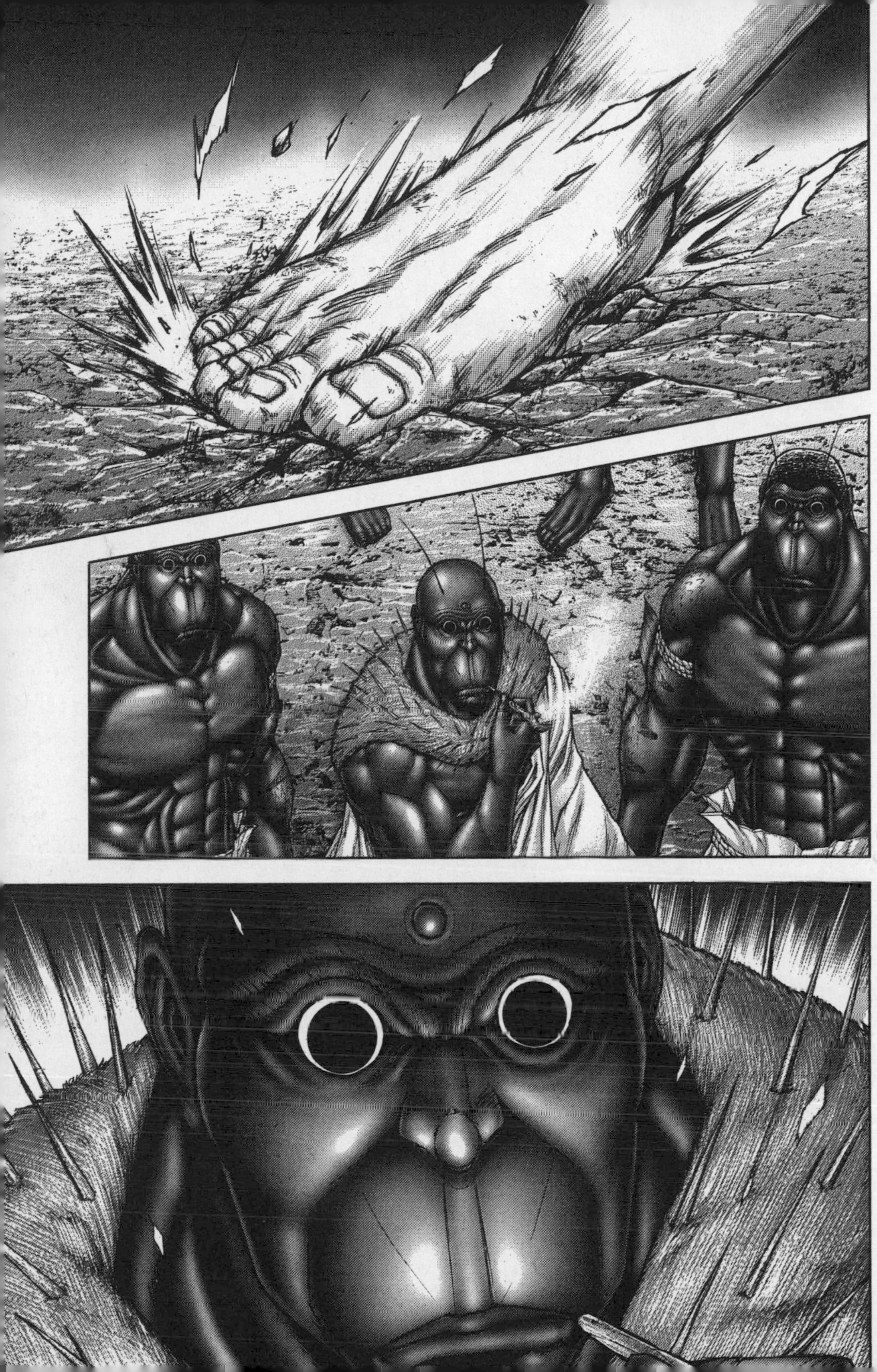

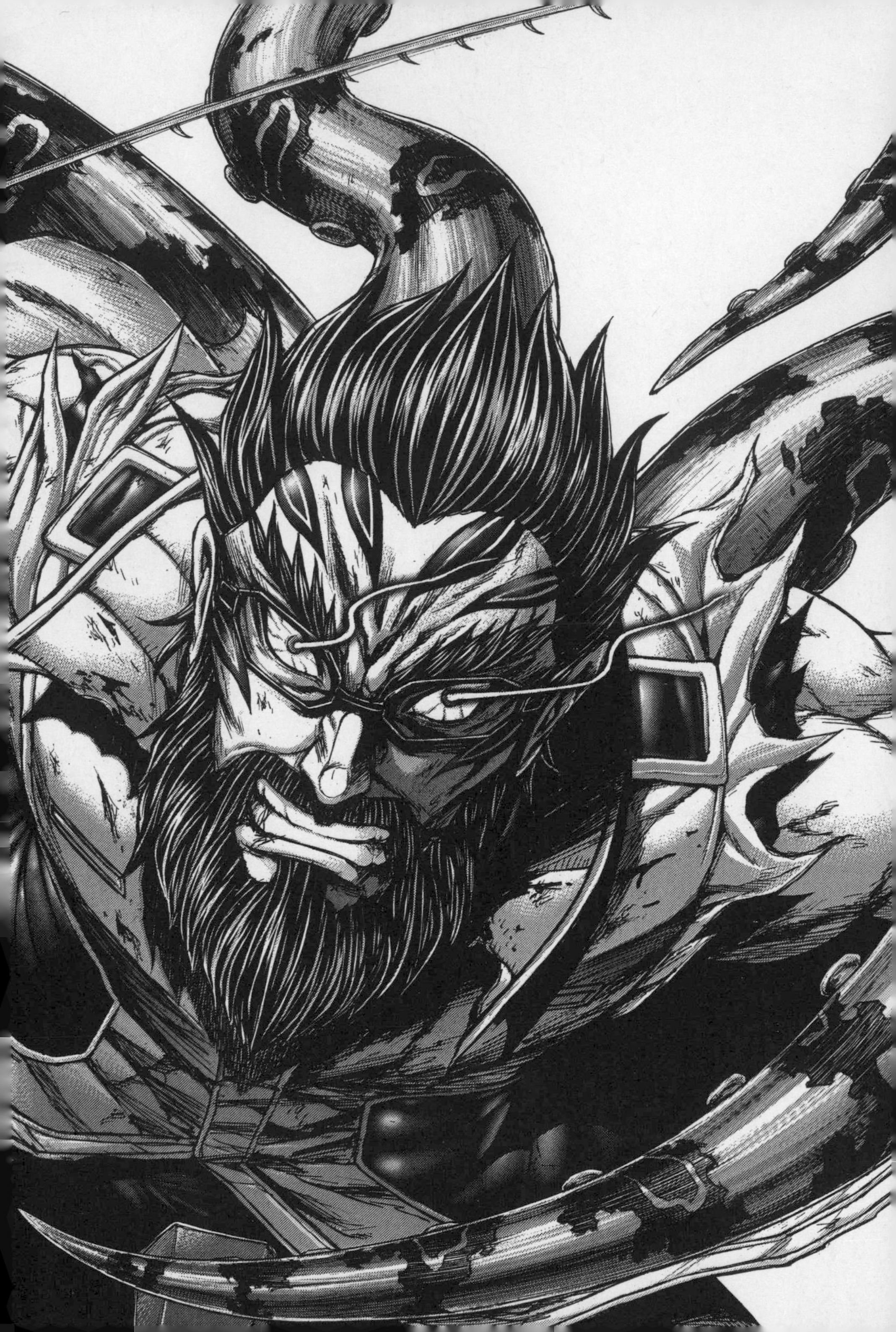

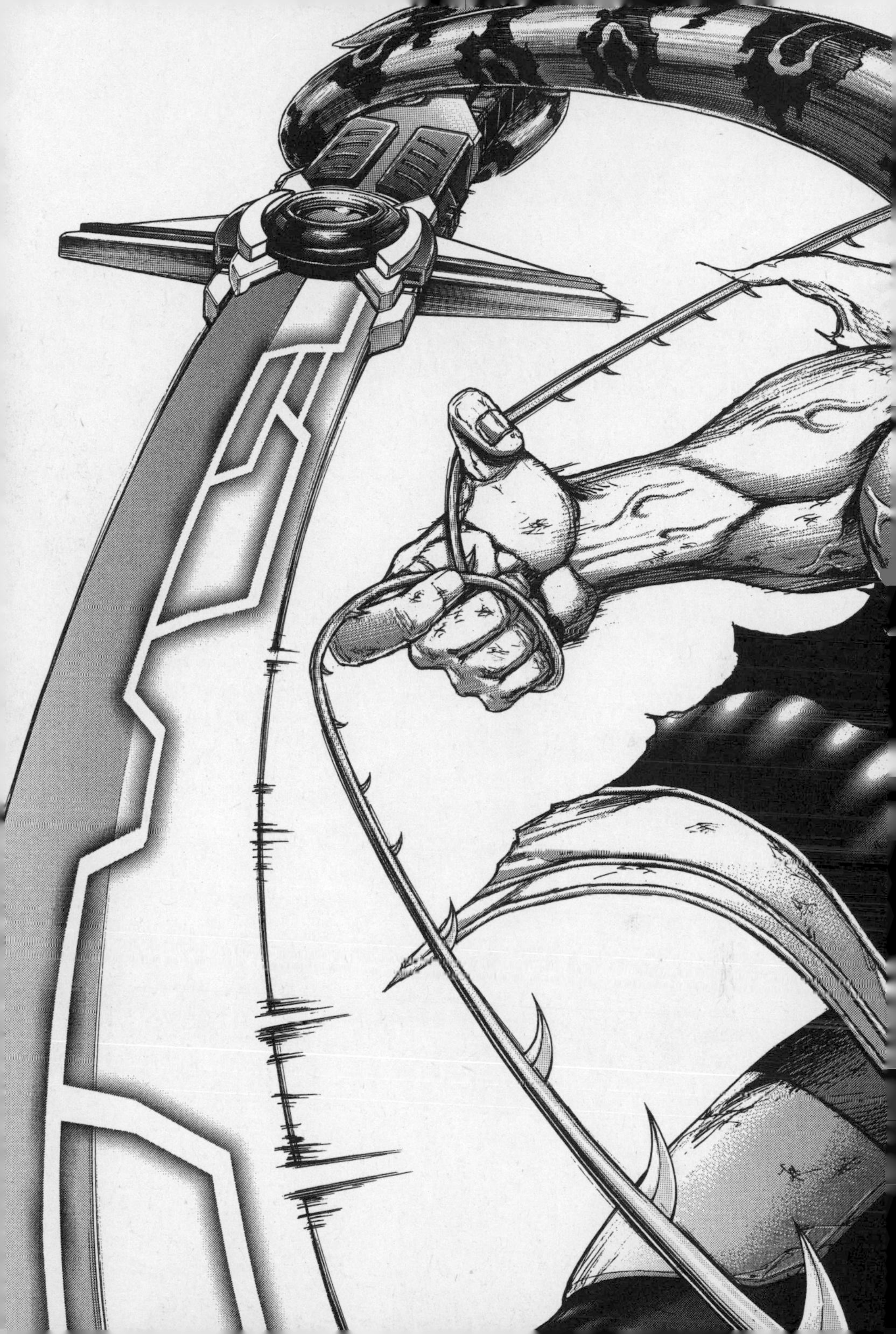

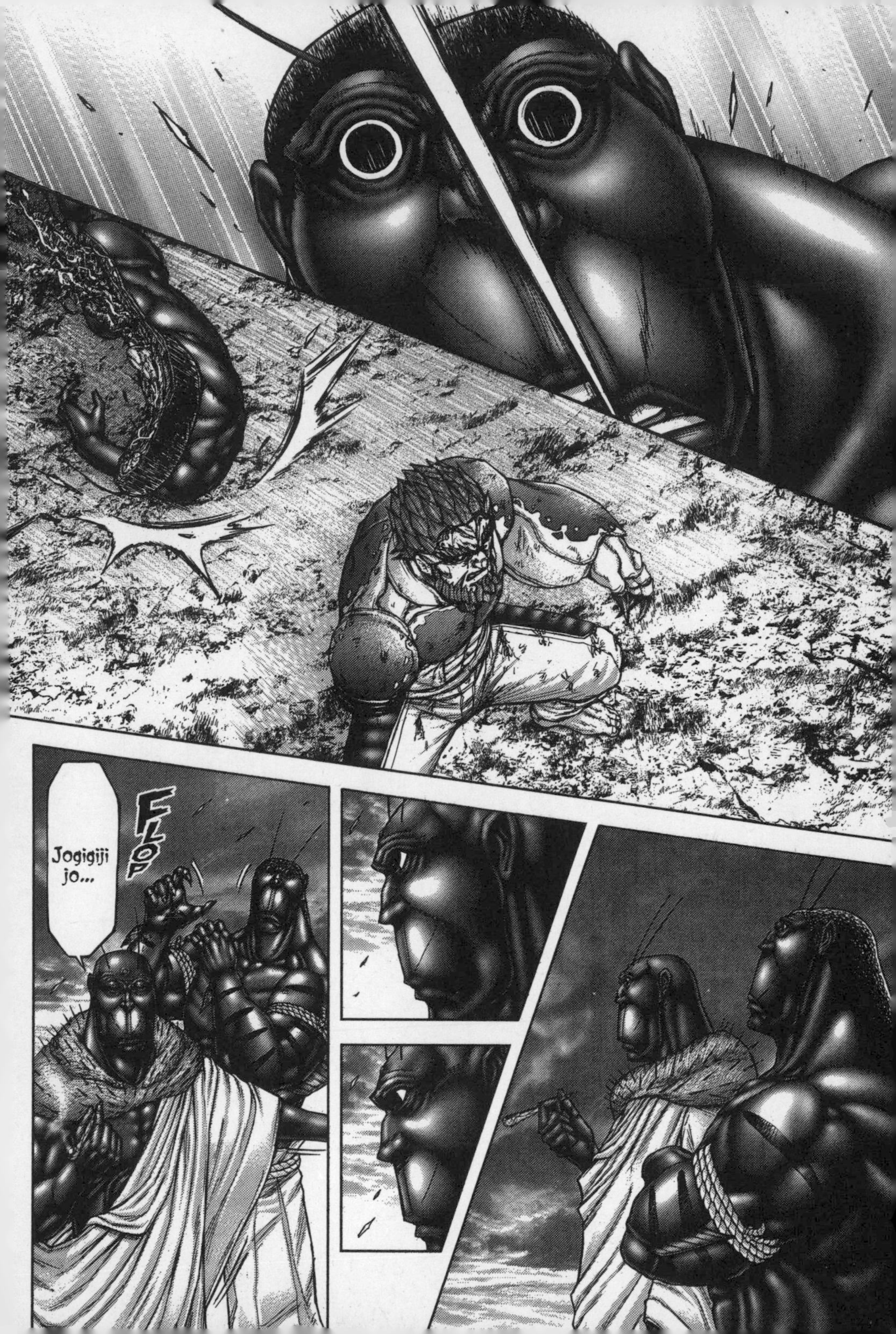
FLOP
Jogigiji jo...

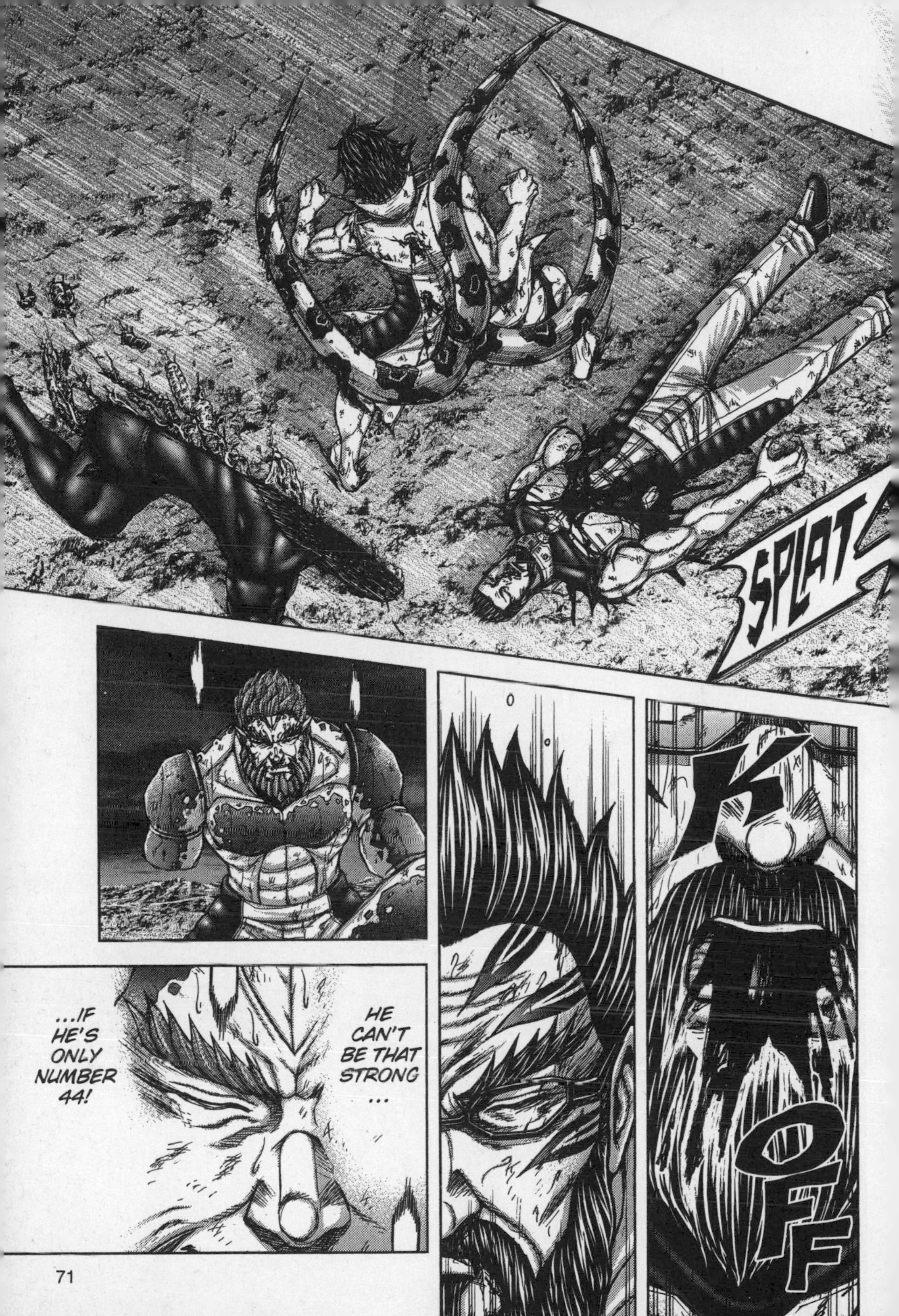
SPLAT
KOFF
HE CAN'T BE THAT STRONG ...
...IF HE'S ONLY NUMBER 44!

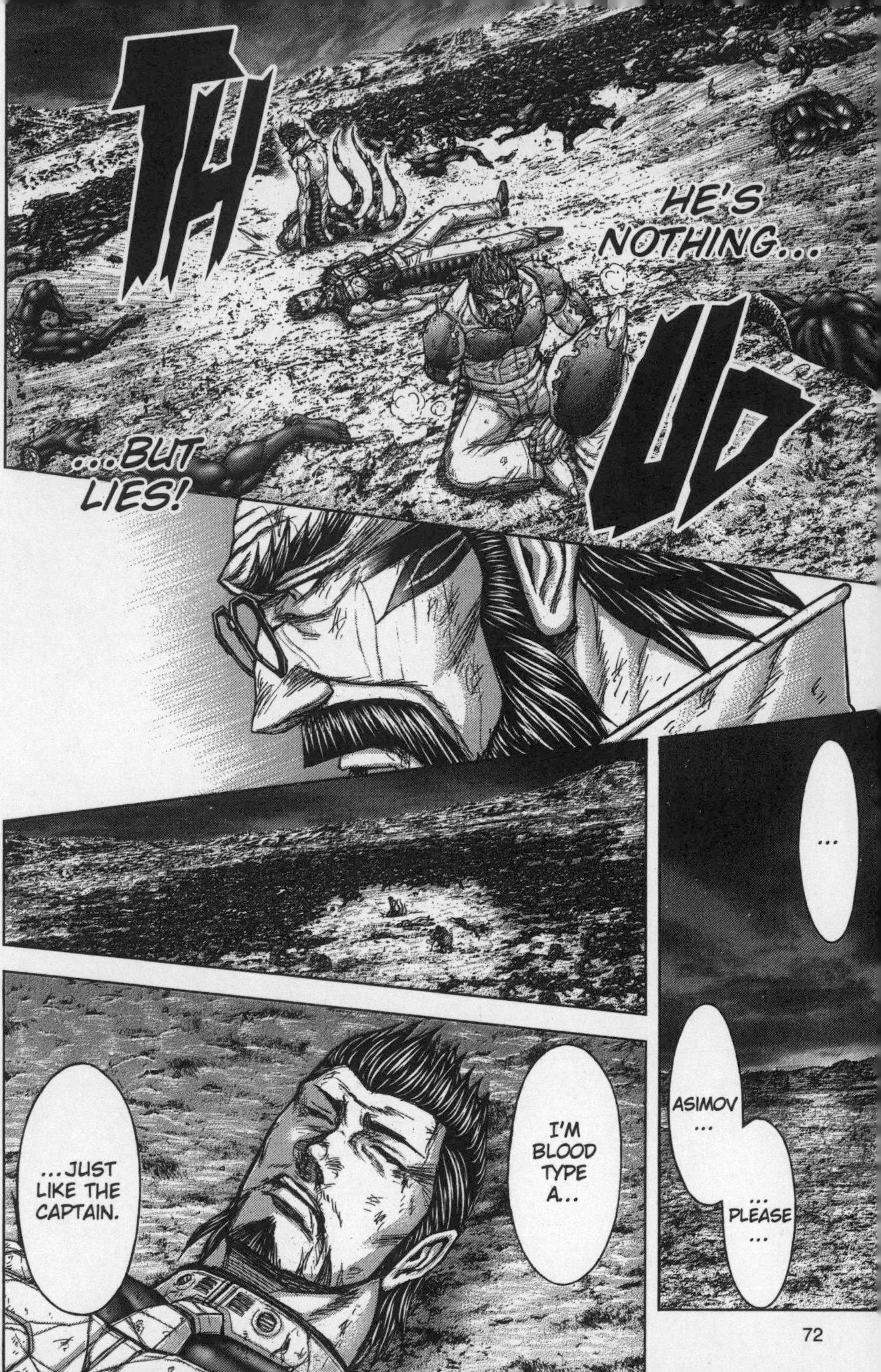
HE'S NOTHING...
...BUT LIES!
THUD
...
ASIMOV ...
... PLEASE ...
I'M BLOOD TYPE A...
...JUST LIKE THE CAPTAIN.

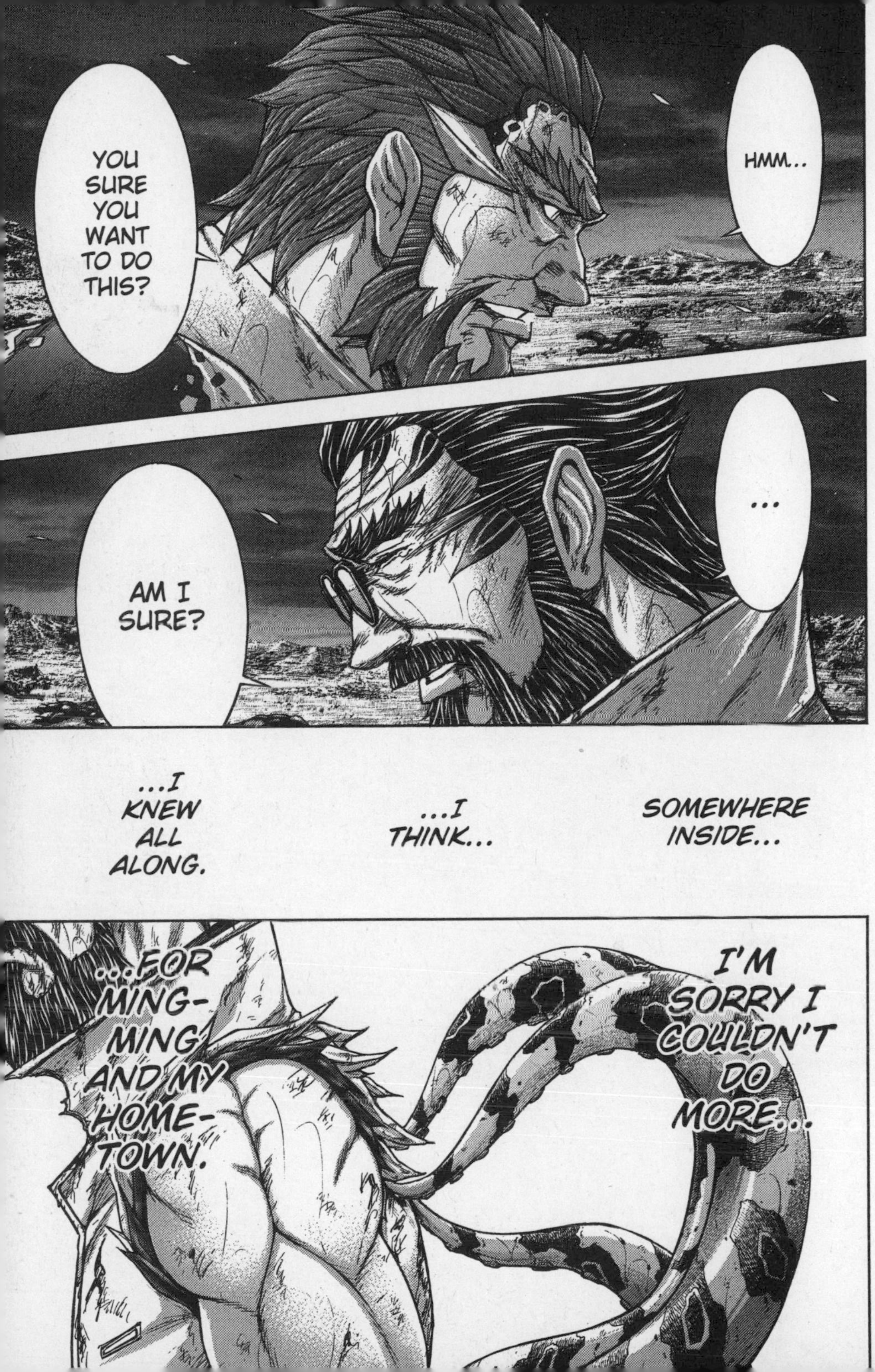
HMM...
YOU SURE YOU WANT TO DO THIS?
...
AM I SURE?
SOMEWHERE INSIDE...
...I THINK...
...I KNEW ALL ALONG.
I'M SORRY I COULDN'T DO MORE...
...FOR MING-MING AND MY HOME-TOWN.

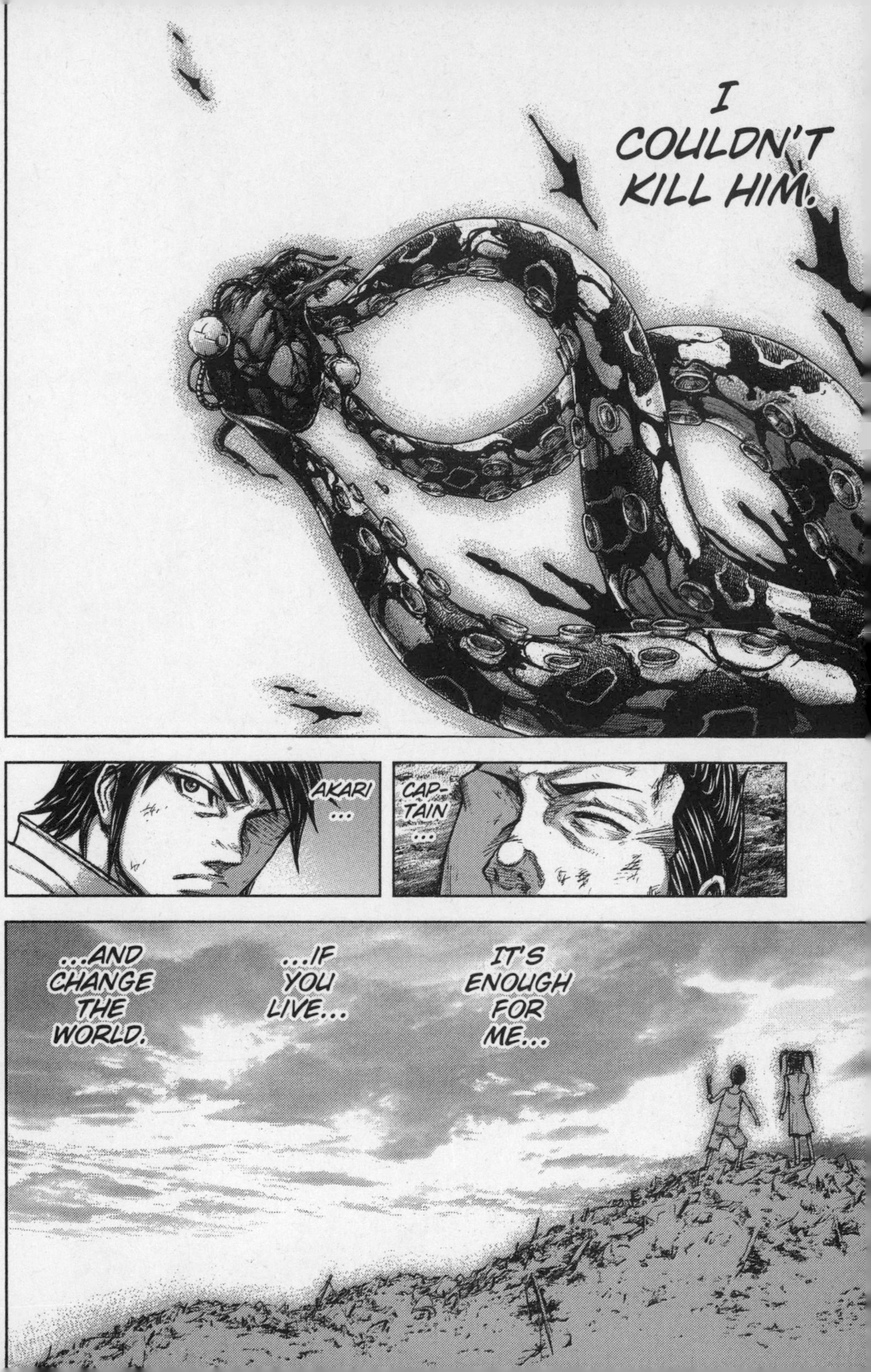
I COULDN'T KILL HIM.
CAP-TAIN ...
AKARI ...
IT'S ENOUGH FOR ME...
...IF YOU LIVE...
...AND CHANGE THE WORLD.

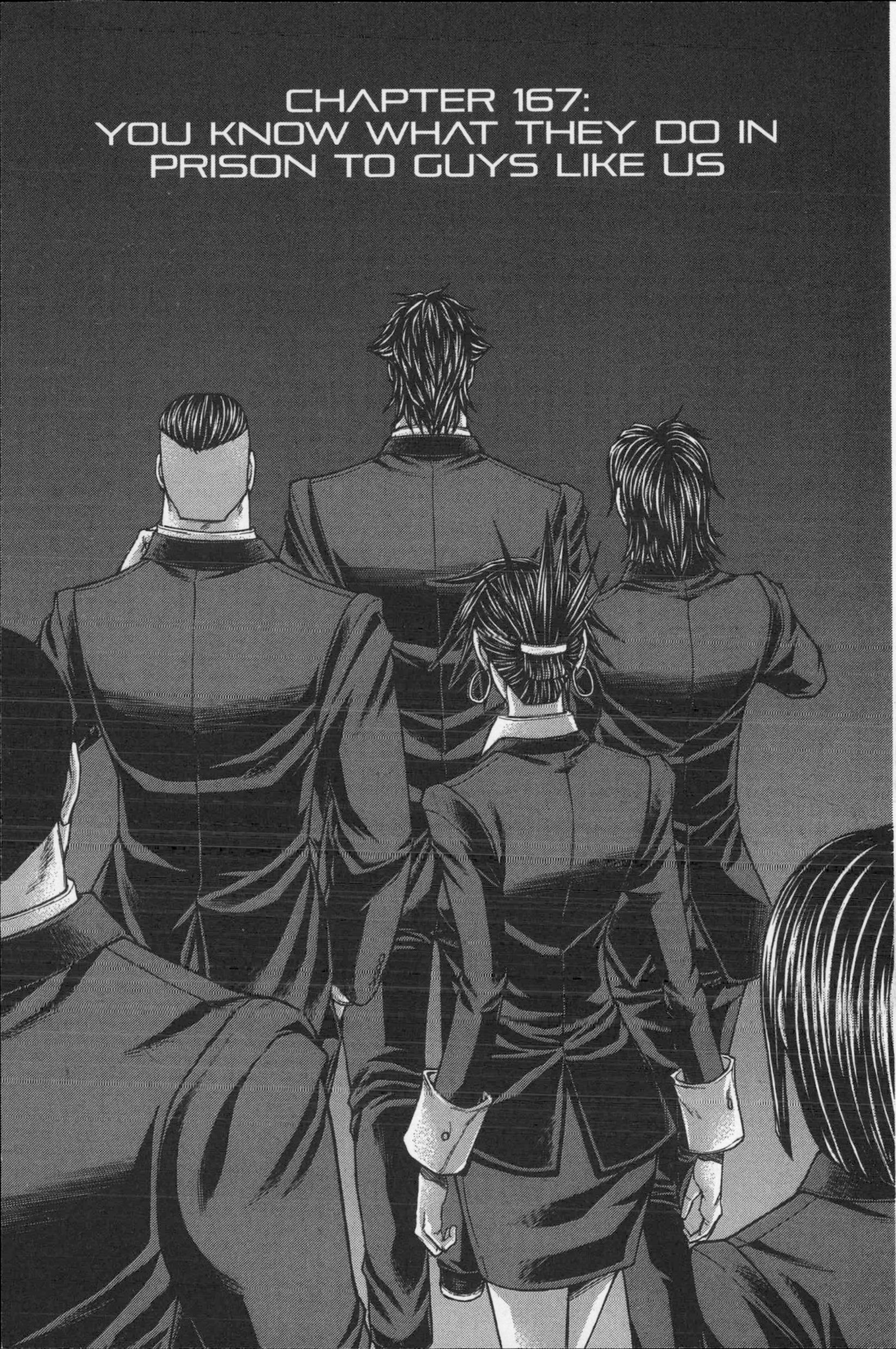
CHAPTER 167:
YOU KNOW WHAT THEY DO IN PRISON TO GUYS LIKE US

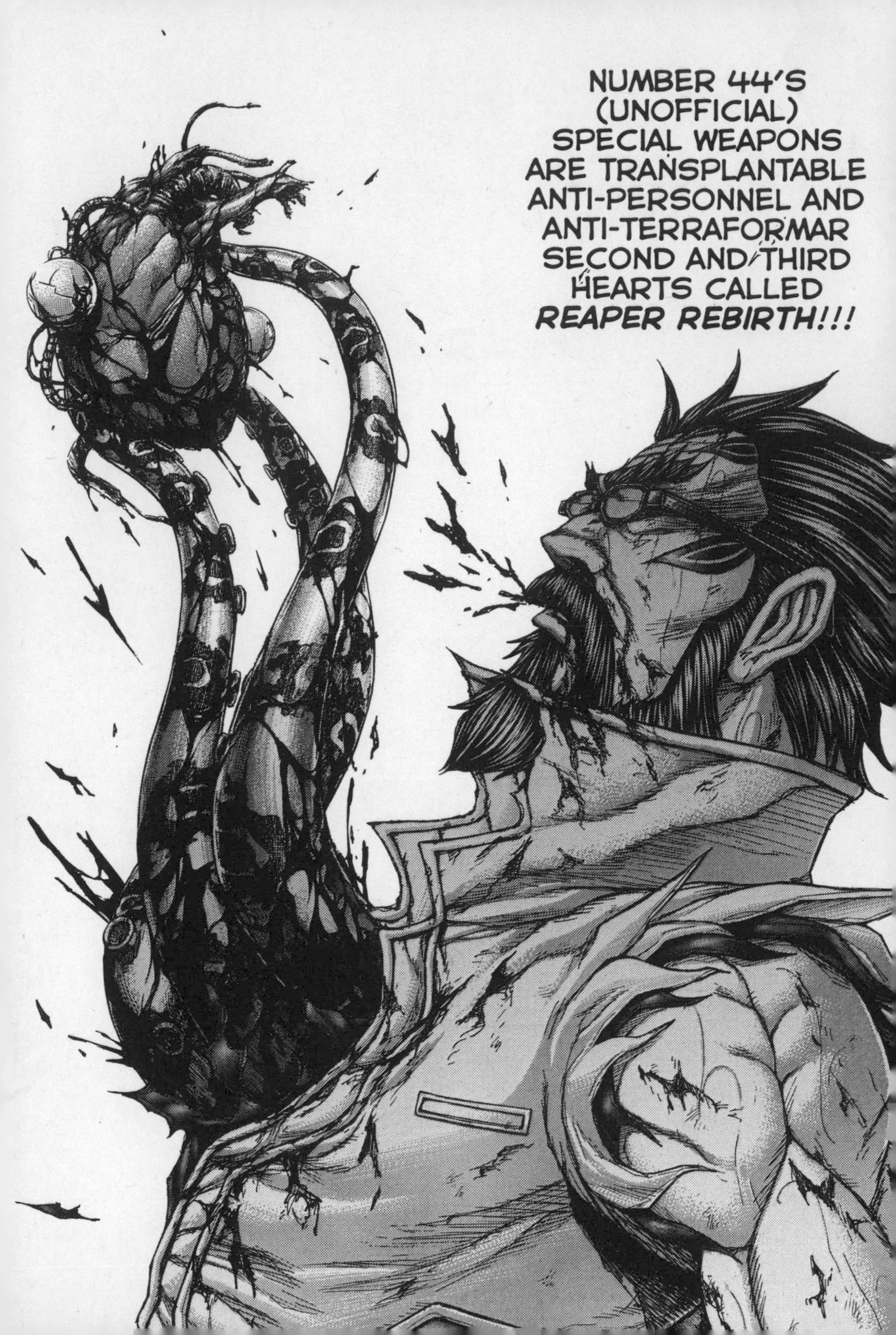
NUMBER 44'S (UNOFFICIAL) SPECIAL WEAPONS ARE TRANSPLANTABLE ANTI-PERSONNEL AND ANTI-TERRAFORMAR SECOND AND THIRD HEARTS CALLED *REAPER REBIRTH!!!*

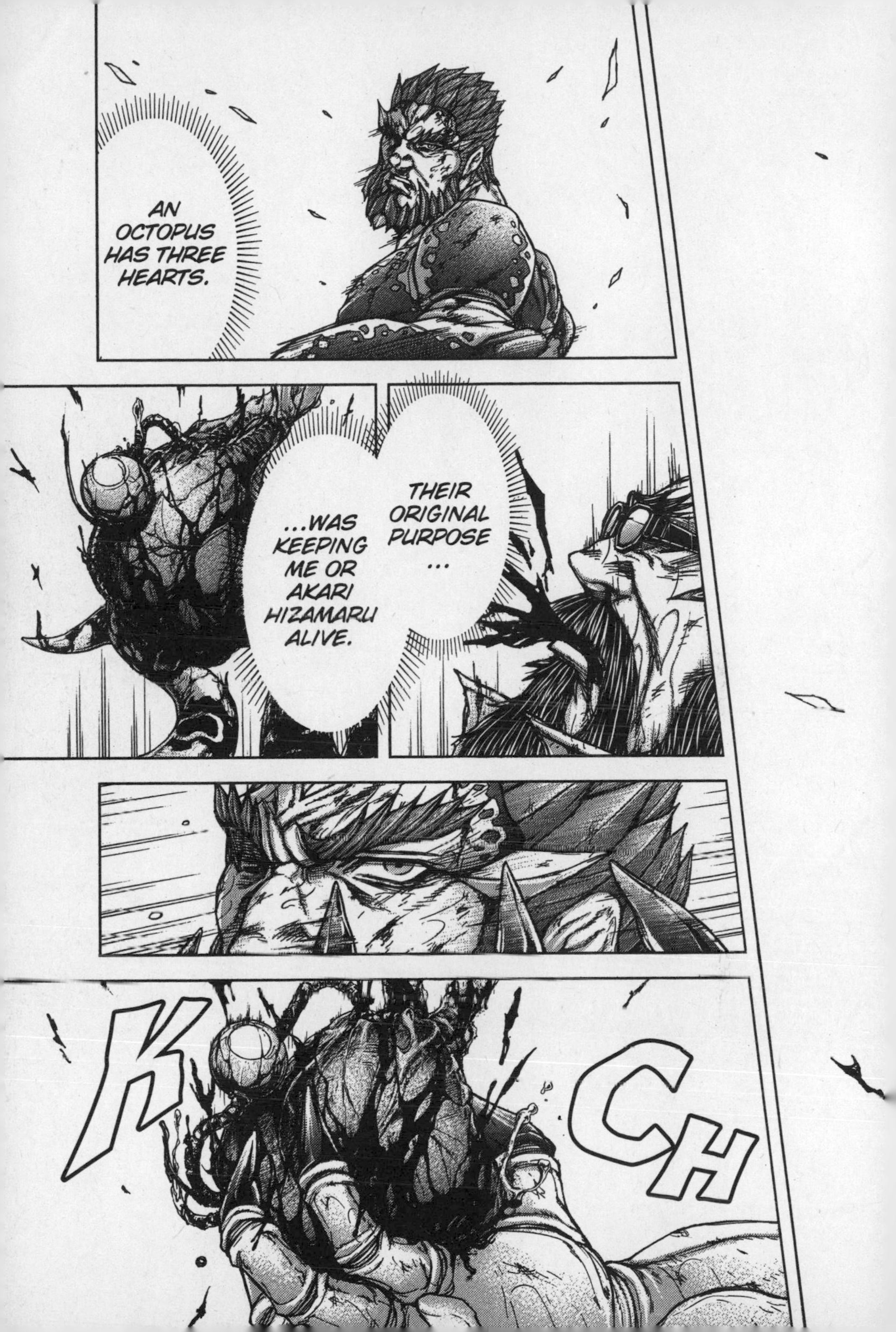
AN OCTOPUS HAS THREE HEARTS.
THEIR ORIGINAL PURPOSE ...
...WAS KEEPING ME OR AKARI HIZAMARU ALIVE.
KCH

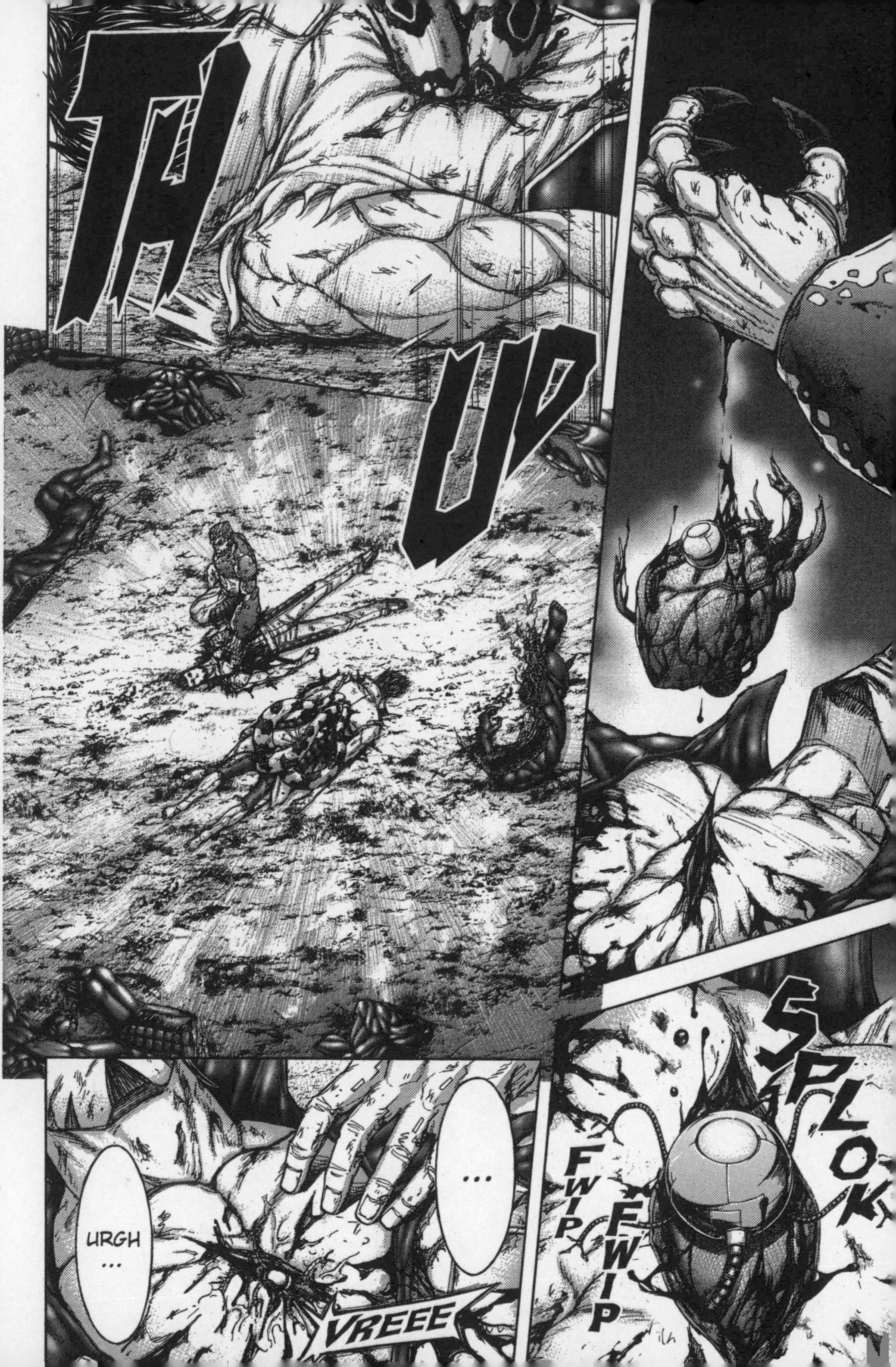
TH
UD
SPLOK
FWIP
FWIP
...
URGH ...
VREEE

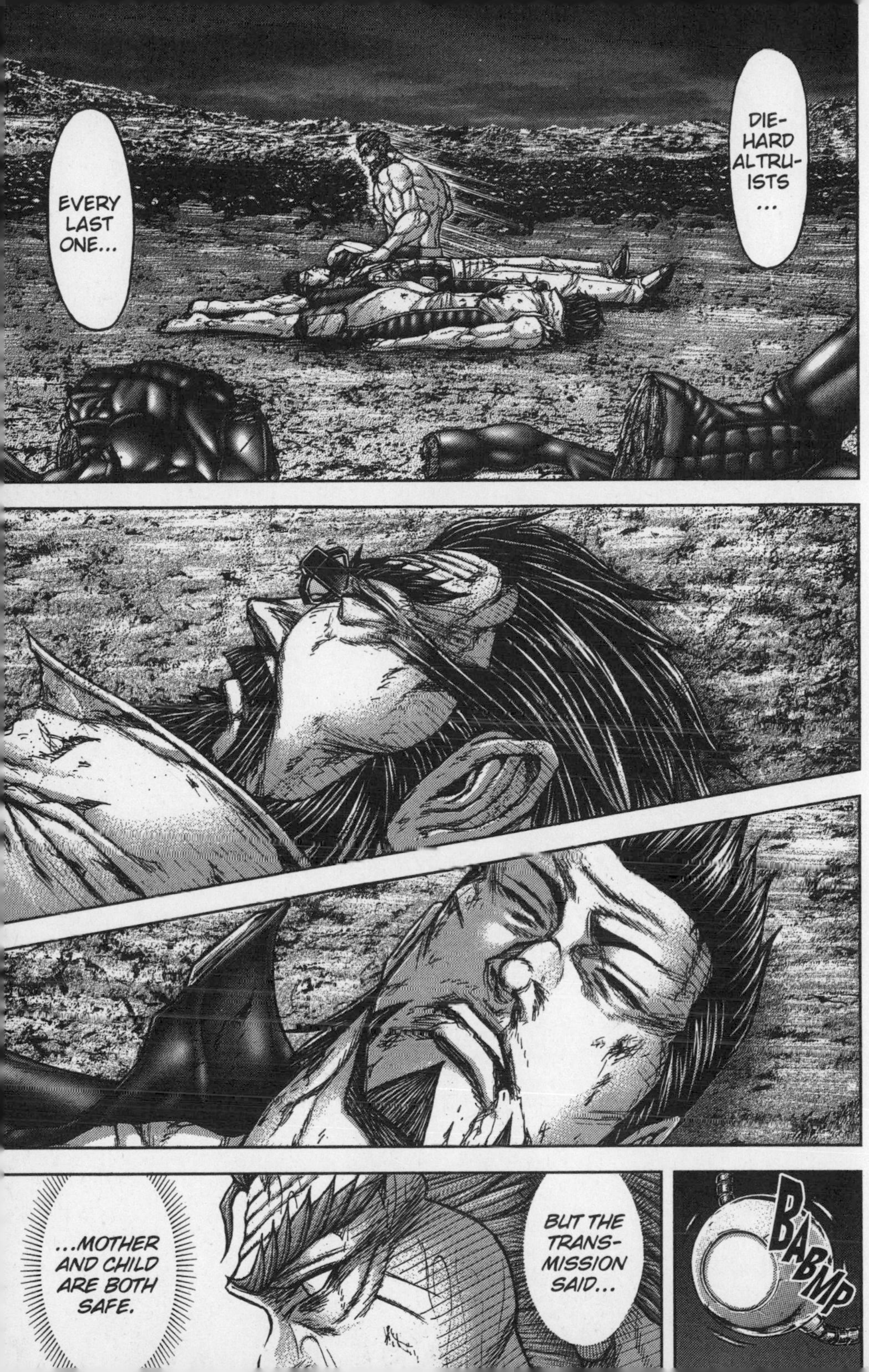
DIE-HARD ALTRU-ISTS...
EVERY LAST ONE...
BABMP
BUT THE TRANS-MISSION SAID...
...MOTHER AND CHILD ARE BOTH SAFE.

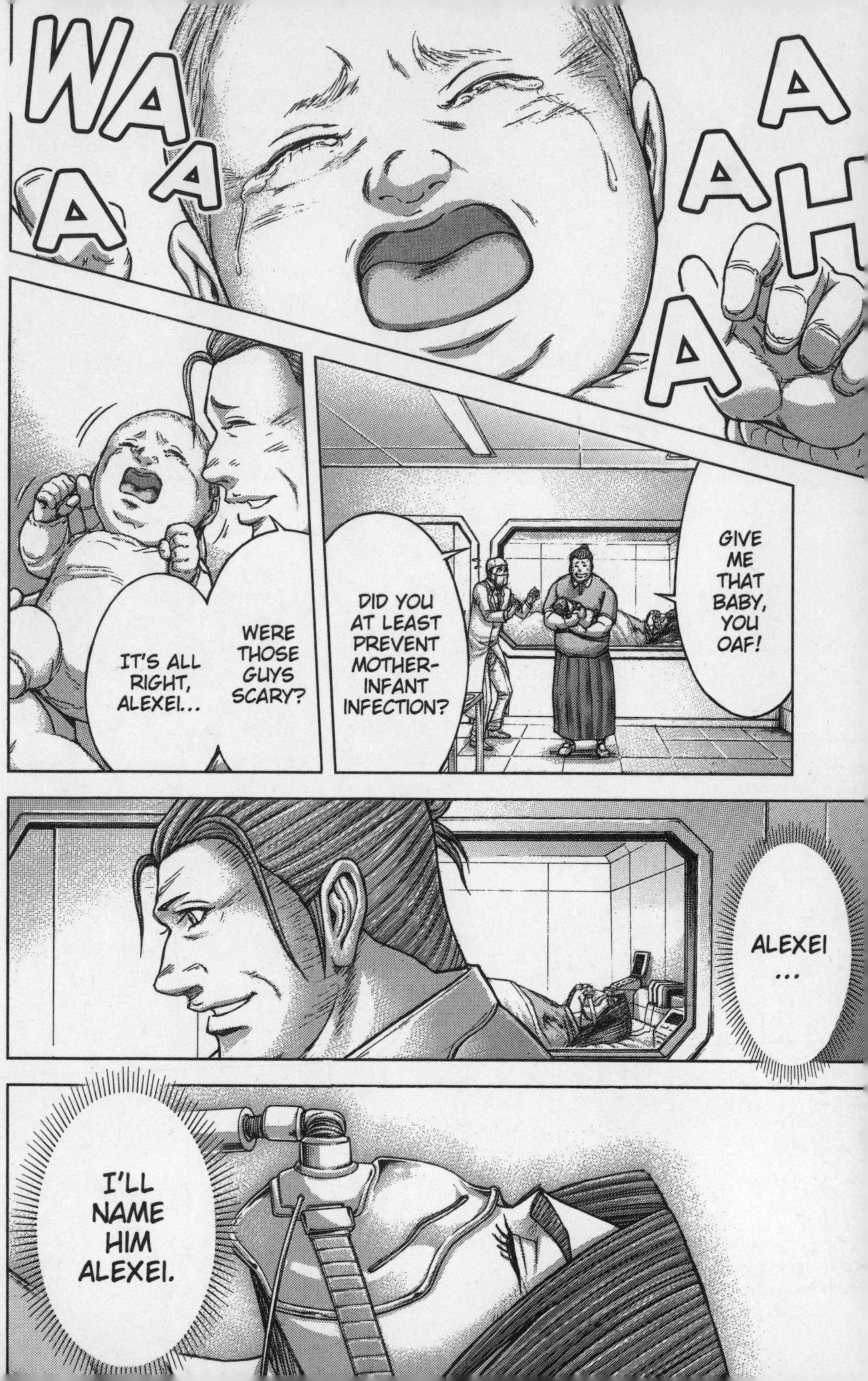
WAAA
AAHA
GIVE ME THAT BABY, YOU OAF!
DID YOU AT LEAST PREVENT MOTHER-INFANT INFECTION?
WERE THOSE GUYS SCARY?
IT'S ALL RIGHT, ALEXEI...
ALEXEI ...
I'LL NAME HIM ALEXEI.

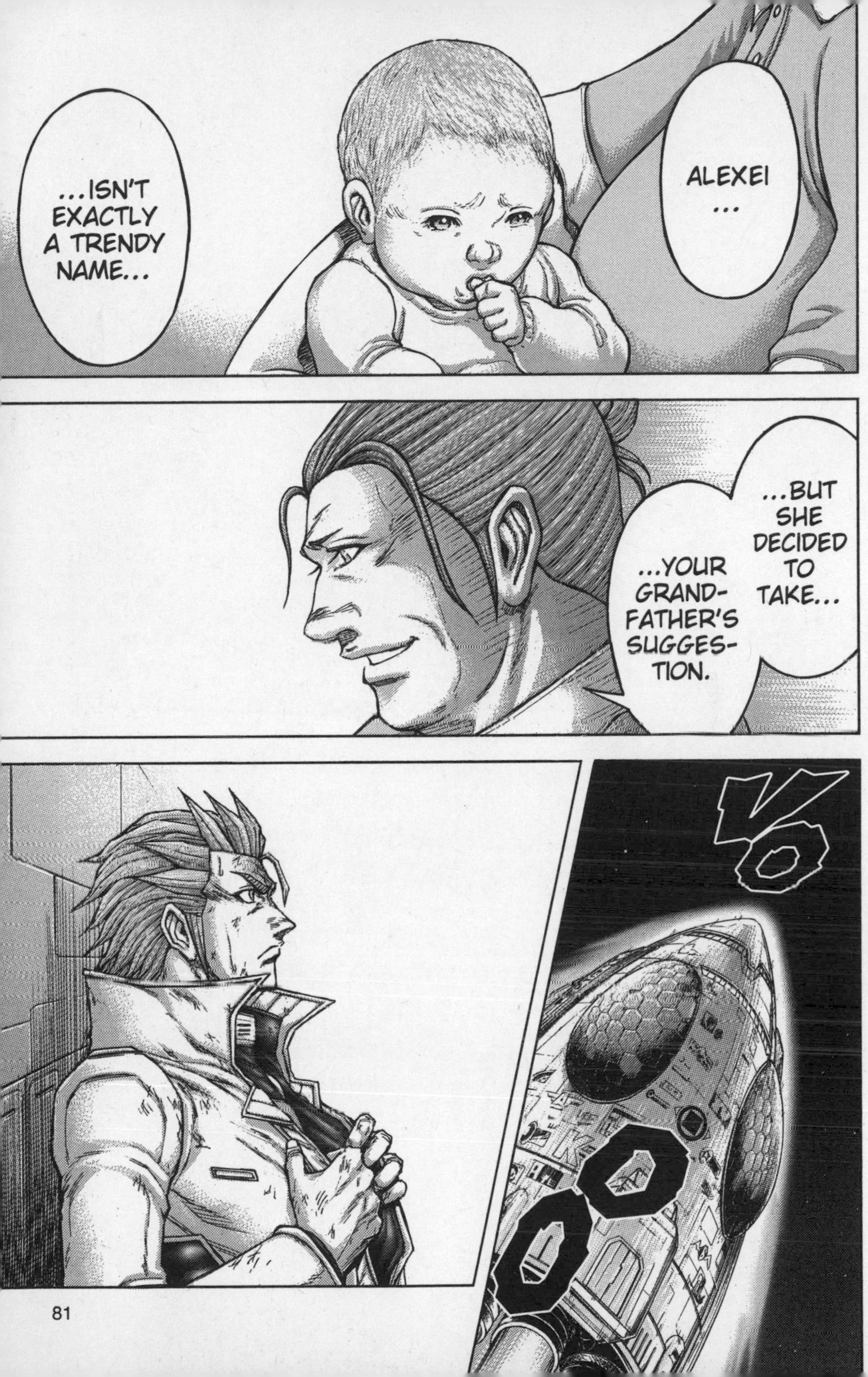
ALEXEI ...
...ISN'T EXACTLY A TRENDY NAME...
...BUT SHE DECIDED TO TAKE...
...YOUR GRAND-FATHER'S SUGGES-TION.

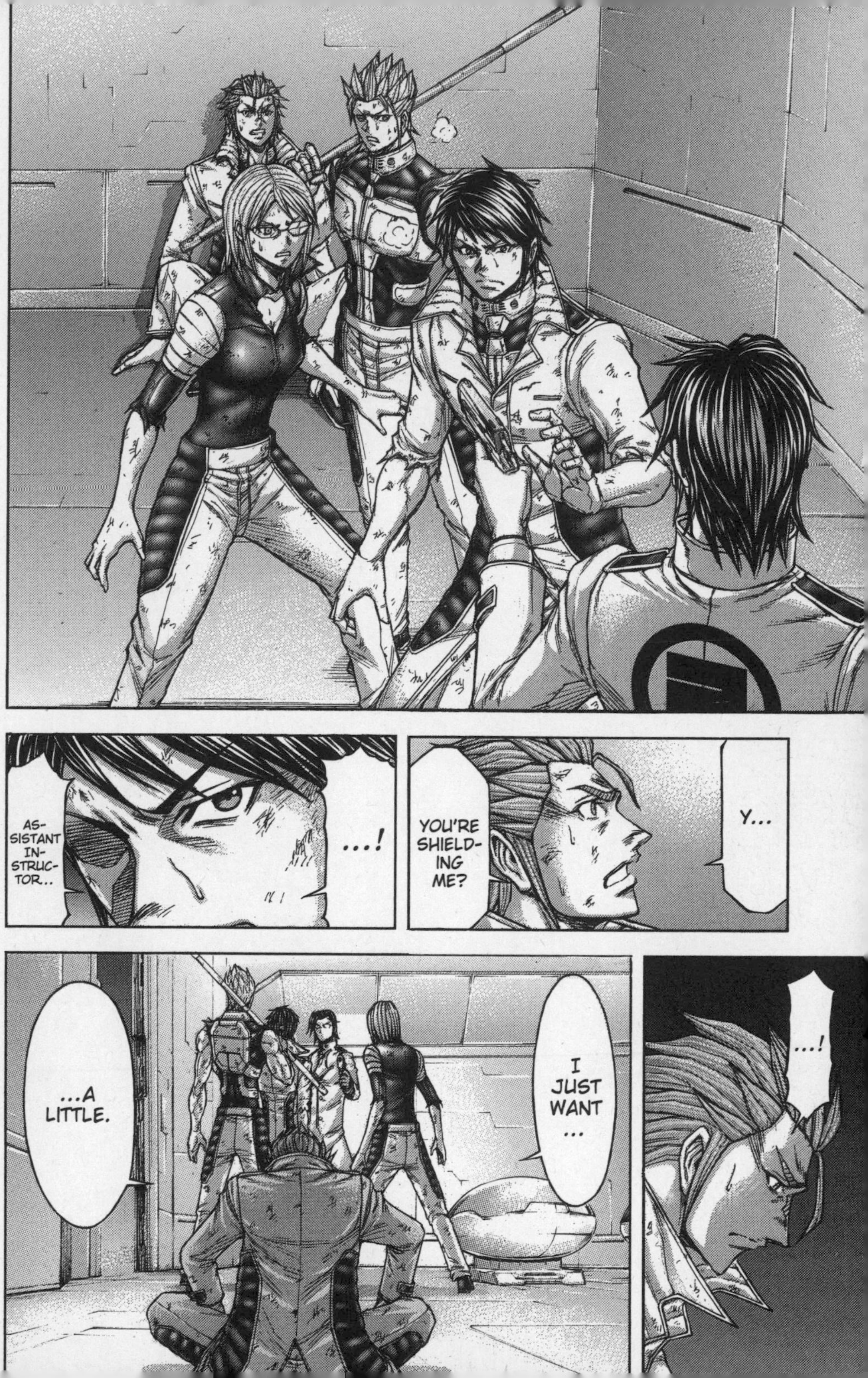
Y...
YOU'RE SHIELDING ME?
...!
ASSISTANT INSTRUCTOR..
...!
I JUST WANT...
...A LITTLE.

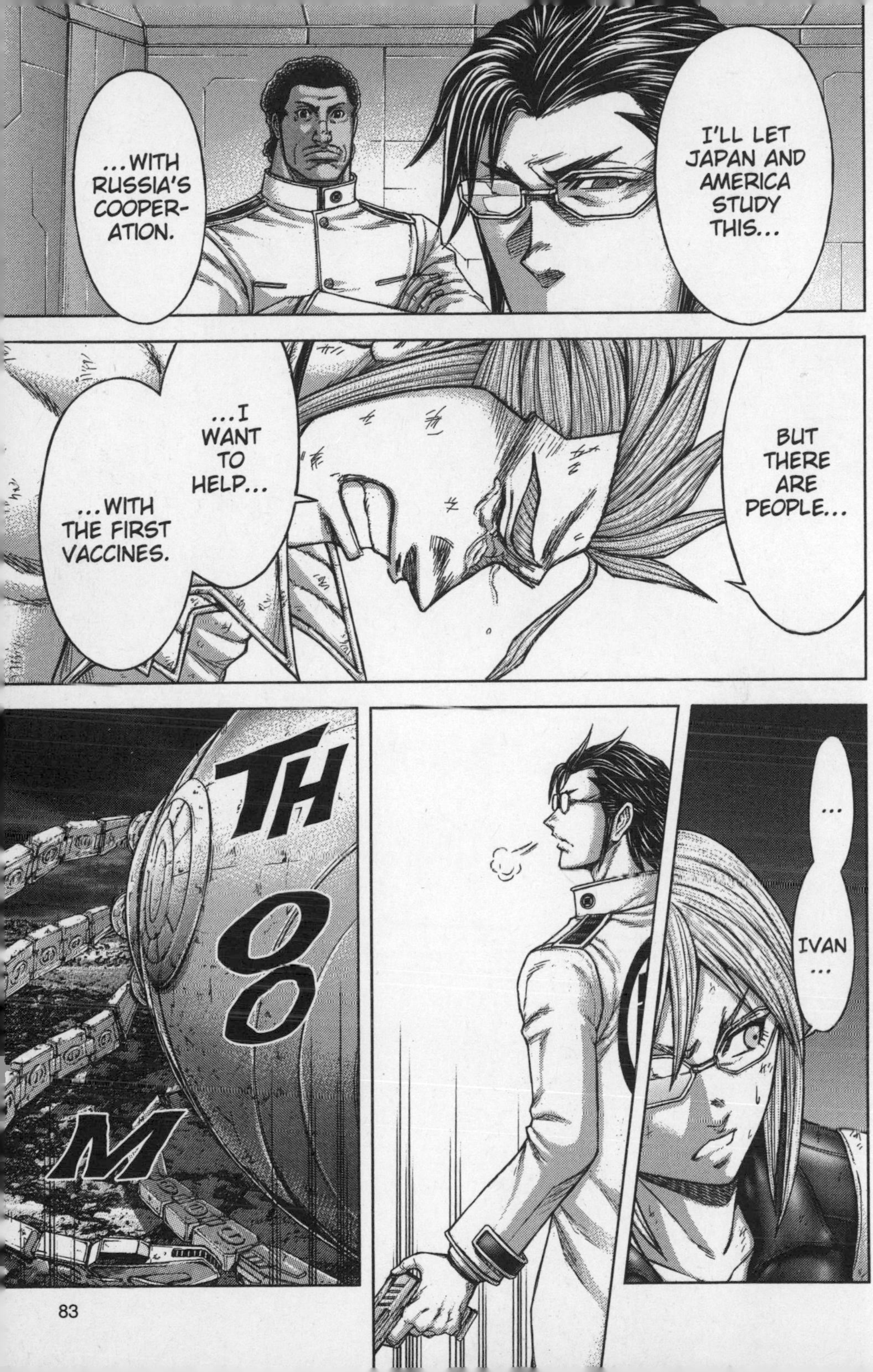
I'LL LET JAPAN AND AMERICA STUDY THIS...
...WITH RUSSIA'S COOPER-ATION.
BUT THERE ARE PEOPLE...
...I WANT TO HELP...
...WITH THE FIRST VACCINES.
...
IVAN ...
TH
M

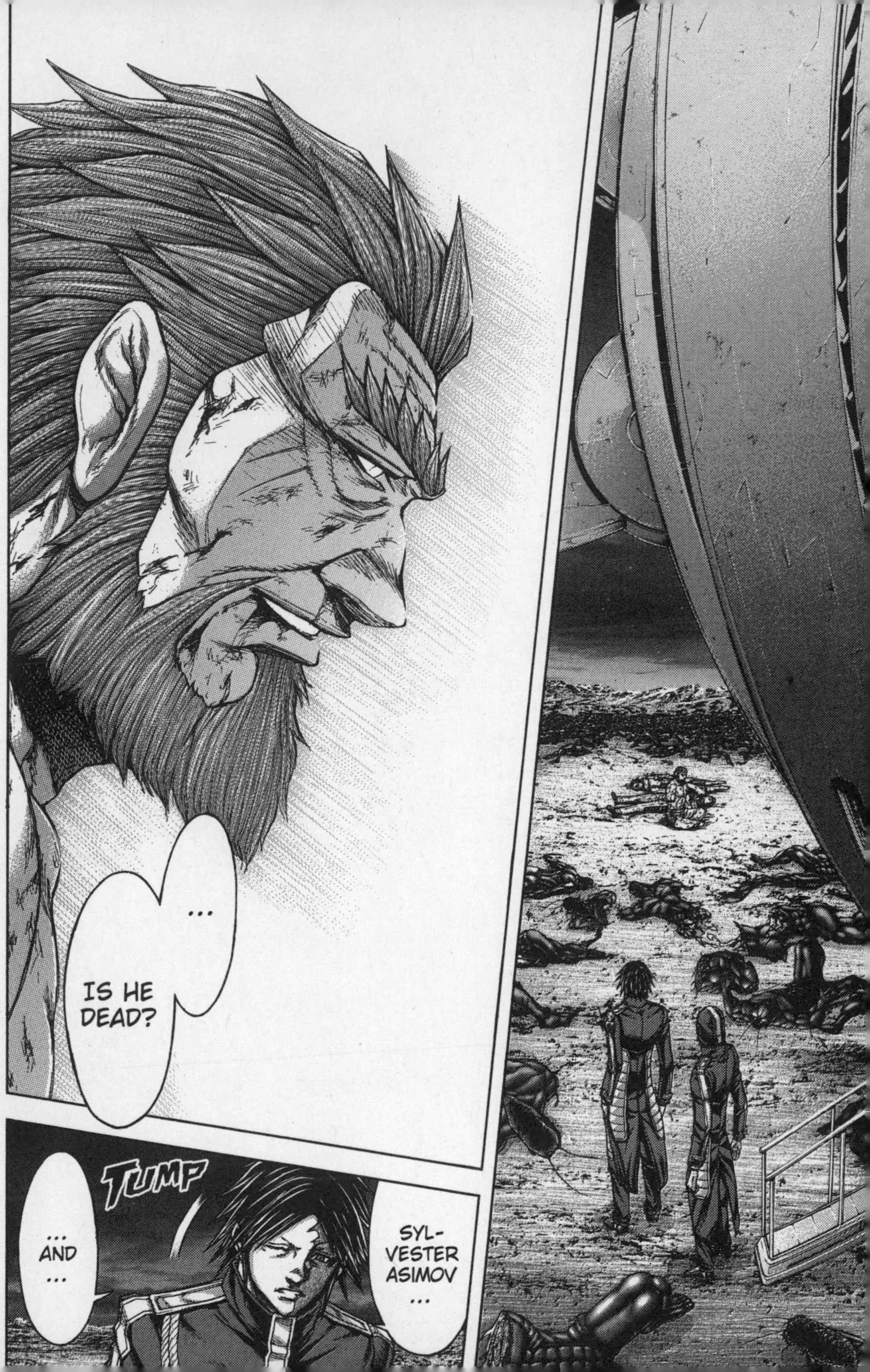
... IS HE DEAD?
SYL-VESTER ASIMOV ...
TUMP
... AND ...

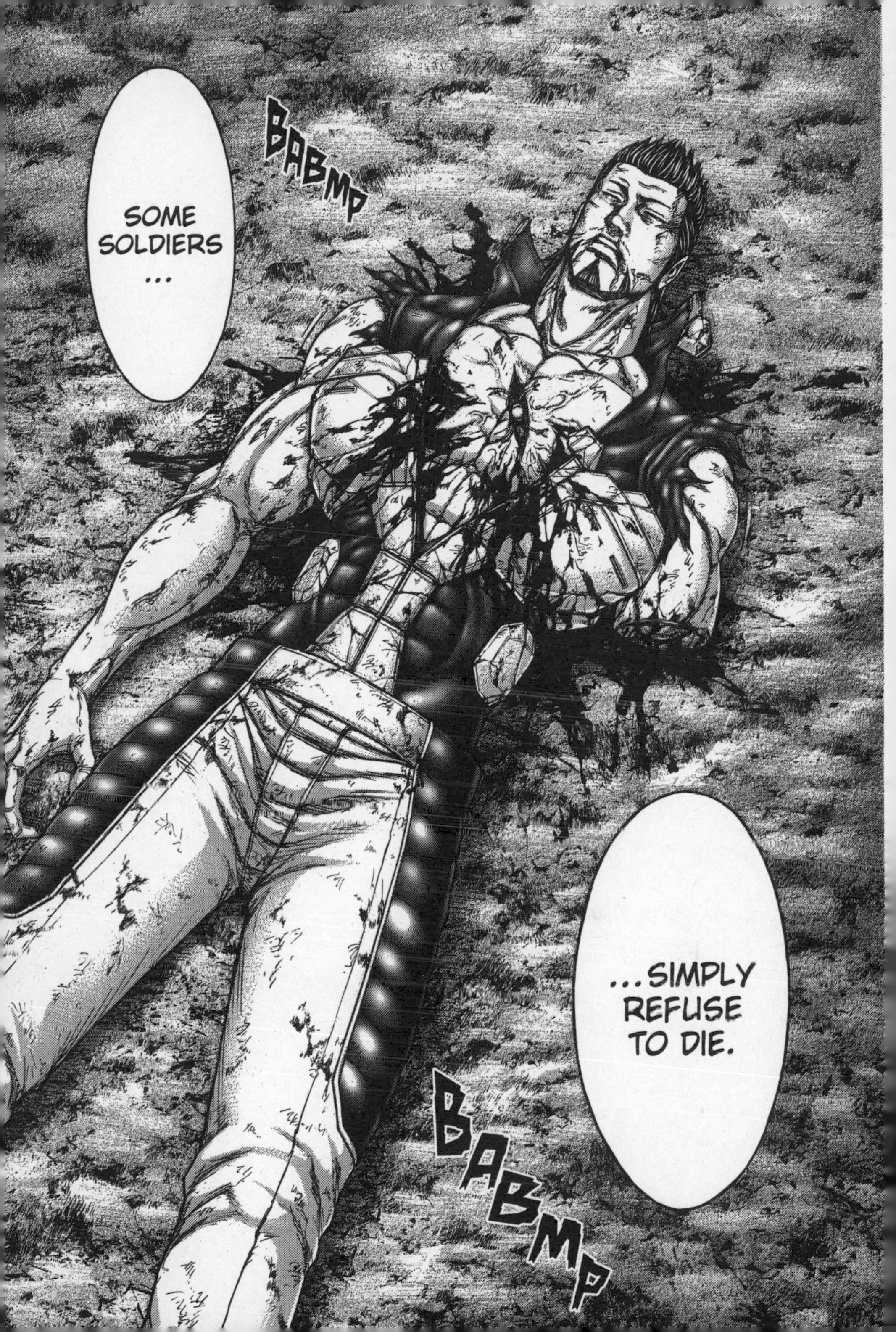
BABMP
SOME SOLDIERS ...
...SIMPLY REFUSE TO DIE.
BABMP

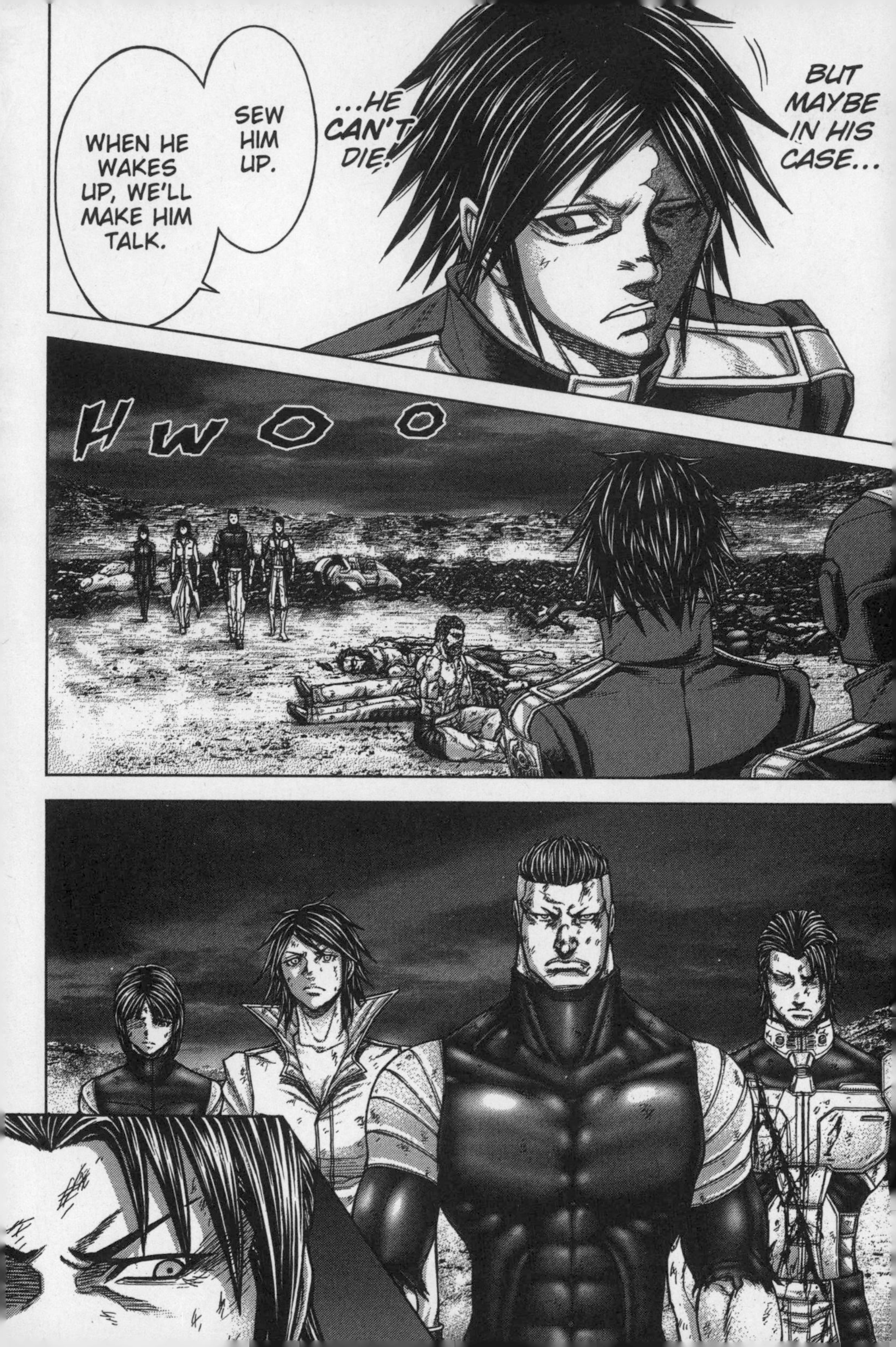
BUT MAYBE IN HIS CASE...
...HE CAN'T DIE!
SEW HIM UP.
WHEN HE WAKES UP, WE'LL MAKE HIM TALK.
HWOO

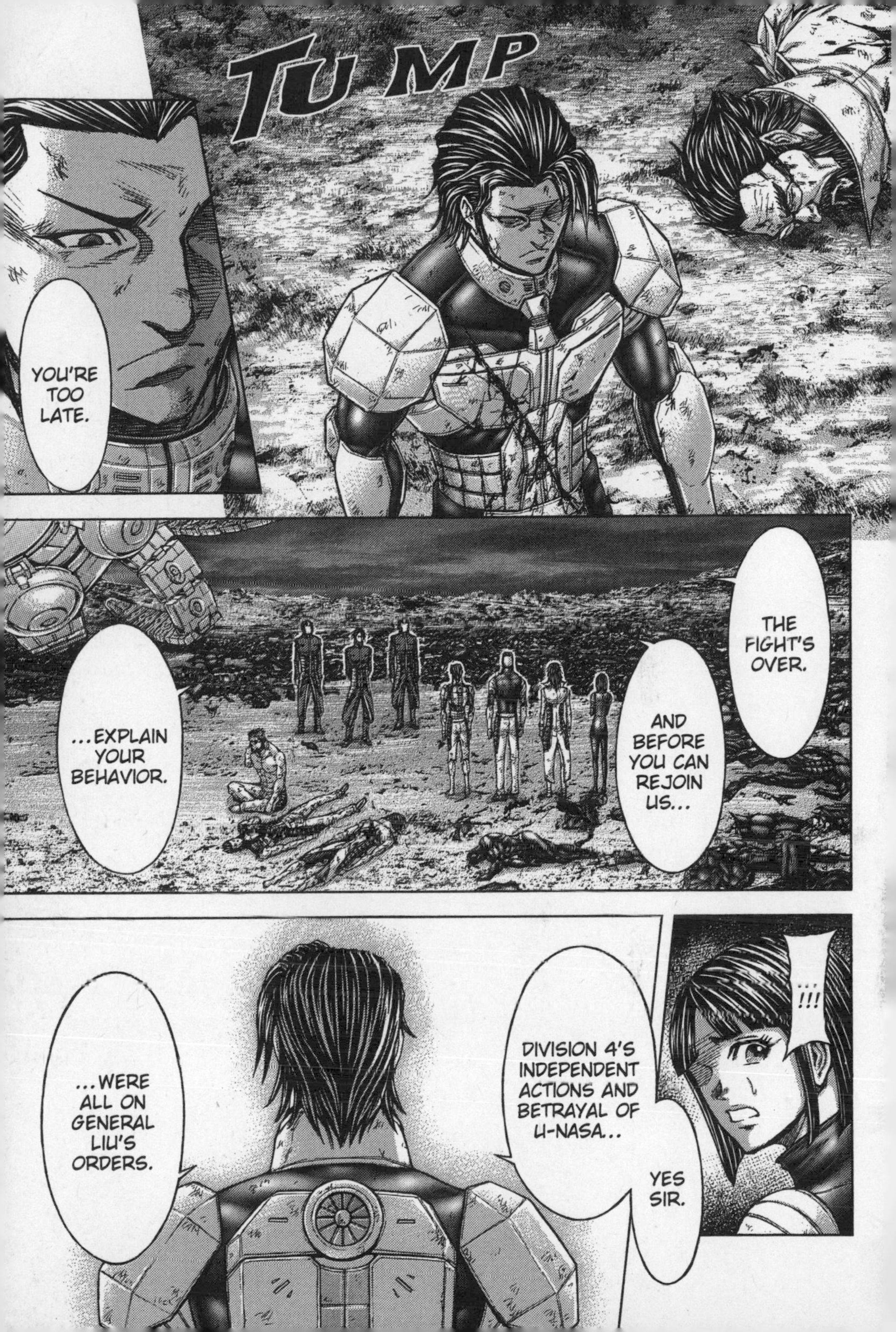
TUMP
YOU'RE TOO LATE.
THE FIGHT'S OVER.
AND BEFORE YOU CAN REJOIN US...
...EXPLAIN YOUR BEHAVIOR.
...!!!
DIVISION 4'S INDEPENDENT ACTIONS AND BETRAYAL OF U-NASA...
YES SIR.
...WERE ALL ON GENERAL LIU'S ORDERS.

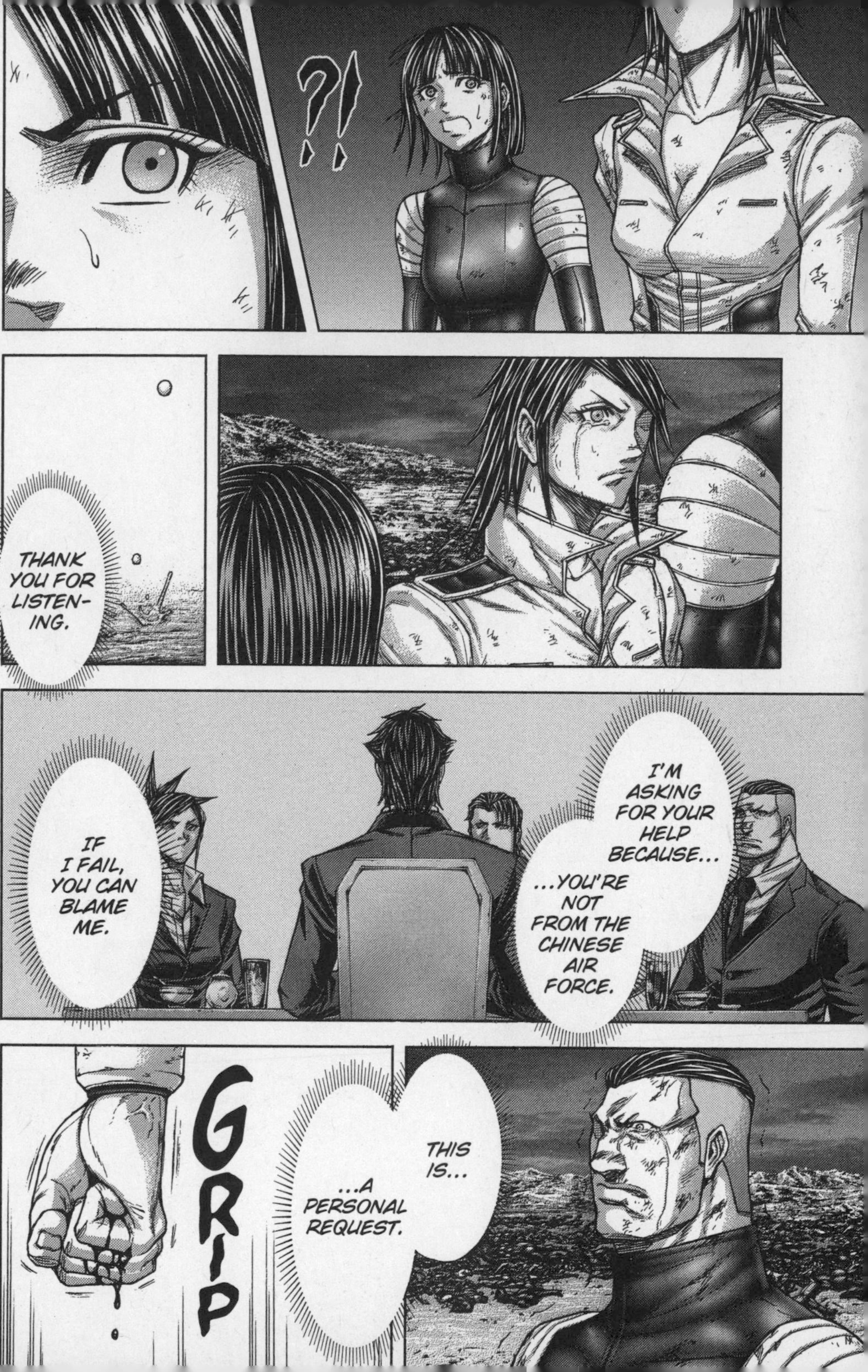
?!
THANK YOU FOR LISTEN-ING.
I'M ASKING FOR YOUR HELP BECAUSE...
...YOU'RE NOT FROM THE CHINESE AIR FORCE.
IF I FAIL, YOU CAN BLAME ME.
THIS IS...
...A PERSONAL REQUEST.
GRIP

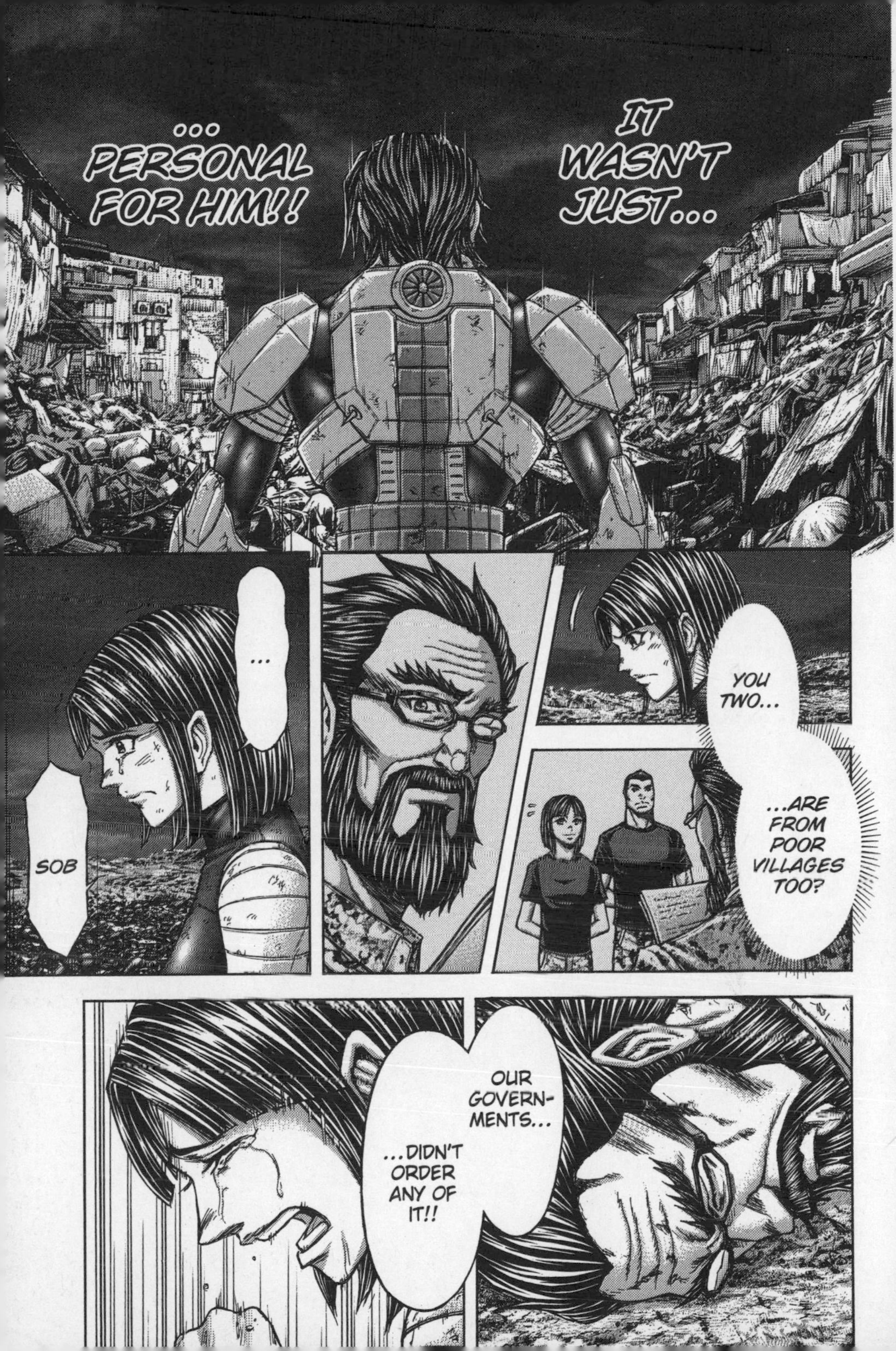
IT WASN'T JUST...
...PERSONAL FOR HIM!!
YOU TWO...
...ARE FROM POOR VILLAGES TOO?
...
SOB
OUR GOVERN-MENTS...
...DIDN'T ORDER ANY OF IT!!

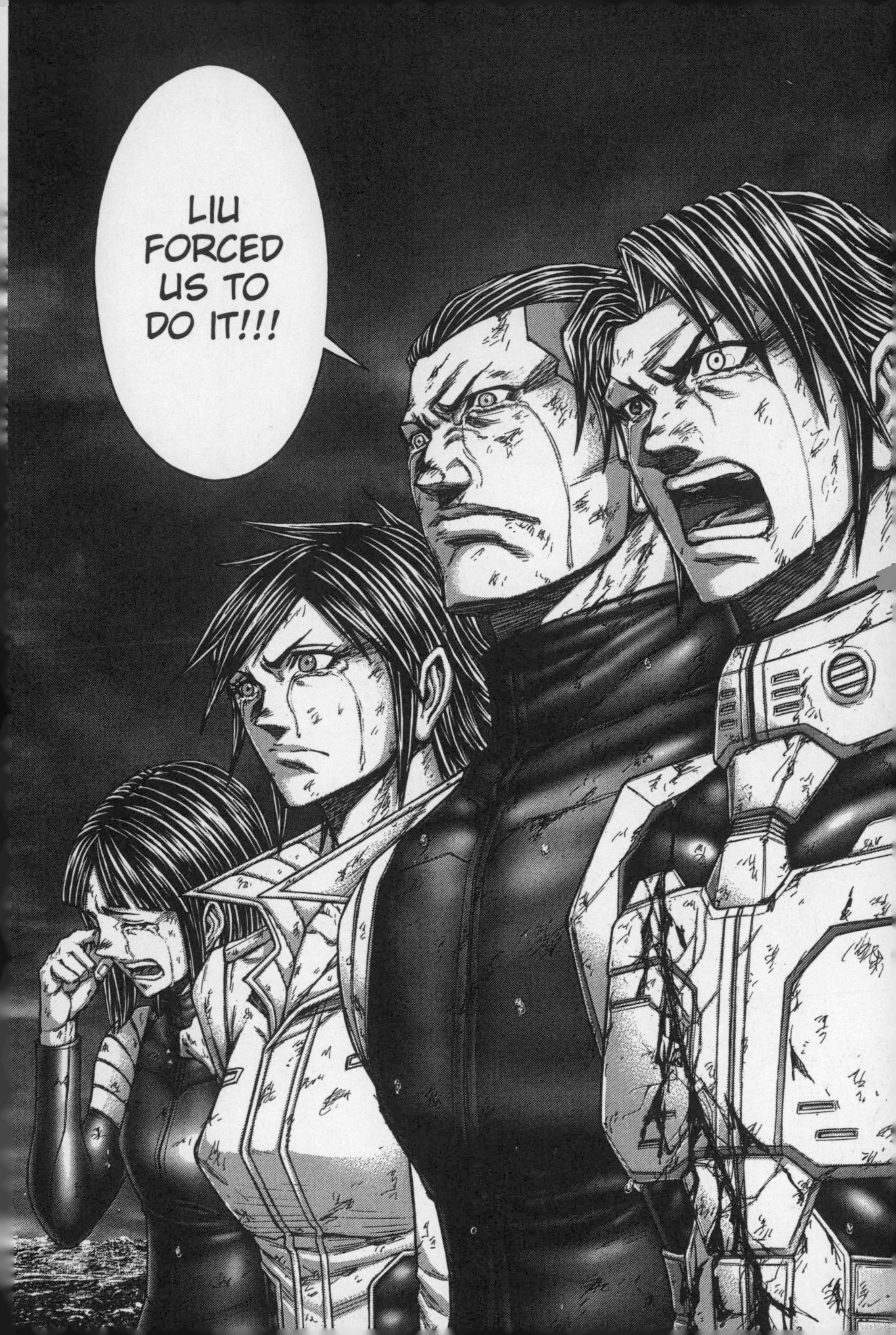
LIU FORCED US TO DO IT!!!

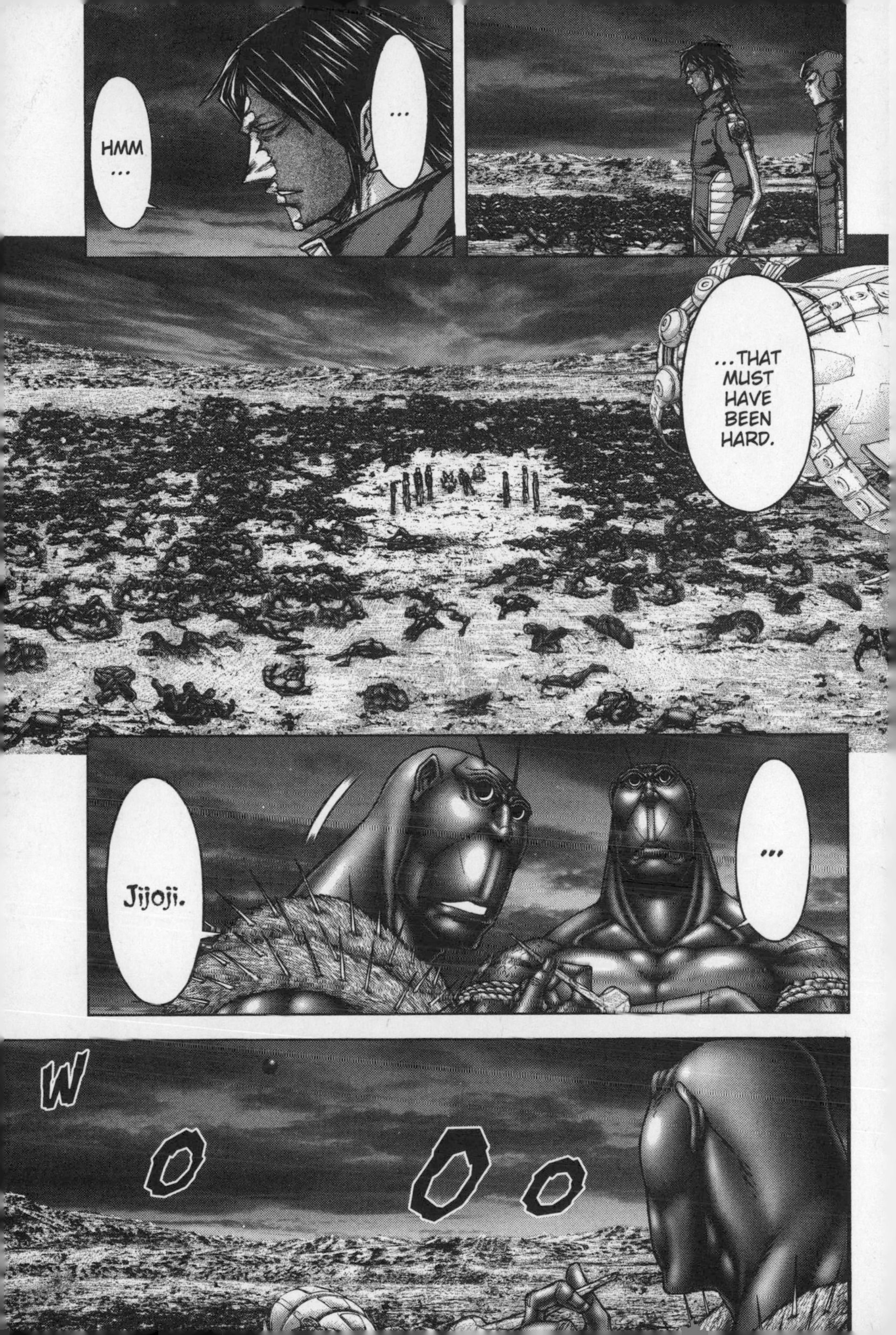
...
HMM ...
...THAT MUST HAVE BEEN HARD.
...
Jijoji.
WOOOO

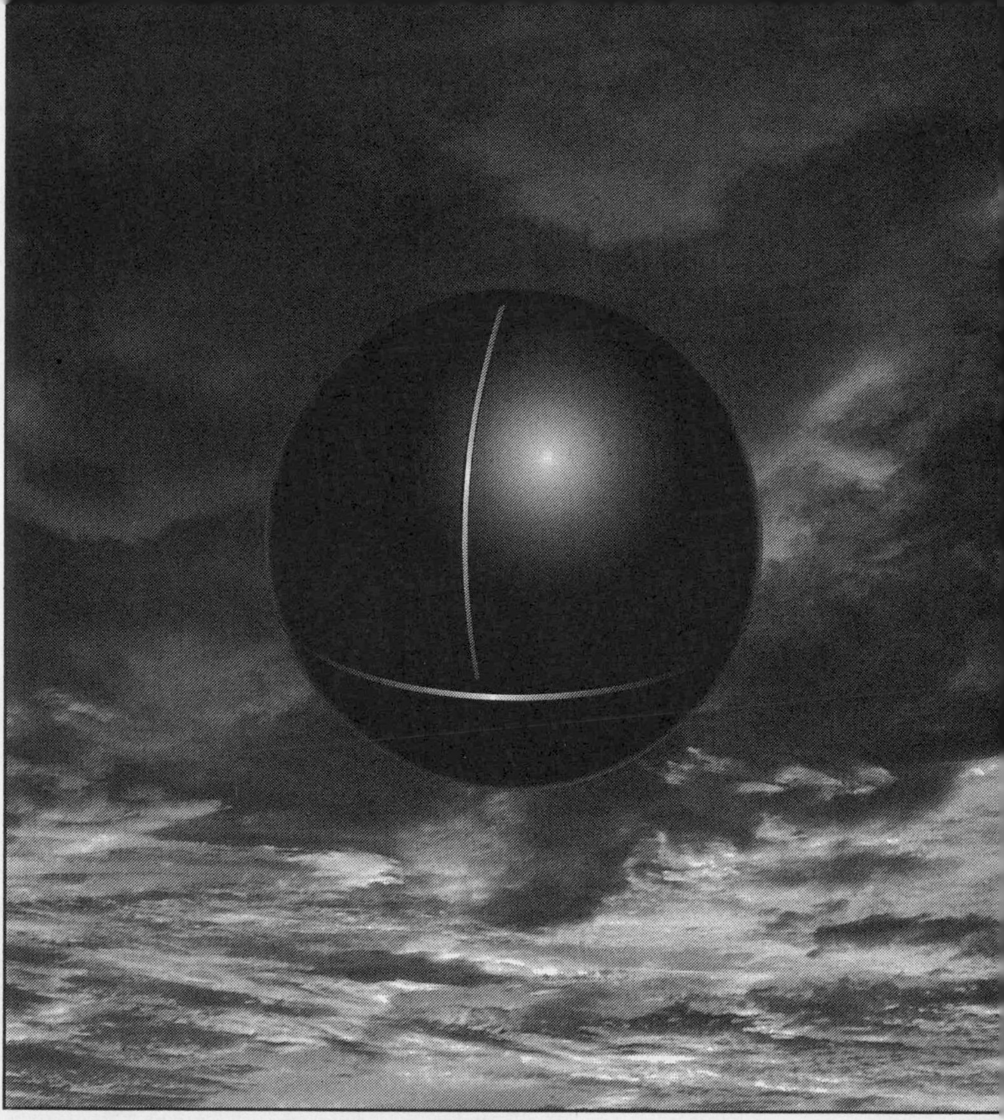
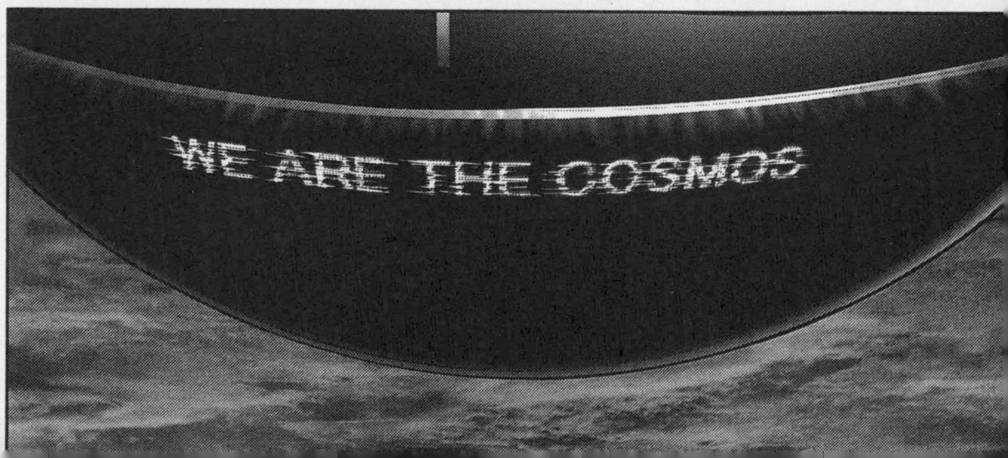
WE ARE THE COSMOS

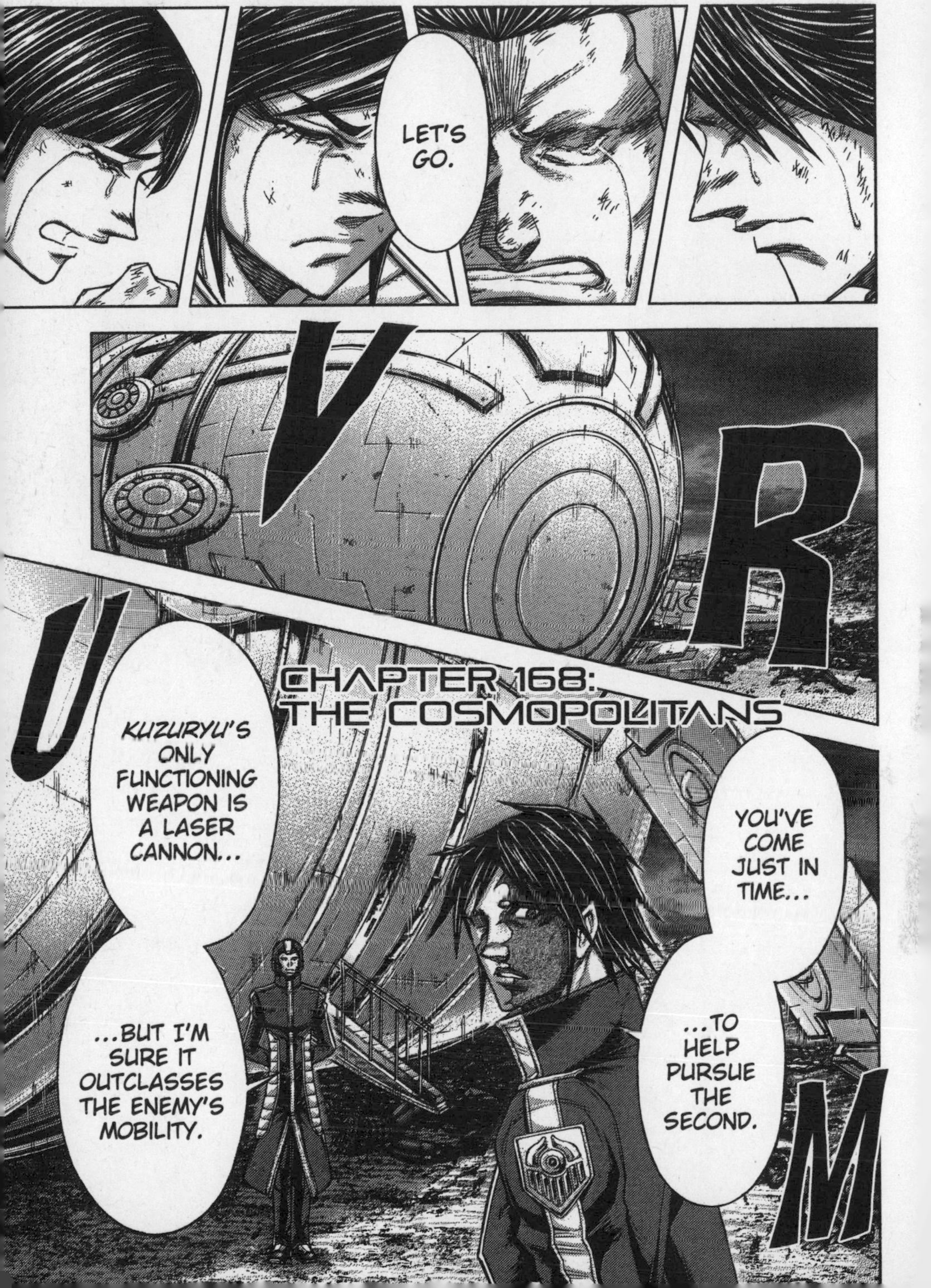
LET'S GO.
VRUM
CHAPTER 168: THE COSMOPOLITANS
YOU'VE COME JUST IN TIME...
...TO HELP PURSUE THE SECOND.
KUZURYU'S ONLY FUNCTIONING WEAPON IS A LASER CANNON...
...BUT I'M SURE IT OUTCLASSES THE ENEMY'S MOBILITY.

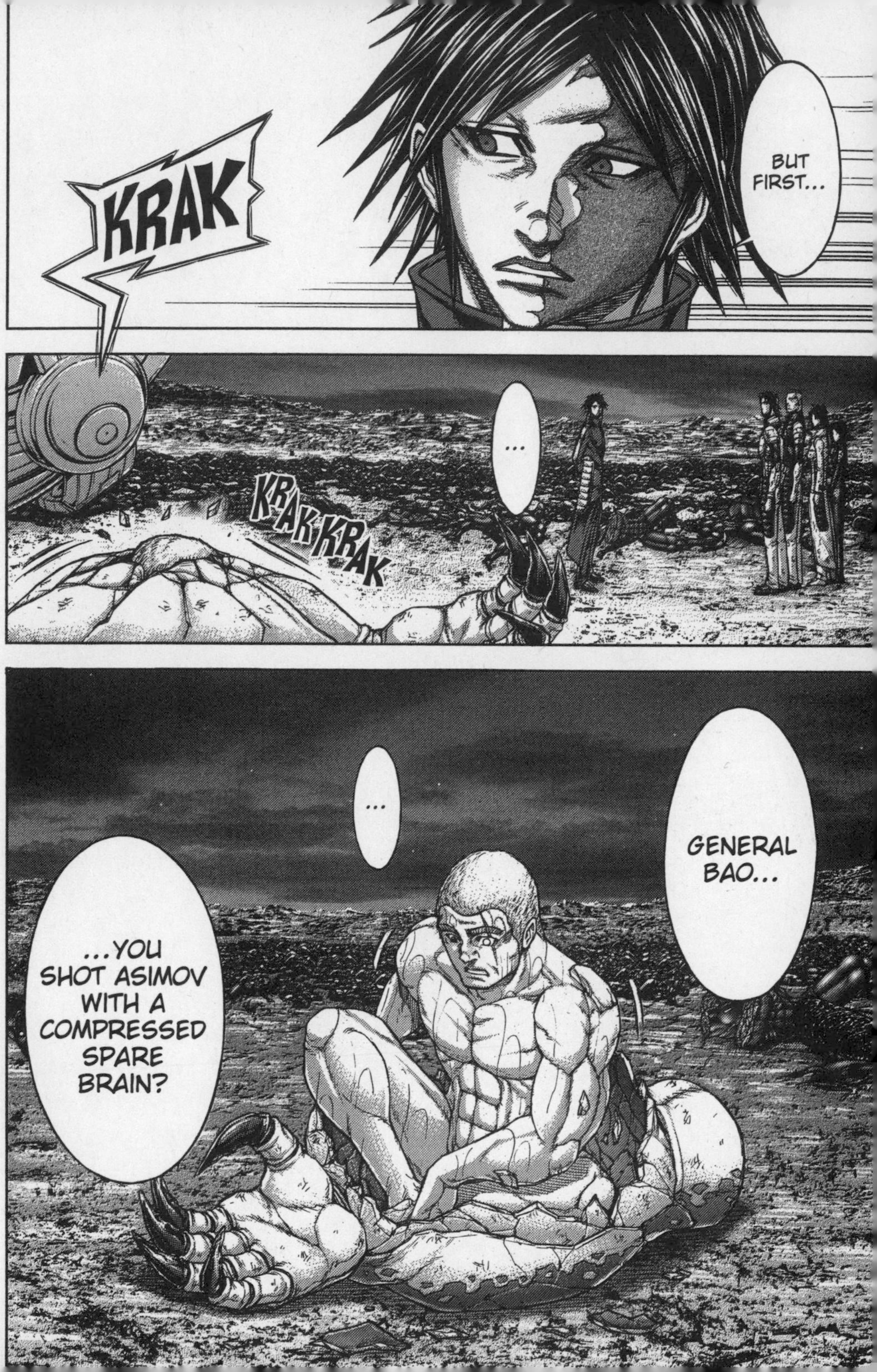
BUT FIRST...
KRAK
...
KRAK KRAK KRAK
GENERAL BAO...
...
...YOU SHOT ASIMOV WITH A COMPRESSED SPARE BRAIN?

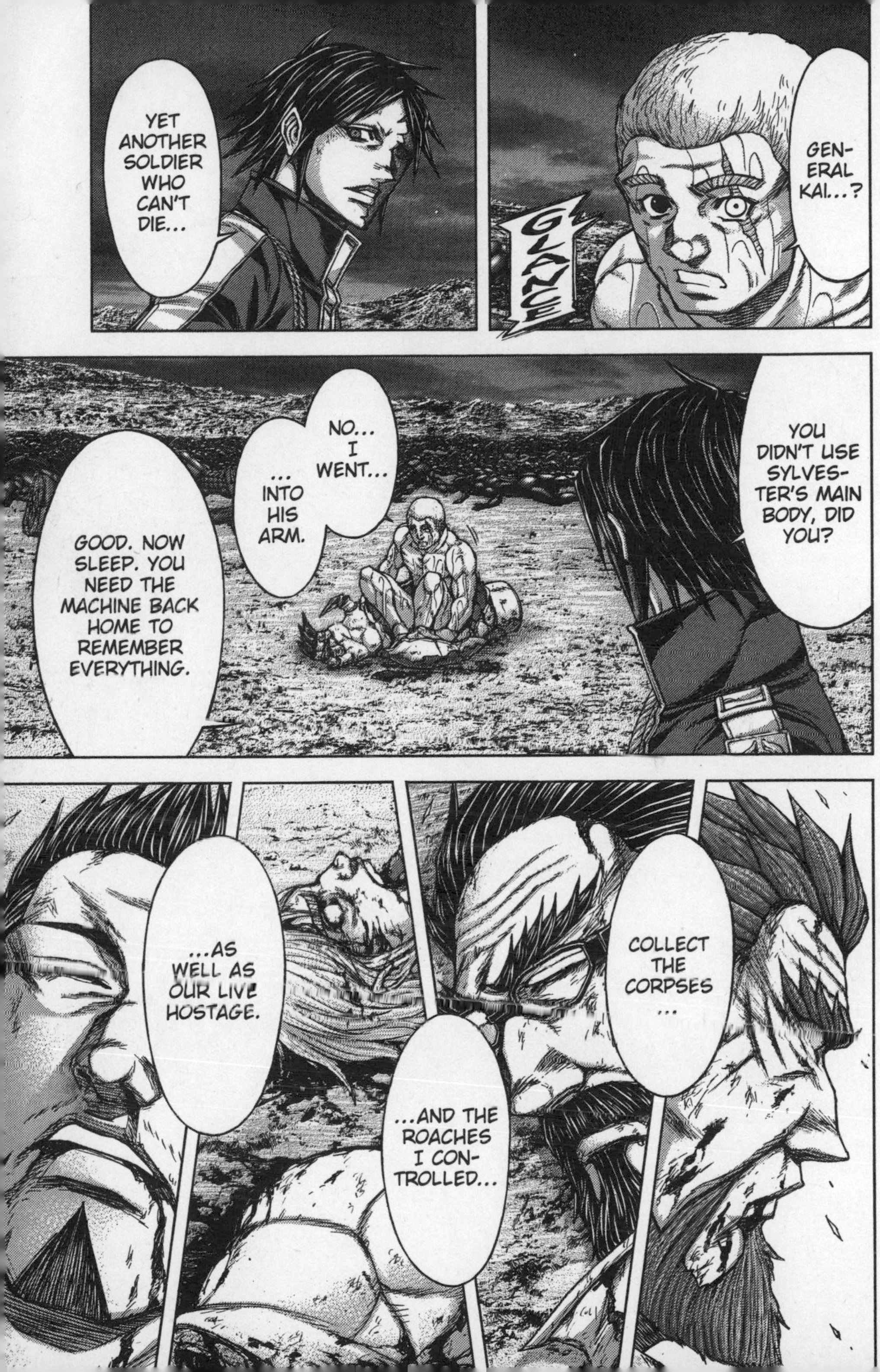
GEN-ERAL KAI...?
GLANCE
YET ANOTHER SOLDIER WHO CAN'T DIE...
YOU DIDN'T USE SYLVES-TER'S MAIN BODY, DID YOU?
NO... I WENT...
... INTO HIS ARM.
GOOD. NOW SLEEP. YOU NEED THE MACHINE BACK HOME TO REMEMBER EVERYTHING.
COLLECT THE CORPSES ...
...AND THE ROACHES I CON-TROLLED...
...AS WELL AS OUR LIVE HOSTAGE.

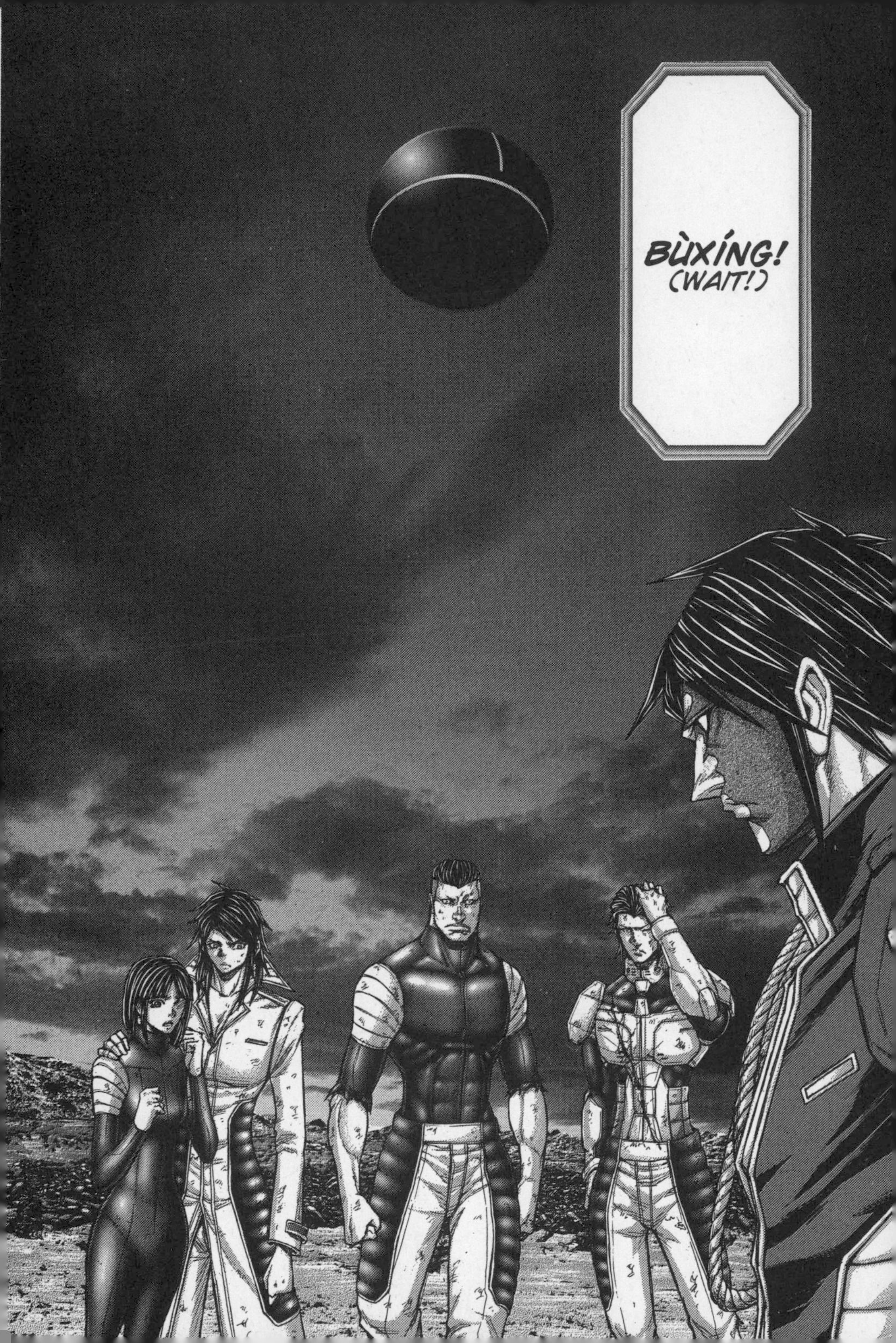
BÙXÍNG!
(WAIT!)

IF YOU CAPTURE THE SECOND OR KILL THE FIRST...

...YOU'LL REGRET IT.

ZING

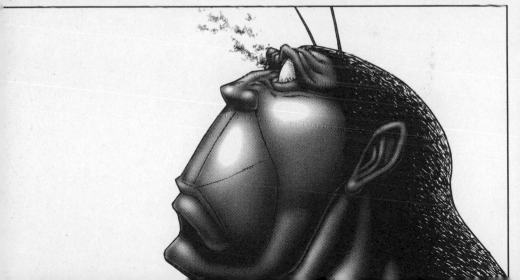

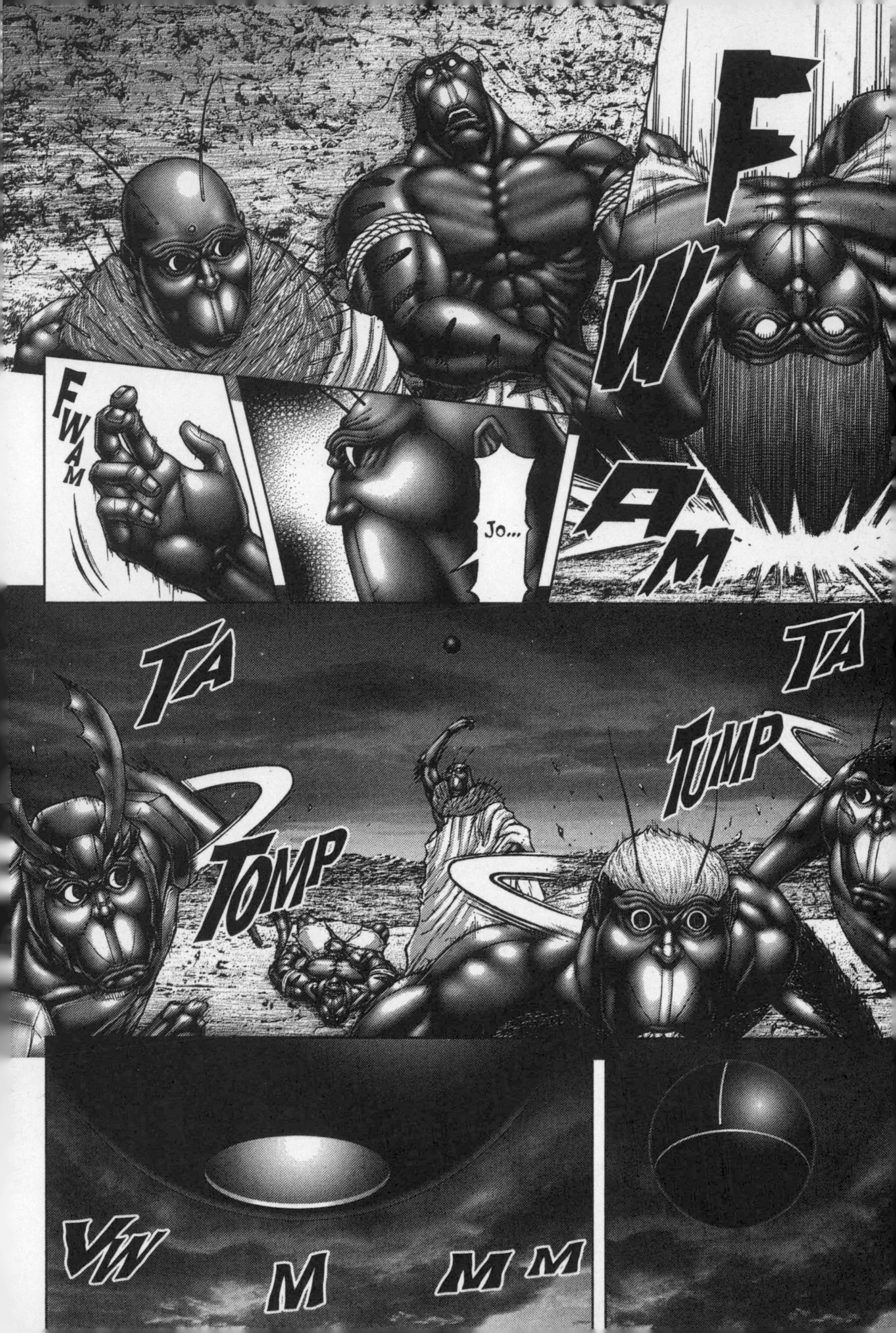
FWAM
JO...
FWAM
TA
TUMP
TA
TOMP
VWMMM

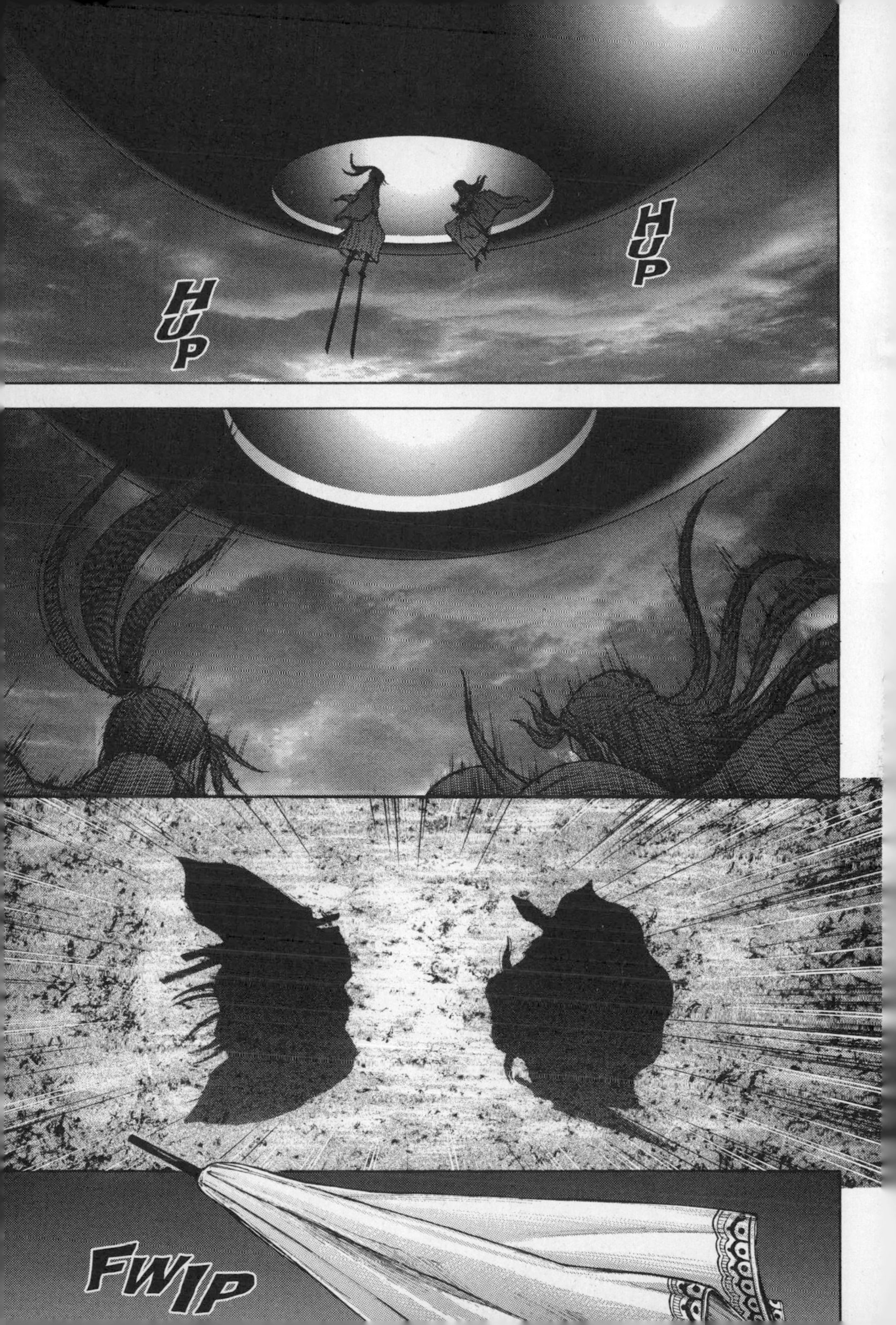
HUP
HUP
FWIP

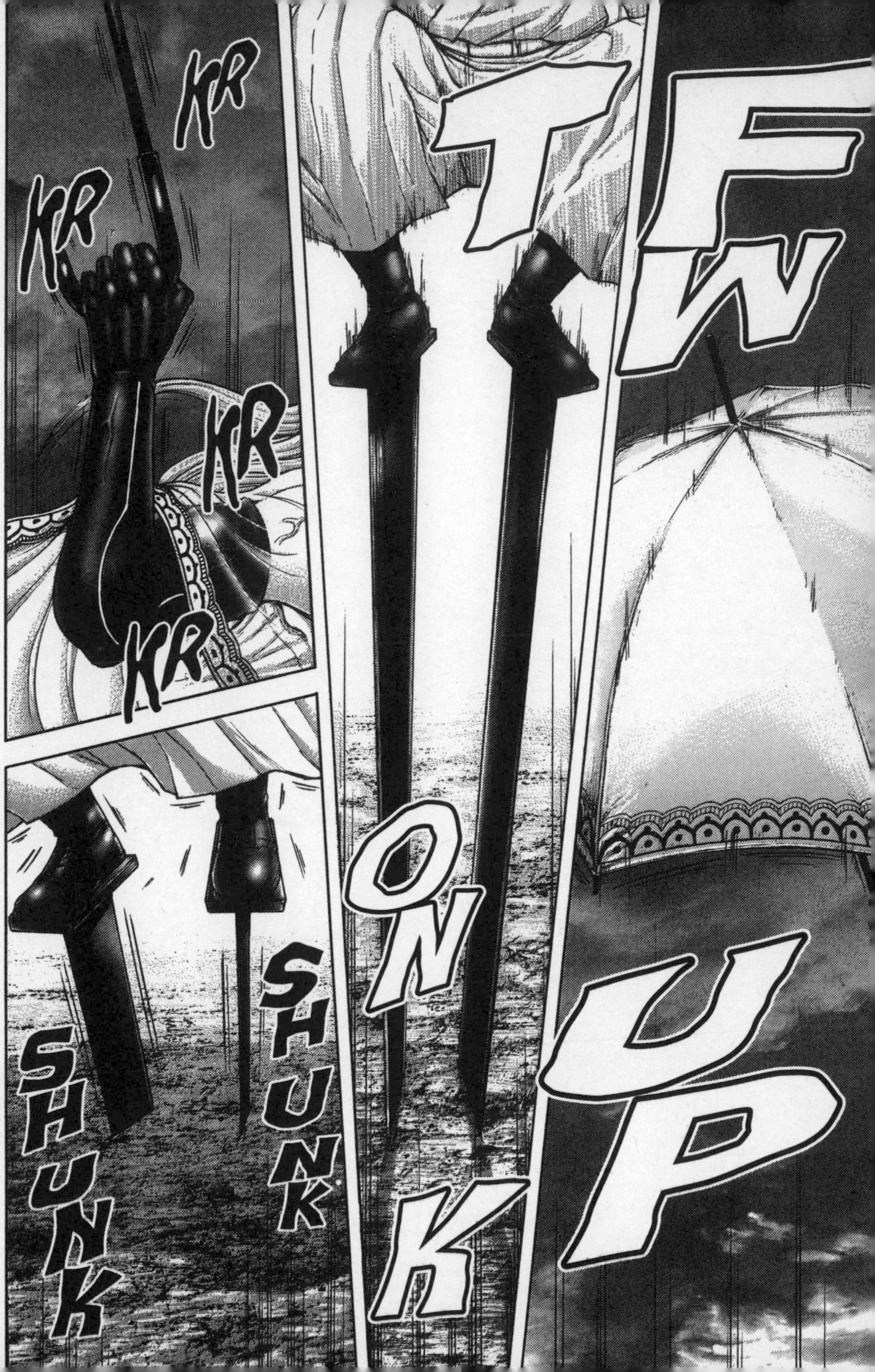
FWUP
TONK
KR
KR
KR
KR
SHUNK
SHUNK

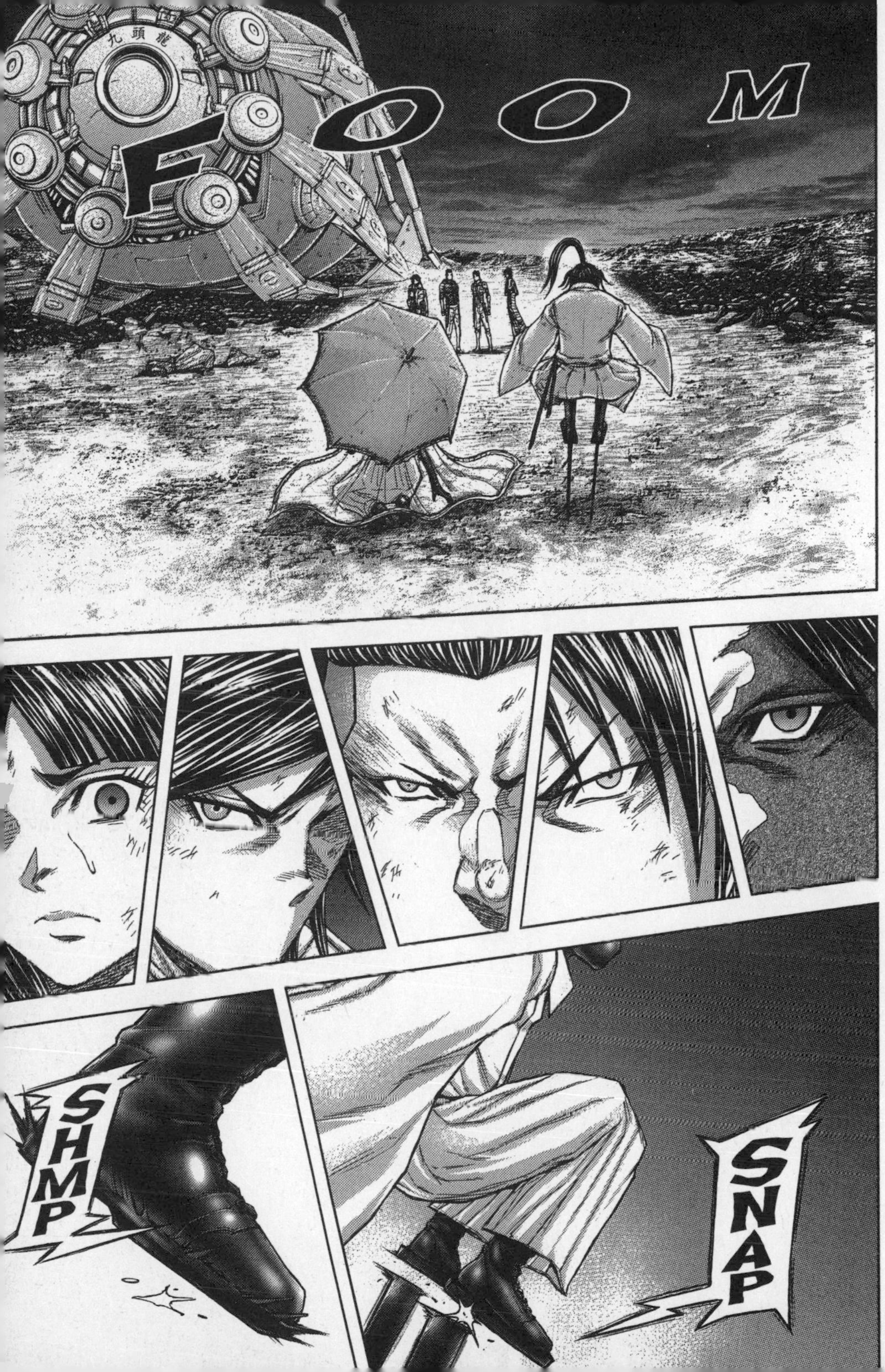
九頭龍
FOOOM
SNAP
SHMP

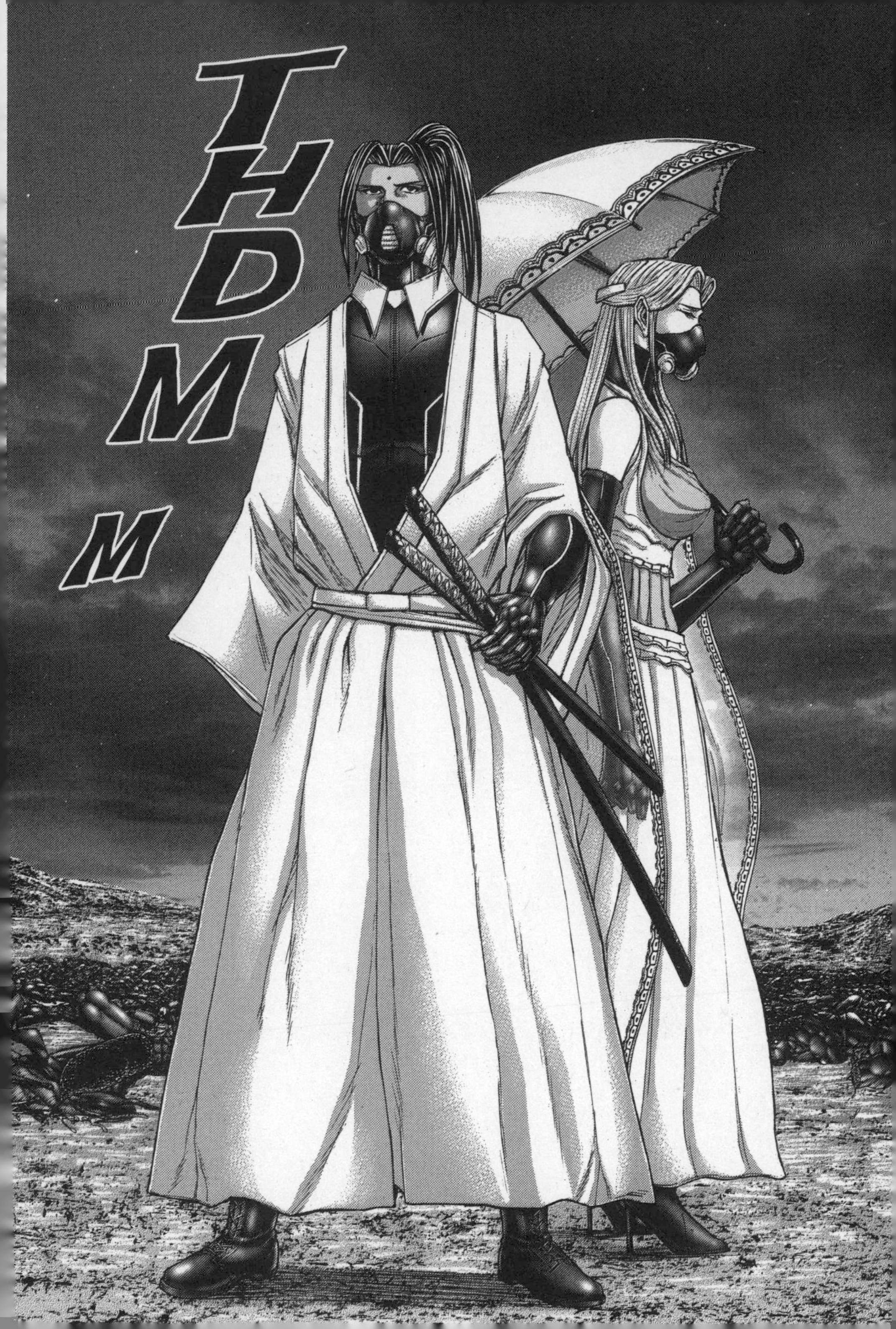
THDM
M

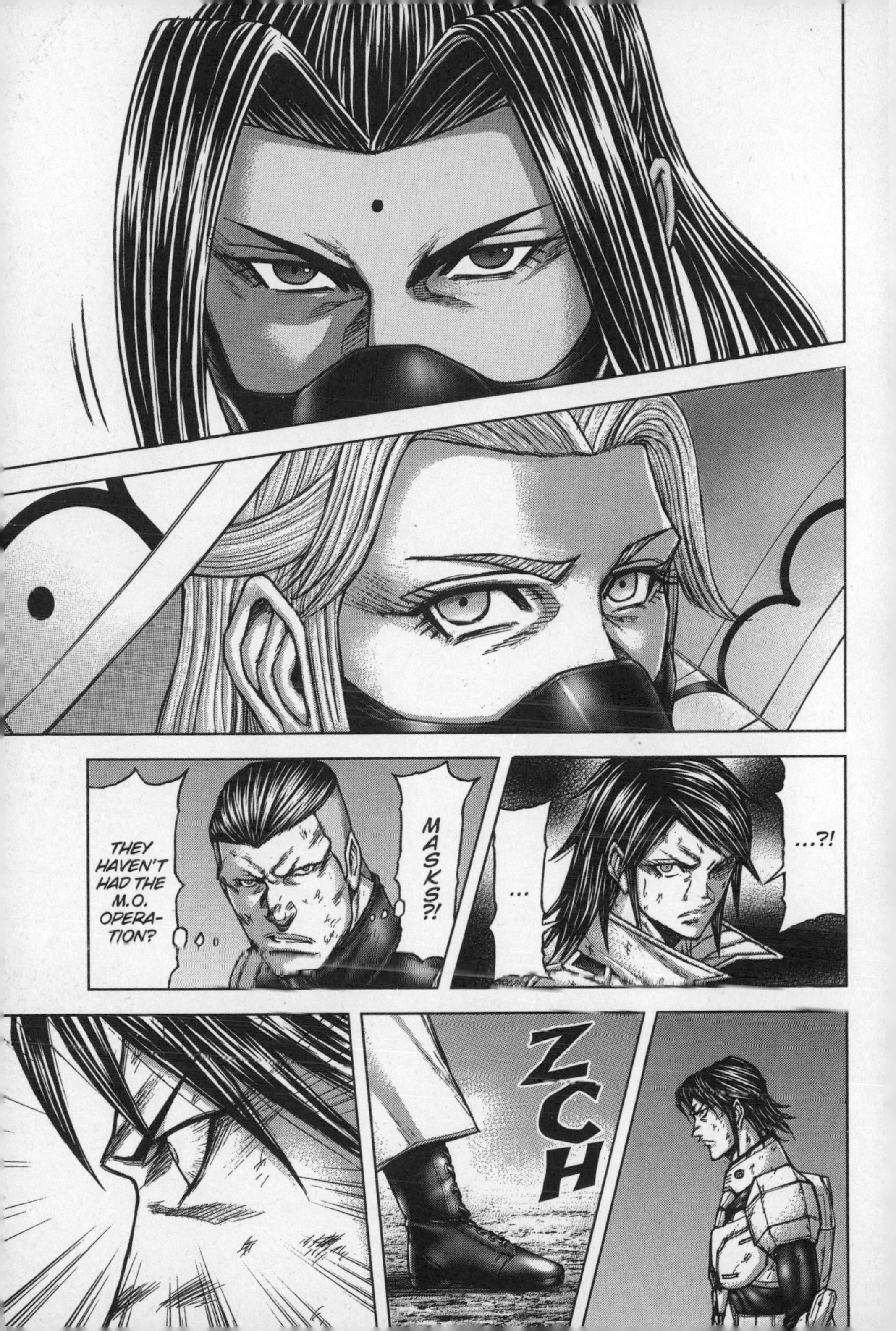
...?!
...
MASKS?!
THEY HAVEN'T HAD THE M.O. OPERATION?
ZCH

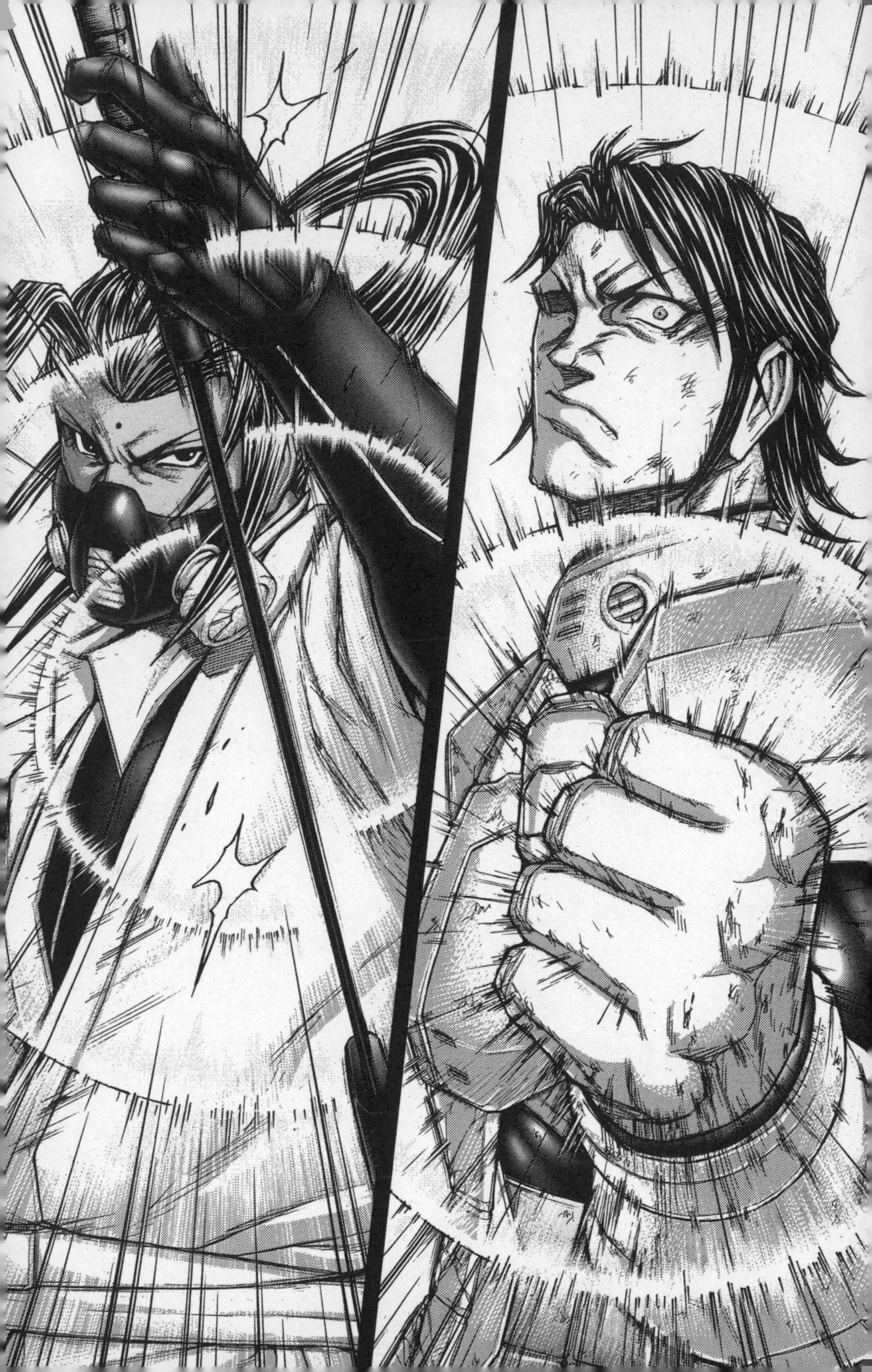

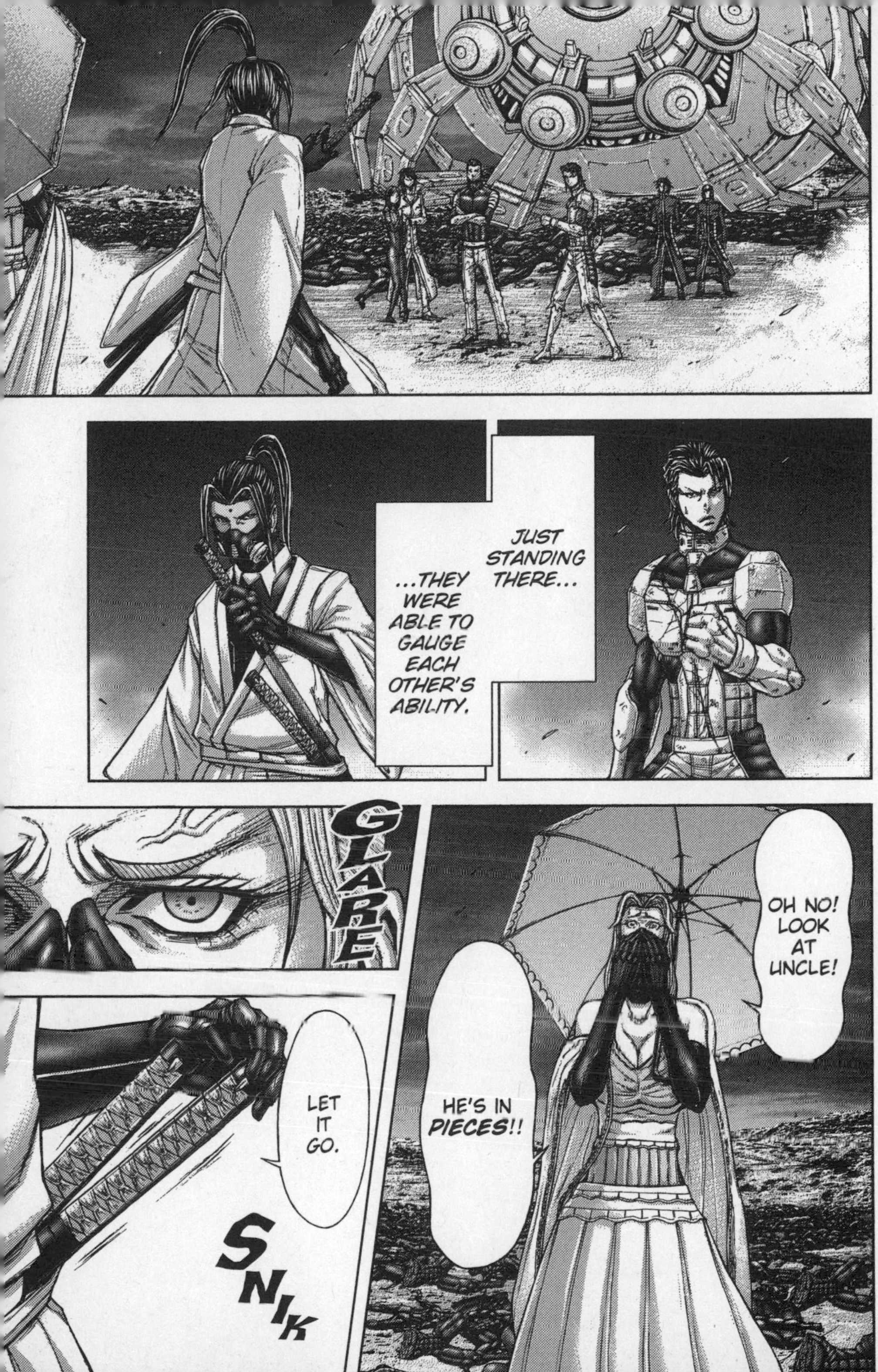
JUST STANDING THERE...
...THEY WERE ABLE TO GAUGE EACH OTHER'S ABILITY.
OH NO! LOOK AT UNCLE!
HE'S IN PIECES!!
GLARE
LET IT GO.
SNIK

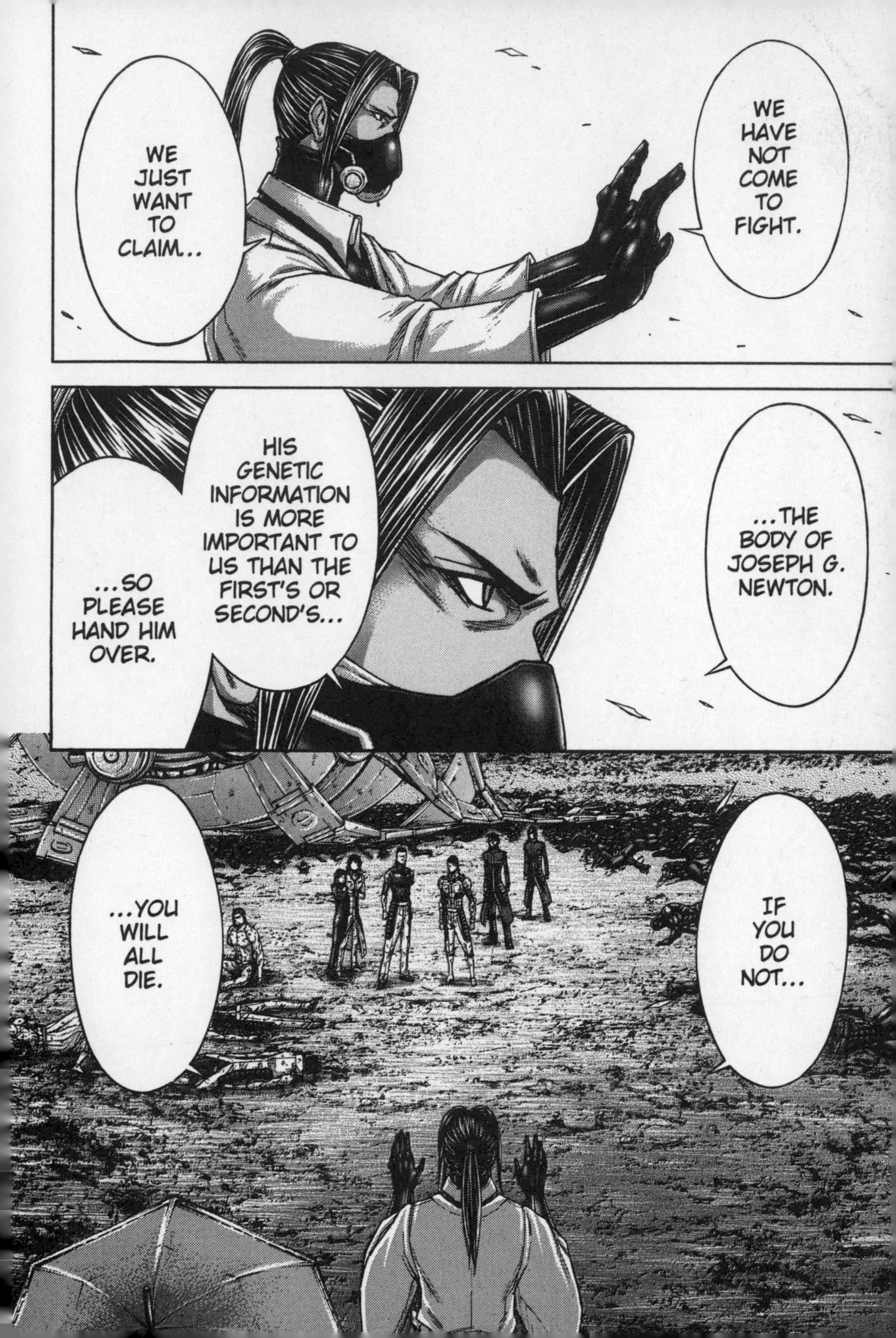
WE HAVE NOT COME TO FIGHT.
WE JUST WANT TO CLAIM...
...THE BODY OF JOSEPH G. NEWTON.
HIS GENETIC INFORMATION IS MORE IMPORTANT TO US THAN THE FIRST'S OR SECOND'S...
...SO PLEASE HAND HIM OVER.
IF YOU DO NOT...
...YOU WILL ALL DIE.

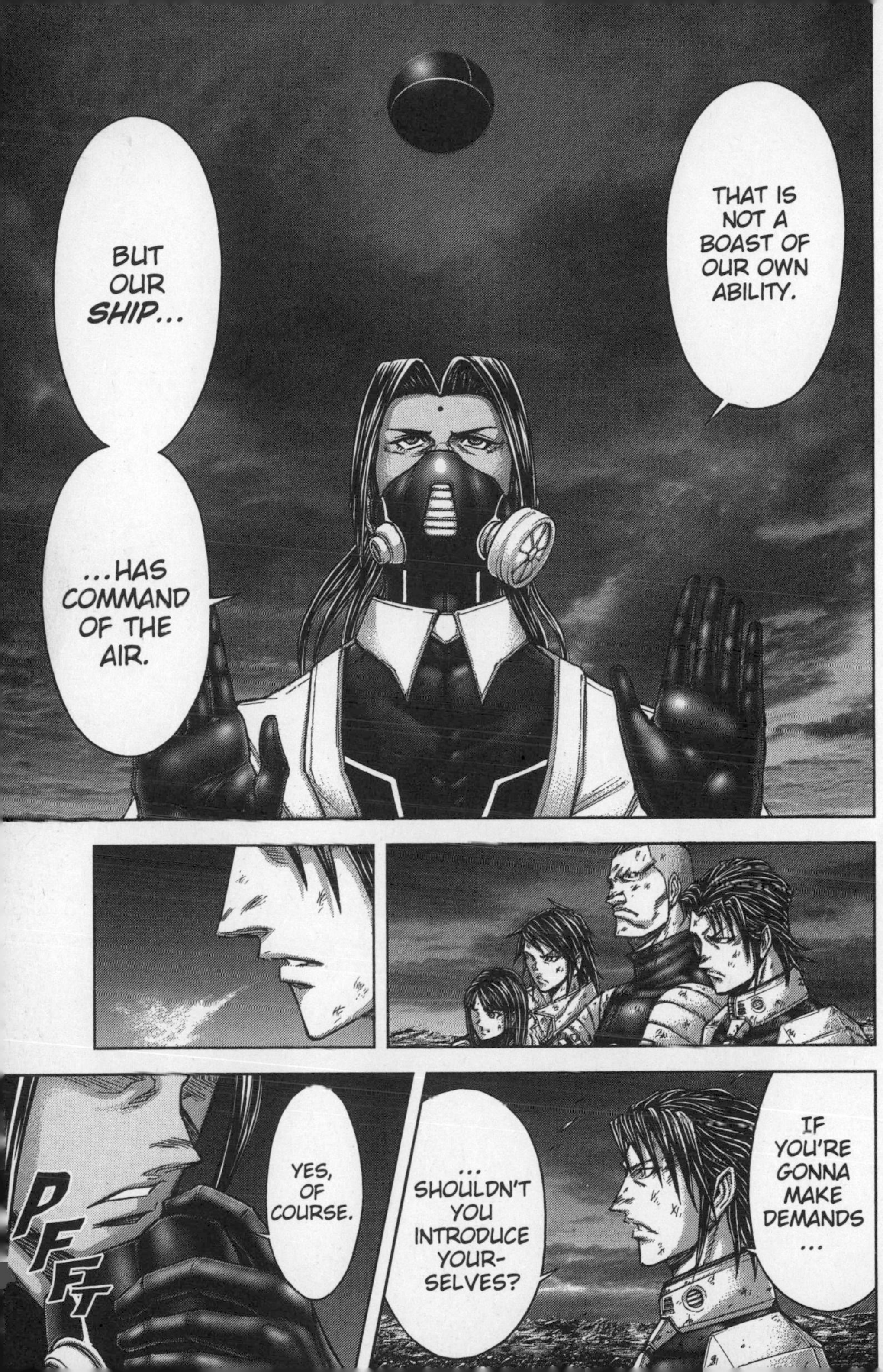
THAT IS NOT A BOAST OF OUR OWN ABILITY.
BUT OUR *SHIP*...
...HAS COMMAND OF THE AIR.
IF YOU'RE GONNA MAKE DEMANDS ...
... SHOULDN'T YOU INTRODUCE YOUR-SELVES?
YES, OF COURSE.
PFFT

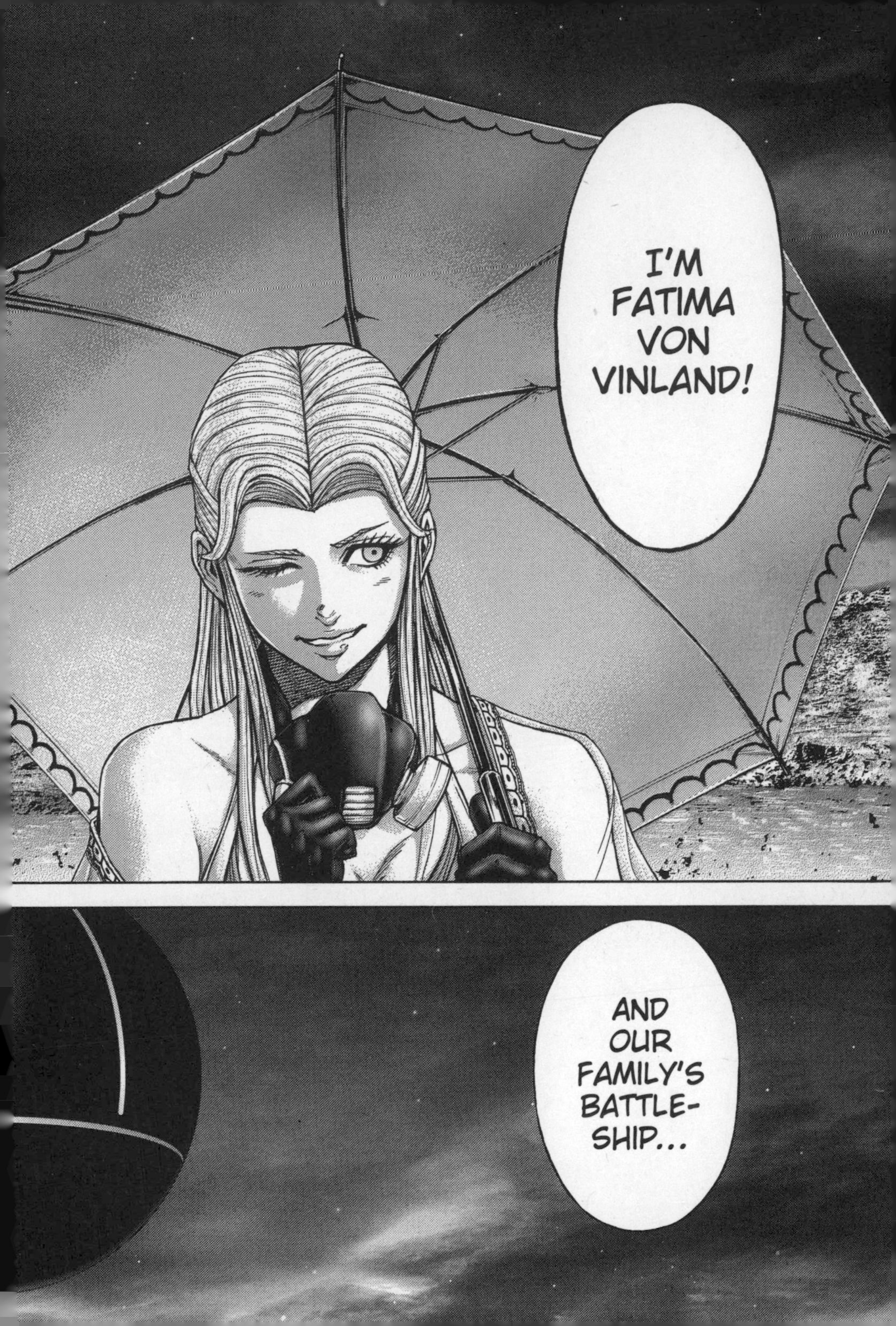
I'M FATIMA VON VINLAND!
AND OUR FAMILY'S BATTLE-SHIP...

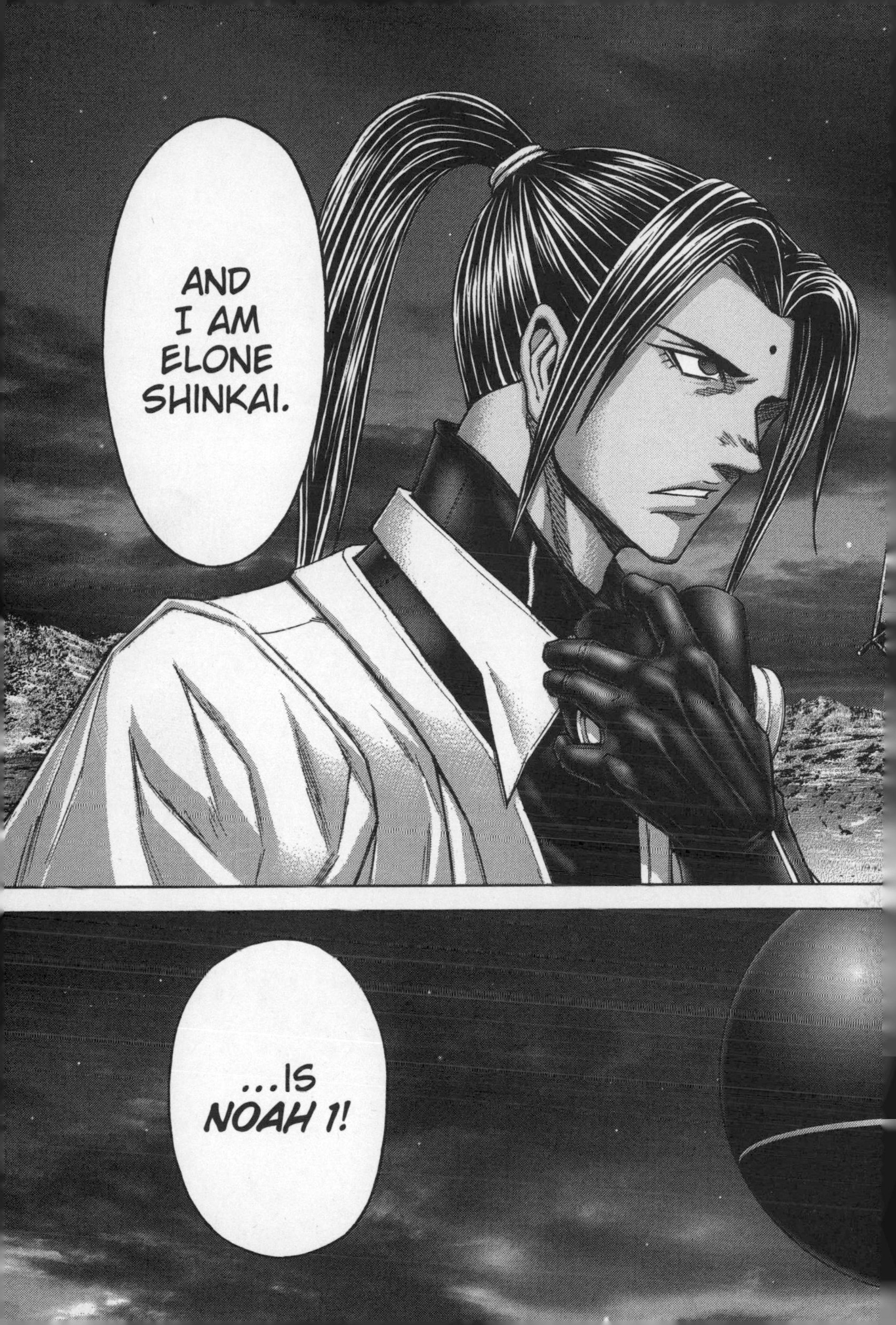
AND I AM ELONE SHINKAI.
...IS *NOAH 1*!

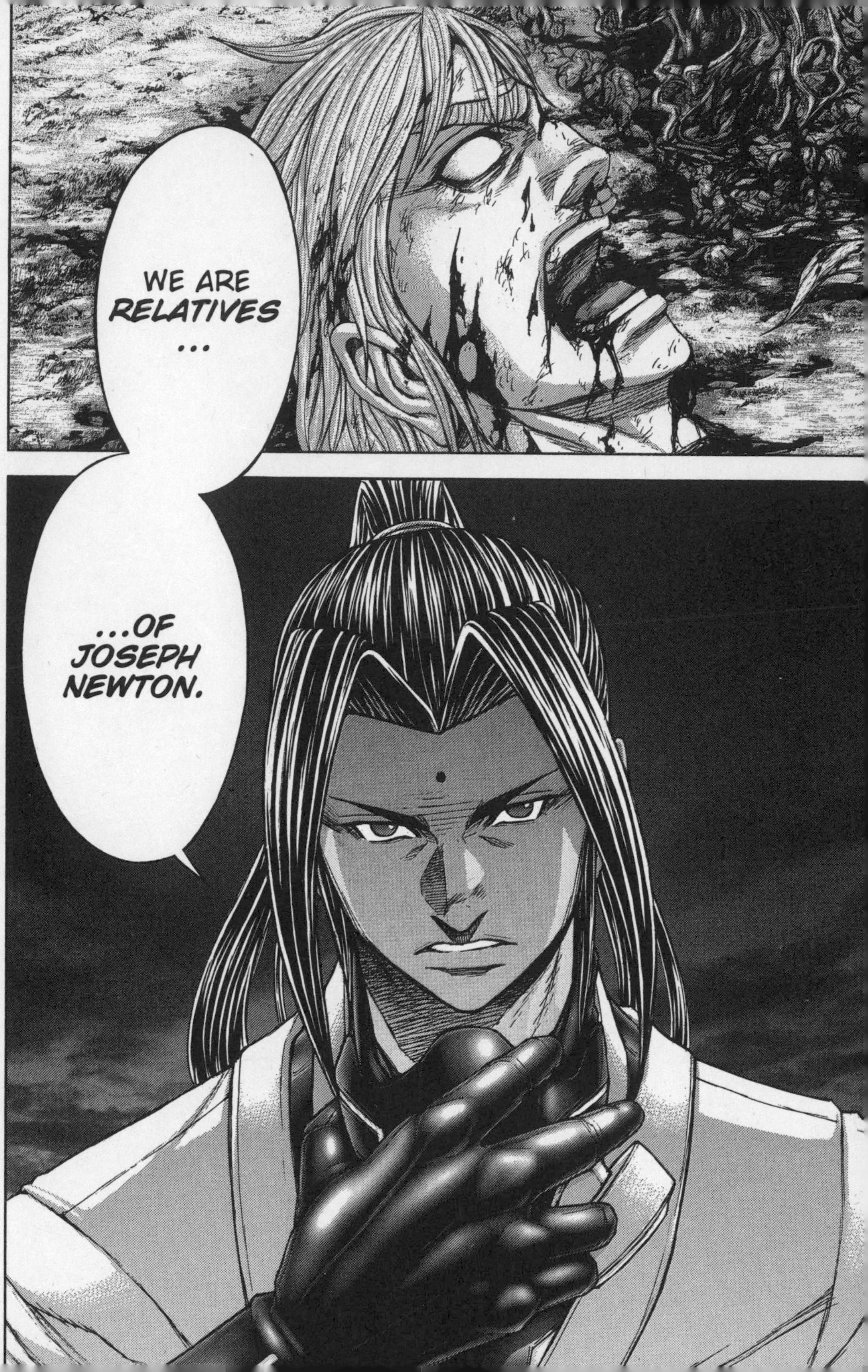
WE ARE RELATIVES ...
...OF JOSEPH NEWTON.

難儀 (nangi)
1. Difficulty
2. Suffering
3. Something troublesome
4. Poverty

General Kai uses this word in panel 3 on page 91. When I heard that people in eastern Japan don't use this word, I was shocked. Apparently, using this word to describe situations such as having a cold is part of the Niigata dialect.

Then what do you say when you have a cold? Darui (languid) isn't quite right...

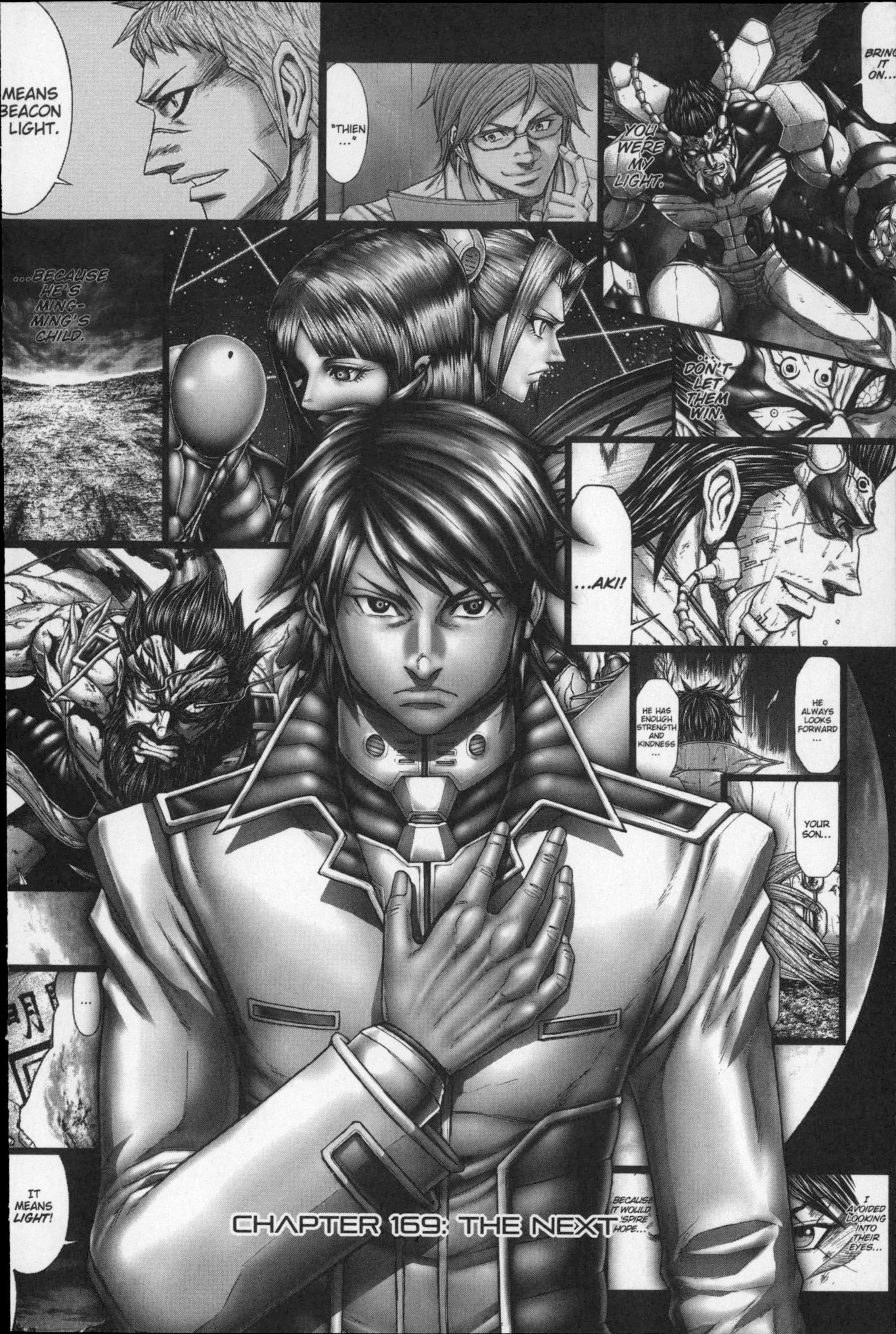
BRING IT ON...
YOU WERE MY LIGHT.
"THIEN..."
MEANS BEACON LIGHT.
DON'T LET THEM WIN.
...BECAUSE HE'S MING-MING'S CHILD.
...AKI!
HE ALWAYS LOOKS FORWARD...
HE HAS ENOUGH STRENGTH AND KINDNESS...
YOUR SON...
...
I AVOIDED LOOKING INTO THEIR EYES...
BECAUSE IT WOULD SPIRE HOPE...
IT MEANS LIGHT!
CHAPTER 169: THE NEXT

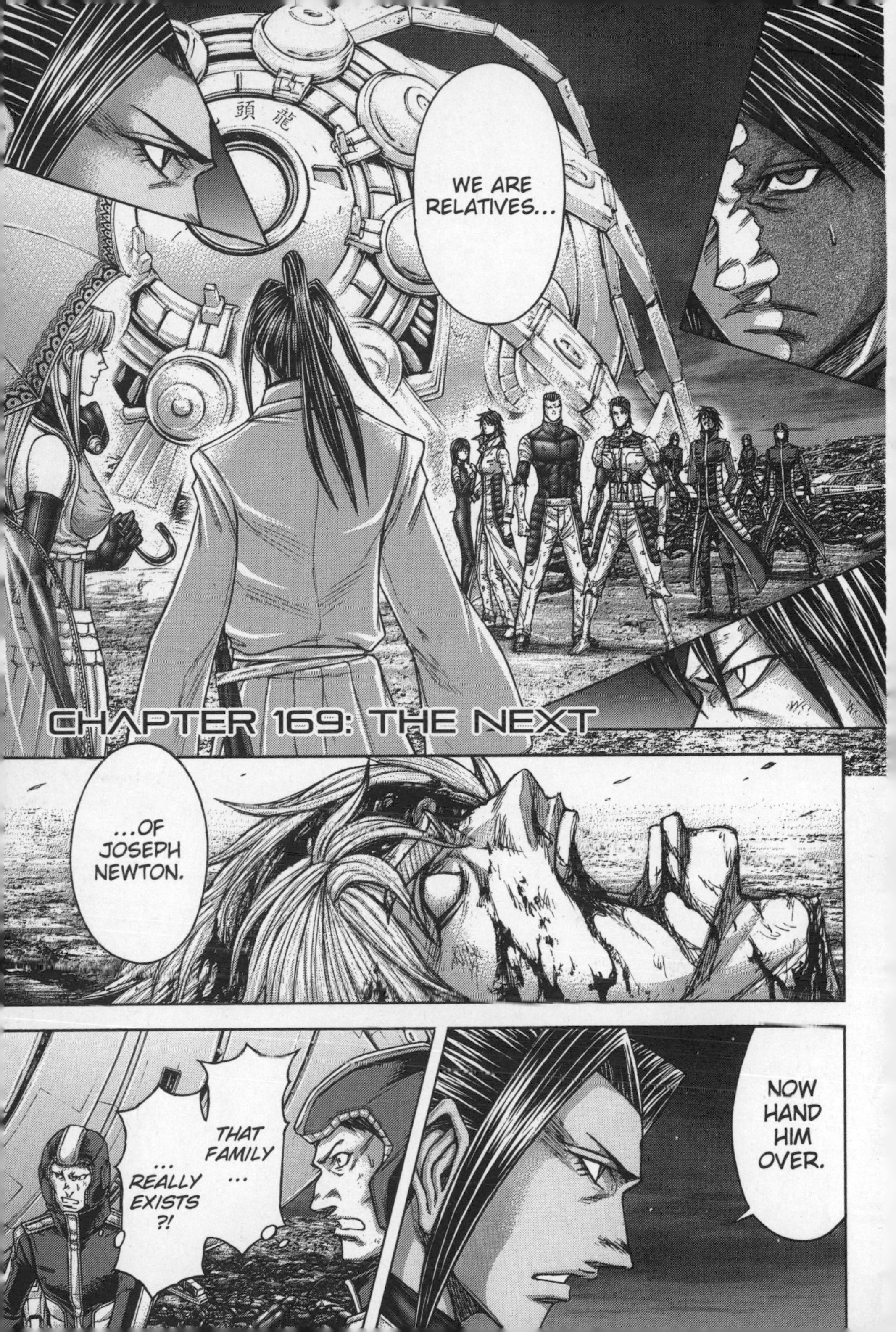
WE ARE RELATIVES...
CHAPTER 169: THE NEXT
...OF JOSEPH NEWTON.
NOW HAND HIM OVER.
THAT FAMILY ...
... REALLY EXISTS ?!

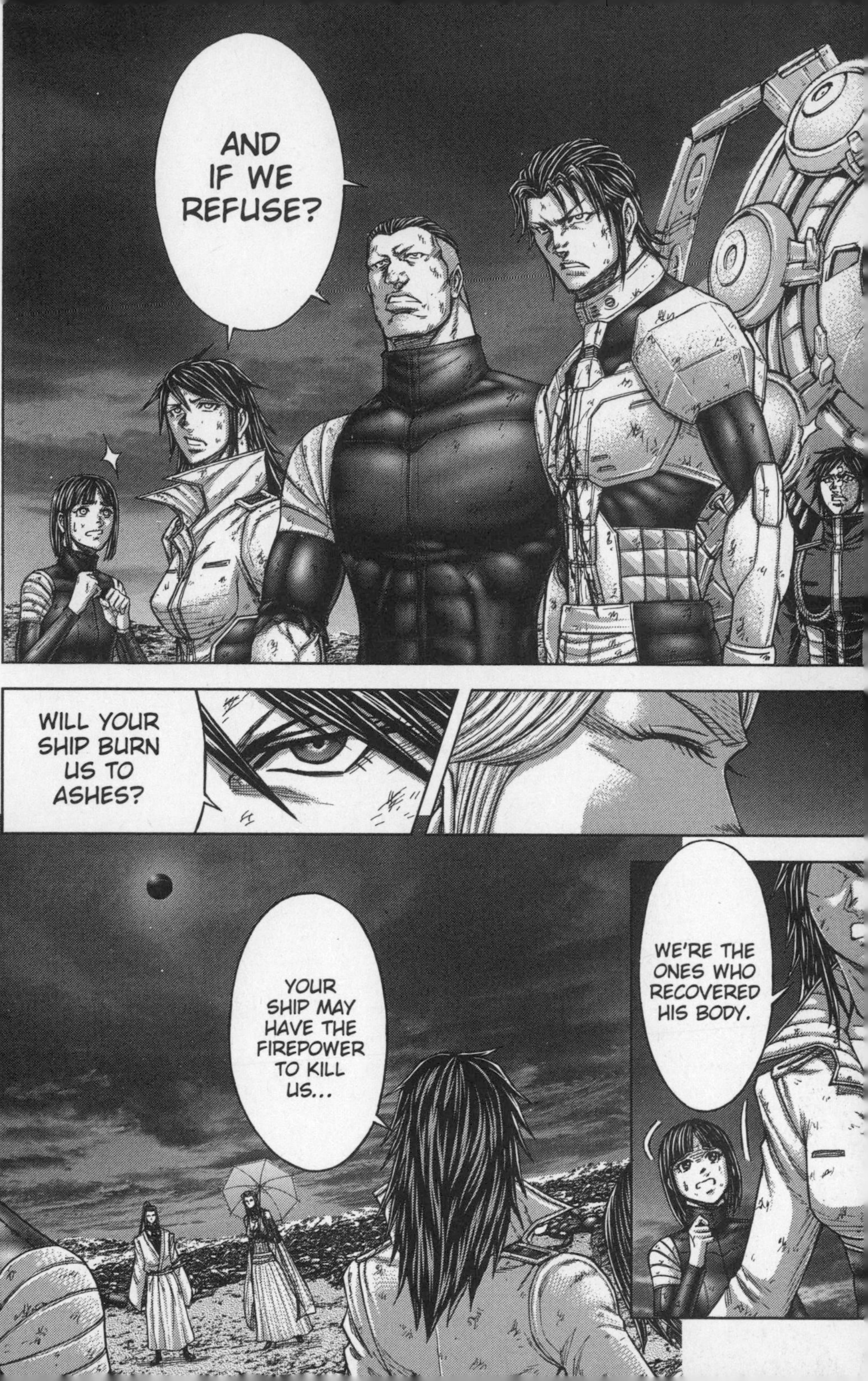
AND IF WE REFUSE?
WILL YOUR SHIP BURN US TO ASHES?
WE'RE THE ONES WHO RECOVERED HIS BODY.
YOUR SHIP MAY HAVE THE FIREPOWER TO KILL US...

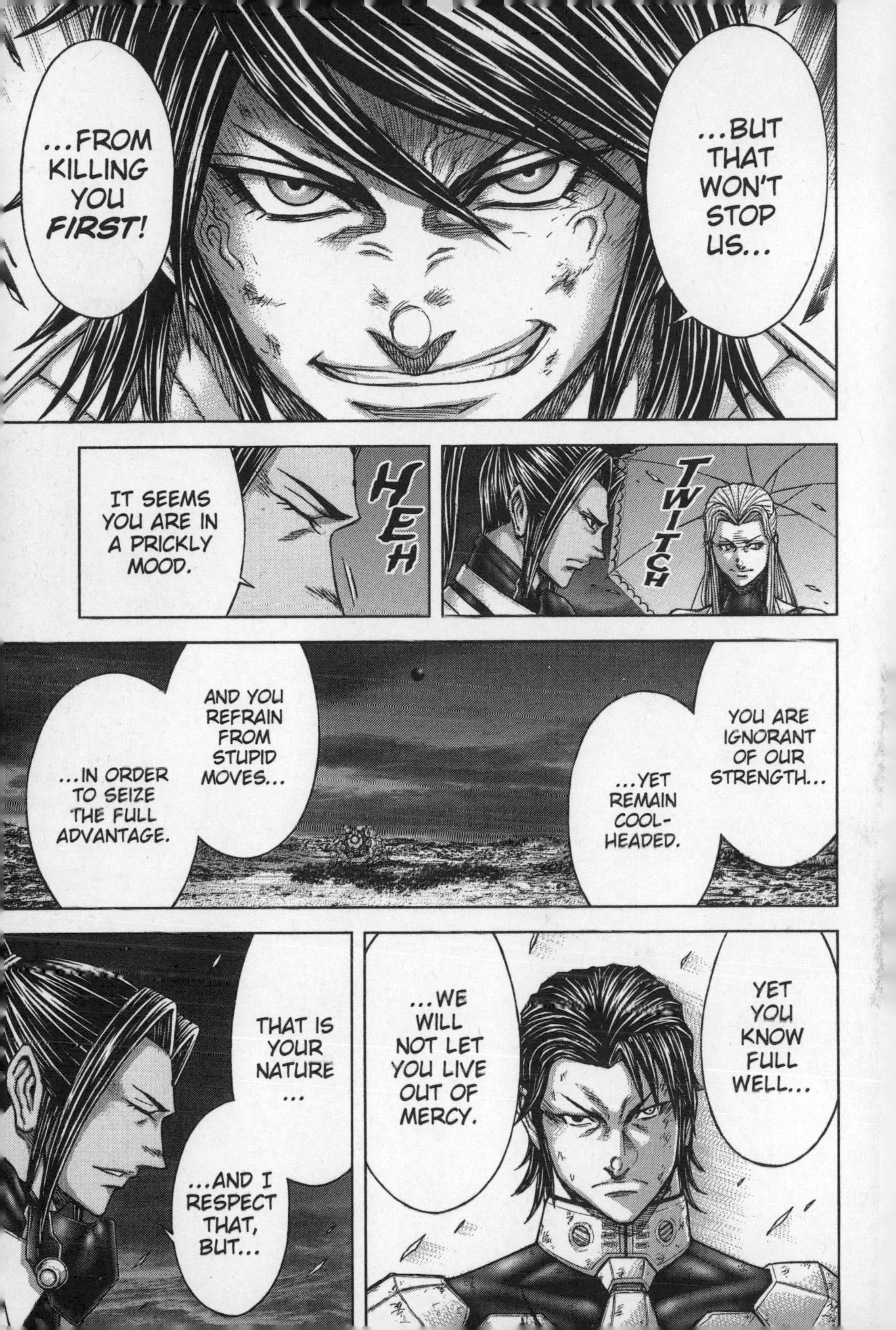
...BUT THAT WON'T STOP US...
...FROM KILLING YOU *FIRST*!
TWITCH
HEH
IT SEEMS YOU ARE IN A PRICKLY MOOD.
YOU ARE IGNORANT OF OUR STRENGTH...
...YET REMAIN COOL-HEADED.
AND YOU REFRAIN FROM STUPID MOVES...
...IN ORDER TO SEIZE THE FULL ADVANTAGE.
YET YOU KNOW FULL WELL...
...WE WILL NOT LET YOU LIVE OUT OF MERCY.
THAT IS YOUR NATURE...
...AND I RESPECT THAT, BUT...

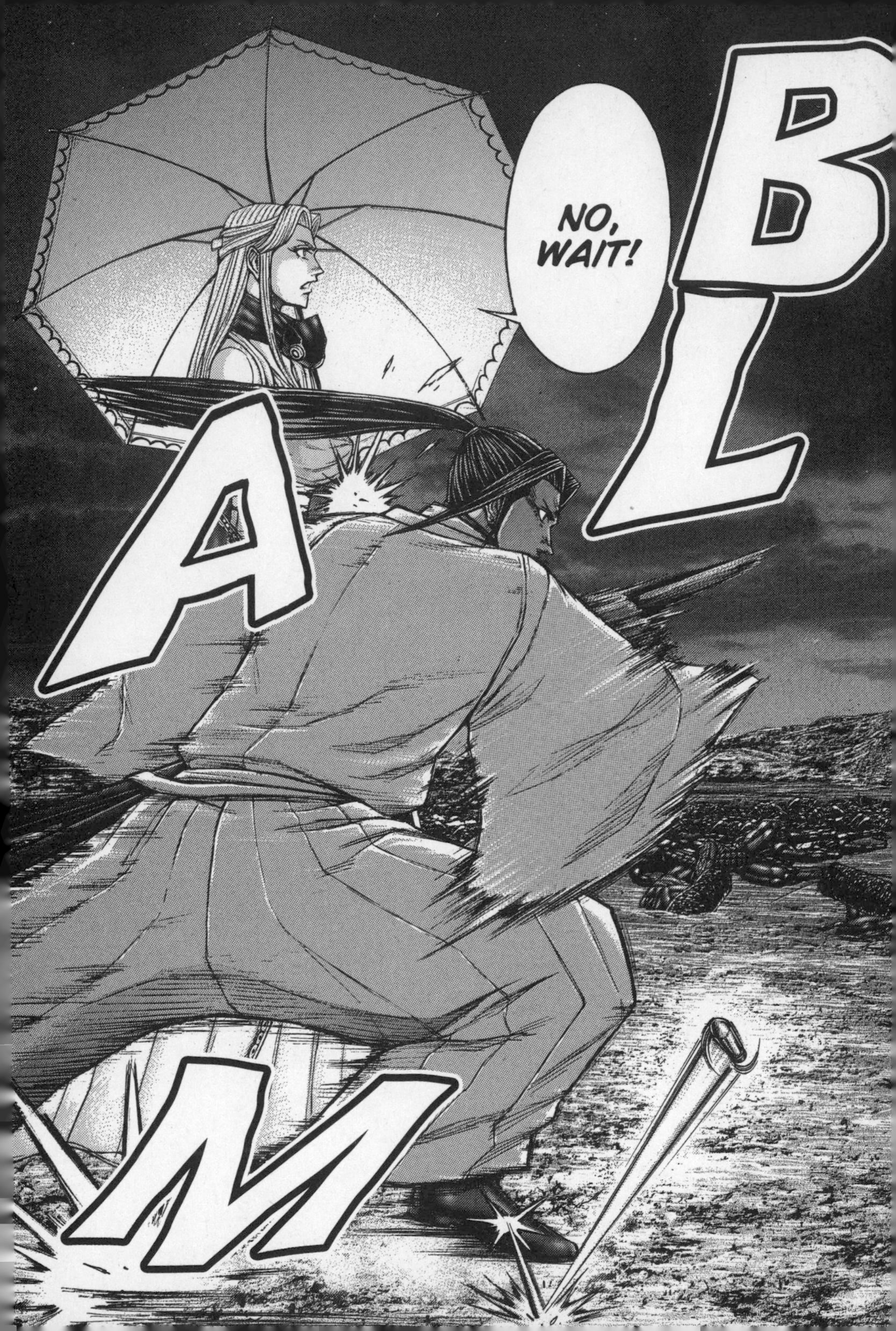
BLAM
NO, WAIT!

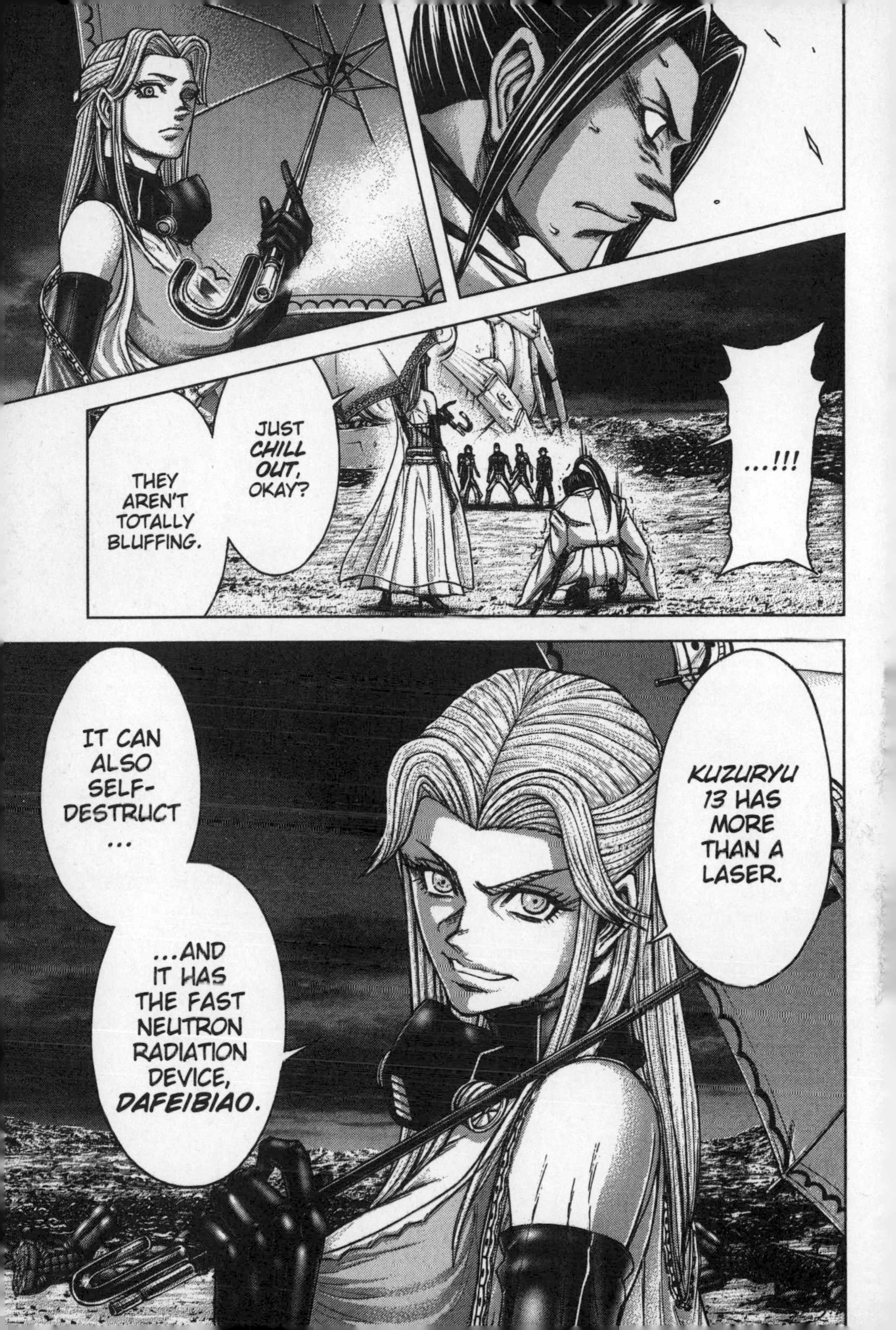
...!!!
JUST CHILL OUT, OKAY?
THEY AREN'T TOTALLY BLUFFING.
KUZURYU 13 HAS MORE THAN A LASER.
IT CAN ALSO SELF-DESTRUCT...
...AND IT HAS THE FAST NEUTRON RADIATION DEVICE, DAFEIBIAO.

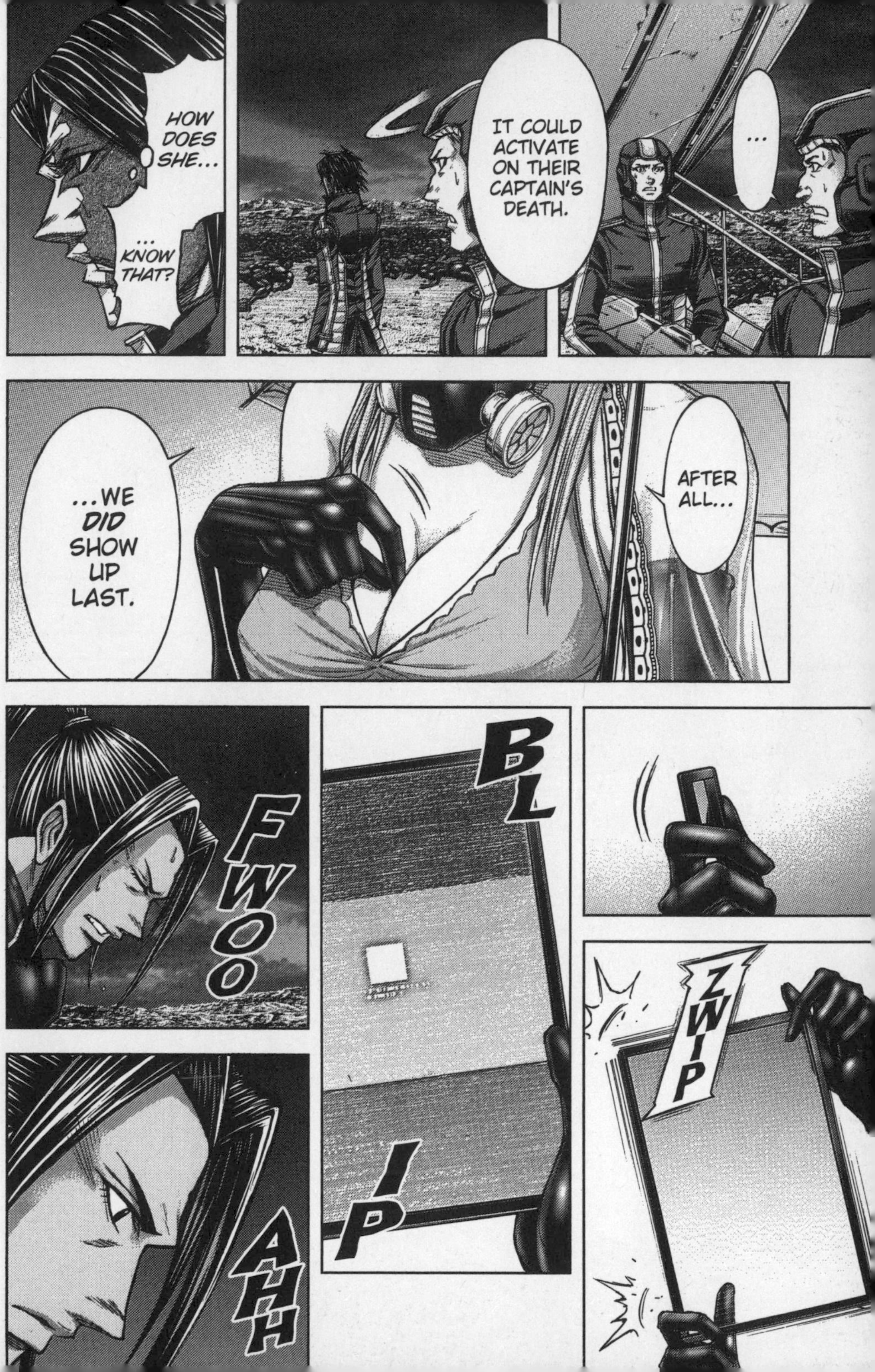
...
IT COULD ACTIVATE ON THEIR CAPTAIN'S DEATH.
HOW DOES SHE...
...KNOW THAT?
AFTER ALL...
...WE *DID* SHOW UP LAST.
ZWIP
BLIP
FWOO
AHH

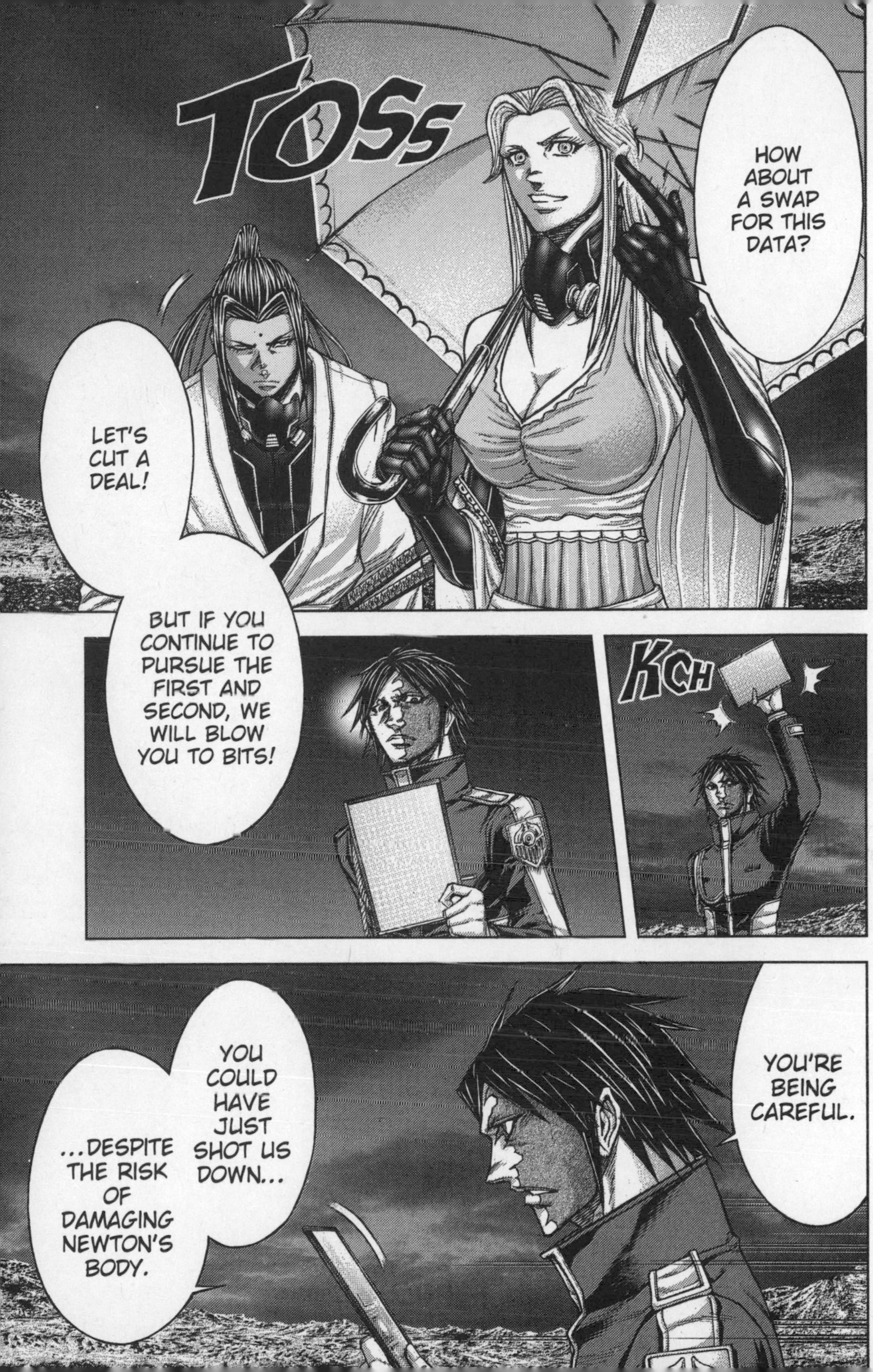
HOW ABOUT A SWAP FOR THIS DATA?
TOSs
LET'S CUT A DEAL!
BUT IF YOU CONTINUE TO PURSUE THE FIRST AND SECOND, WE WILL BLOW YOU TO BITS!
KCH
YOU'RE BEING CAREFUL.
YOU COULD HAVE JUST SHOT US DOWN...
...DESPITE THE RISK OF DAMAGING NEWTON'S BODY.

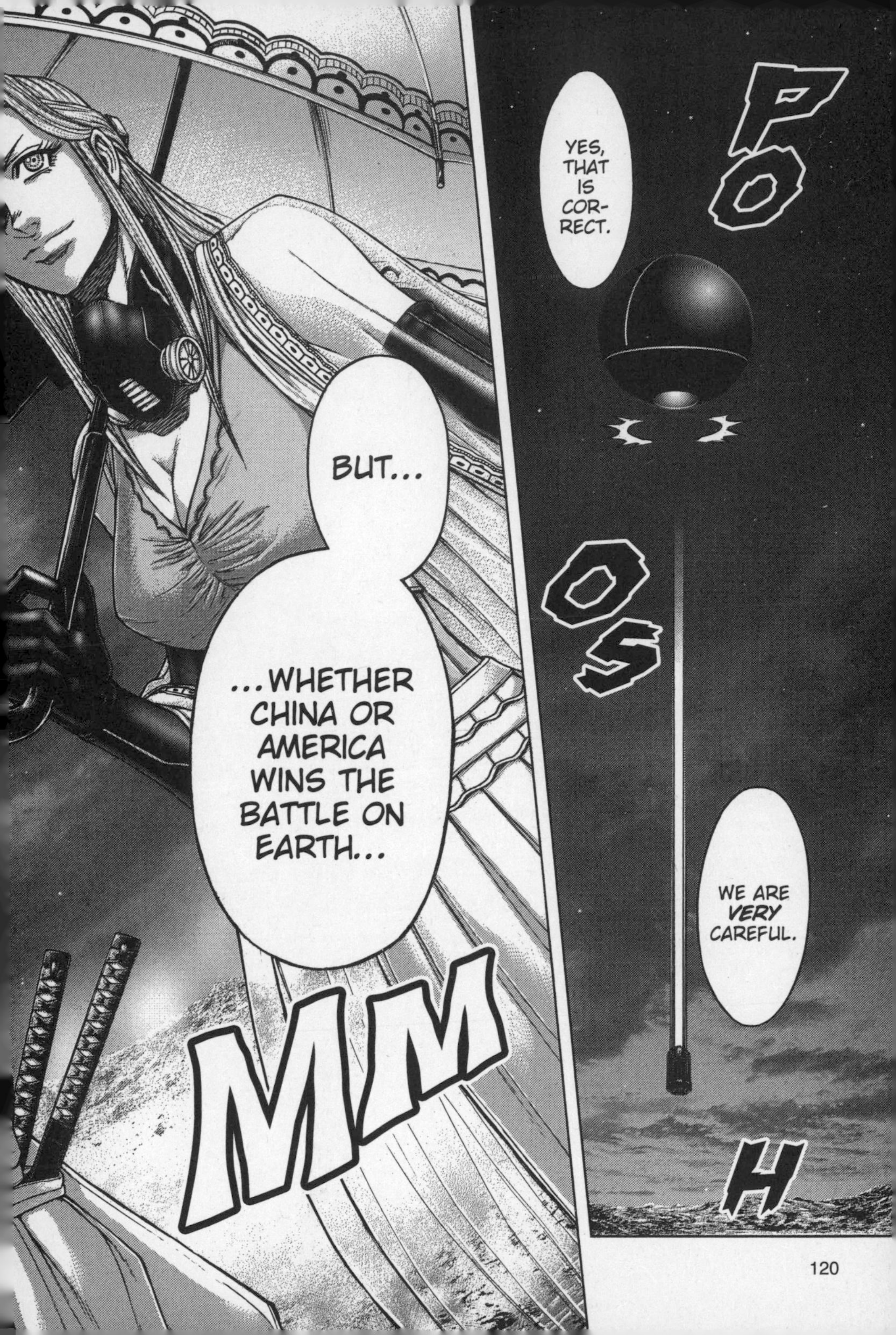
PO
YES, THAT IS COR-RECT.
OS
WE ARE *VERY* CAREFUL.
H
BUT...
...WHETHER CHINA OR AMERICA WINS THE BATTLE ON EARTH...
MM

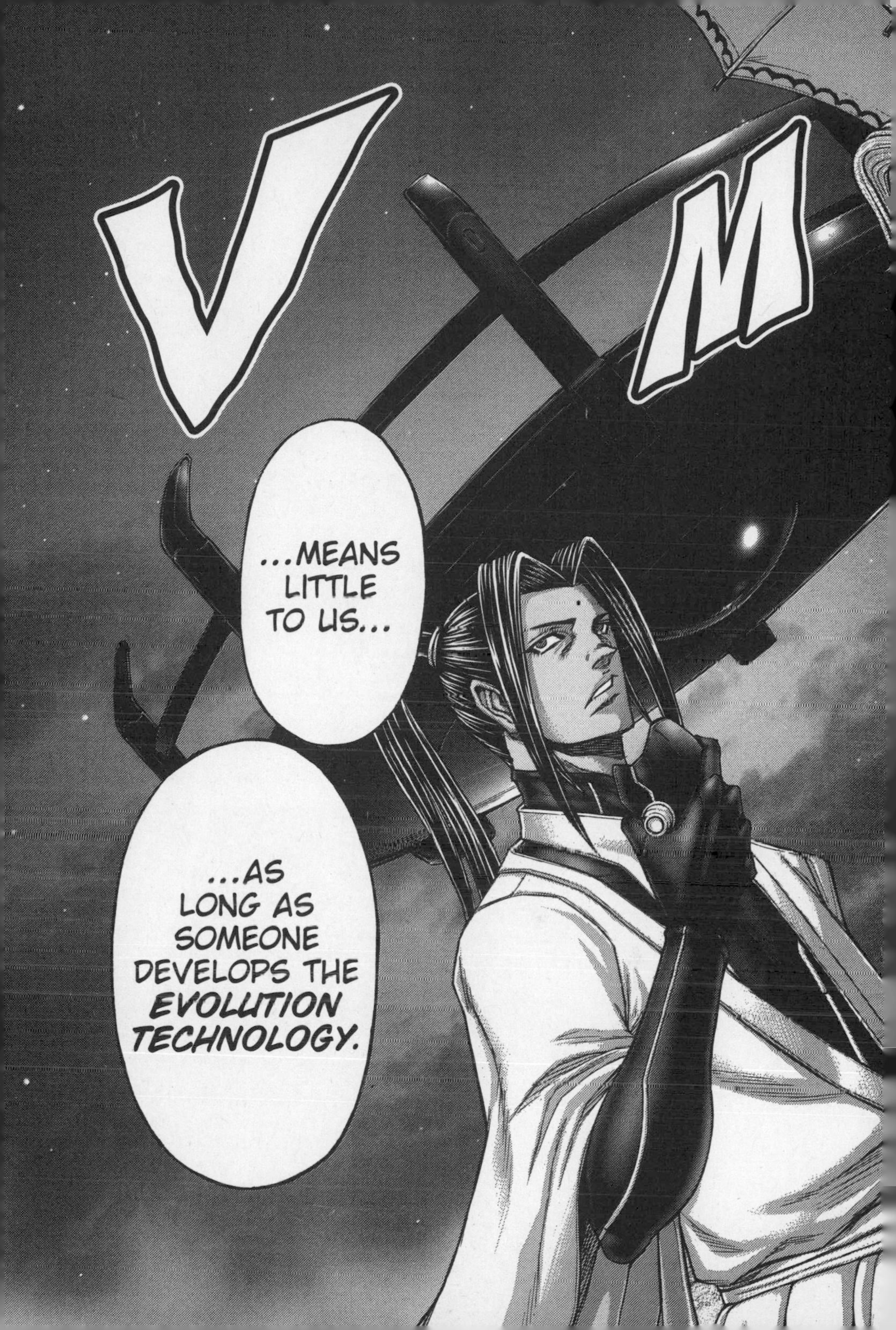
M
V
...MEANS LITTLE TO US...
...AS LONG AS SOMEONE DEVELOPS THE EVOLUTION TECHNOLOGY.

COSMO-
POLITAN
...

...IS EVERY-
WHERE.

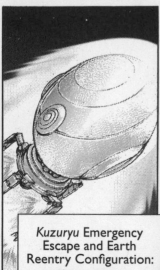

Kuzuryu Emergency Escape and Earth Reentry Configuration:
Dagon

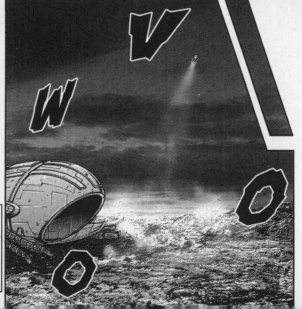

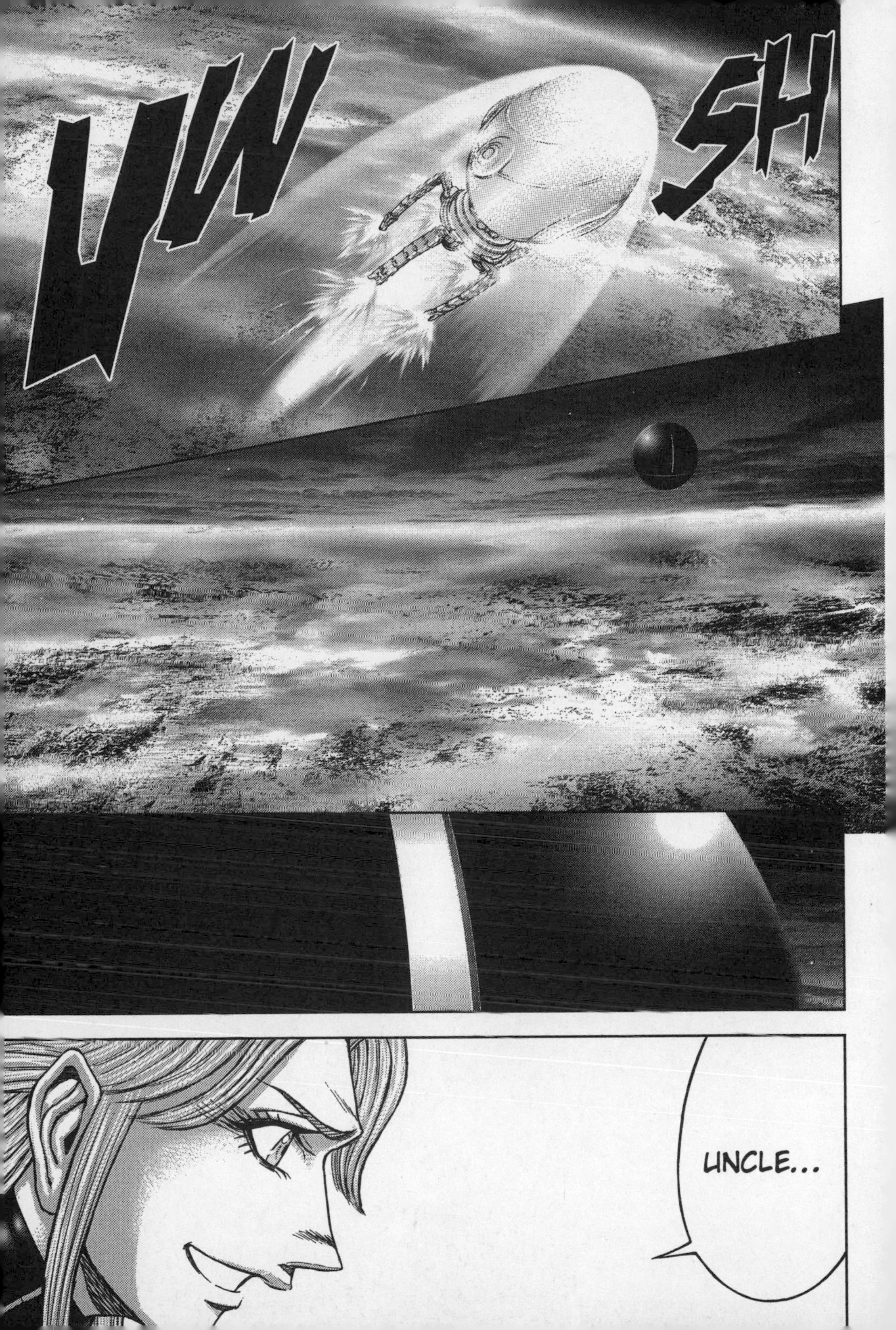
VWSH
UNCLE...

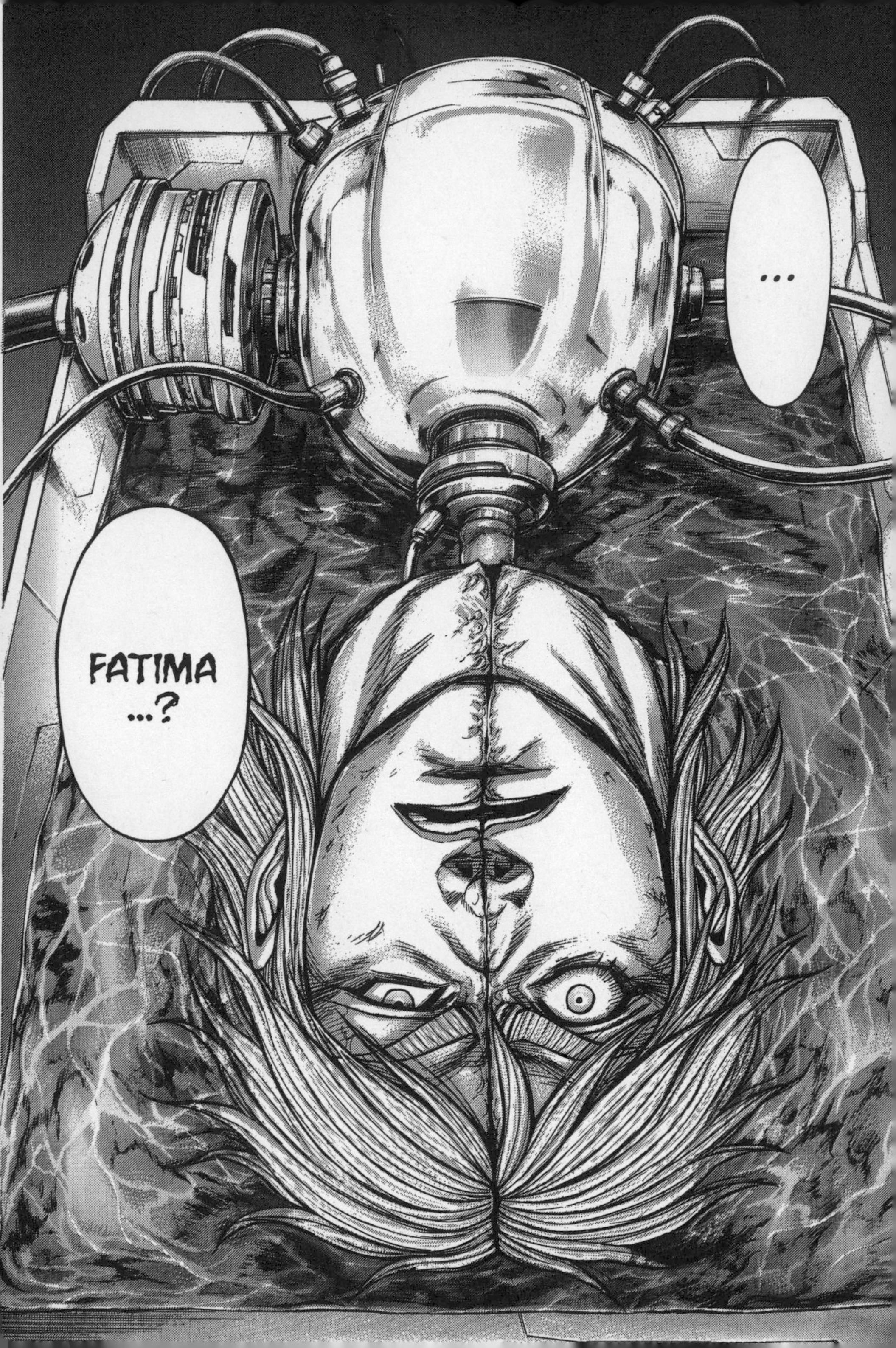
...
FATIMA ...?

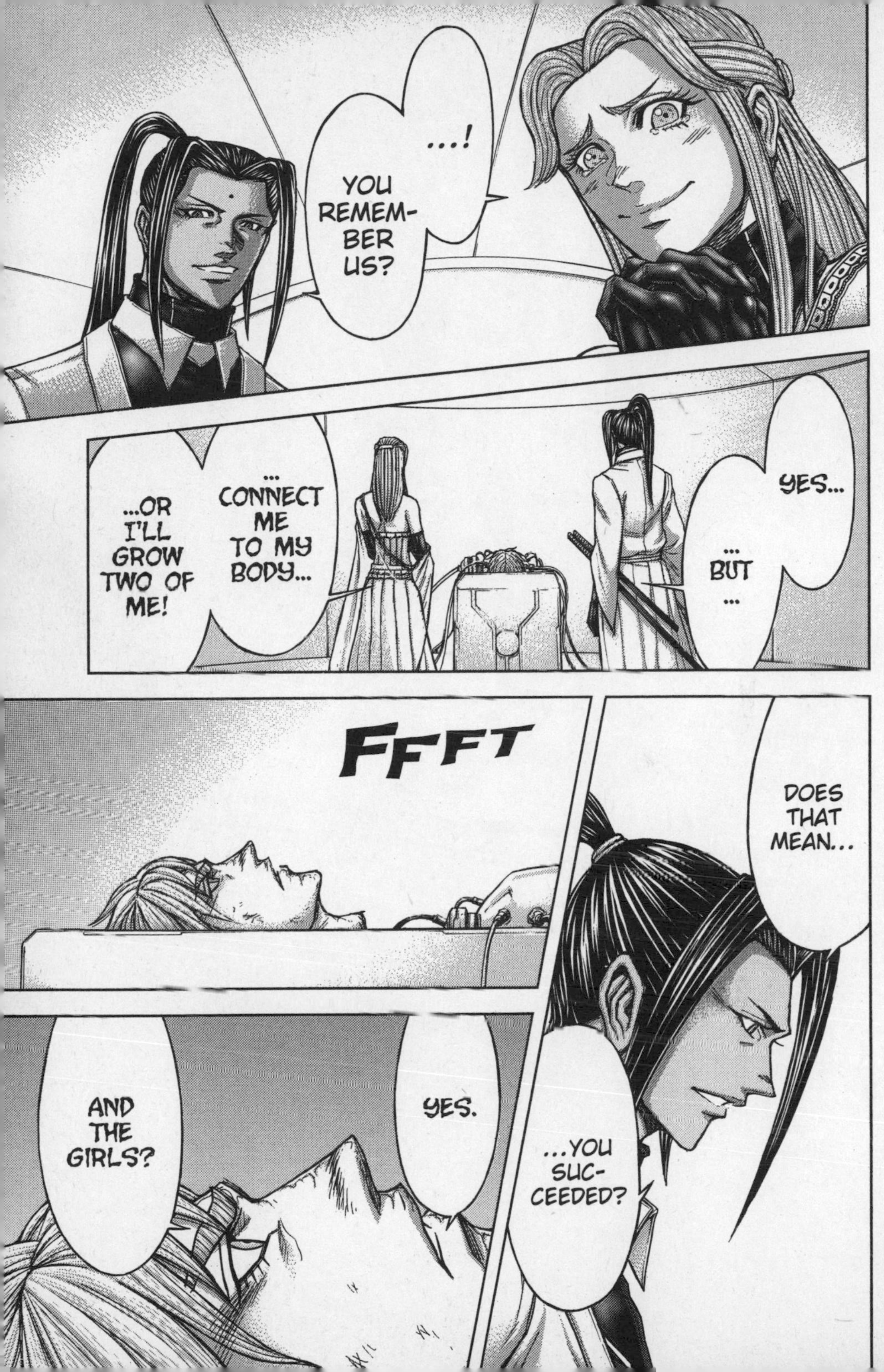
...!
YOU REMEM-BER US?
YES...
... BUT ...
... CONNECT ME TO MY BODY...
...OR I'LL GROW TWO OF ME!
DOES THAT MEAN...
...YOU SUC-CEEDED?
FFFT
YES.
AND THE GIRLS?

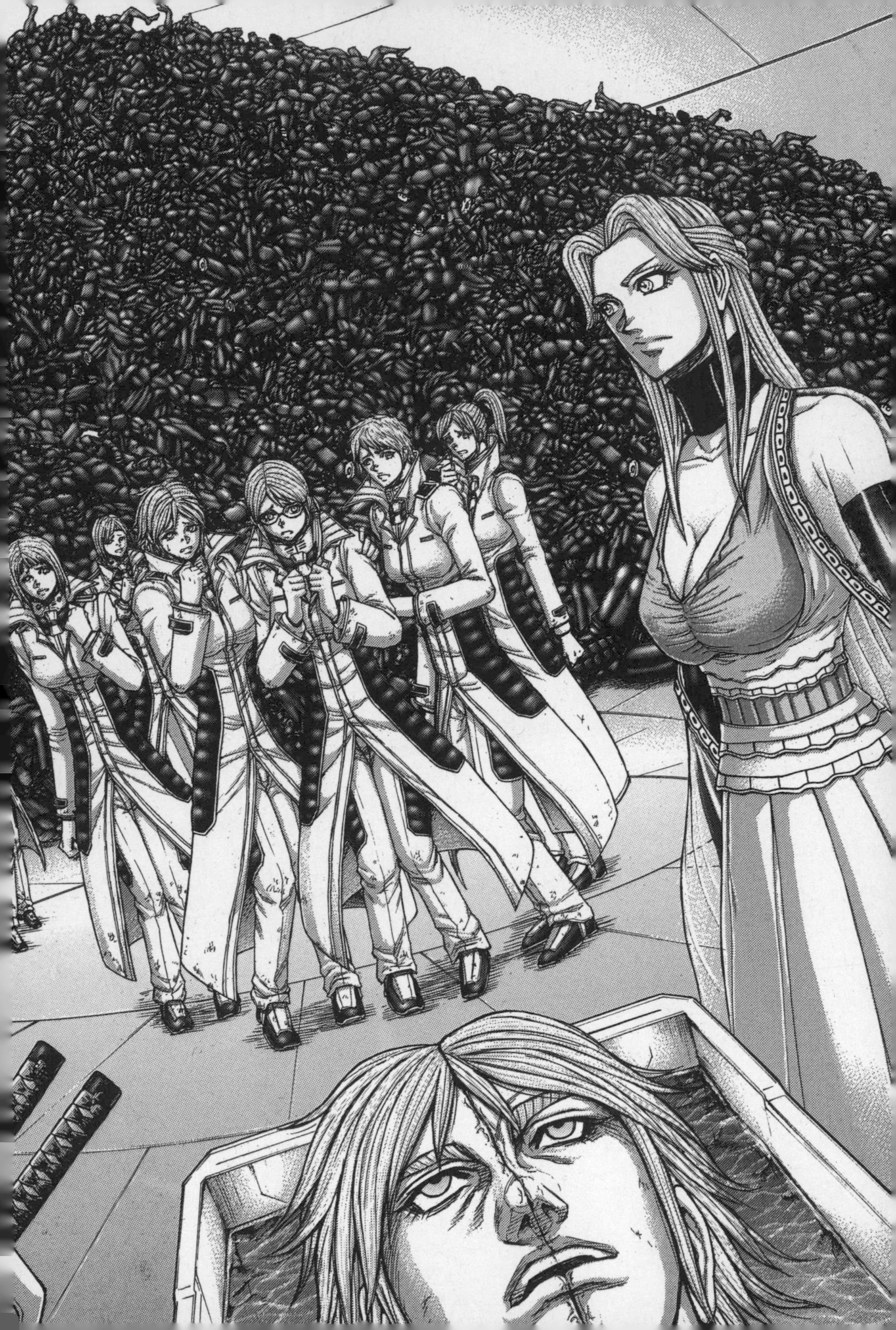

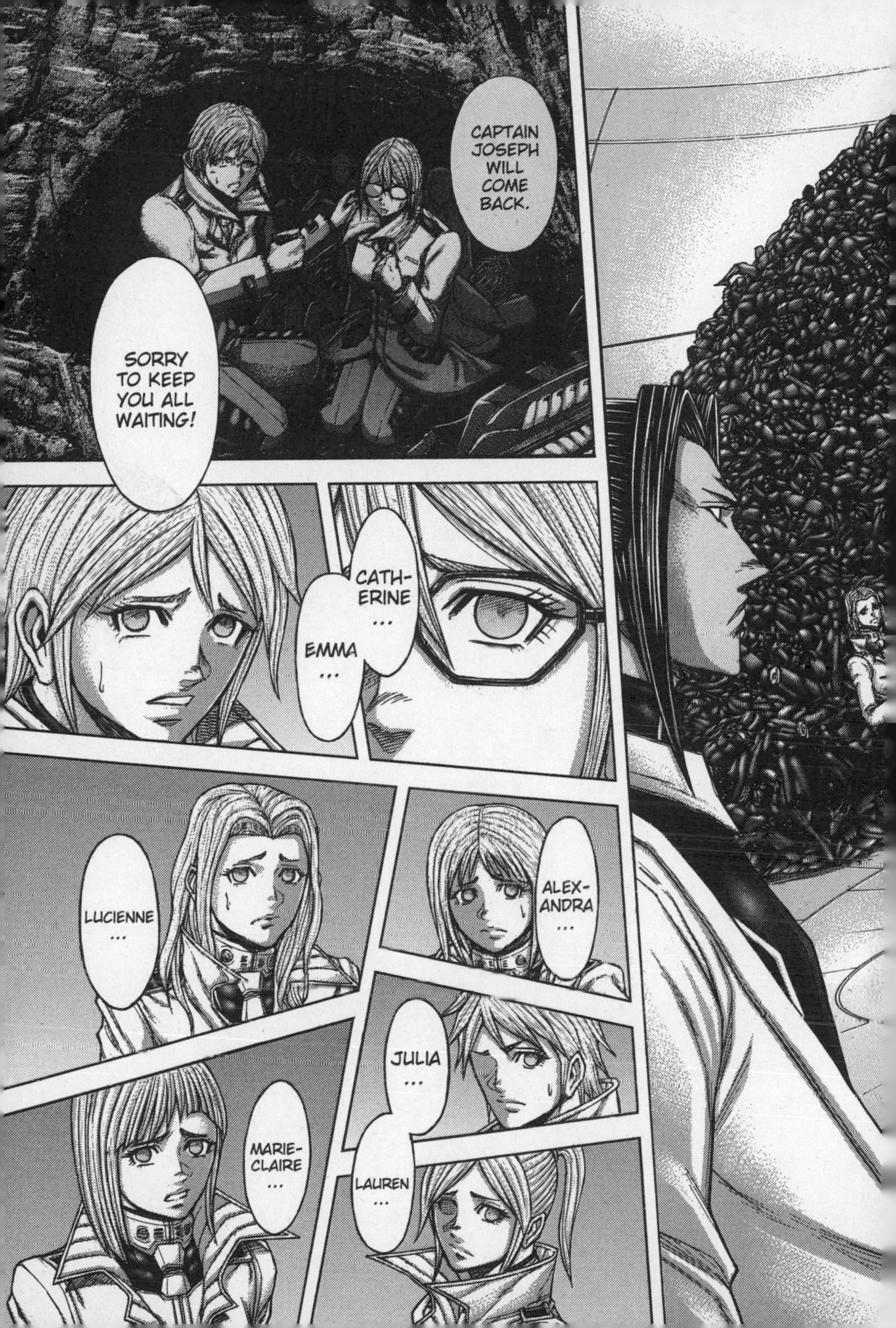
CAPTAIN JOSEPH WILL COME BACK.
SORRY TO KEEP YOU ALL WAITING!
CATHERINE...
EMMA...
ALEXANDRA...
LUCIENNE...
JULIA...
LAUREN...
MARIE-CLAIRE...

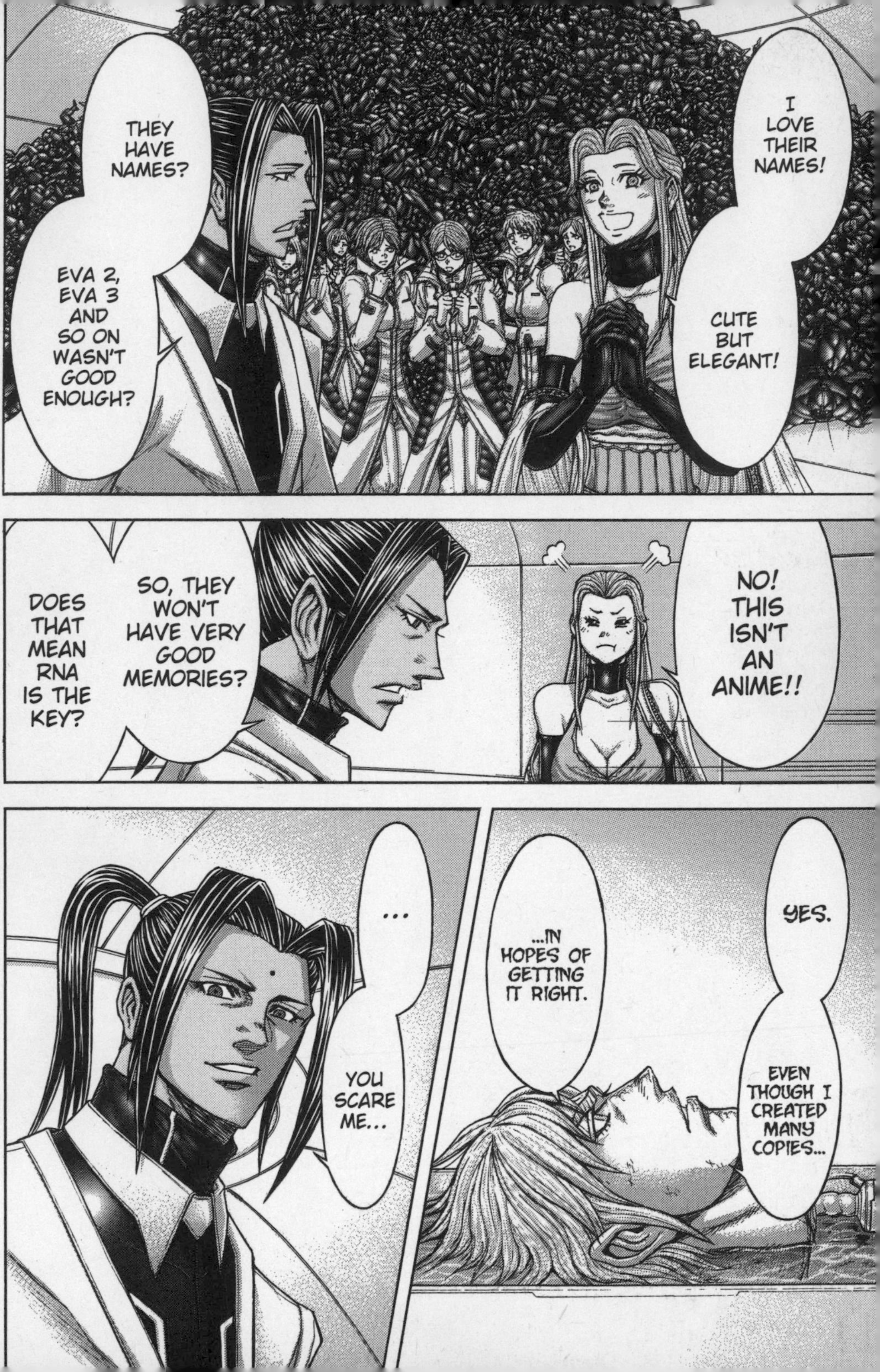
I LOVE THEIR NAMES!
CUTE BUT ELEGANT!
THEY HAVE NAMES?
EVA 2, EVA 3 AND SO ON WASN'T GOOD ENOUGH?
NO! THIS ISN'T AN ANIME!!
SO, THEY WON'T HAVE VERY GOOD MEMORIES?
DOES THAT MEAN RNA IS THE KEY?
YES.
EVEN THOUGH I CREATED MANY COPIES...
...IN HOPES OF GETTING IT RIGHT.
...
YOU SCARE ME...

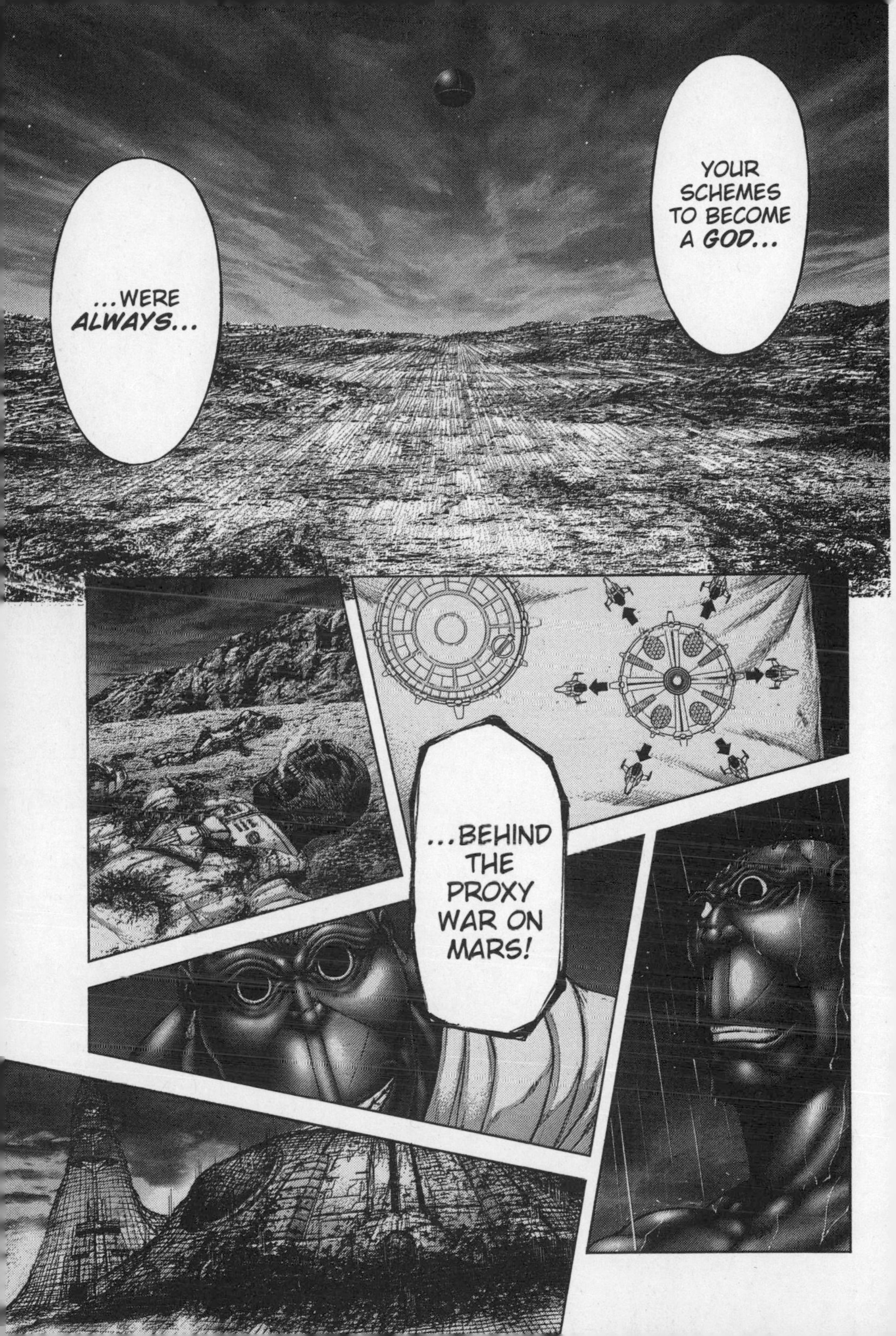
YOUR SCHEMES TO BECOME A GOD...
...WERE ALWAYS...
...BEHIND THE PROXY WAR ON MARS!

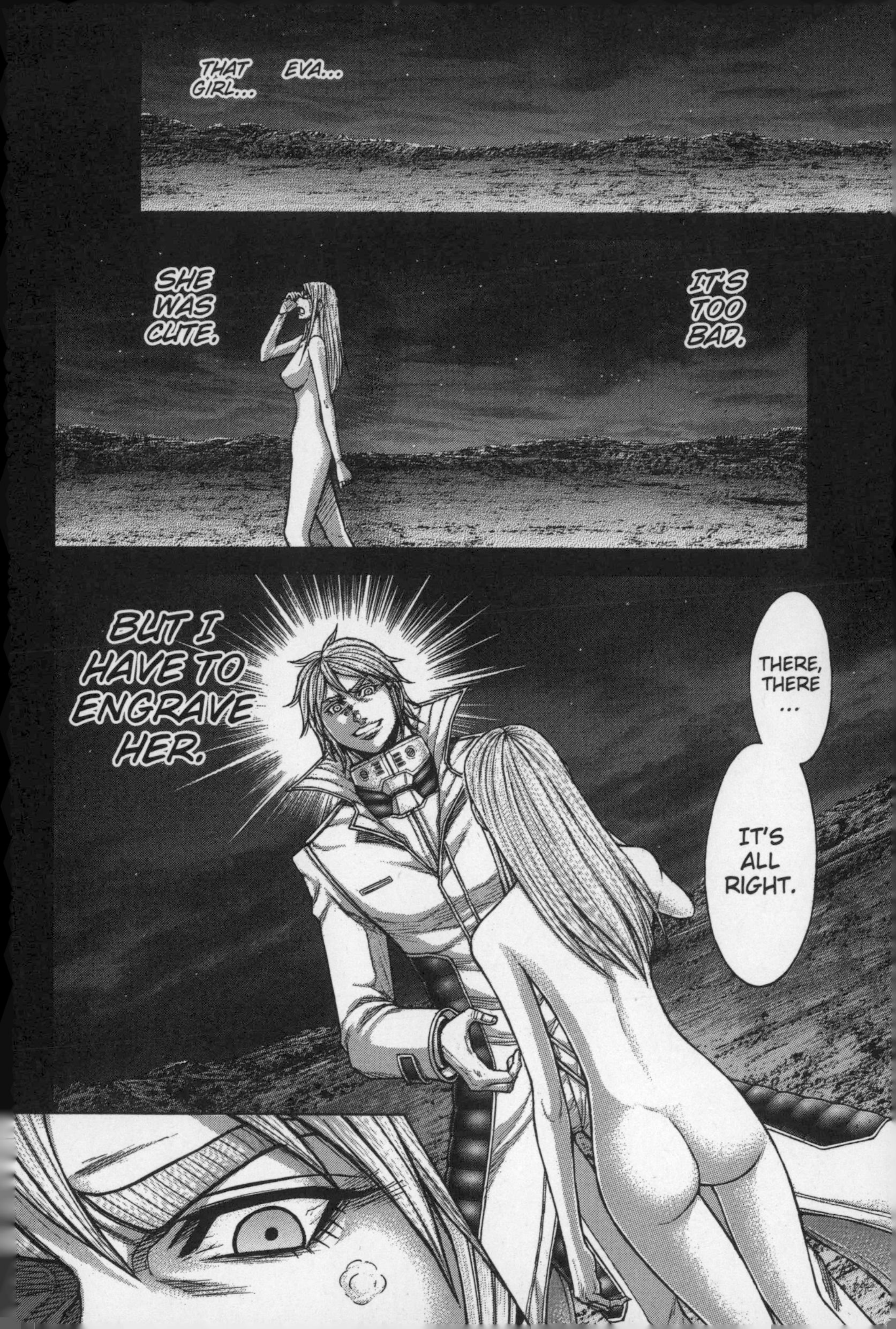
EVA...
THAT GIRL...
IT'S TOO BAD.
SHE WAS CUTE.
THERE, THERE ...
IT'S ALL RIGHT.
BUT I HAVE TO ENGRAVE HER.

CHAPTER 170: THE TREE OF LIFE

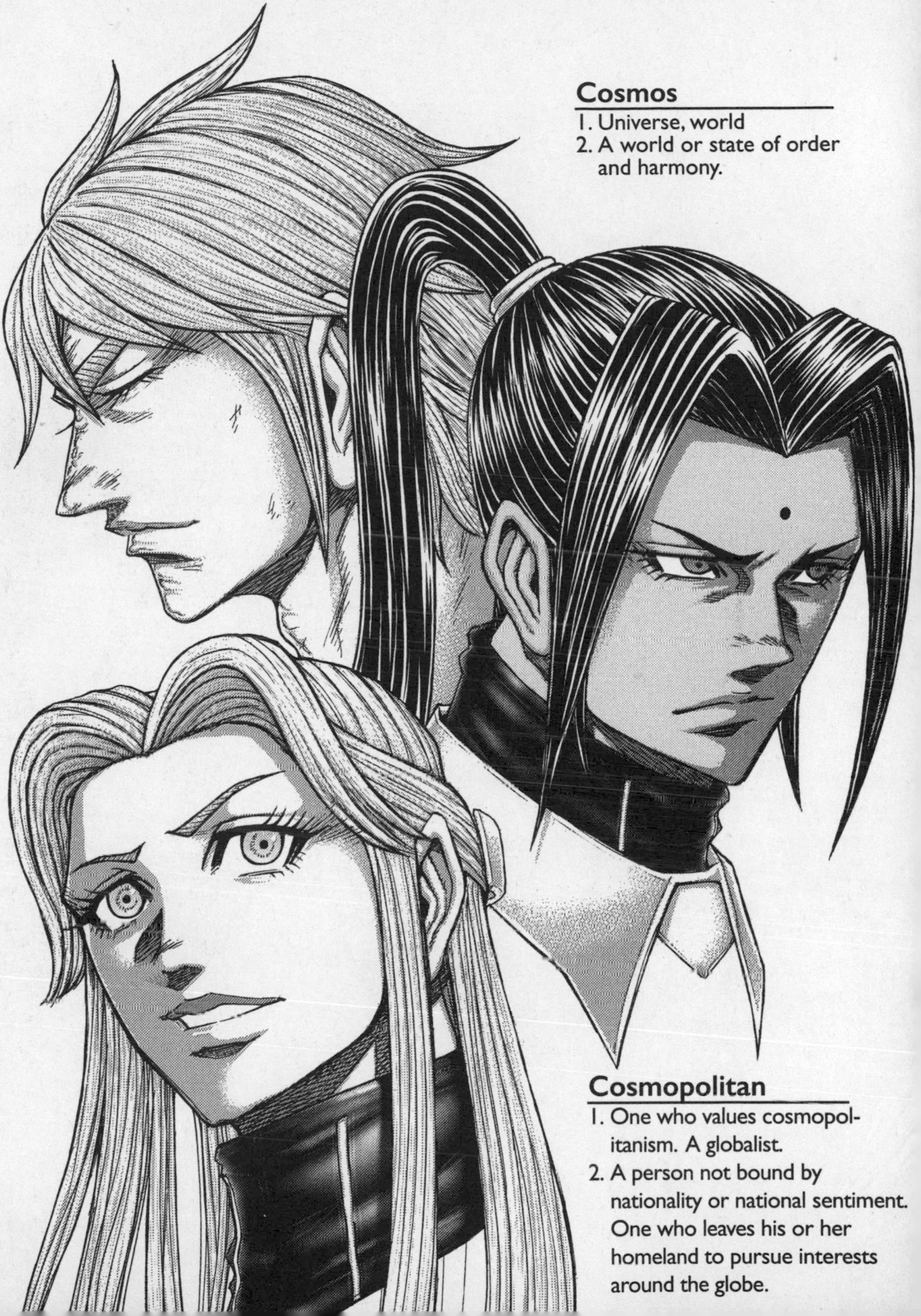

Cosmos

1. Universe, world
2. A world or state of order and harmony.

Cosmopolitan

1. One who values cosmopolitanism. A globalist.
2. A person not bound by nationality or national sentiment. One who leaves his or her homeland to pursue interests around the globe.

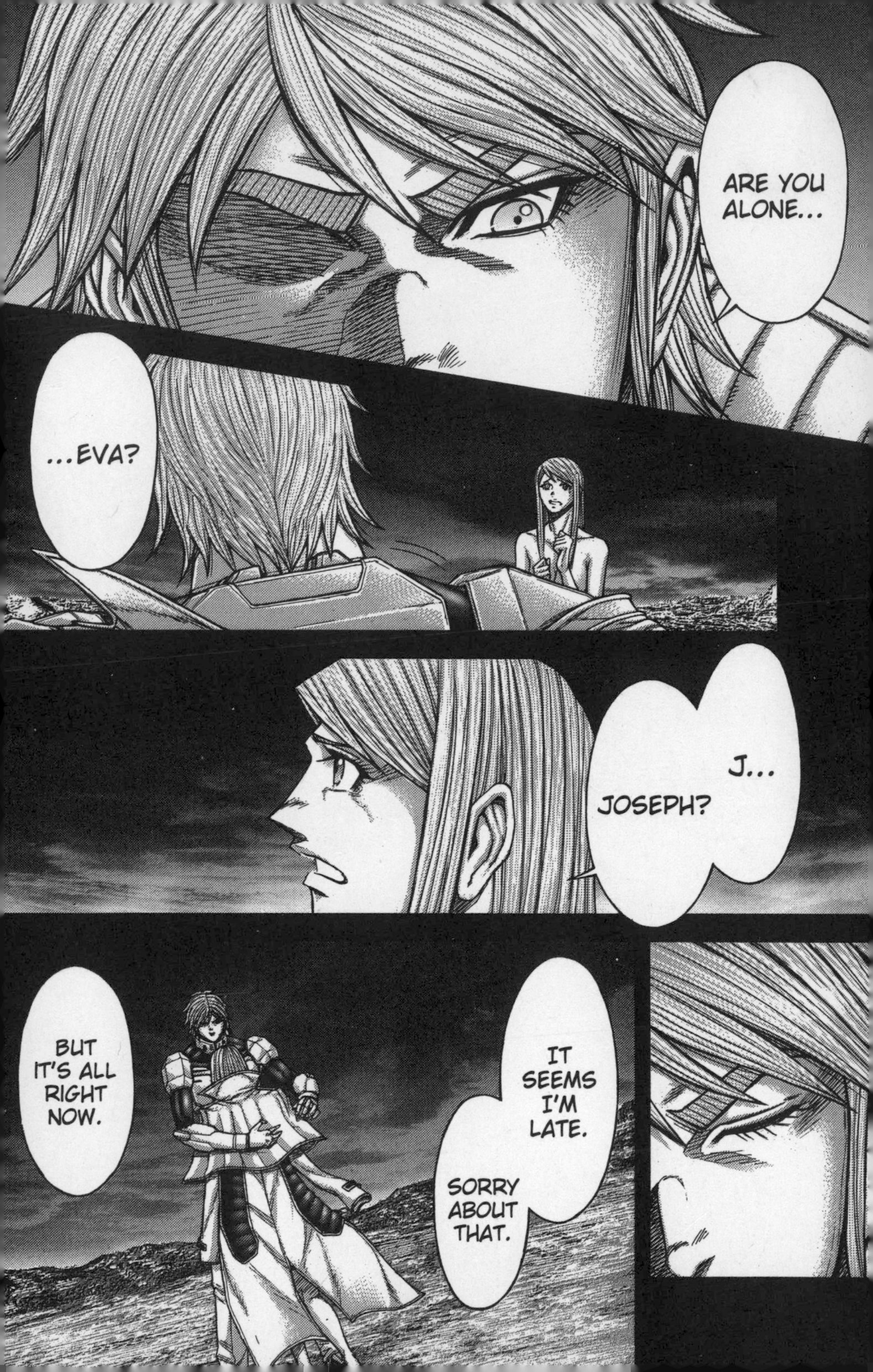
ARE YOU ALONE...
...EVA?
J...
JOSEPH?
IT SEEMS I'M LATE.
SORRY ABOUT THAT.
BUT IT'S ALL RIGHT NOW.

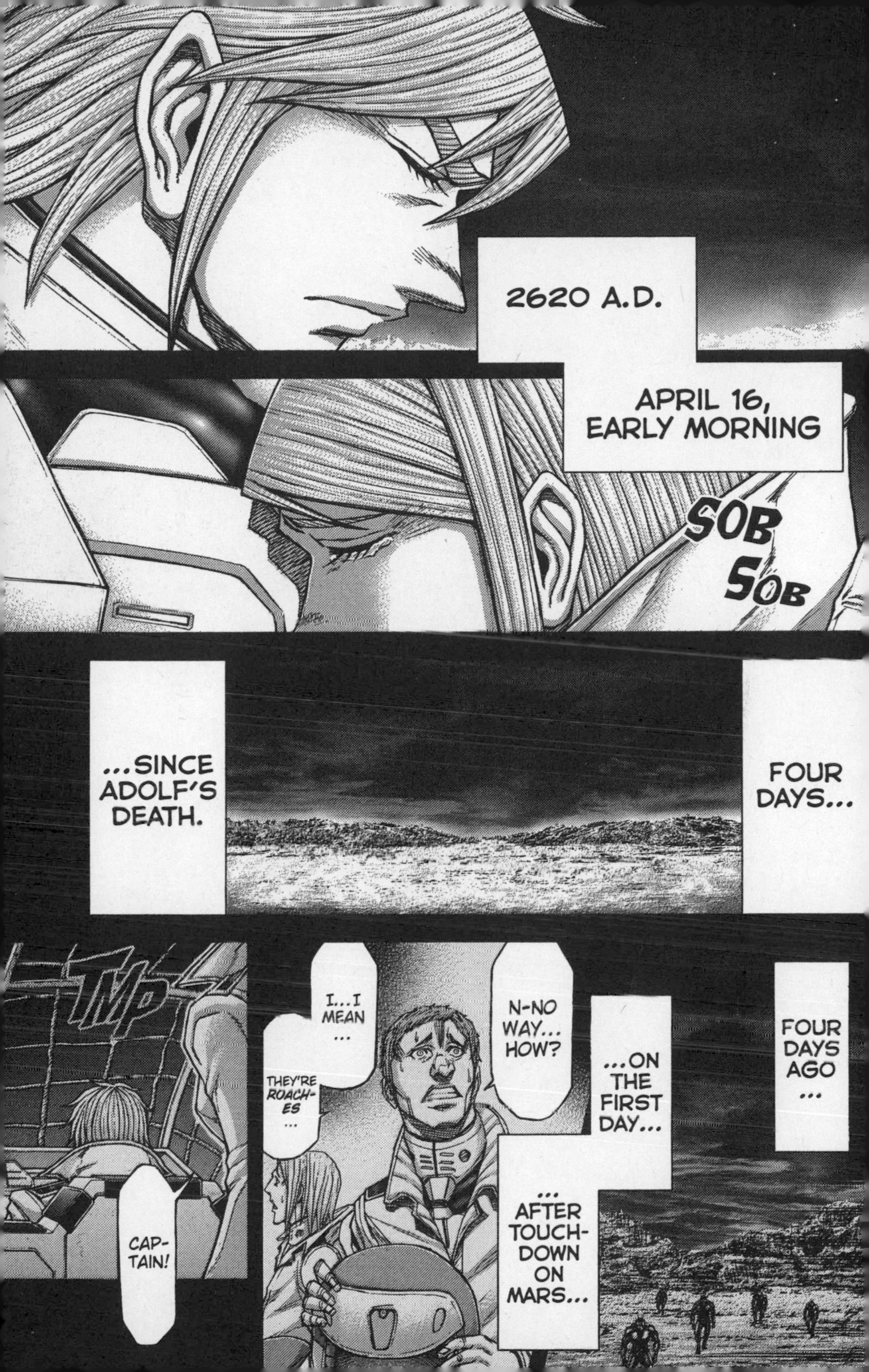
2620 A.D.
APRIL 16, EARLY MORNING
SOB SOB
FOUR DAYS...
...SINCE ADOLF'S DEATH.
FOUR DAYS AGO...
...ON THE FIRST DAY...
...AFTER TOUCH-DOWN ON MARS...
N-NO WAY... HOW?
I... I MEAN...
THEY'RE ROACH-ES...
TMP
CAP-TAIN!

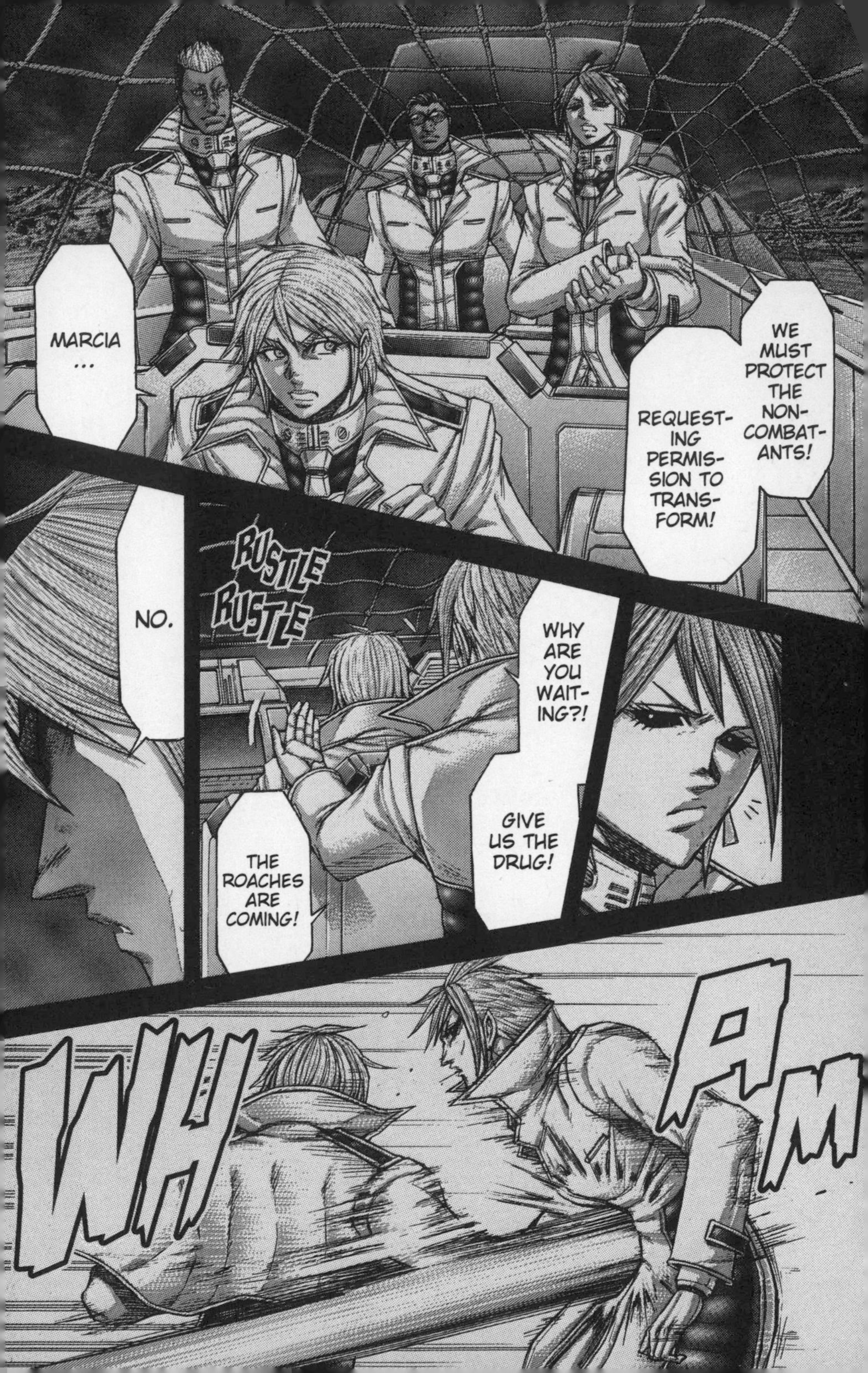
WE MUST PROTECT THE NON-COMBATANTS!
REQUESTING PERMISSION TO TRANSFORM!
MARCIA...
WHY ARE YOU WAITING?!
GIVE US THE DRUG!
RUSTLE RUSTLE
THE ROACHES ARE COMING!
NO.
WHAM

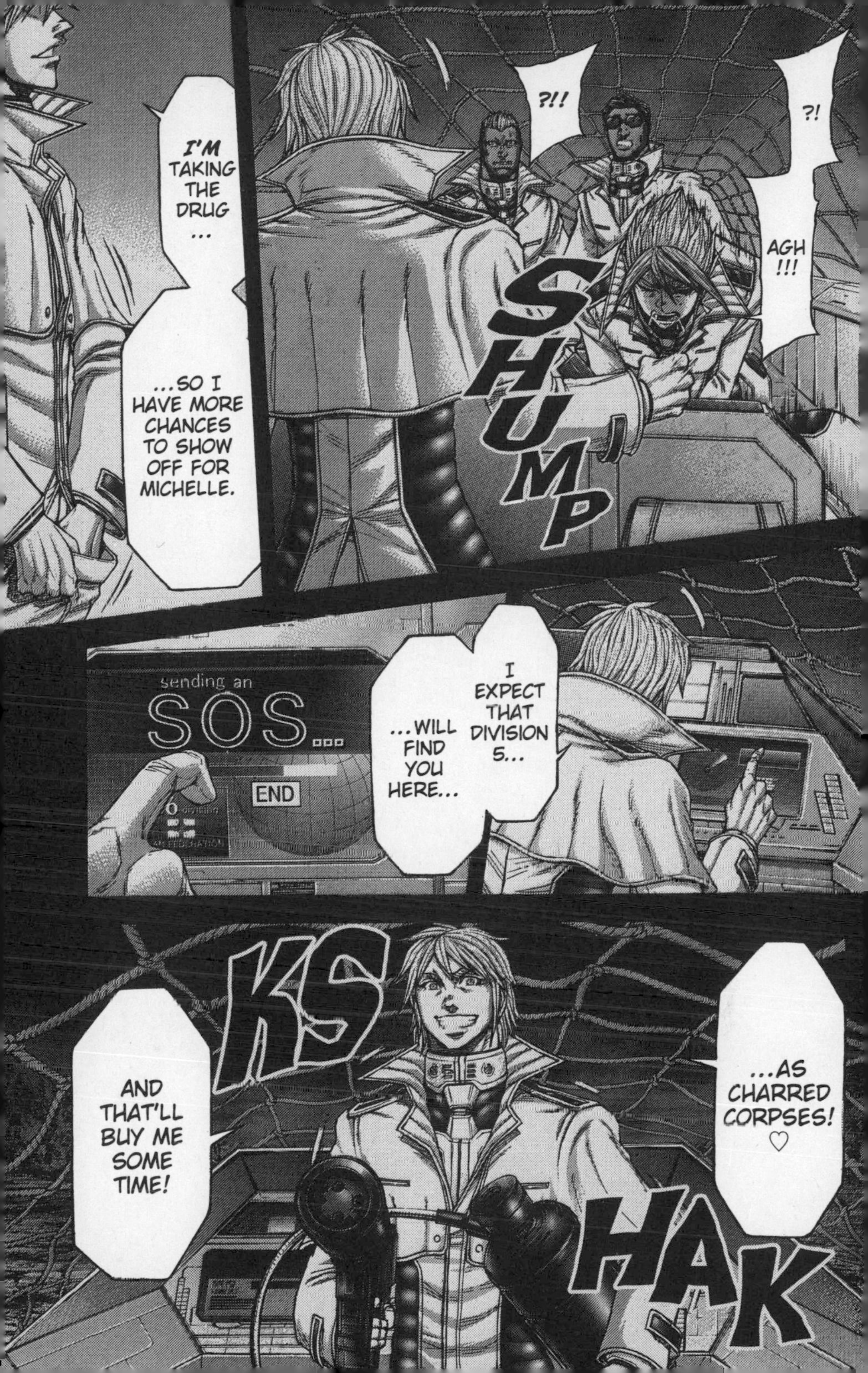
?!
?!!
AGH!!!
SHUMP
I'M TAKING THE DRUG...
...SO I HAVE MORE CHANCES TO SHOW OFF FOR MICHELLE.
I EXPECT THAT DIVISION 5...
...WILL FIND YOU HERE...
sending an SOS...
END
...AS CHARRED CORPSES! ♡
KS
HAK
AND THAT'LL BUY ME SOME TIME!

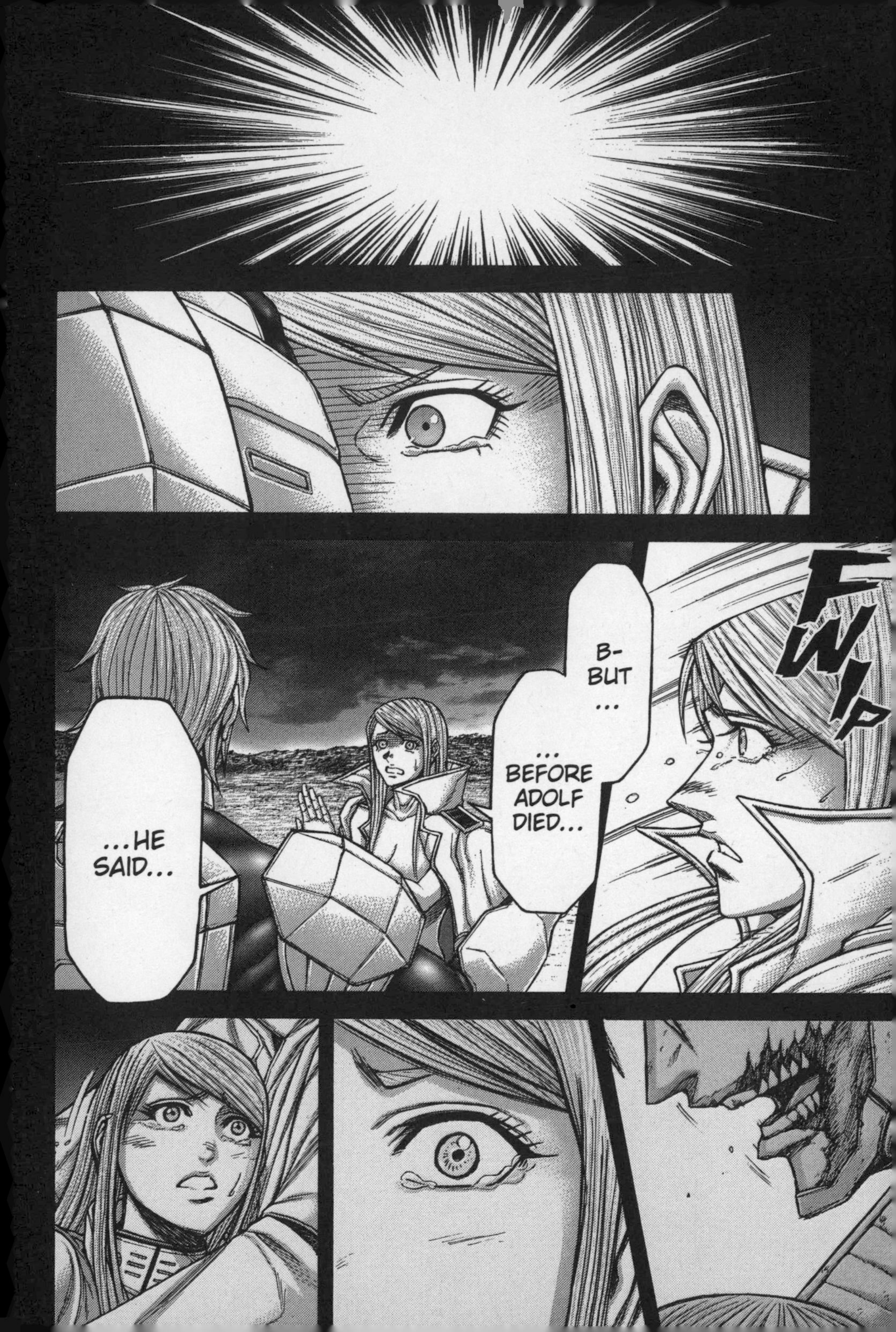
FWIP
B-BUT...
...BEFORE ADOLF DIED...
...HE SAID...

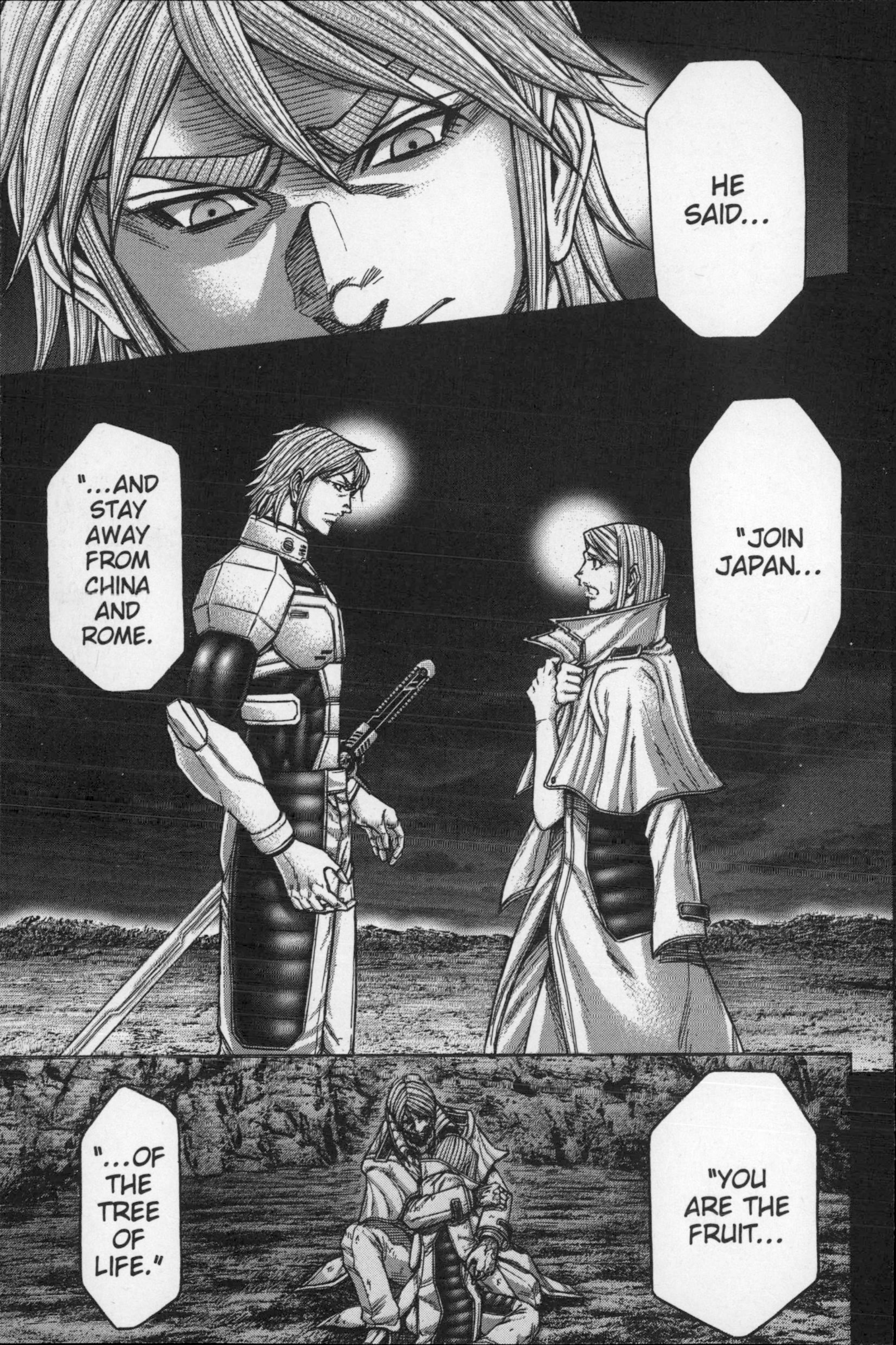
HE SAID...
"JOIN JAPAN...
"...AND STAY AWAY FROM CHINA AND ROME.
"YOU ARE THE FRUIT...
"...OF THE TREE OF LIFE."

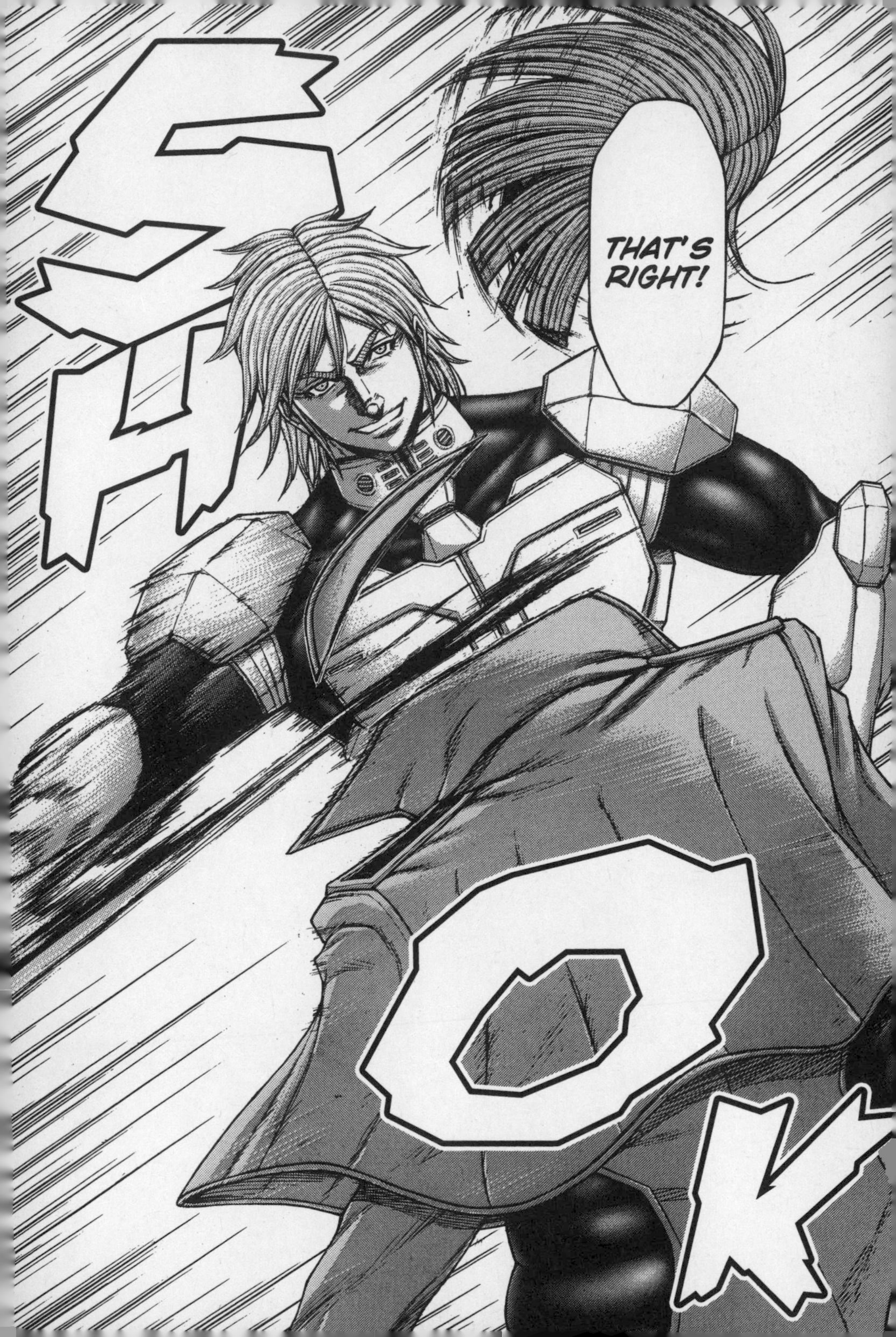
THAT'S RIGHT!

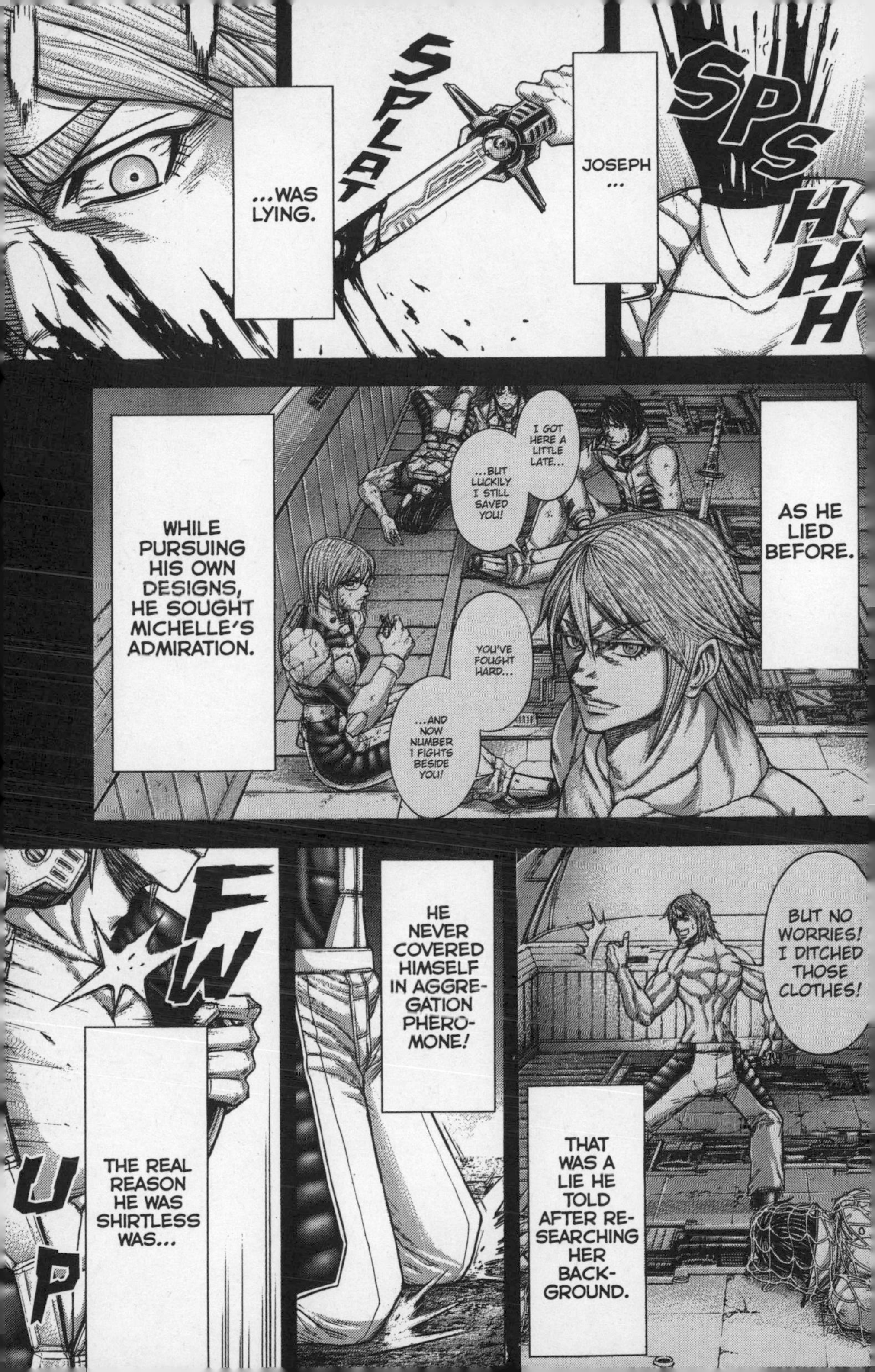
SPSHHH
JOSEPH...
SPLAT
...WAS LYING.
AS HE LIED BEFORE.
I GOT HERE A LITTLE LATE...
...BUT LUCKILY I STILL SAVED YOU!
YOU'VE FOUGHT HARD...
...AND NOW NUMBER 1 FIGHTS BESIDE YOU!
WHILE PURSUING HIS OWN DESIGNS, HE SOUGHT MICHELLE'S ADMIRATION.
BUT NO WORRIES! I DITCHED THOSE CLOTHES!
THAT WAS A LIE HE TOLD AFTER RESEARCHING HER BACKGROUND.
HE NEVER COVERED HIMSELF IN AGGREGATION PHEROMONE!
FWUP
THE REAL REASON HE WAS SHIRTLESS WAS...

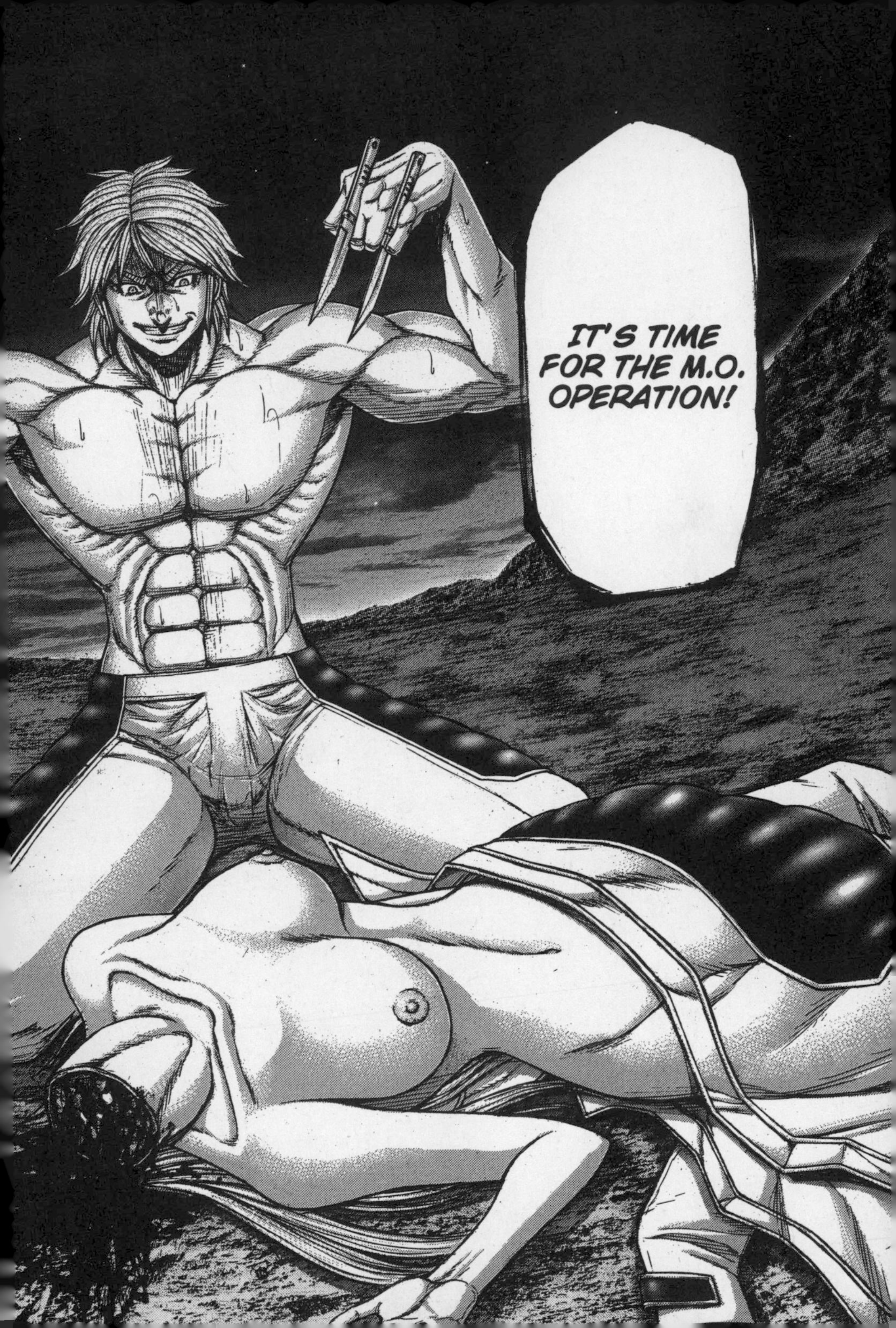
IT'S TIME FOR THE M.O. OPERATION!

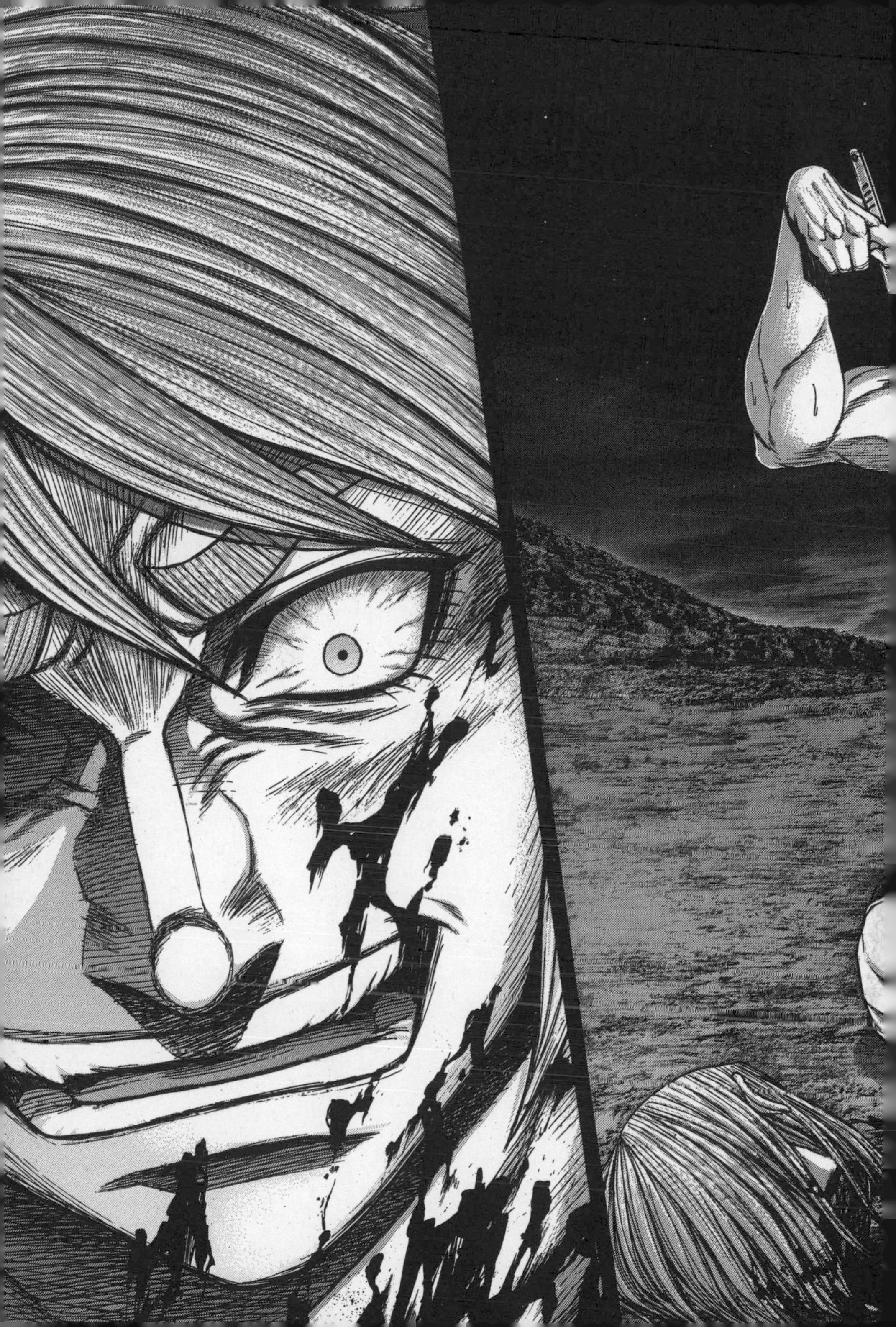

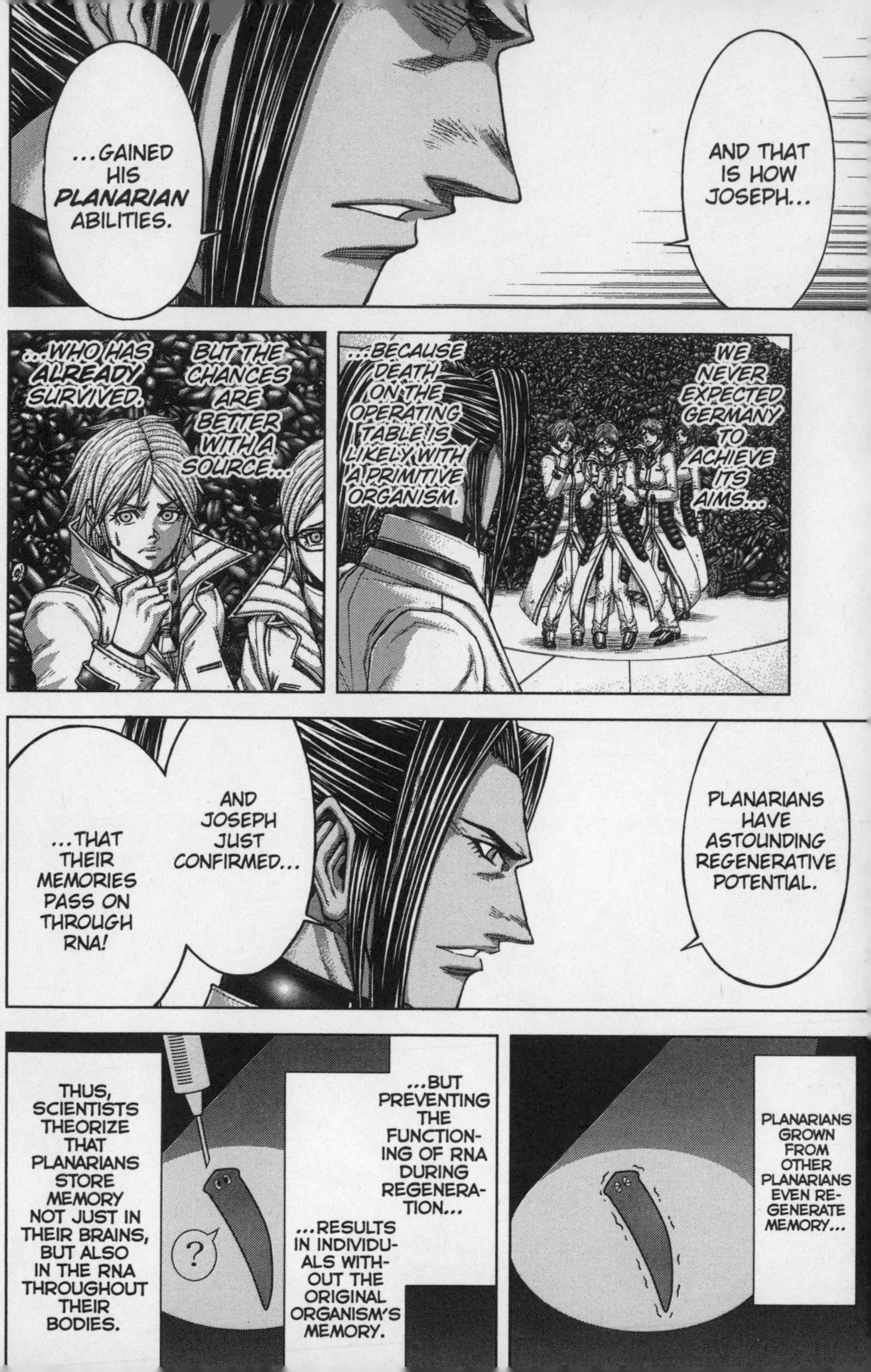
AND THAT IS HOW JOSEPH...
...GAINED HIS PLANARIAN ABILITIES.
WE NEVER EXPECTED GERMANY TO ACHIEVE ITS AIMS...
...BECAUSE DEATH ON THE OPERATING TABLE IS LIKELY WITH A PRIMITIVE ORGANISM.
BUT THE CHANCES ARE BETTER WITH A SOURCE...
...WHO HAS ALREADY SURVIVED.
PLANARIANS HAVE ASTOUNDING REGENERATIVE POTENTIAL.
AND JOSEPH JUST CONFIRMED...
...THAT THEIR MEMORIES PASS ON THROUGH RNA!
PLANARIANS GROWN FROM OTHER PLANARIANS EVEN REGENERATE MEMORY...
...BUT PREVENTING THE FUNCTIONING OF RNA DURING REGENERATION...
...RESULTS IN INDIVIDUALS WITHOUT THE ORIGINAL ORGANISM'S MEMORY.
?
THUS, SCIENTISTS THEORIZE THAT PLANARIANS STORE MEMORY NOT JUST IN THEIR BRAINS, BUT ALSO IN THE RNA THROUGHOUT THEIR BODIES.

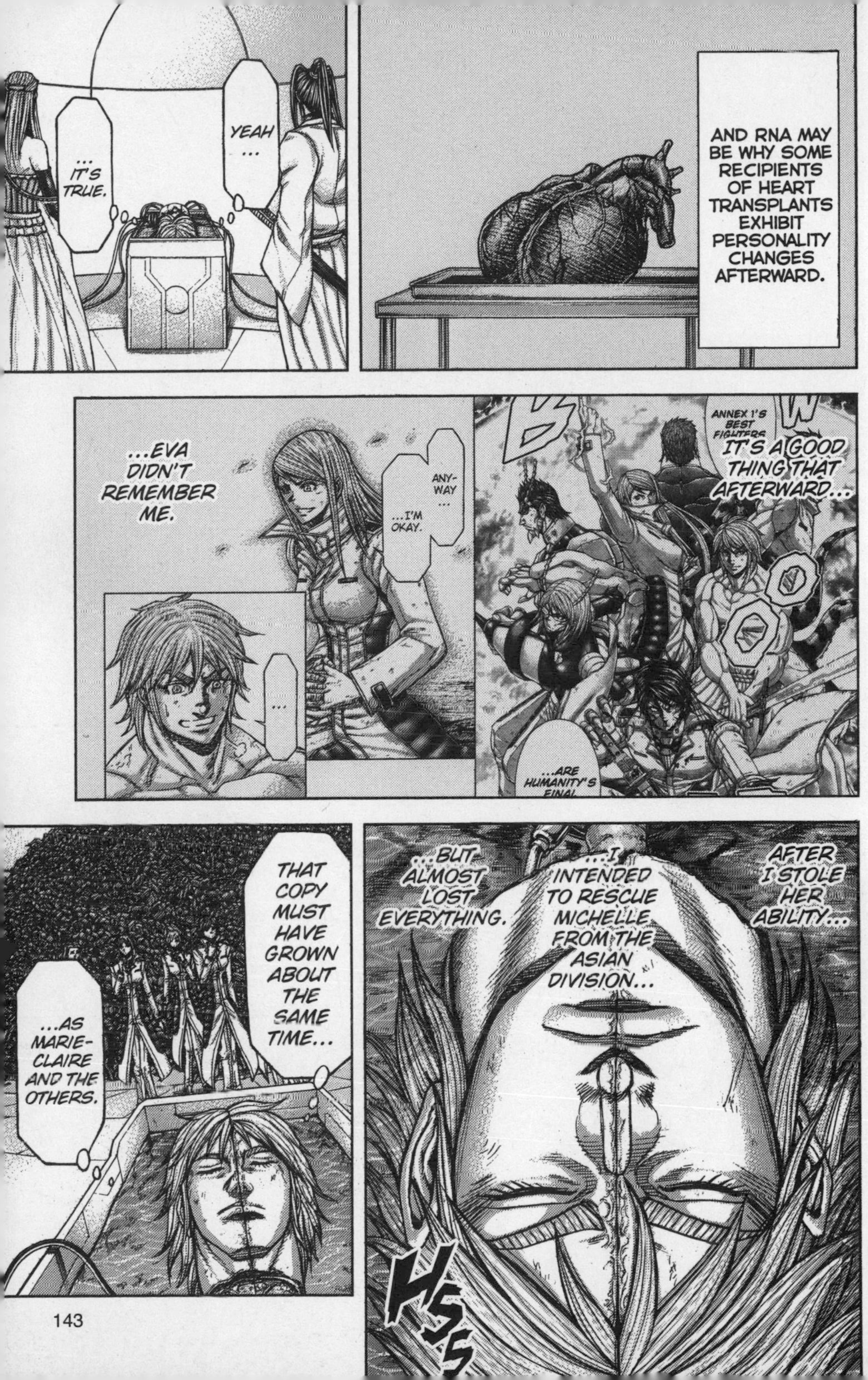

AND RNA MAY BE WHY SOME RECIPIENTS OF HEART TRANSPLANTS EXHIBIT PERSONALITY CHANGES AFTERWARD.
YEAH ...
... IT'S TRUE.
ANNEX 1'S BEST FIGHTERS
IT'S A GOOD THING THAT AFTERWARD...
...ARE HUMANITY'S FINAL
ANY-WAY ...
...I'M OKAY.
...EVA DIDN'T REMEMBER ME.
...
AFTER I STOLE HER ABILITY...
...I INTENDED TO RESCUE MICHELLE FROM THE ASIAN DIVISION...
...BUT ALMOST LOST EVERYTHING.
HSS
THAT COPY MUST HAVE GROWN ABOUT THE SAME TIME...
...AS MARIE-CLAIRE AND THE OTHERS.

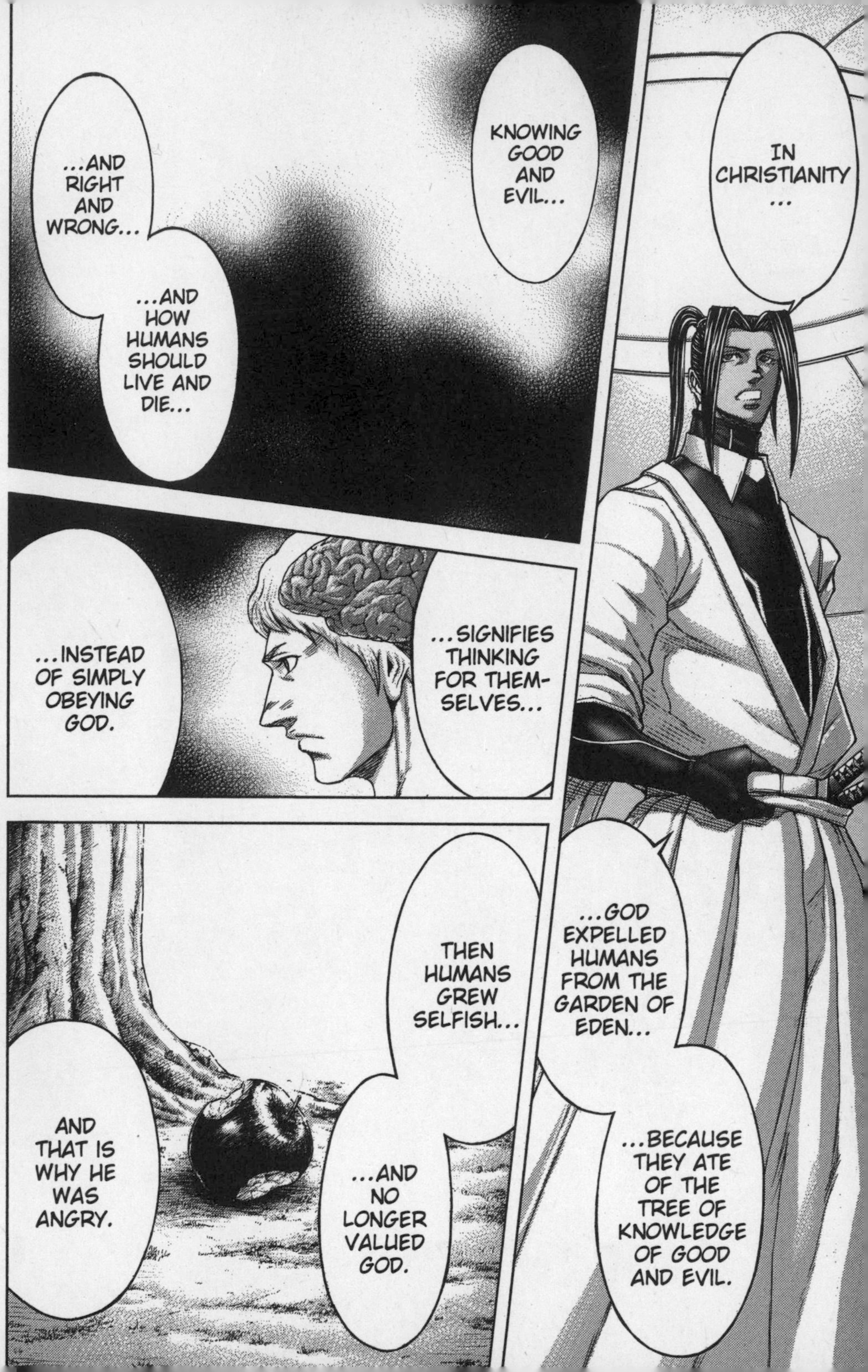
IN CHRISTIANITY...
...GOD EXPELLED HUMANS FROM THE GARDEN OF EDEN...
...BECAUSE THEY ATE OF THE TREE OF KNOWLEDGE OF GOOD AND EVIL.
KNOWING GOOD AND EVIL...
...AND RIGHT AND WRONG...
...AND HOW HUMANS SHOULD LIVE AND DIE...
...SIGNIFIES THINKING FOR THEM-SELVES...
...INSTEAD OF SIMPLY OBEYING GOD.
THEN HUMANS GREW SELFISH...
...AND NO LONGER VALUED GOD.
AND THAT IS WHY HE WAS ANGRY.

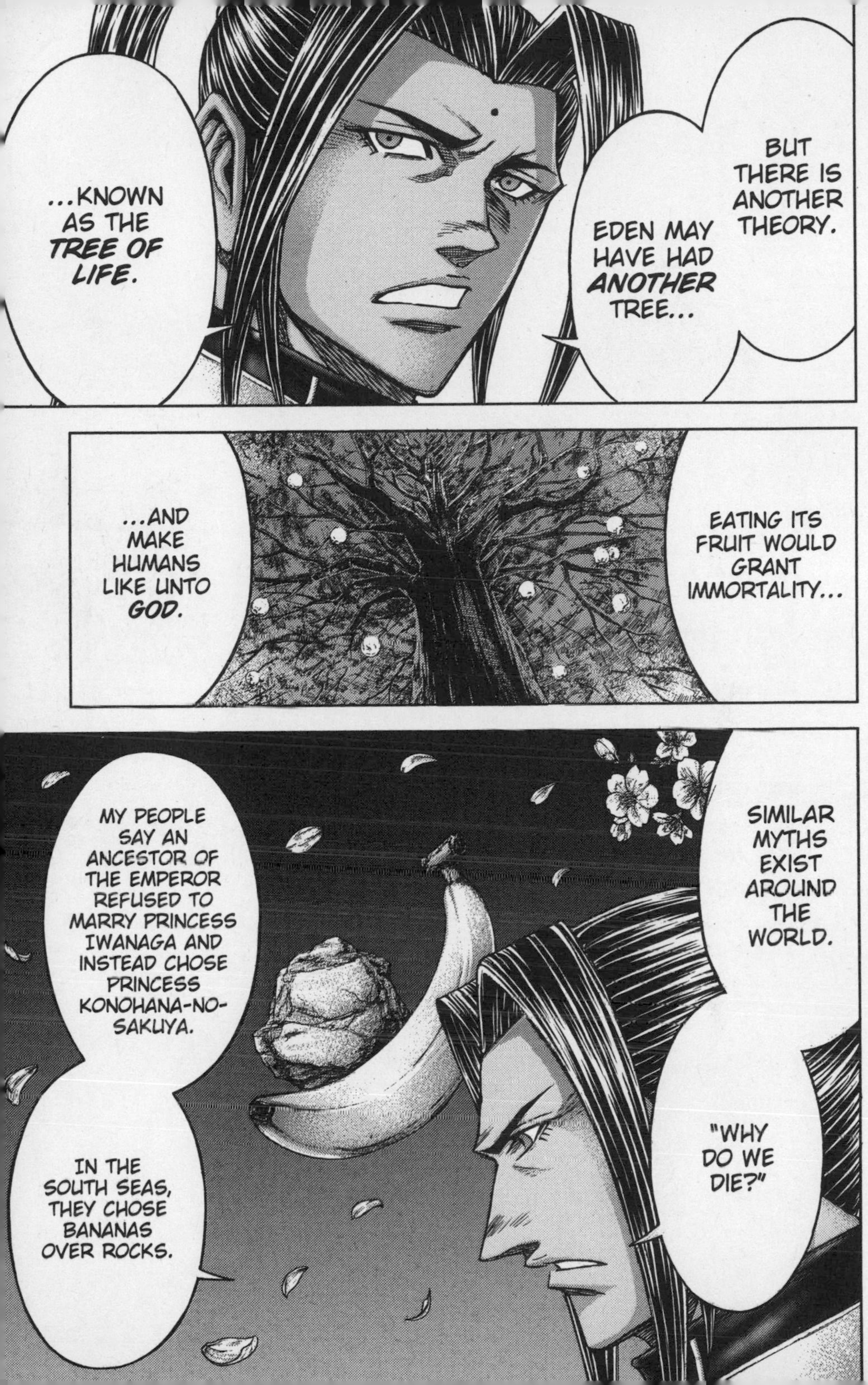
BUT THERE IS ANOTHER THEORY.
EDEN MAY HAVE HAD ANOTHER TREE...
...KNOWN AS THE TREE OF LIFE.
EATING ITS FRUIT WOULD GRANT IMMORTALITY...
...AND MAKE HUMANS LIKE UNTO GOD.
SIMILAR MYTHS EXIST AROUND THE WORLD.
"WHY DO WE DIE?"
MY PEOPLE SAY AN ANCESTOR OF THE EMPEROR REFUSED TO MARRY PRINCESS IWANAGA AND INSTEAD CHOSE PRINCESS KONOHANA-NO-SAKUYA.
IN THE SOUTH SEAS, THEY CHOSE BANANAS OVER ROCKS.

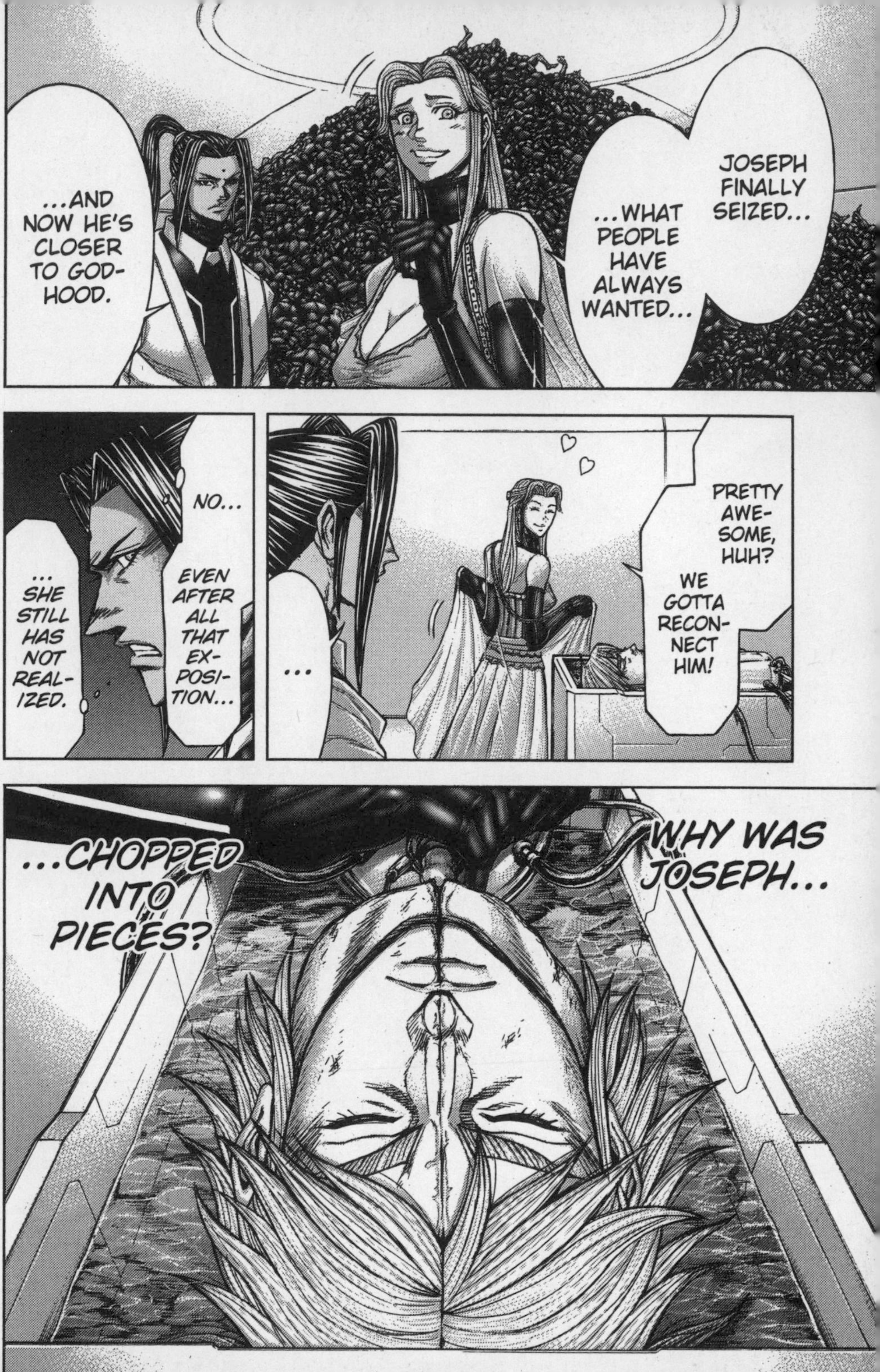
JOSEPH FINALLY SEIZED...
...WHAT PEOPLE HAVE ALWAYS WANTED...
...AND NOW HE'S CLOSER TO GOD-HOOD.
PRETTY AWE-SOME, HUH?
WE GOTTA RECON-NECT HIM!
...
NO...
EVEN AFTER ALL THAT EX-POSI-TION...
...SHE STILL HAS NOT REAL-IZED.
WHY WAS JOSEPH...
...CHOPPED INTO PIECES?

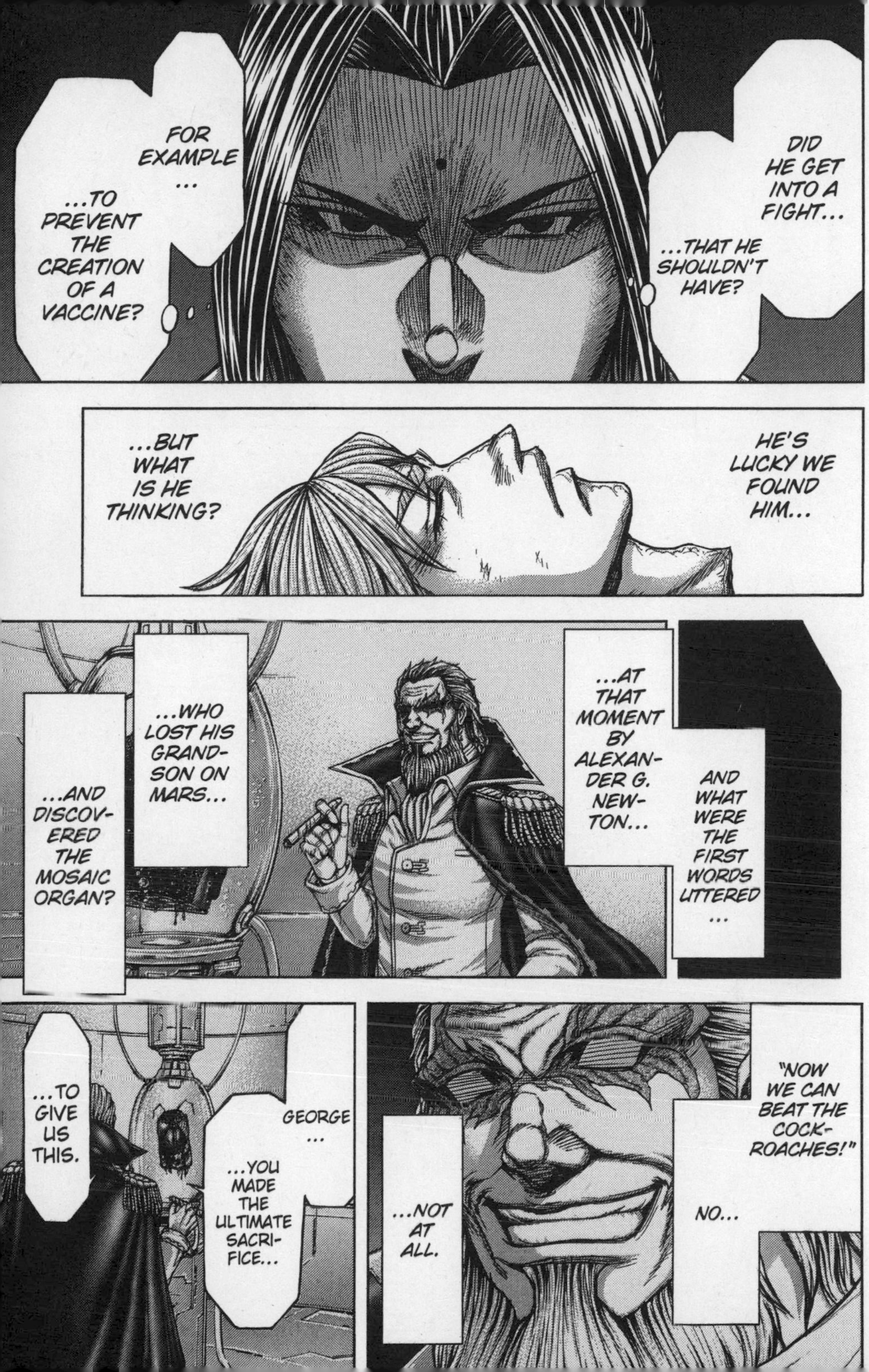
DID HE GET INTO A FIGHT...
...THAT HE SHOULDN'T HAVE?
FOR EXAMPLE...
...TO PREVENT THE CREATION OF A VACCINE?
HE'S LUCKY WE FOUND HIM...
...BUT WHAT IS HE THINKING?
AND WHAT WERE THE FIRST WORDS UTTERED...
...AT THAT MOMENT BY ALEXANDER G. NEWTON...
...WHO LOST HIS GRANDSON ON MARS...
...AND DISCOVERED THE MOSAIC ORGAN?
"NOW WE CAN BEAT THE COCKROACHES!"
NO...
...NOT AT ALL.
GEORGE...
...YOU MADE THE ULTIMATE SACRIFICE...
...TO GIVE US THIS.

I SUR-
PASS
...

...HU-
MAN-
ITY!

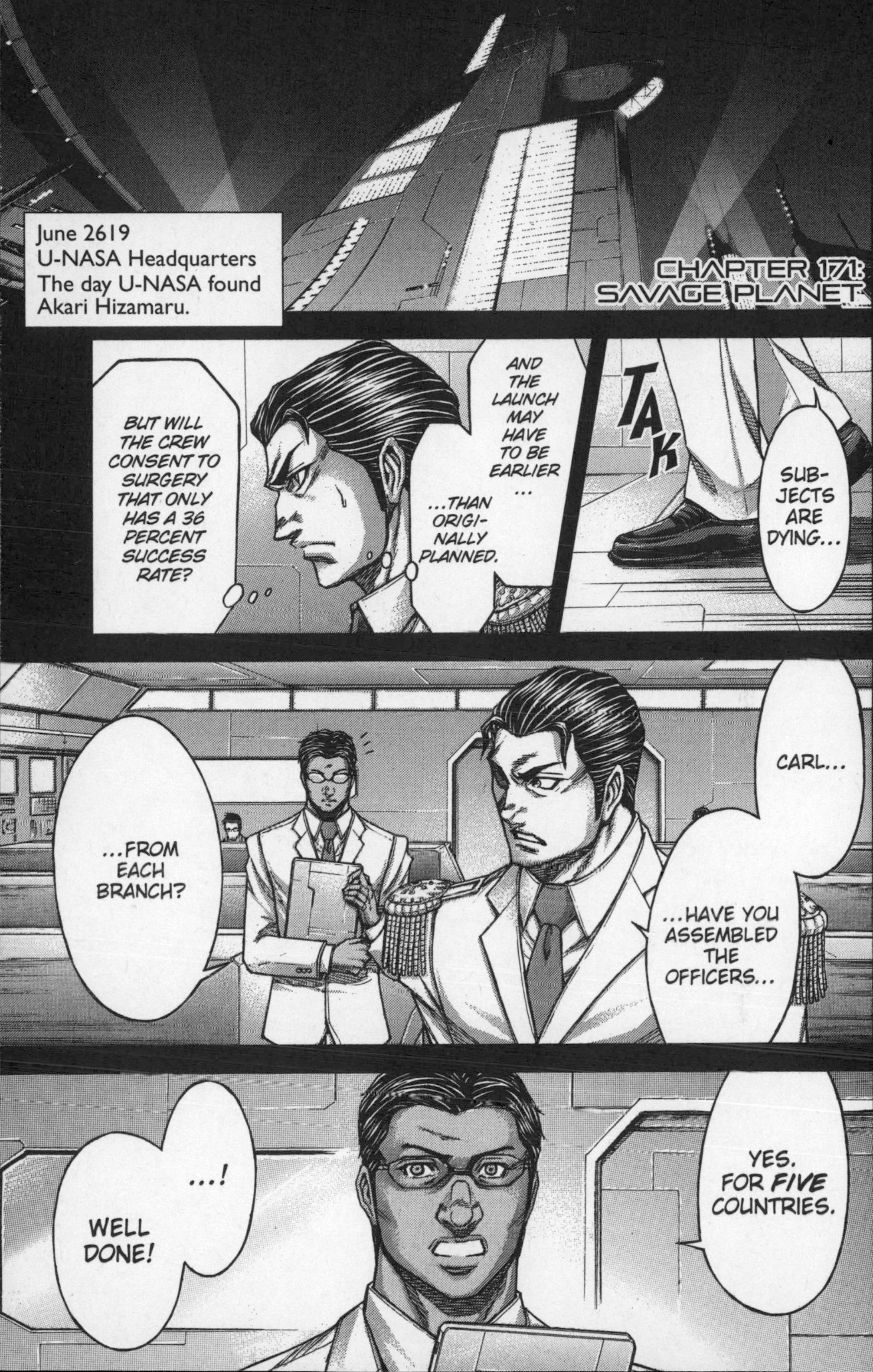
CHAPTER 171: SAVAGE PLANET
June 2619 U-NASA Headquarters The day U-NASA found Akari Hizamaru.
TAK
SUB-JECTS ARE DYING...
AND THE LAUNCH MAY HAVE TO BE EARLIER...
...THAN ORIGI-NALLY PLANNED.
BUT WILL THE CREW CONSENT TO SURGERY THAT ONLY HAS A 36 PERCENT SUCCESS RATE?
CARL...
...HAVE YOU ASSEMBLED THE OFFICERS...
...FROM EACH BRANCH?
YES. FOR *FIVE* COUNTRIES.
...!
WELL DONE!

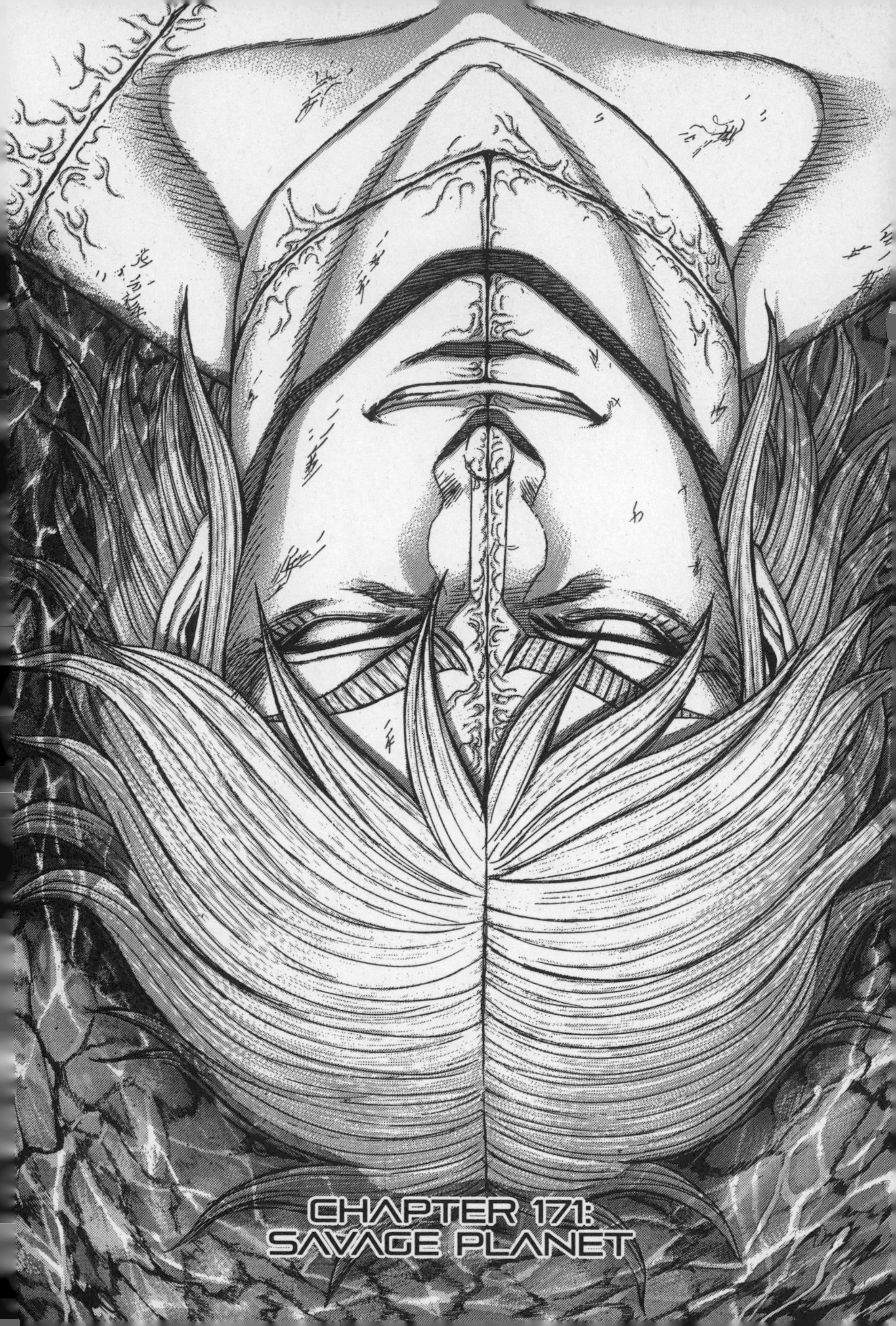
CHAPTER 171:
SAVAGE PLANET

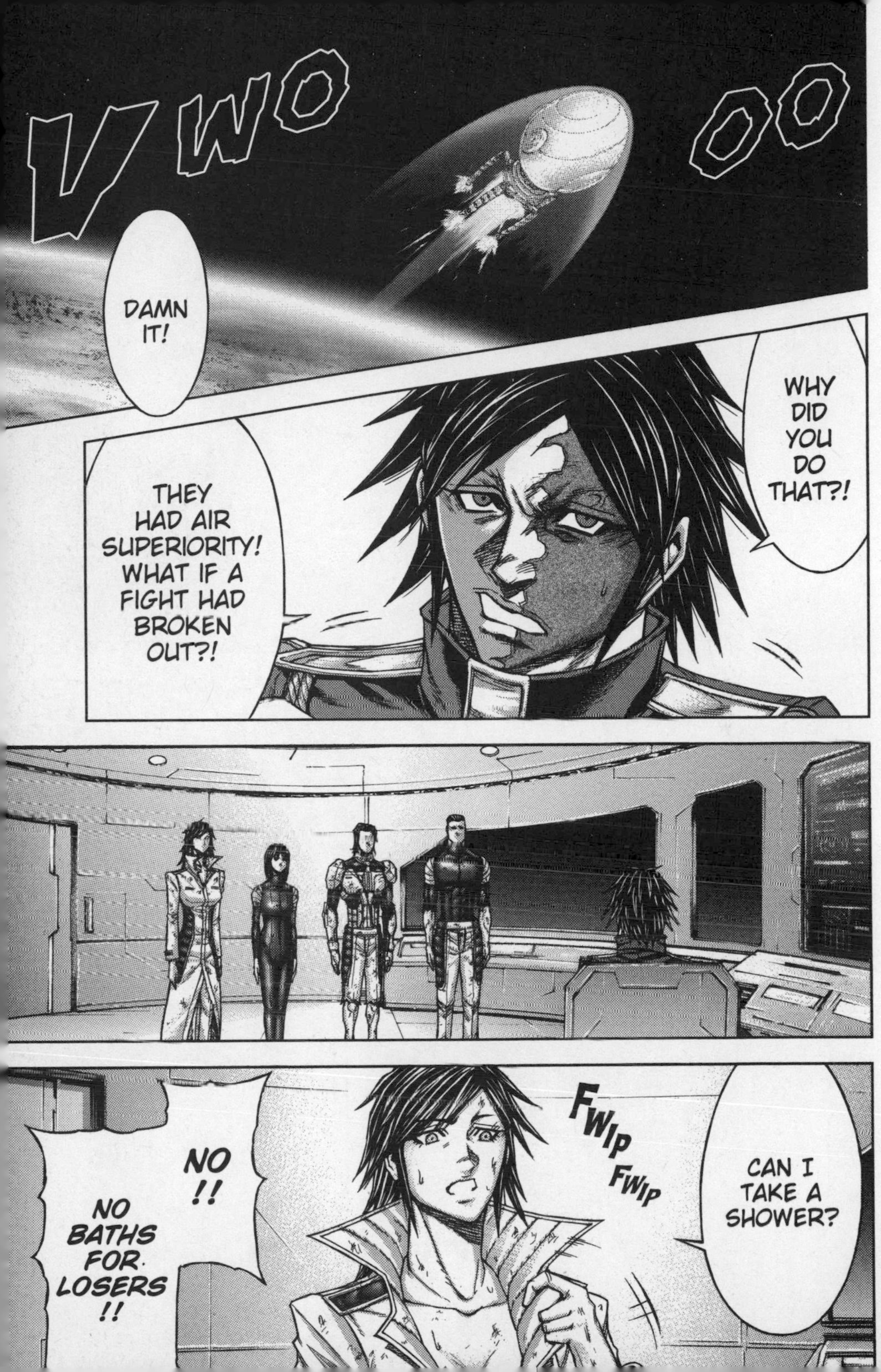
VWO OO
DAMN IT!
WHY DID YOU DO THAT?!
THEY HAD AIR SUPERIORITY! WHAT IF A FIGHT HAD BROKEN OUT?!
CAN I TAKE A SHOWER?
FWIP FWIP
NO!!
NO BATHS FOR LOSERS!!

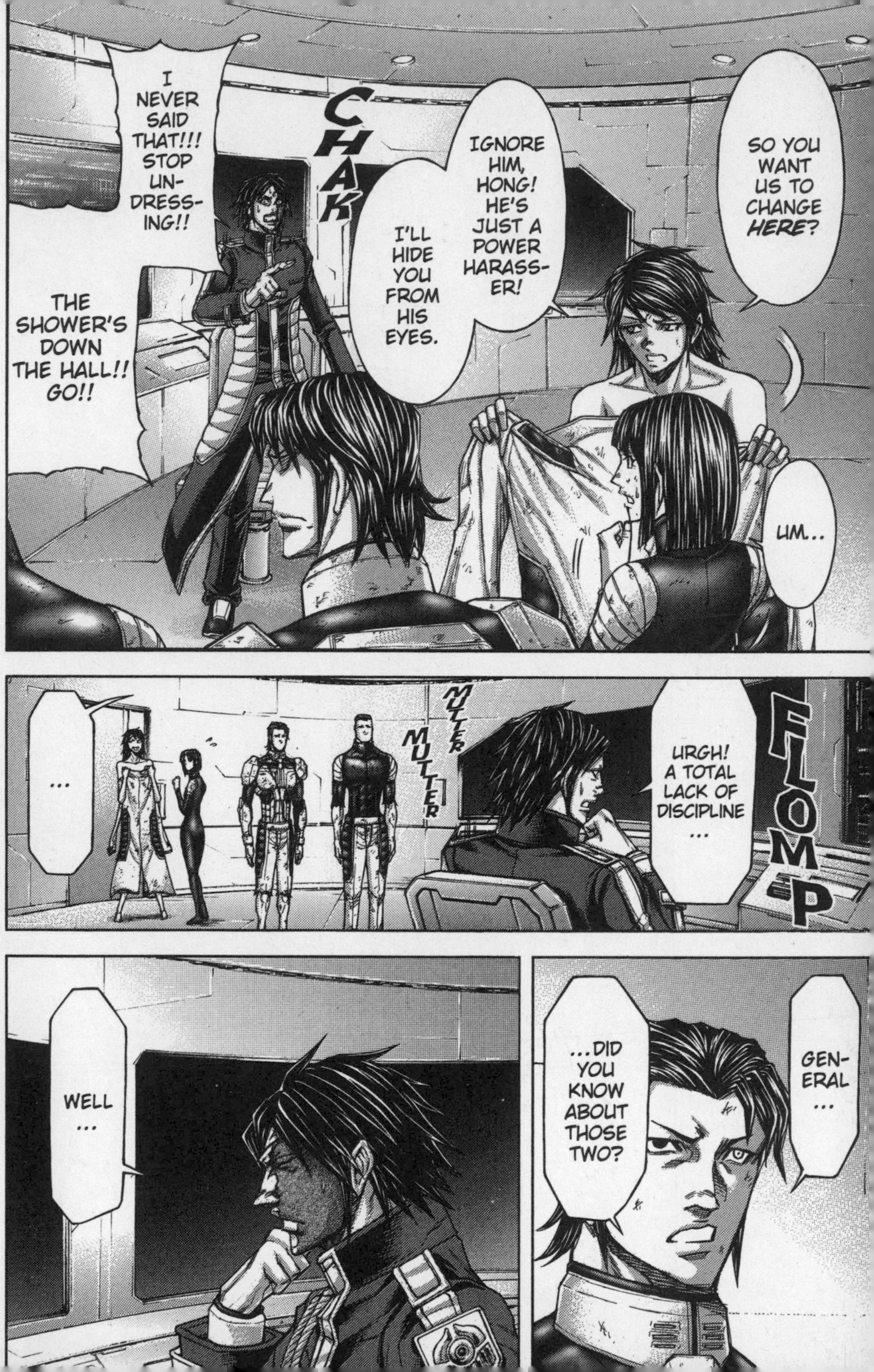
SO YOU WANT US TO CHANGE *HERE*?
UM...
IGNORE HIM, HONG! HE'S JUST A POWER HARASSER!
I'LL HIDE YOU FROM HIS EYES.
CHAK
I NEVER SAID THAT!!! STOP UNDRESSING!!
THE SHOWER'S DOWN THE HALL!! GO!!
FLOMP
URGH! A TOTAL LACK OF DISCIPLINE...
MUTTER MUTTER
...
GENERAL...
...DID YOU KNOW ABOUT THOSE TWO?
WELL...

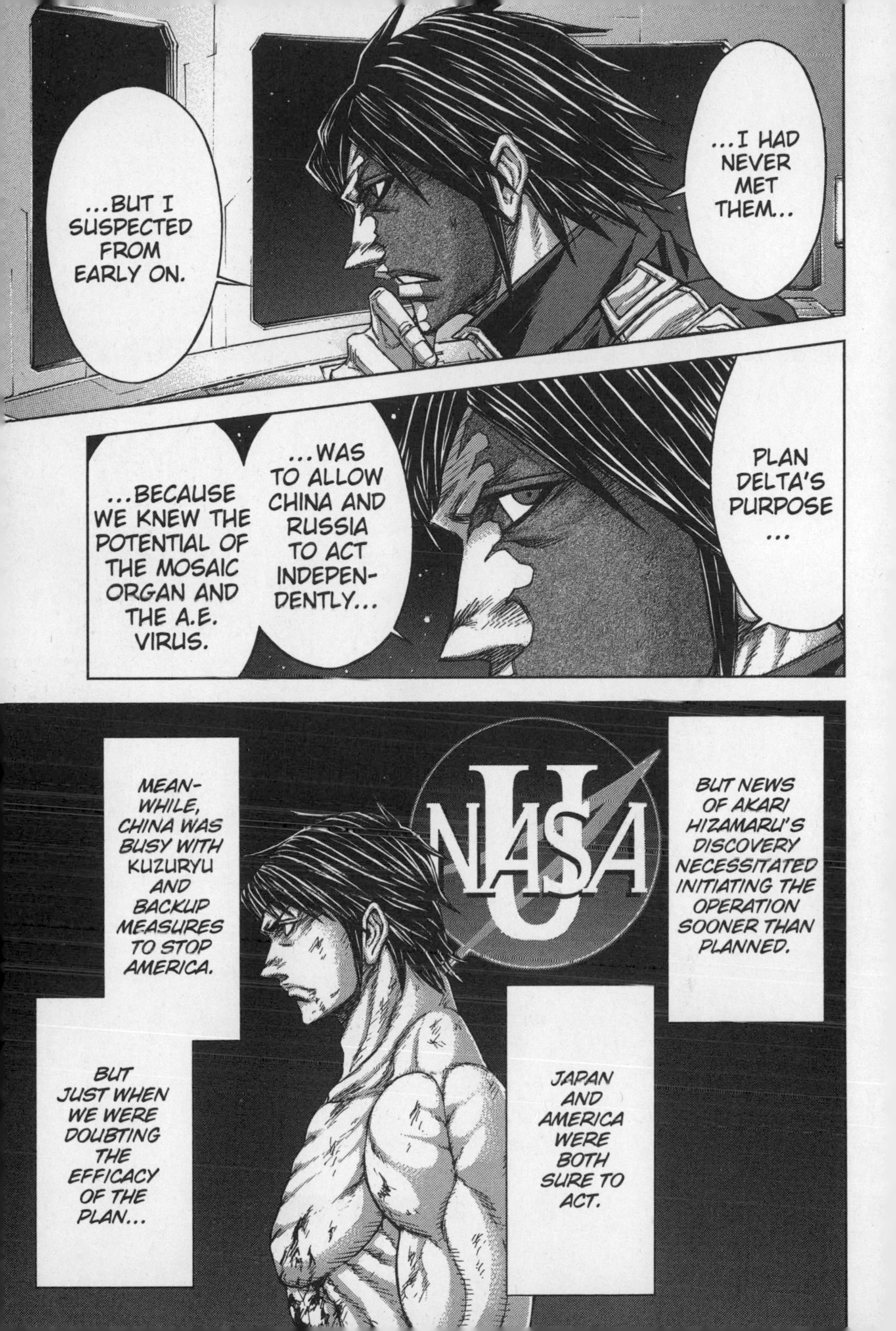
...I HAD NEVER MET THEM...
...BUT I SUSPECTED FROM EARLY ON.
PLAN DELTA'S PURPOSE ...
...WAS TO ALLOW CHINA AND RUSSIA TO ACT INDEPEN-DENTLY...
...BECAUSE WE KNEW THE POTENTIAL OF THE MOSAIC ORGAN AND THE A.E. VIRUS.
BUT NEWS OF AKARI HIZAMARU'S DISCOVERY NECESSITATED INITIATING THE OPERATION SOONER THAN PLANNED.
MEAN-WHILE, CHINA WAS BUSY WITH KUZURYU AND BACKUP MEASURES TO STOP AMERICA.
JAPAN AND AMERICA WERE BOTH SURE TO ACT.
BUT JUST WHEN WE WERE DOUBTING THE EFFICACY OF THE PLAN...

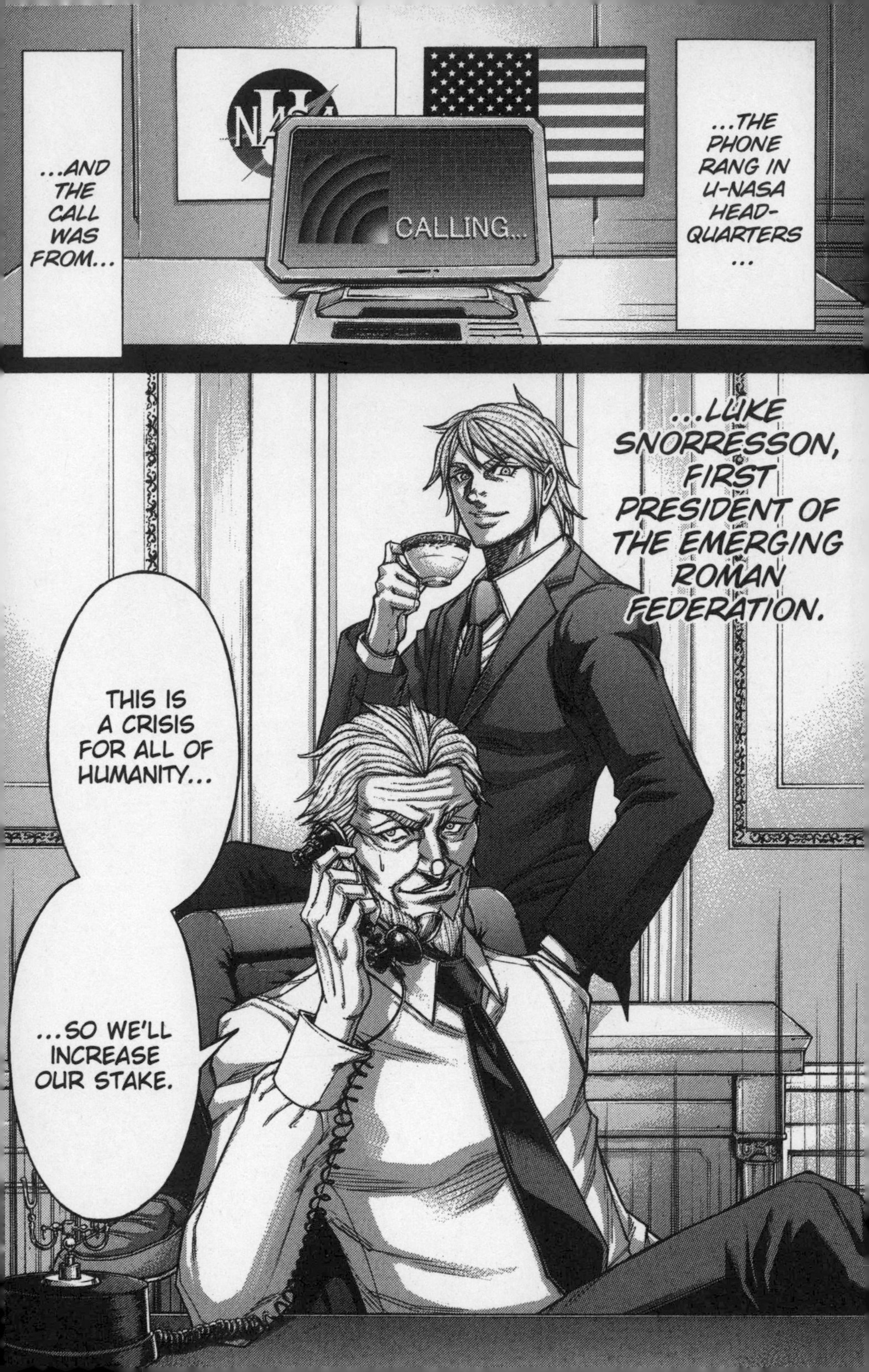
...THE PHONE RANG IN U-NASA HEAD-QUARTERS...
CALLING...
...AND THE CALL WAS FROM...
...LUKE SNORRESSON, FIRST PRESIDENT OF THE EMERGING ROMAN FEDERATION.
THIS IS A CRISIS FOR ALL OF HUMANITY...
...SO WE'LL INCREASE OUR STAKE.

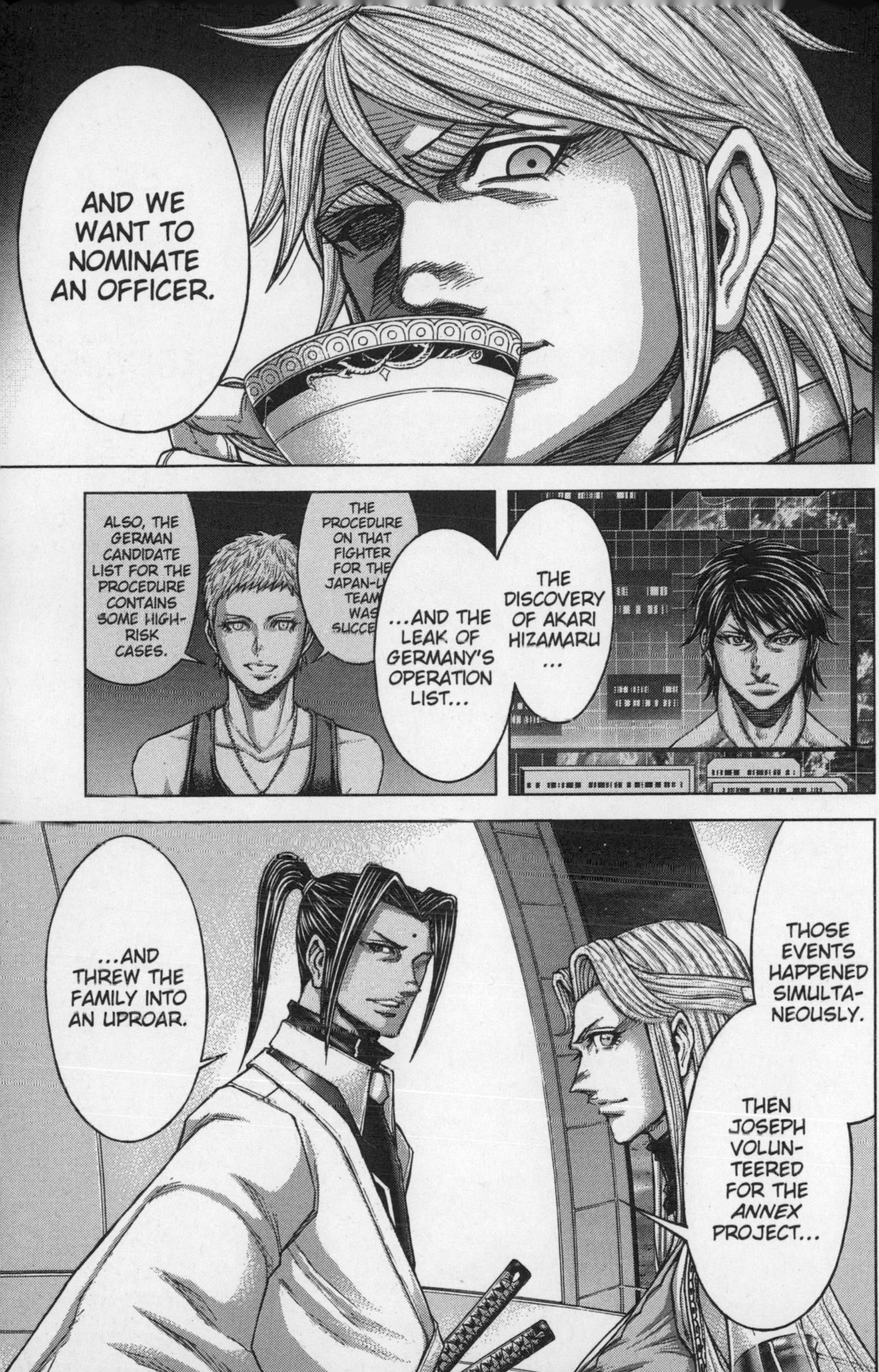
AND WE WANT TO NOMINATE AN OFFICER.
THE DISCOVERY OF AKARI HIZAMARU ...
...AND THE LEAK OF GERMANY'S OPERATION LIST...
THE PROCEDURE ON THAT FIGHTER FOR THE JAPAN-U TEAM WAS SUCCE
ALSO, THE GERMAN CANDIDATE LIST FOR THE PROCEDURE CONTAINS SOME HIGH-RISK CASES.
THOSE EVENTS HAPPENED SIMULTANEOUSLY.
THEN JOSEPH VOLUNTEERED FOR THE *ANNEX* PROJECT...
...AND THREW THE FAMILY INTO AN UPROAR.

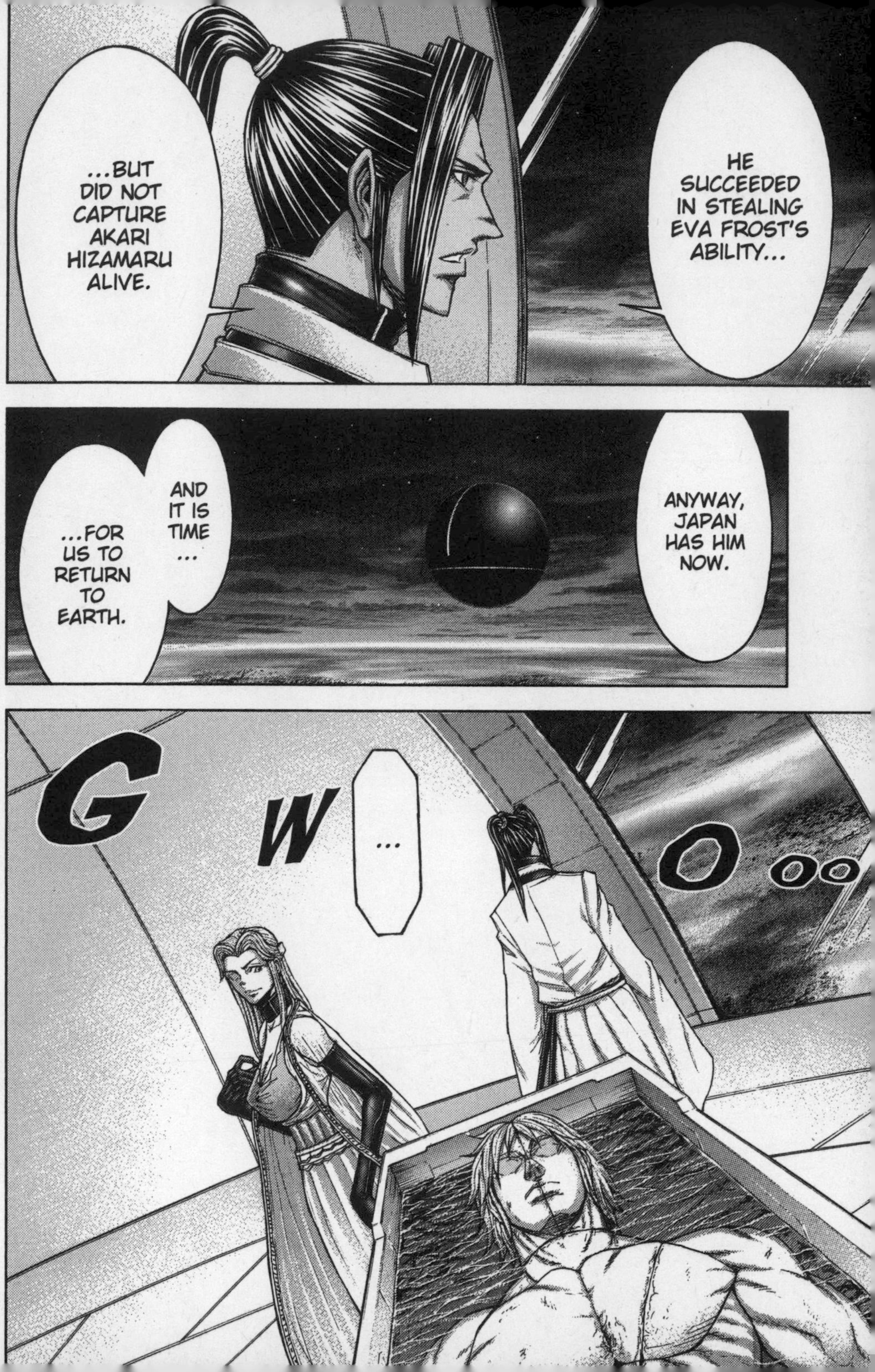
HE SUCCEEDED IN STEALING EVA FROST'S ABILITY...
...BUT DID NOT CAPTURE AKARI HIZAMARU ALIVE.
ANYWAY, JAPAN HAS HIM NOW.
AND IT IS TIME...
...FOR US TO RETURN TO EARTH.
...
GWOOO

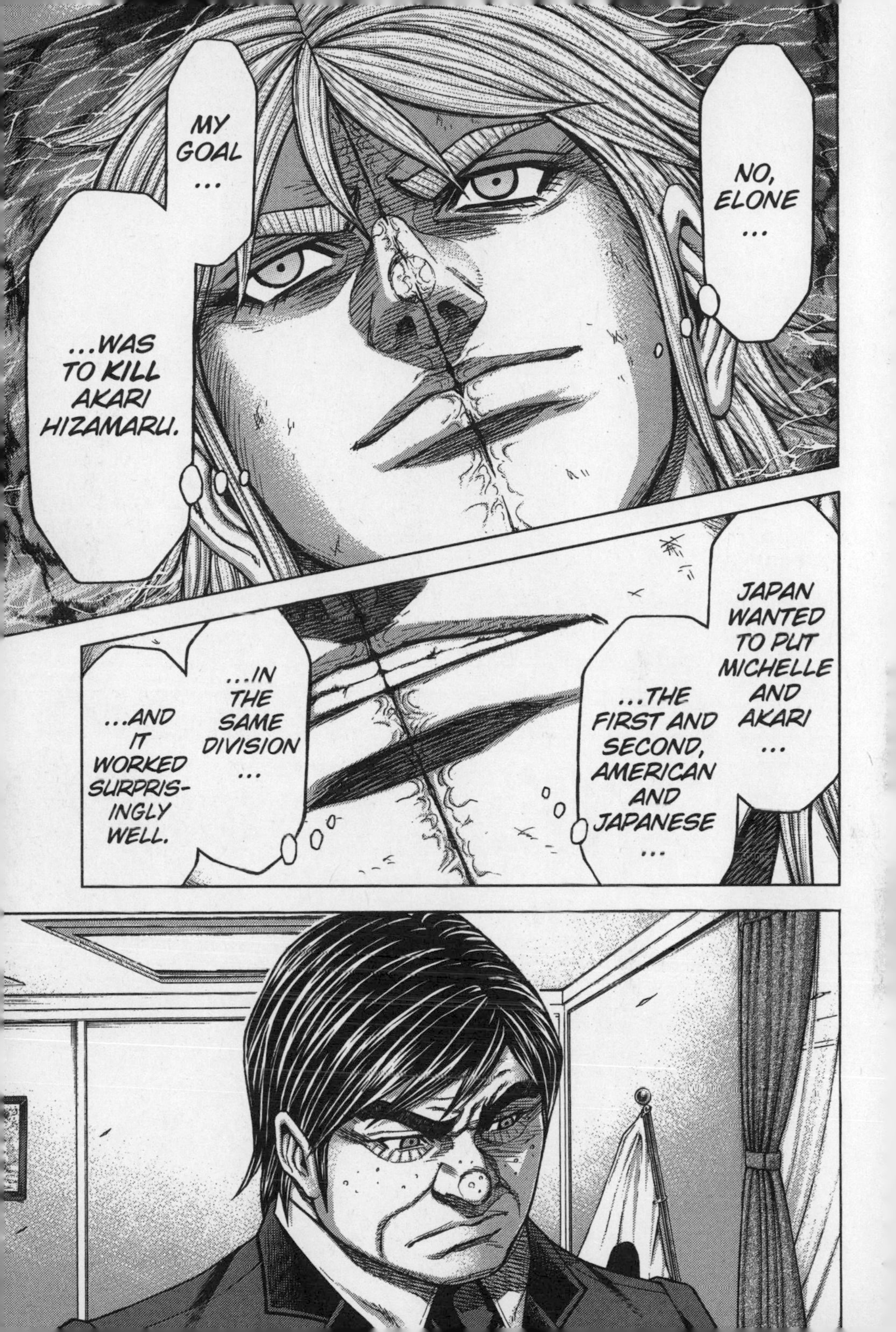
NO, ELONE ...
MY GOAL ...
...WAS TO KILL AKARI HIZAMARU.
JAPAN WANTED TO PUT MICHELLE AND AKARI ...
...THE FIRST AND SECOND, AMERICAN AND JAPANESE ...
...IN THE SAME DIVISION ...
...AND IT WORKED SURPRISINGLY WELL.

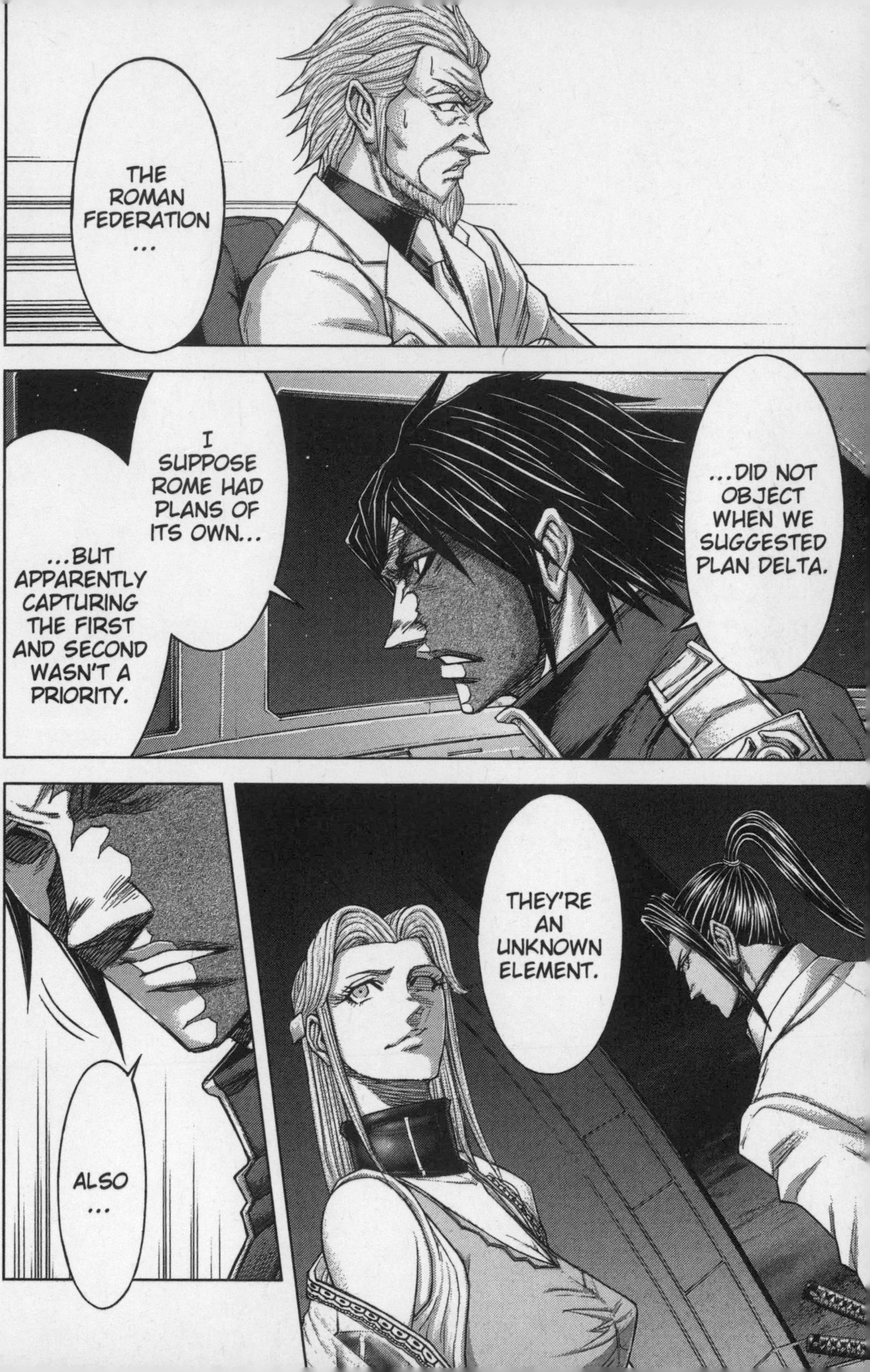
THE ROMAN FEDERATION ...
...DID NOT OBJECT WHEN WE SUGGESTED PLAN DELTA.
I SUPPOSE ROME HAD PLANS OF ITS OWN...
...BUT APPARENTLY CAPTURING THE FIRST AND SECOND WASN'T A PRIORITY.
THEY'RE AN UNKNOWN ELEMENT.
ALSO ...

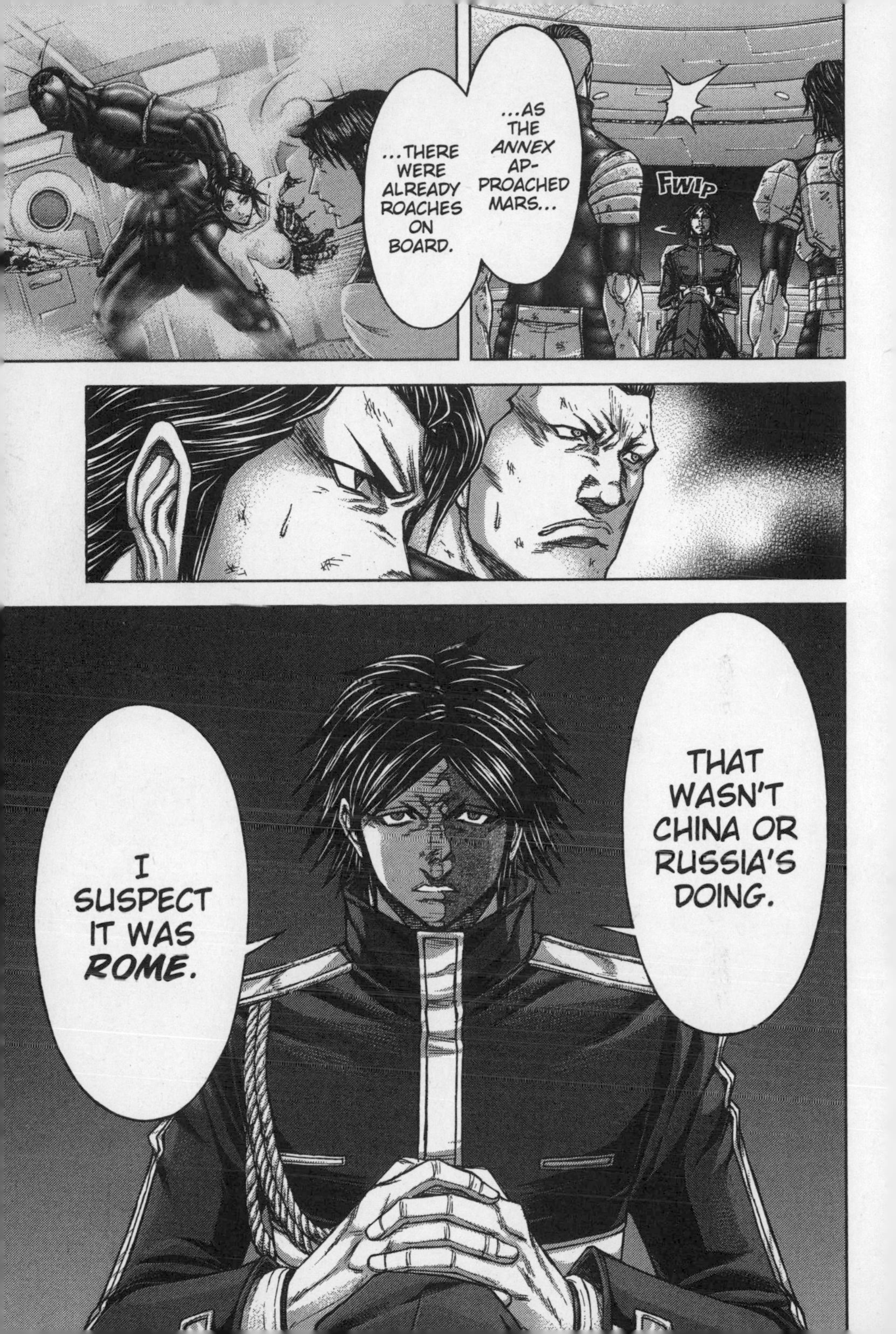
...AS THE ANNEX AP-PROACHED MARS...
FWIP
...THERE WERE ALREADY ROACHES ON BOARD.
THAT WASN'T CHINA OR RUSSIA'S DOING.
I SUSPECT IT WAS *ROME*.

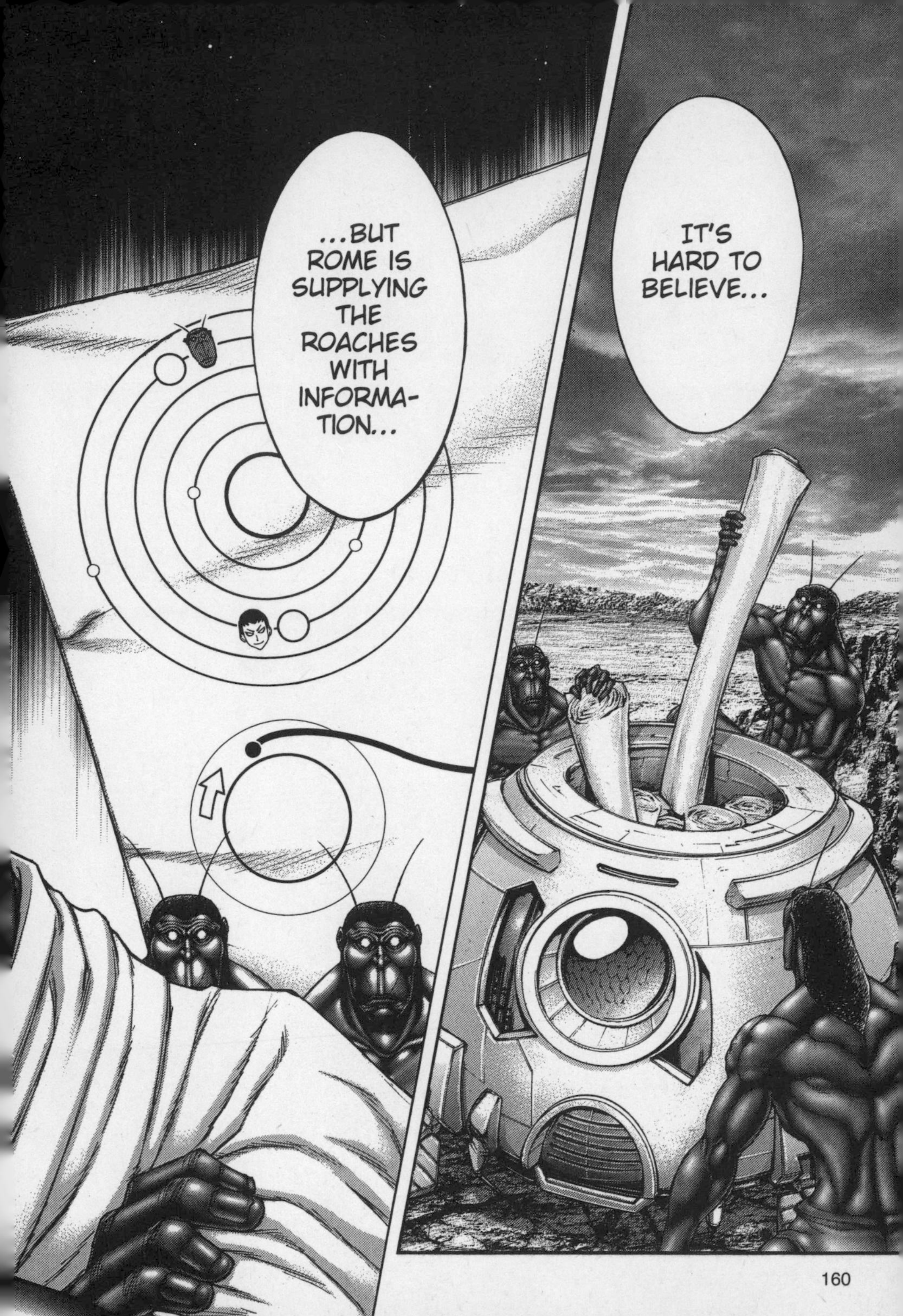
IT'S HARD TO BELIEVE...
...BUT ROME IS SUPPLYING THE ROACHES WITH INFORMATION...

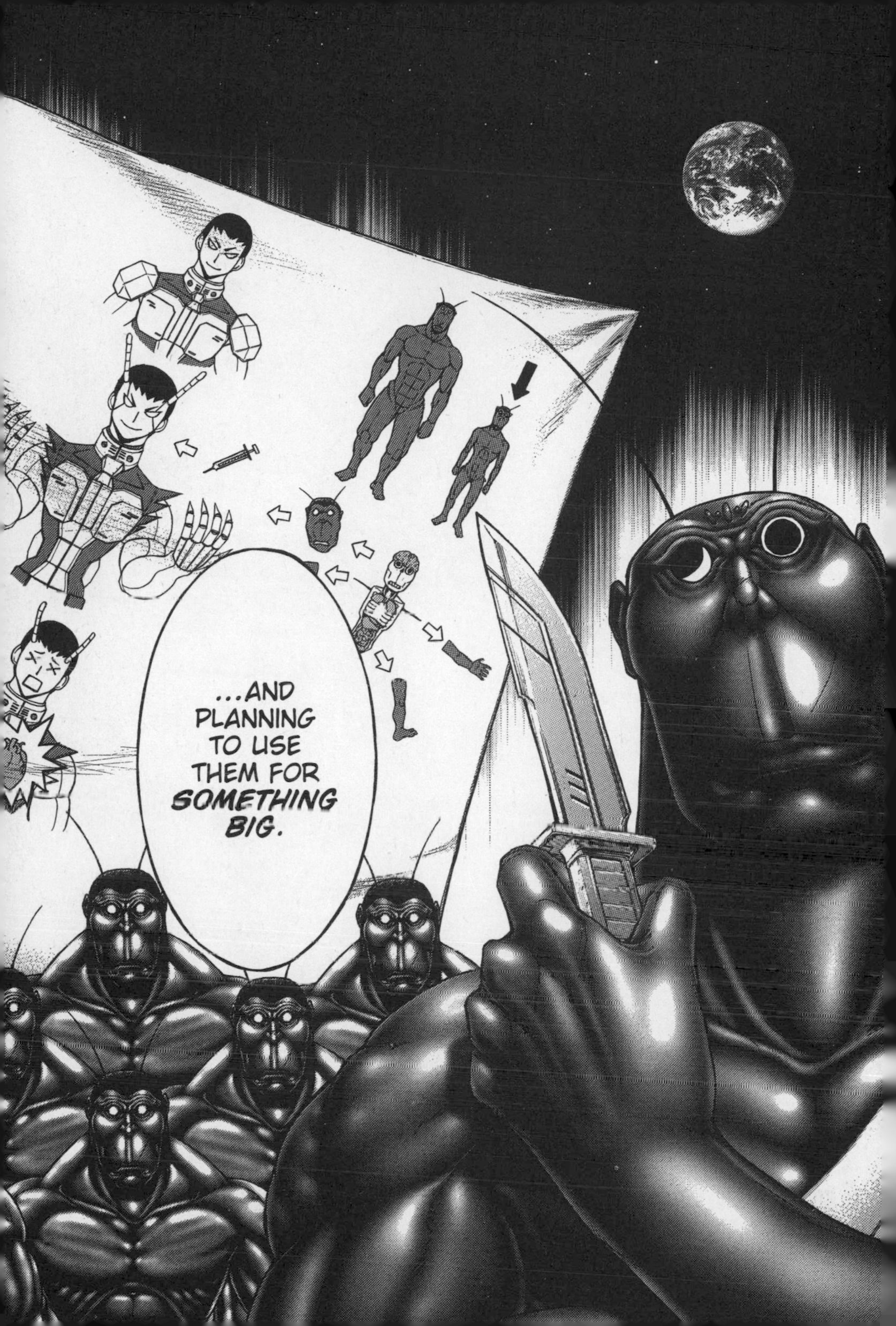
...AND PLANNING TO USE THEM FOR SOMETHING BIG.

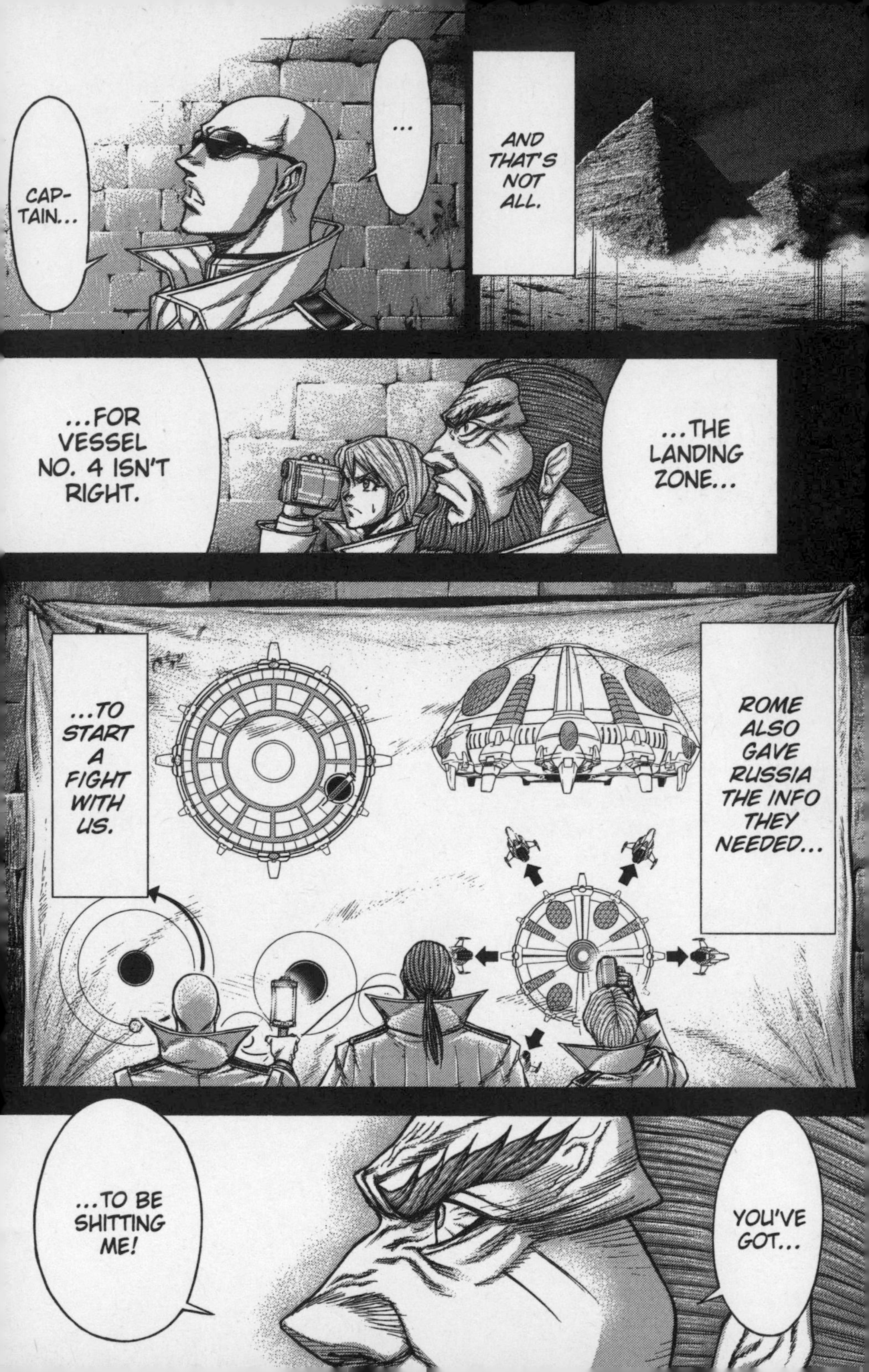
AND THAT'S NOT ALL.
...
CAP-TAIN...
...THE LANDING ZONE...
...FOR VESSEL NO. 4 ISN'T RIGHT.
ROME ALSO GAVE RUSSIA THE INFO THEY NEEDED...
...TO START A FIGHT WITH US.
YOU'VE GOT...
...TO BE SHITTING ME!

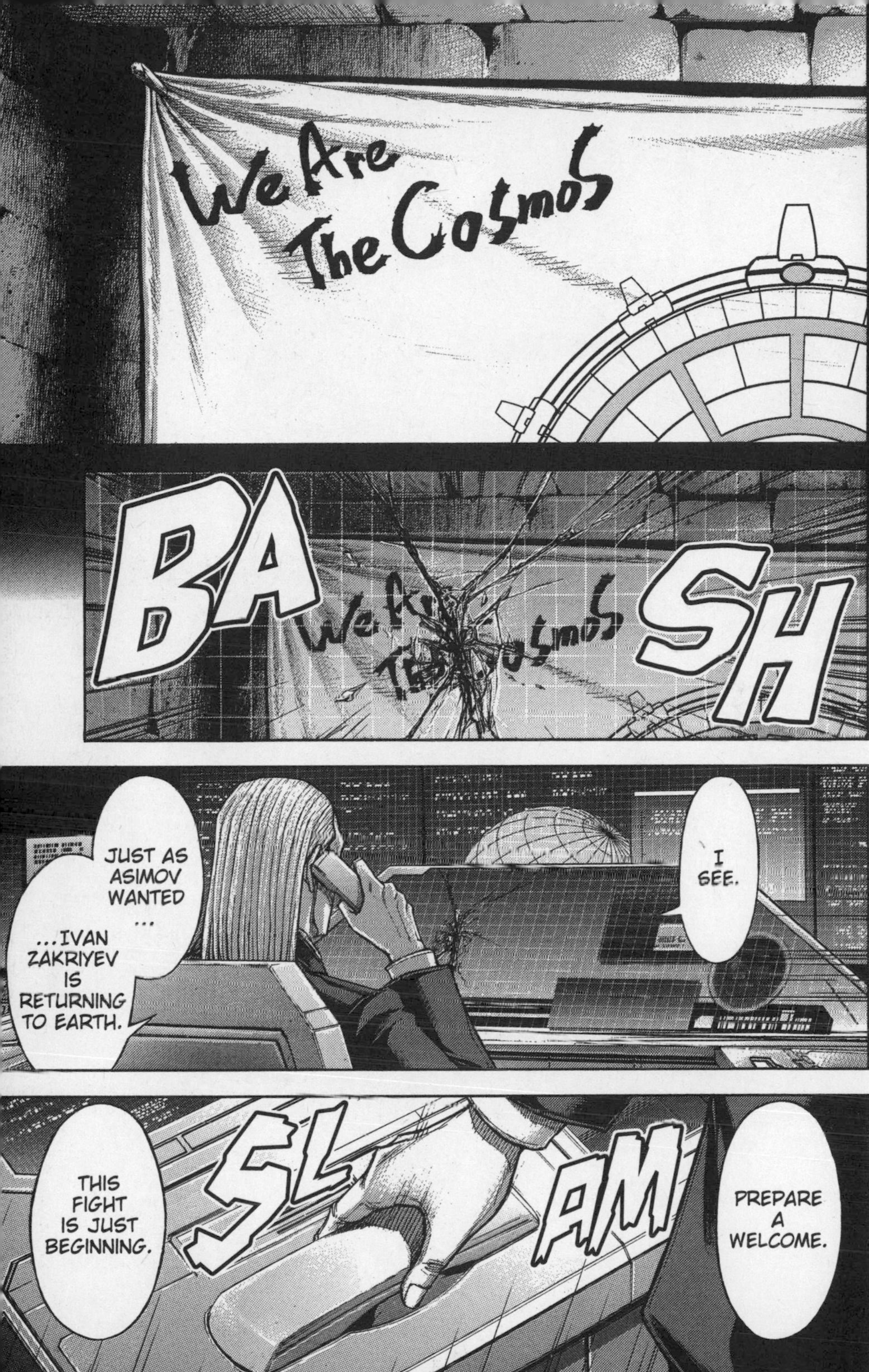
We Are The Cosmos
BASH
We Are The Cosmos
I SEE.
JUST AS ASIMOV WANTED ...
...IVAN ZAKRIYEV IS RETURNING TO EARTH.
PREPARE A WELCOME.
SLAM
THIS FIGHT IS JUST BEGINNING.

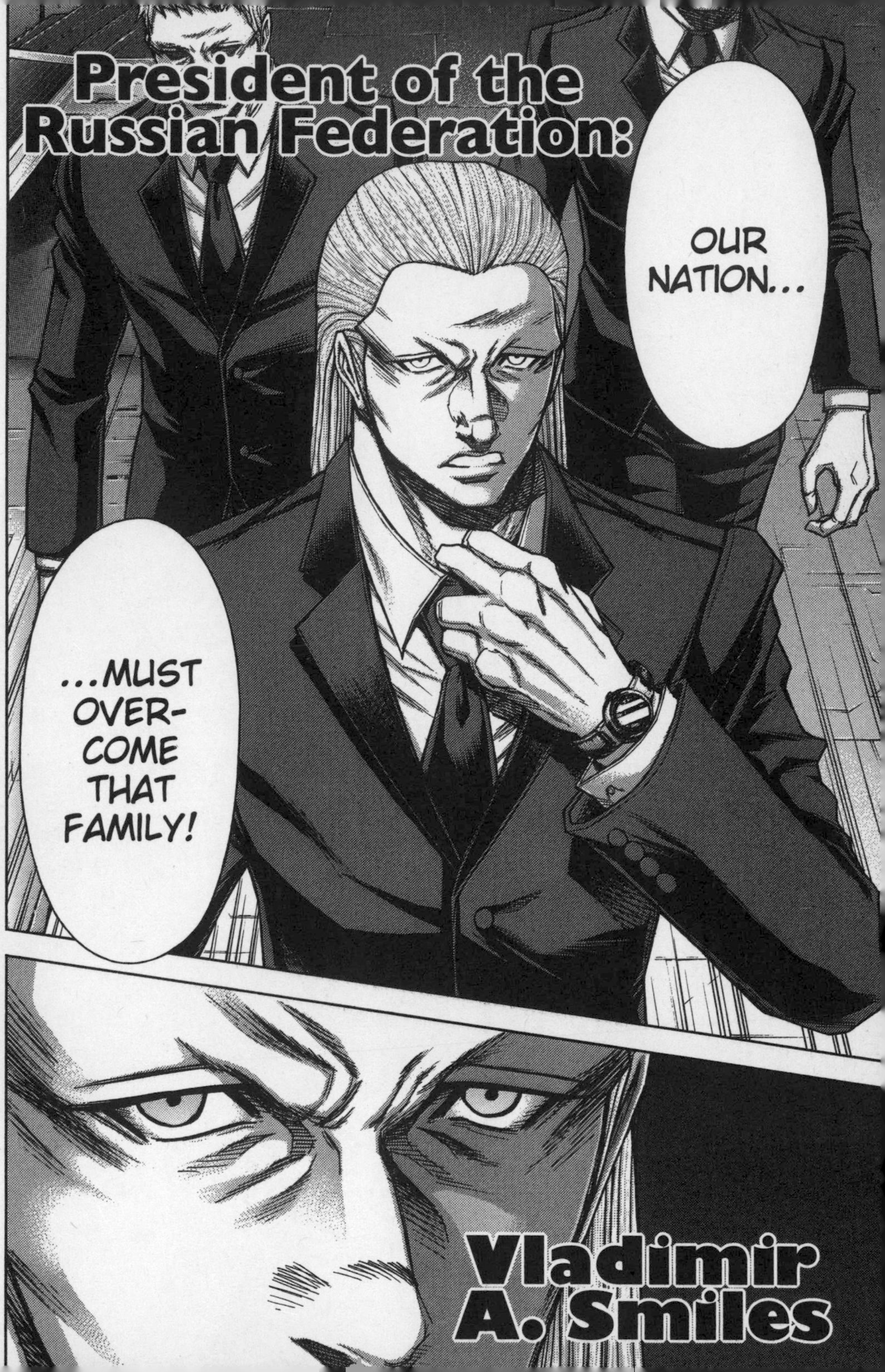
President of the Russian Federation:
OUR NATION...
...MUST OVER-COME THAT FAMILY!
Vladimir A. Smiles

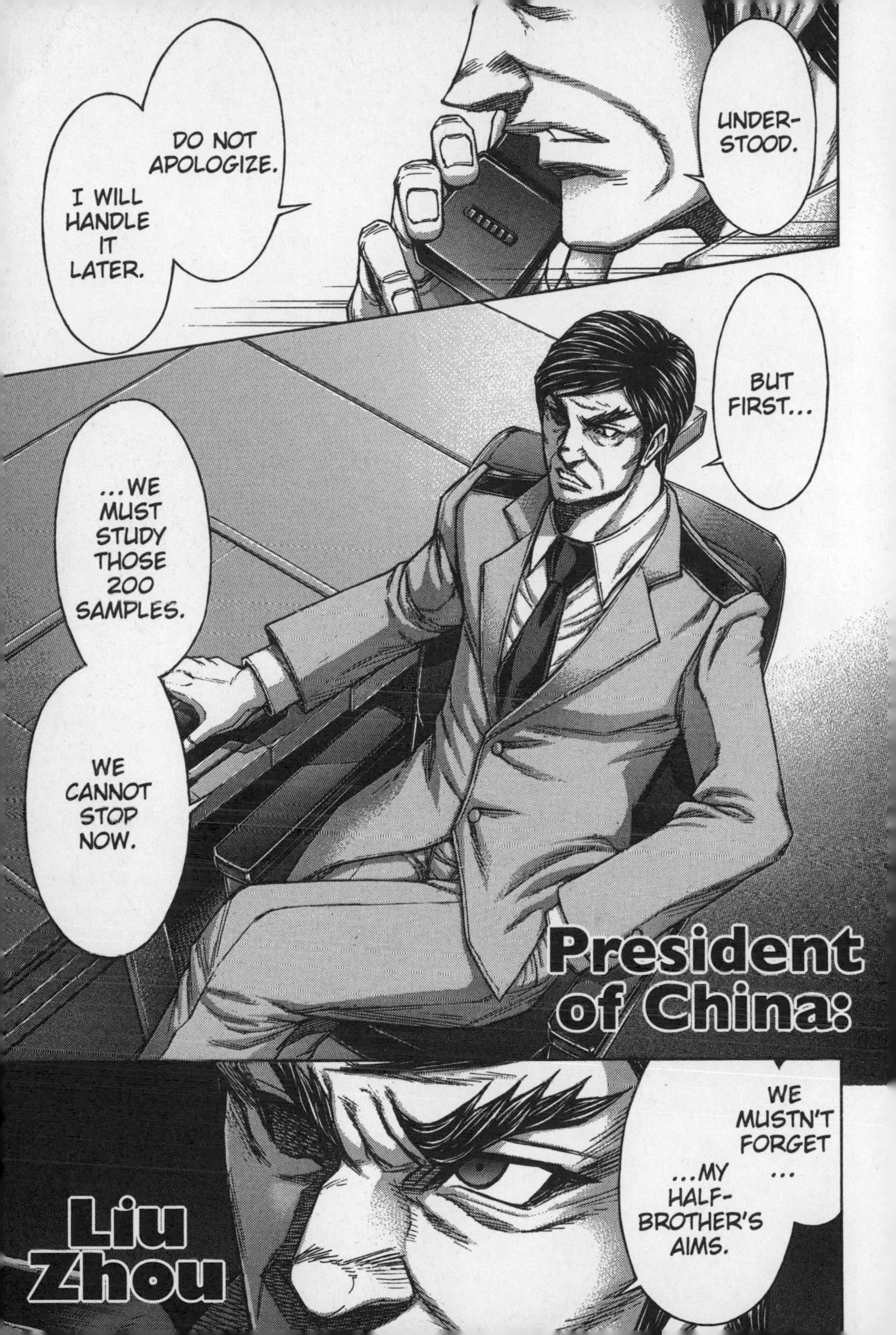
UNDER-STOOD.
DO NOT APOLOGIZE.
I WILL HANDLE IT LATER.
BUT FIRST...
...WE MUST STUDY THOSE 200 SAMPLES.
WE CANNOT STOP NOW.
President of China:
WE MUSTN'T FORGET ...
...MY HALF-BROTHER'S AIMS.
Liu Zhou

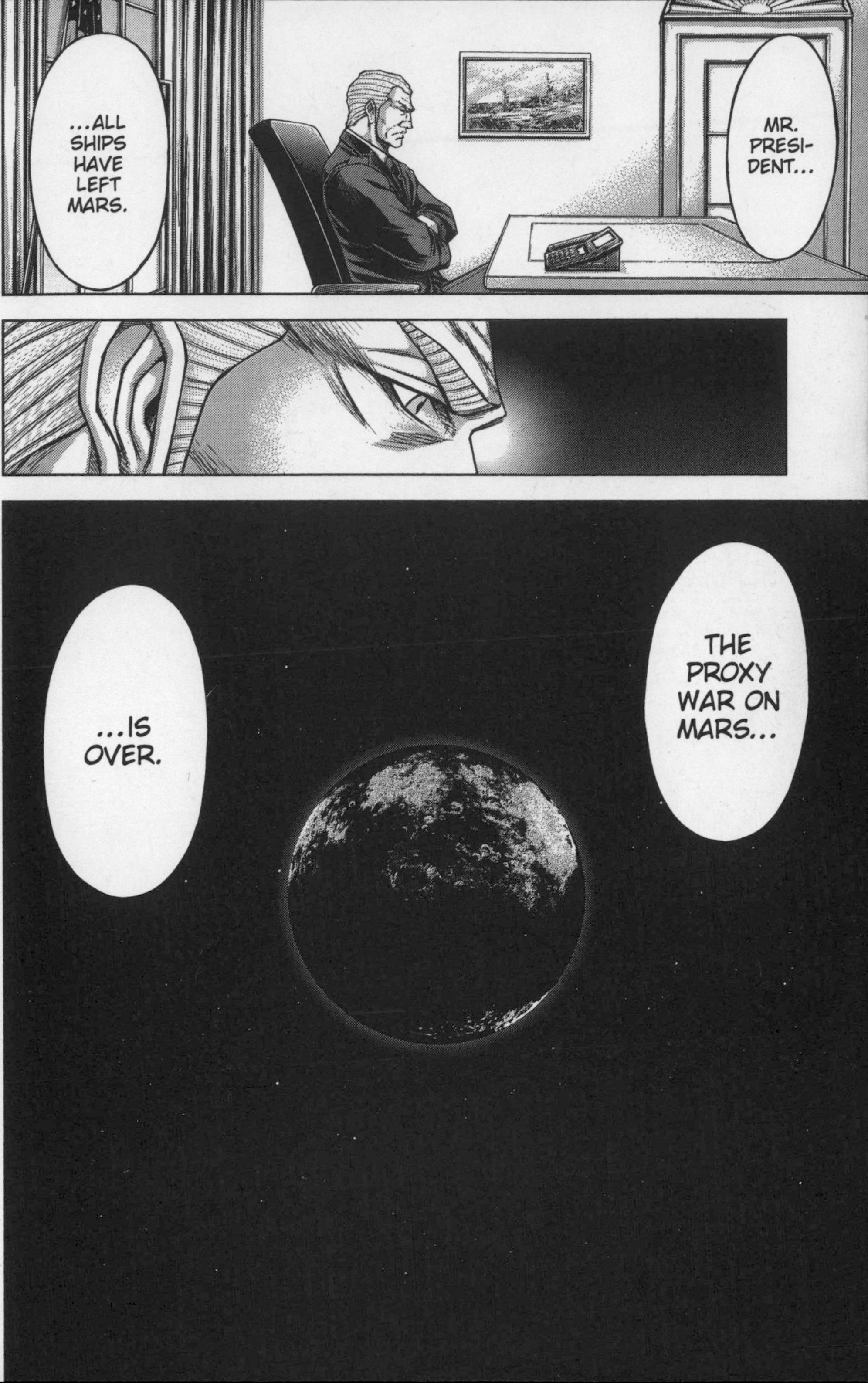
MR. PRESIDENT...
...ALL SHIPS HAVE LEFT MARS.
THE PROXY WAR ON MARS...
...IS OVER.

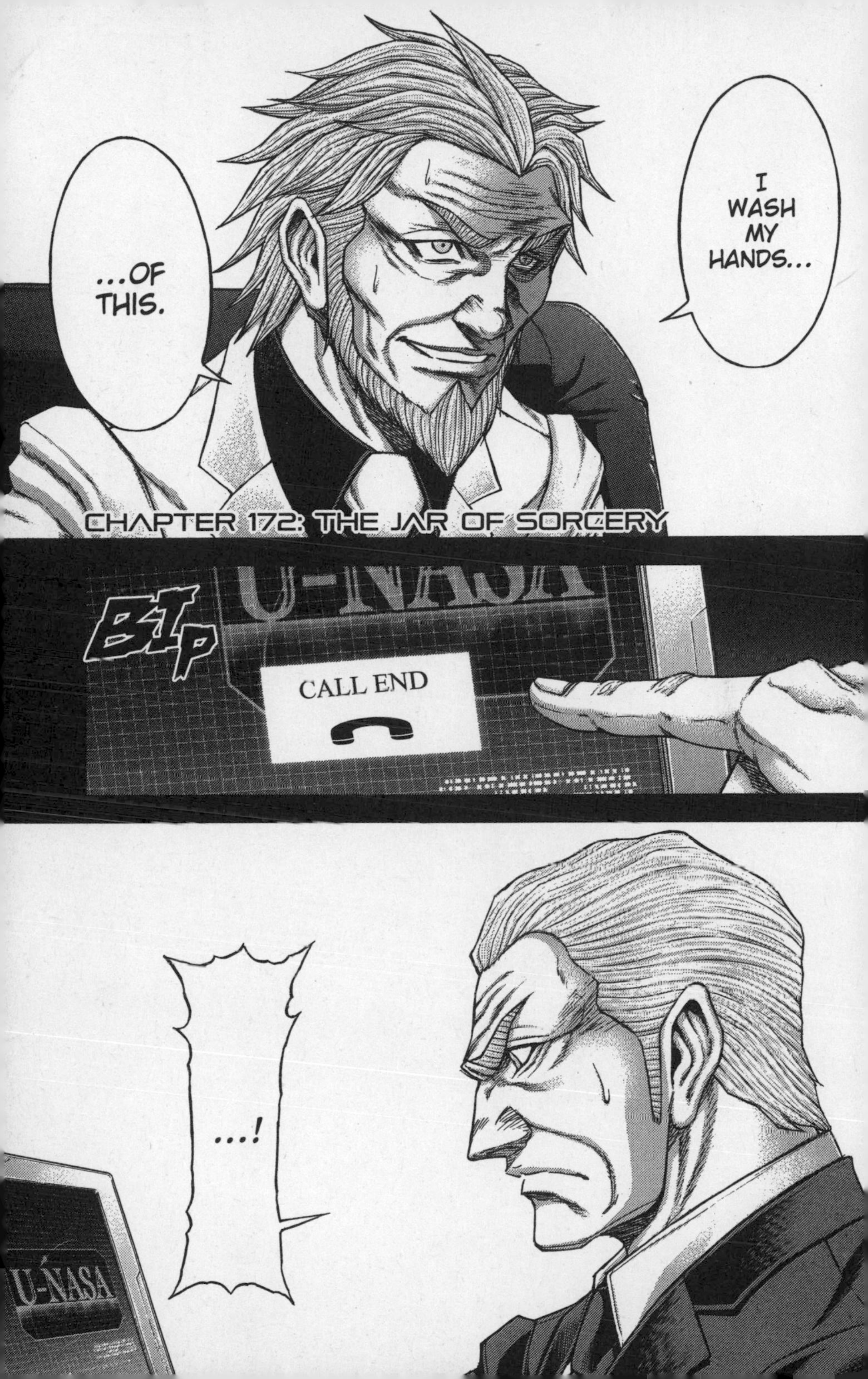
I WASH MY HANDS...
...OF THIS.
CHAPTER 172: THE JAR OF SORCERY
BIP
U-NASA
CALL END
...!
U-NASA

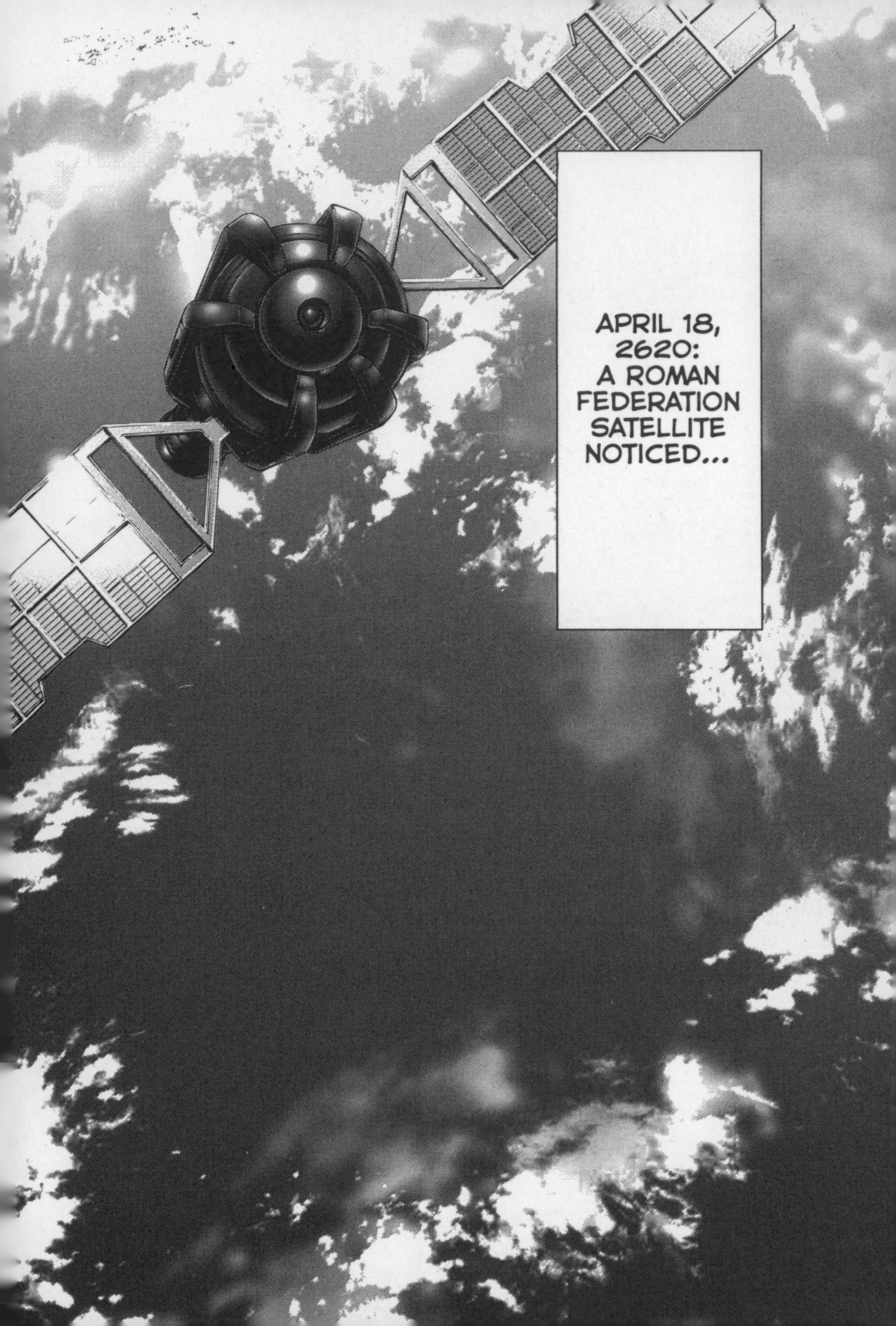
APRIL 18, 2620: A ROMAN FEDERATION SATELLITE NOTICED...

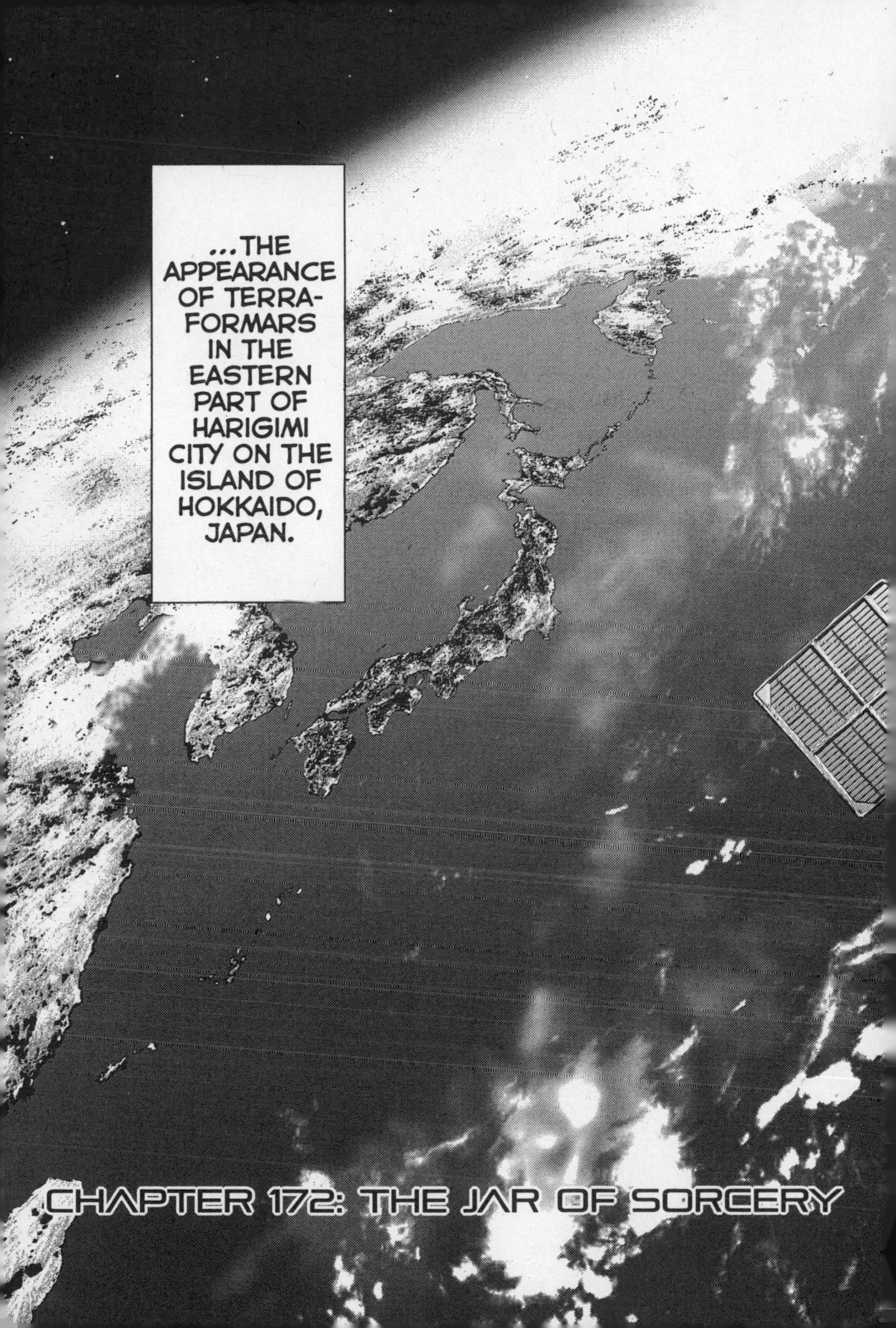
...THE APPEARANCE OF TERRA-FORMARS IN THE EASTERN PART OF HARIGIMI CITY ON THE ISLAND OF HOKKAIDO, JAPAN.
CHAPTER 172: THE JAR OF SORCERY

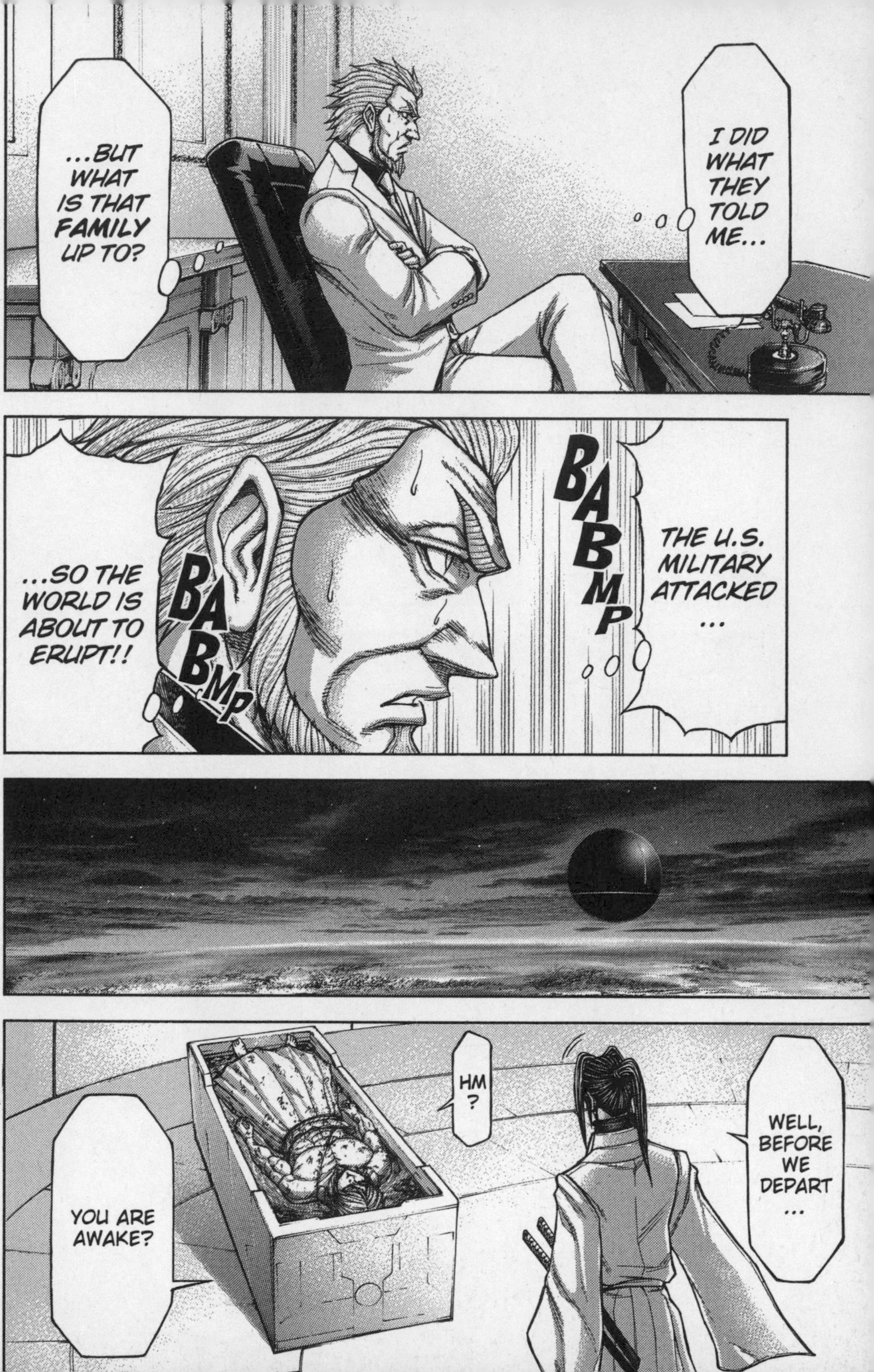
I DID WHAT THEY TOLD ME...
...BUT WHAT IS THAT FAMILY UP TO?
BABMP
THE U.S. MILITARY ATTACKED ...
BABMP
...SO THE WORLD IS ABOUT TO ERUPT!!
WELL, BEFORE WE DEPART ...
HM ?
YOU ARE AWAKE?

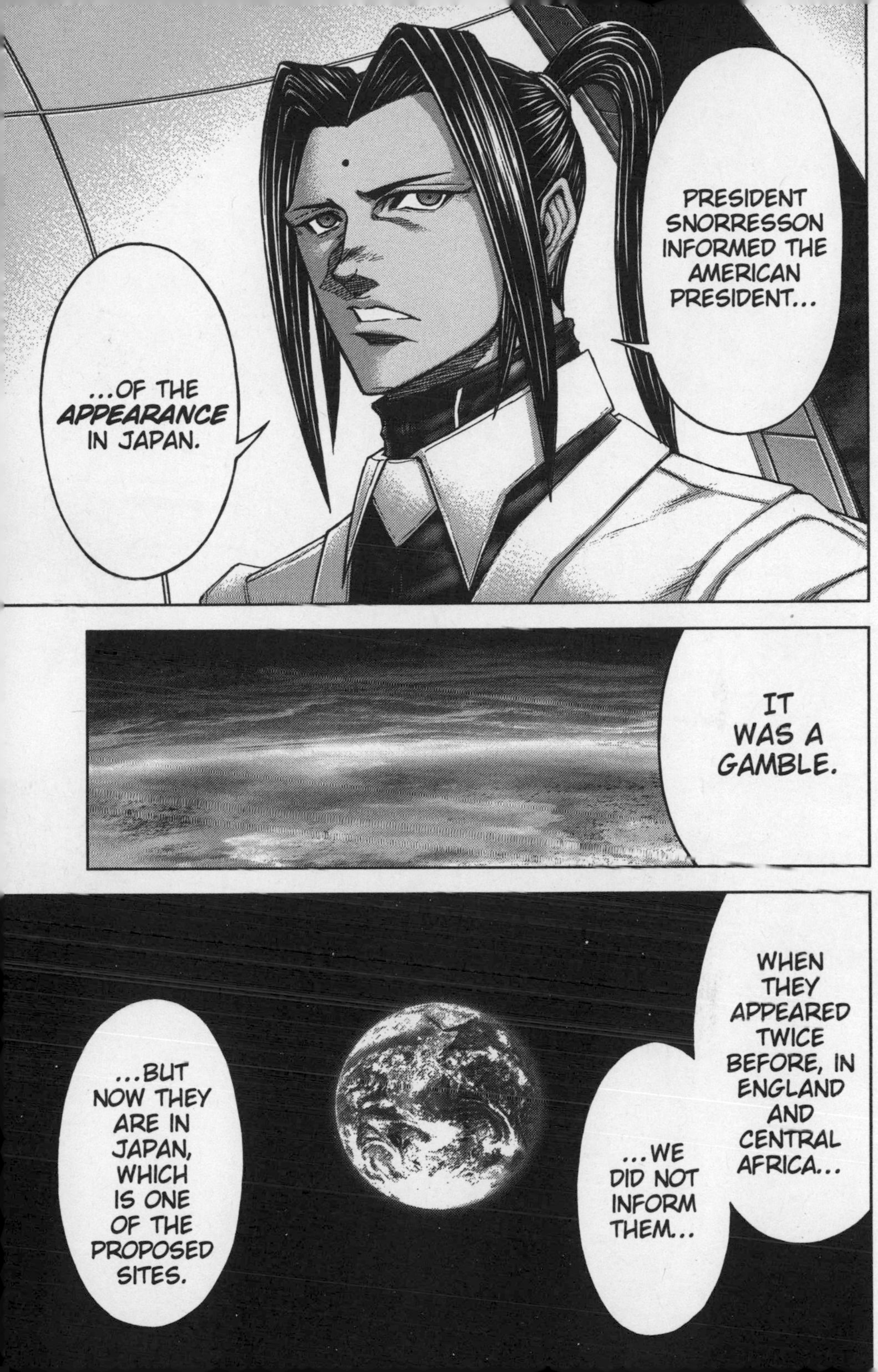
PRESIDENT SNORRESSON INFORMED THE AMERICAN PRESIDENT...
...OF THE *APPEARANCE* IN JAPAN.
IT WAS A GAMBLE.
WHEN THEY APPEARED TWICE BEFORE, IN ENGLAND AND CENTRAL AFRICA...
...WE DID NOT INFORM THEM...
...BUT NOW THEY ARE IN JAPAN, WHICH IS ONE OF THE PROPOSED SITES.

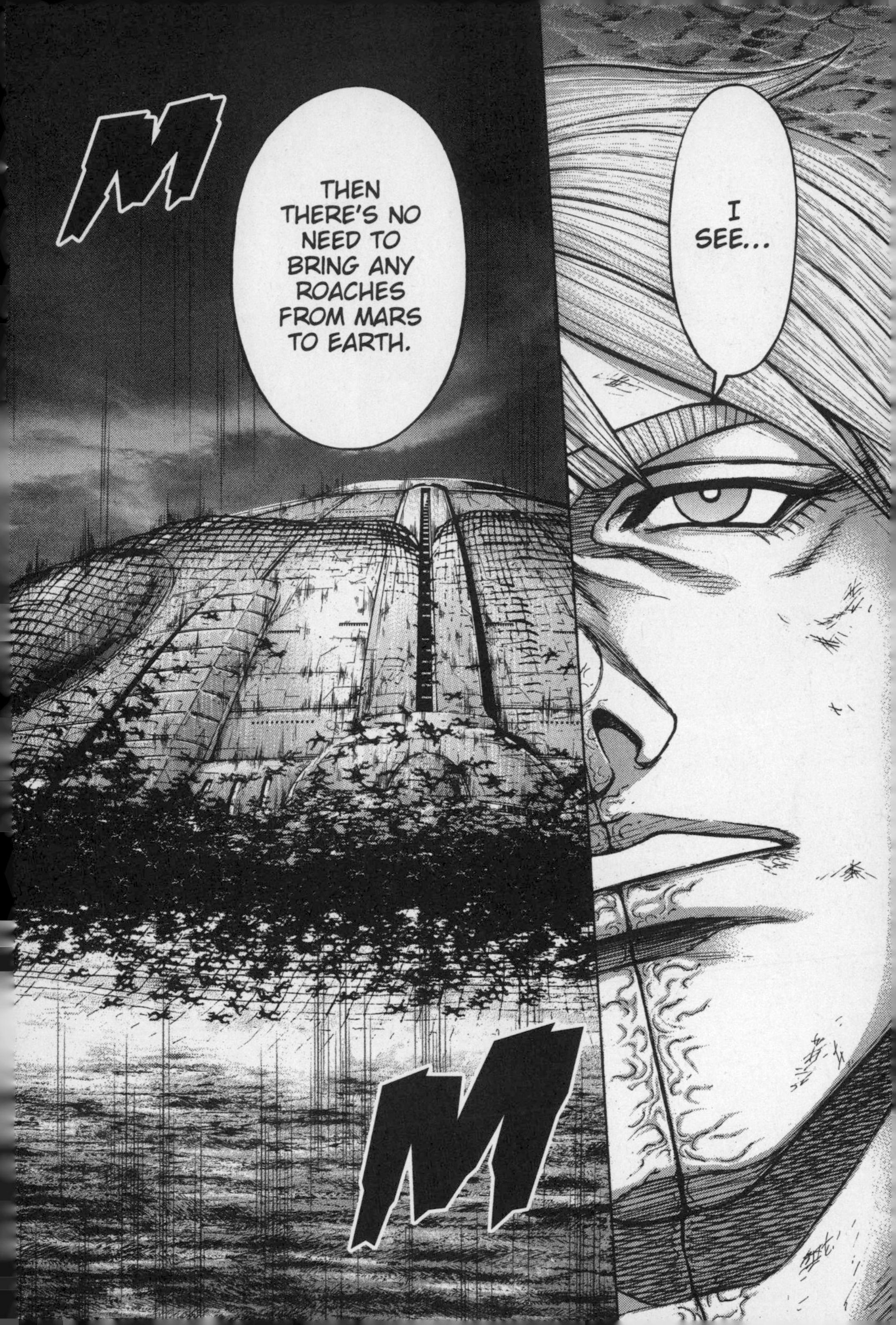
I SEE...
M
THEN THERE'S NO NEED TO BRING ANY ROACHES FROM MARS TO EARTH.
M

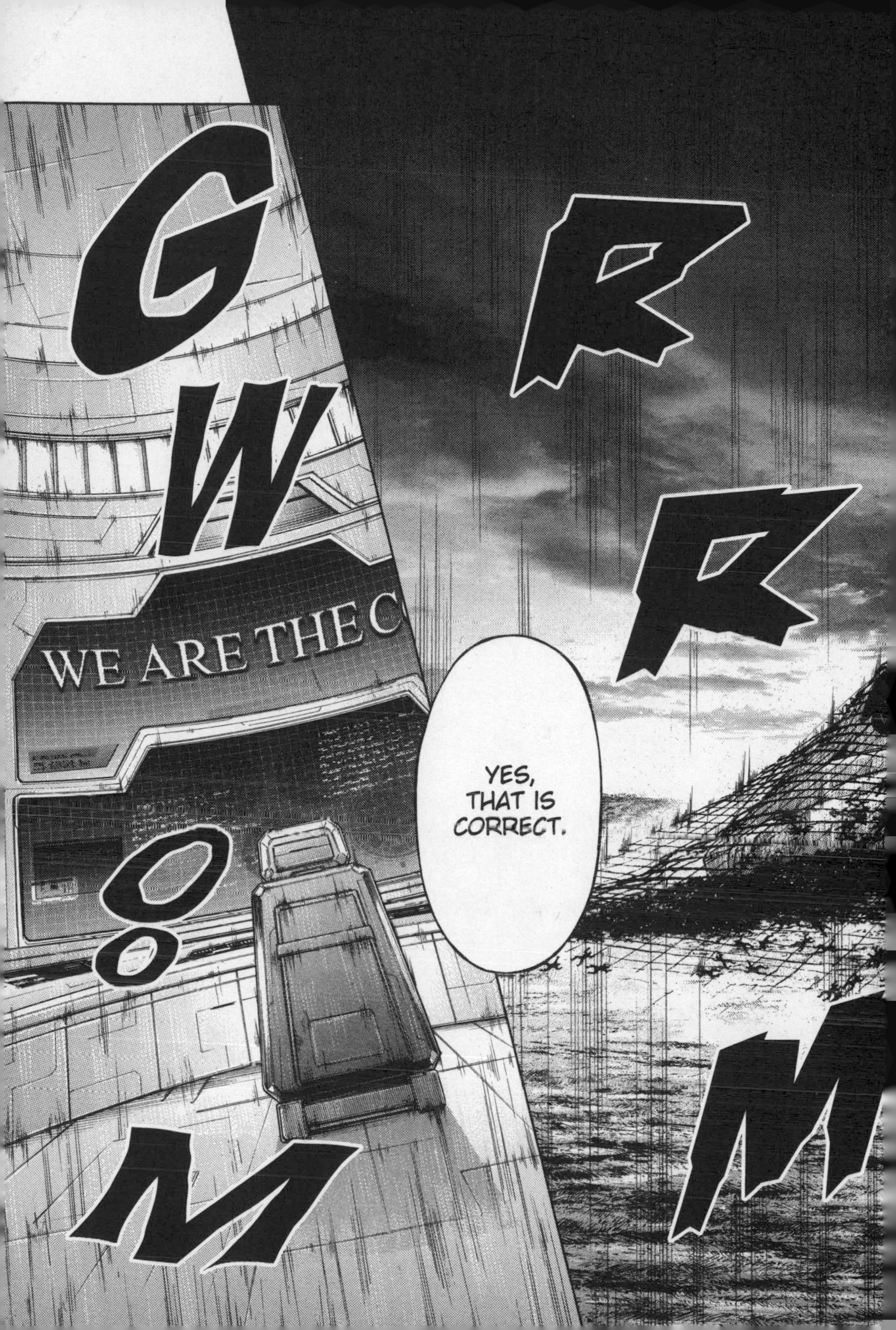
YES, THAT IS CORRECT.
RRM
GWOM
WE ARE THE C

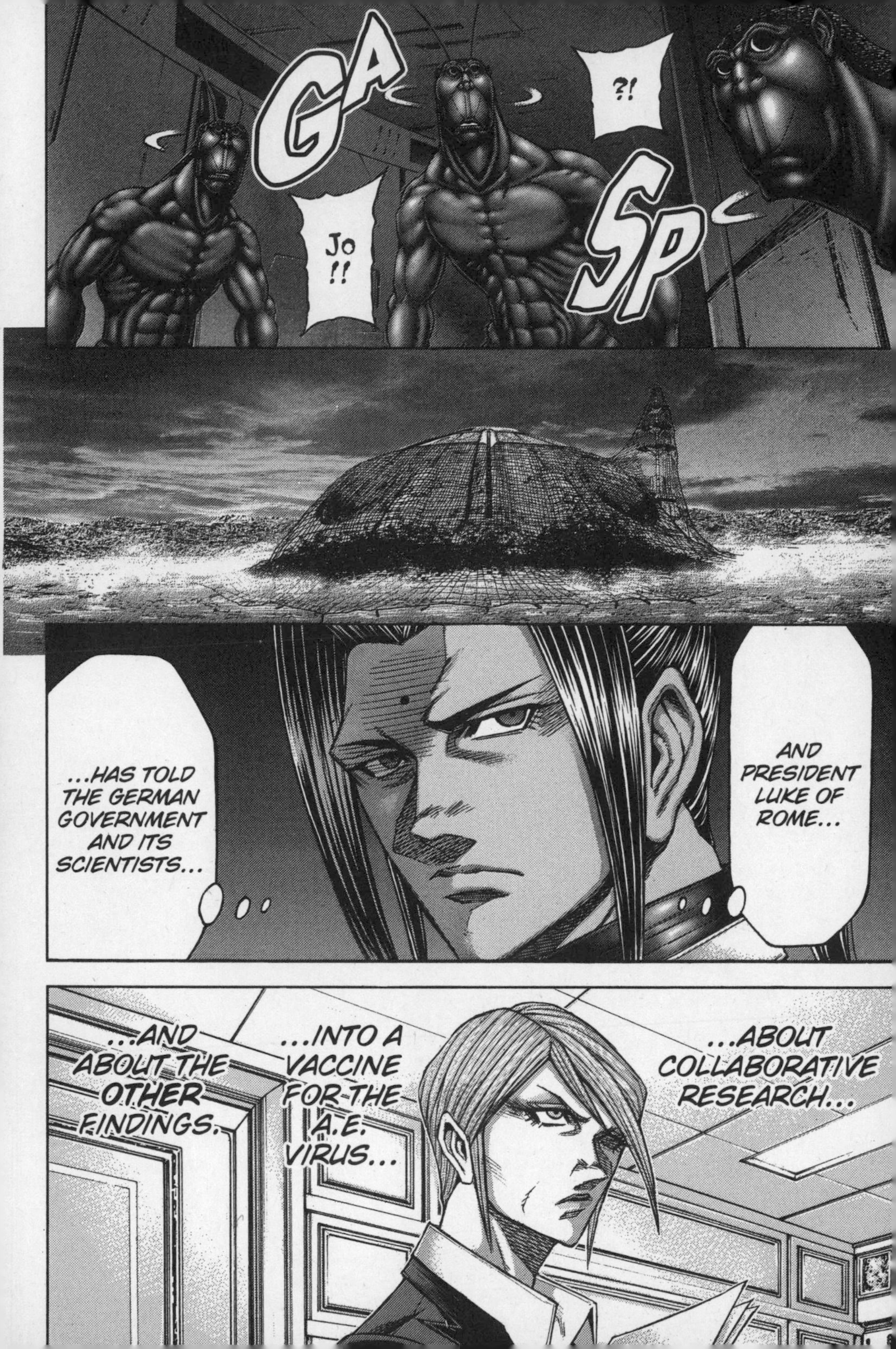
?!
GA
SP
Jo !!
AND PRESIDENT LUKE OF ROME...
...HAS TOLD THE GERMAN GOVERNMENT AND ITS SCIENTISTS...
...ABOUT COLLABORATIVE RESEARCH...
...INTO A VACCINE FOR THE A.E. VIRUS...
...AND ABOUT THE OTHER FINDINGS.

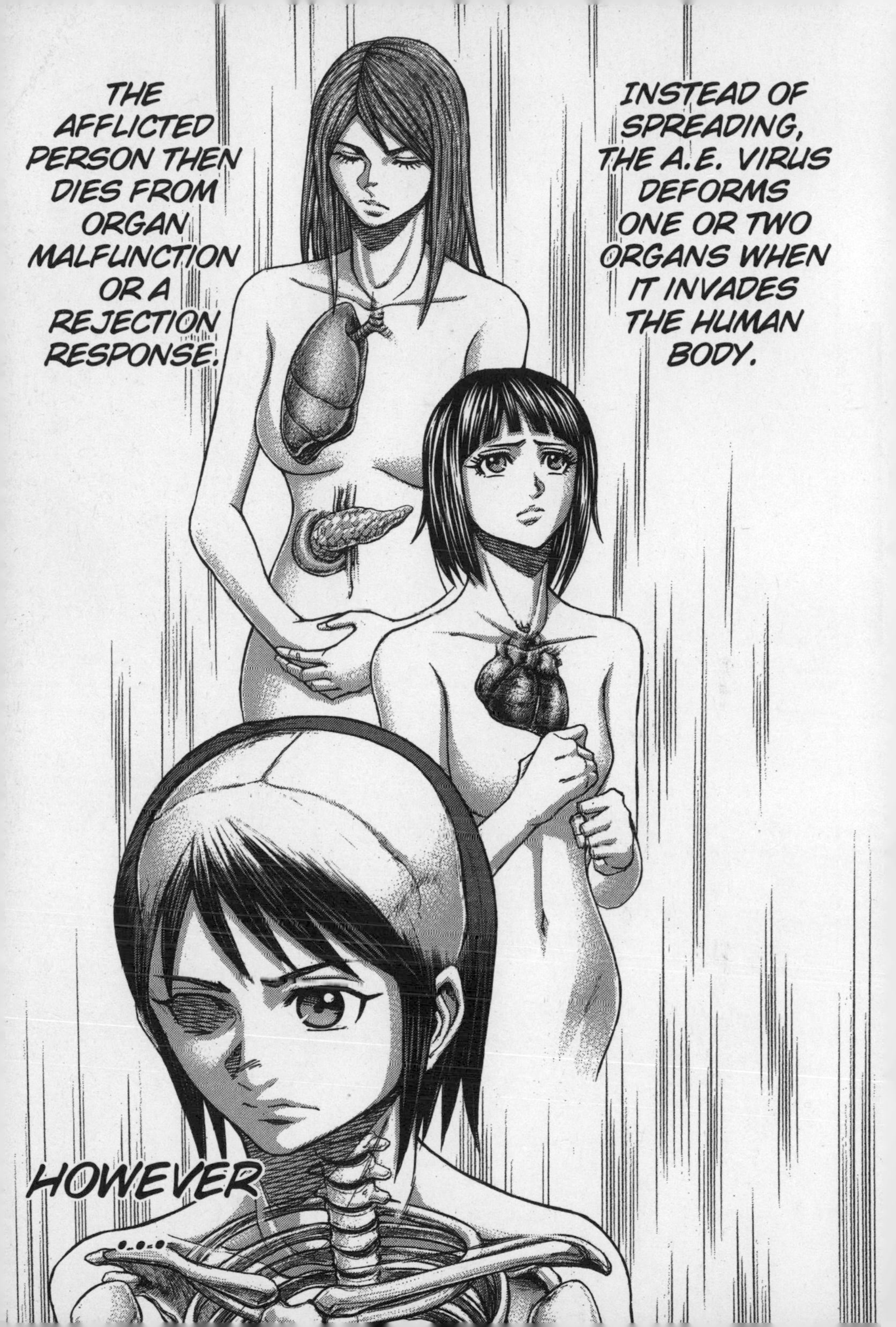
INSTEAD OF SPREADING, THE A.E. VIRUS DEFORMS ONE OR TWO ORGANS WHEN IT INVADES THE HUMAN BODY.
THE AFFLICTED PERSON THEN DIES FROM ORGAN MALFUNCTION OR A REJECTION RESPONSE.
HOWEVER
...

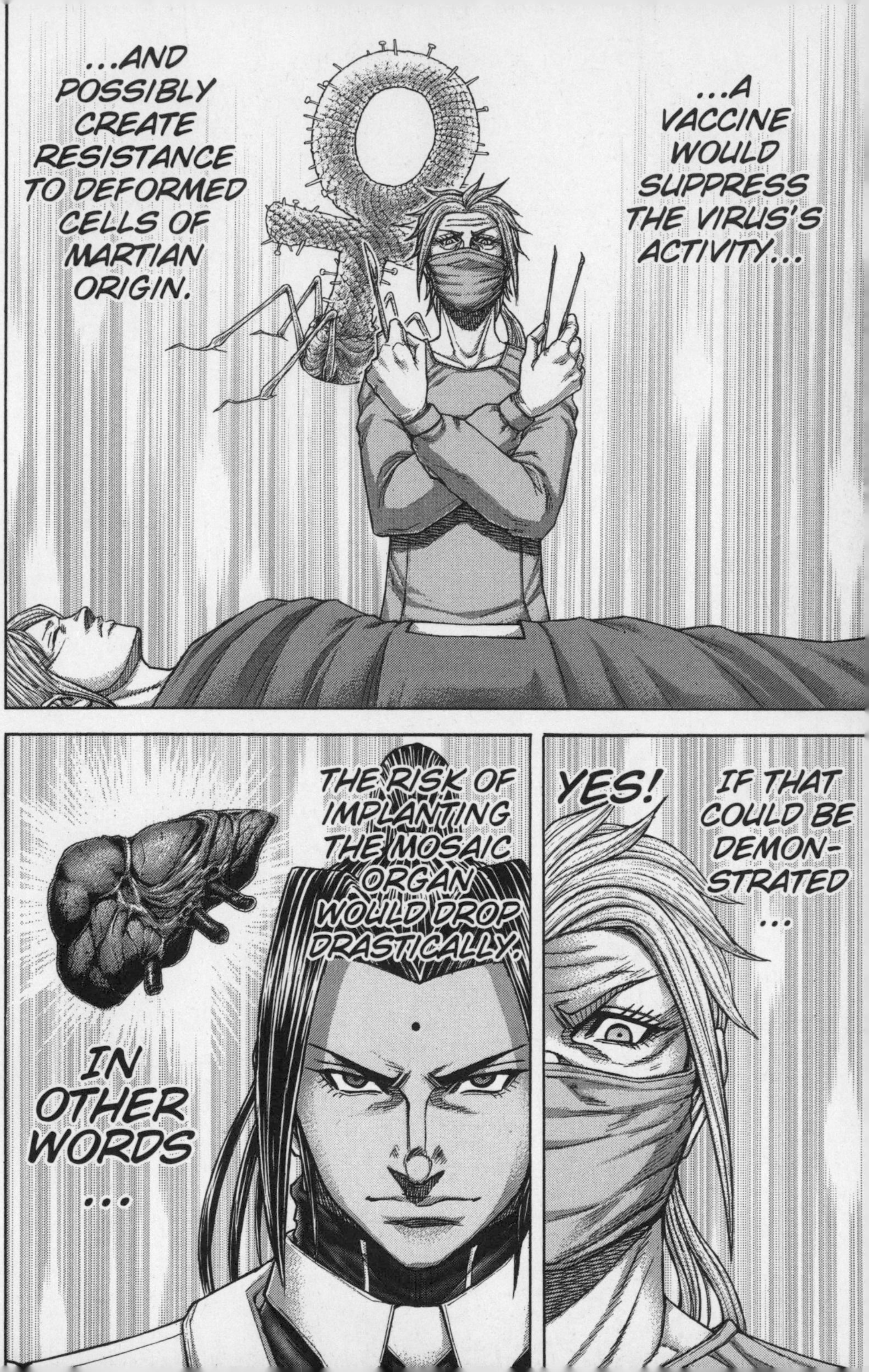
...A VACCINE WOULD SUPPRESS THE VIRUS'S ACTIVITY...
...AND POSSIBLY CREATE RESISTANCE TO DEFORMED CELLS OF MARTIAN ORIGIN.
IF THAT COULD BE DEMON-STRATED...
YES!
THE RISK OF IMPLANTING THE MOSAIC ORGAN WOULD DROP DRASTICALLY.
IN OTHER WORDS...

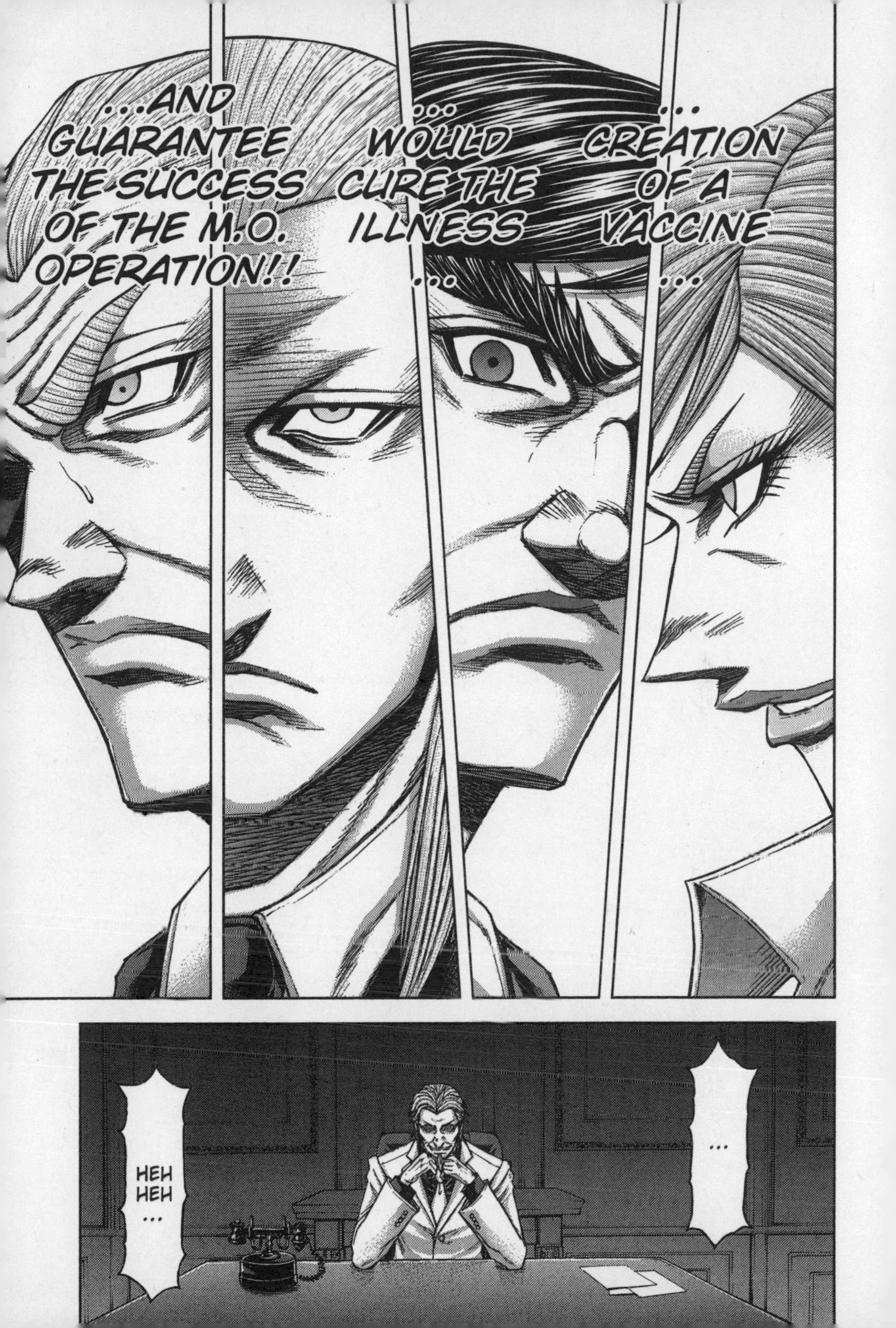
...CREATION OF A VACCINE...
...WOULD CURE THE ILLNESS...
...AND GUARANTEE THE SUCCESS OF THE M.O. OPERATION!!
...
HEH HEH ...

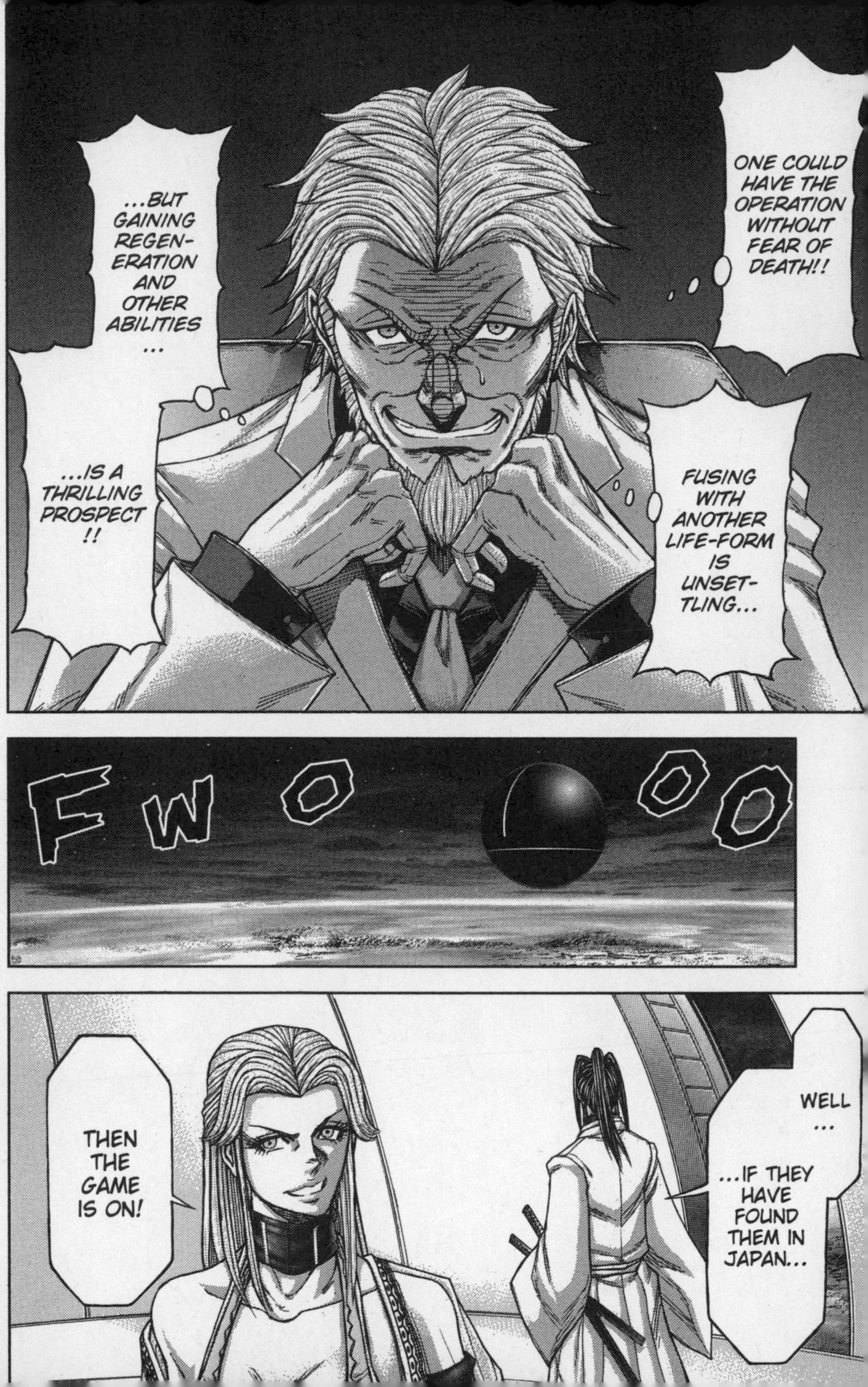
ONE COULD HAVE THE OPERATION WITHOUT FEAR OF DEATH!!
...BUT GAINING REGEN-ERATION AND OTHER ABILITIES...
FUSING WITH ANOTHER LIFE-FORM IS UNSET-TLING...
...IS A THRILLING PROSPECT!!
FWOOOO
WELL...
...IF THEY HAVE FOUND THEM IN JAPAN...
THEN THE GAME IS ON!

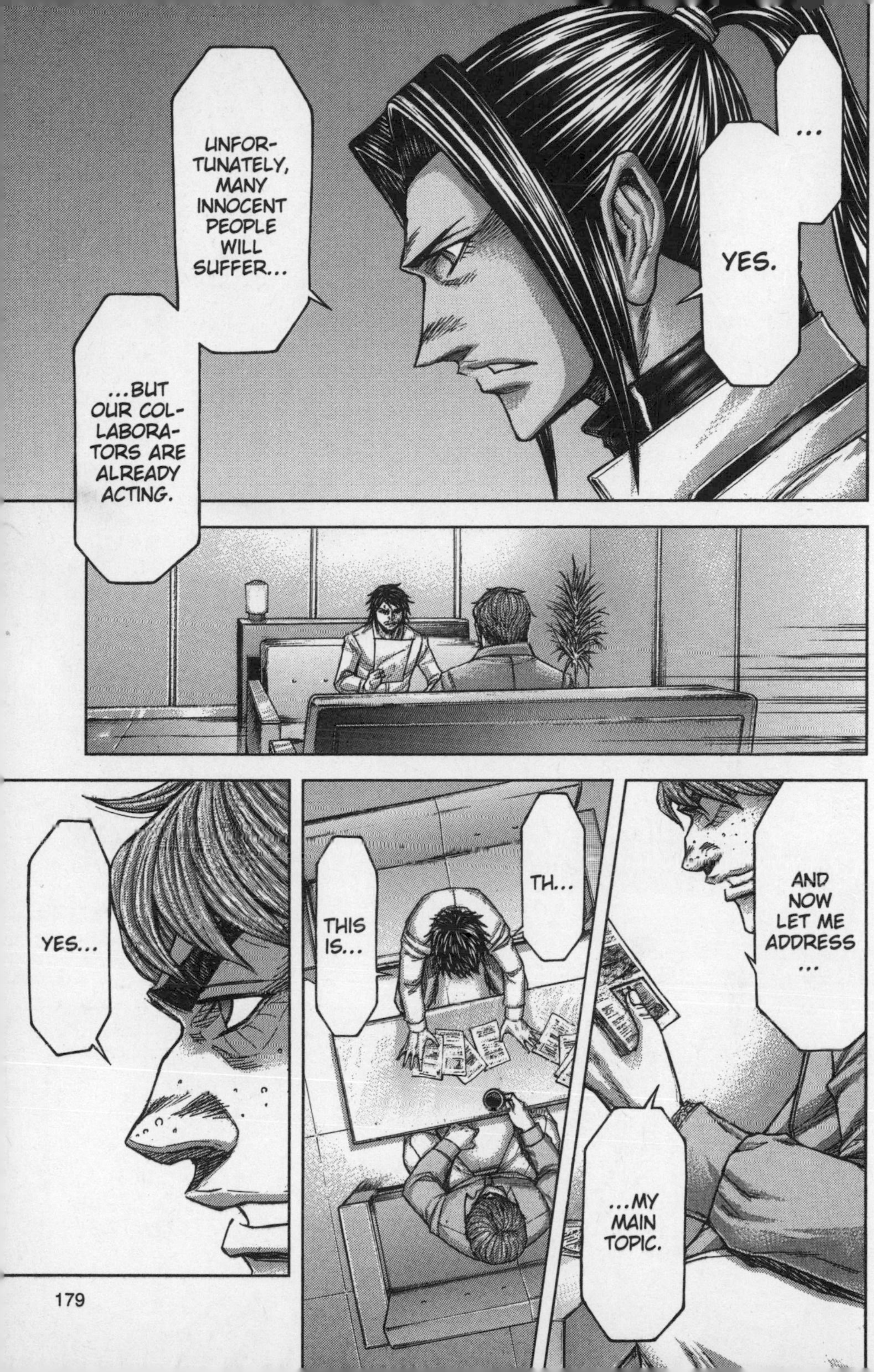
...
YES.
UNFORTUNATELY, MANY INNOCENT PEOPLE WILL SUFFER...
...BUT OUR COLLABORATORS ARE ALREADY ACTING.
AND NOW LET ME ADDRESS ...
...MY MAIN TOPIC.
TH...
THIS IS...
YES...

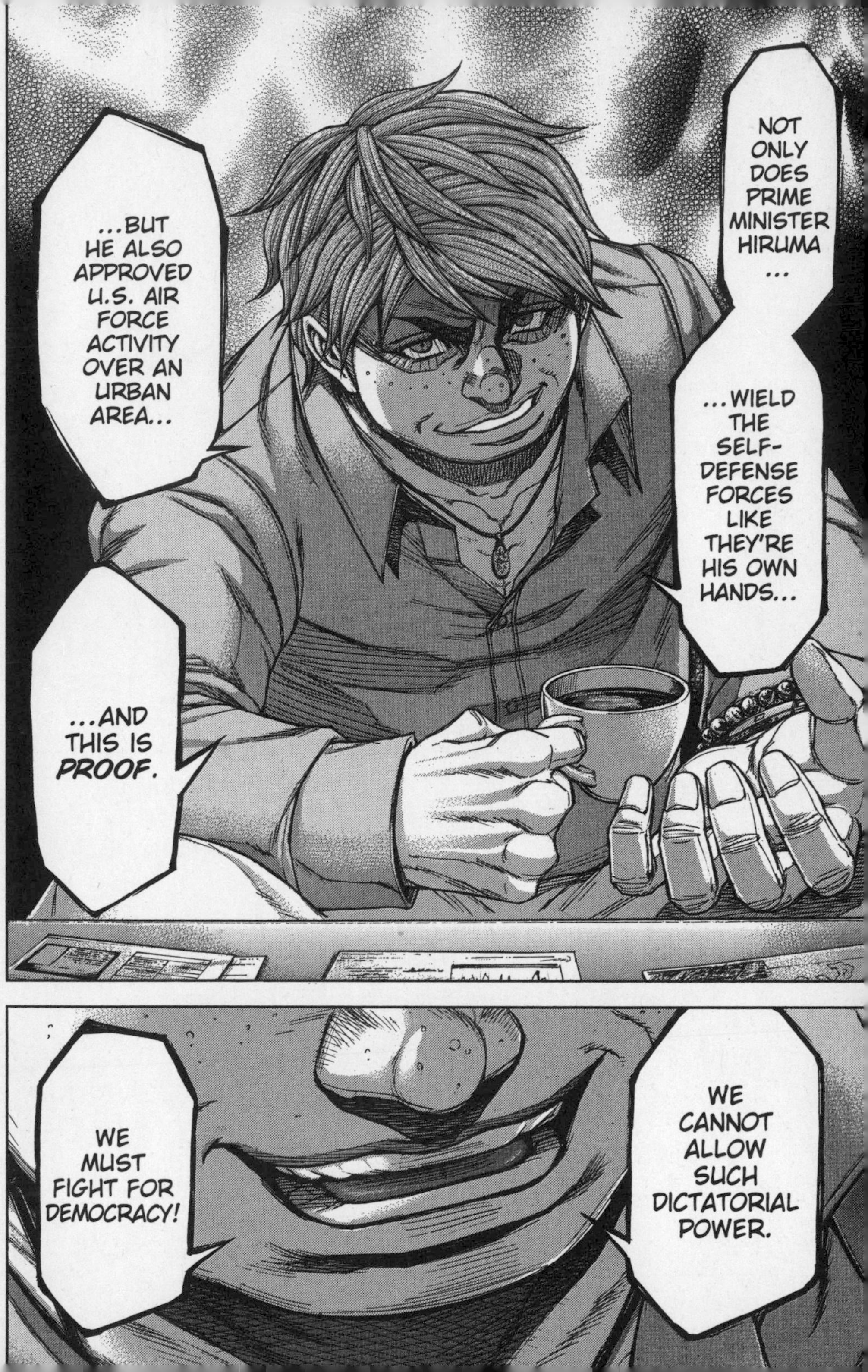
NOT ONLY DOES PRIME MINISTER HIRUMA...
...WIELD THE SELF-DEFENSE FORCES LIKE THEY'RE HIS OWN HANDS...
...BUT HE ALSO APPROVED U.S. AIR FORCE ACTIVITY OVER AN URBAN AREA...
...AND THIS IS *PROOF*.
WE CANNOT ALLOW SUCH DICTATORIAL POWER.
WE MUST FIGHT FOR DEMOCRACY!

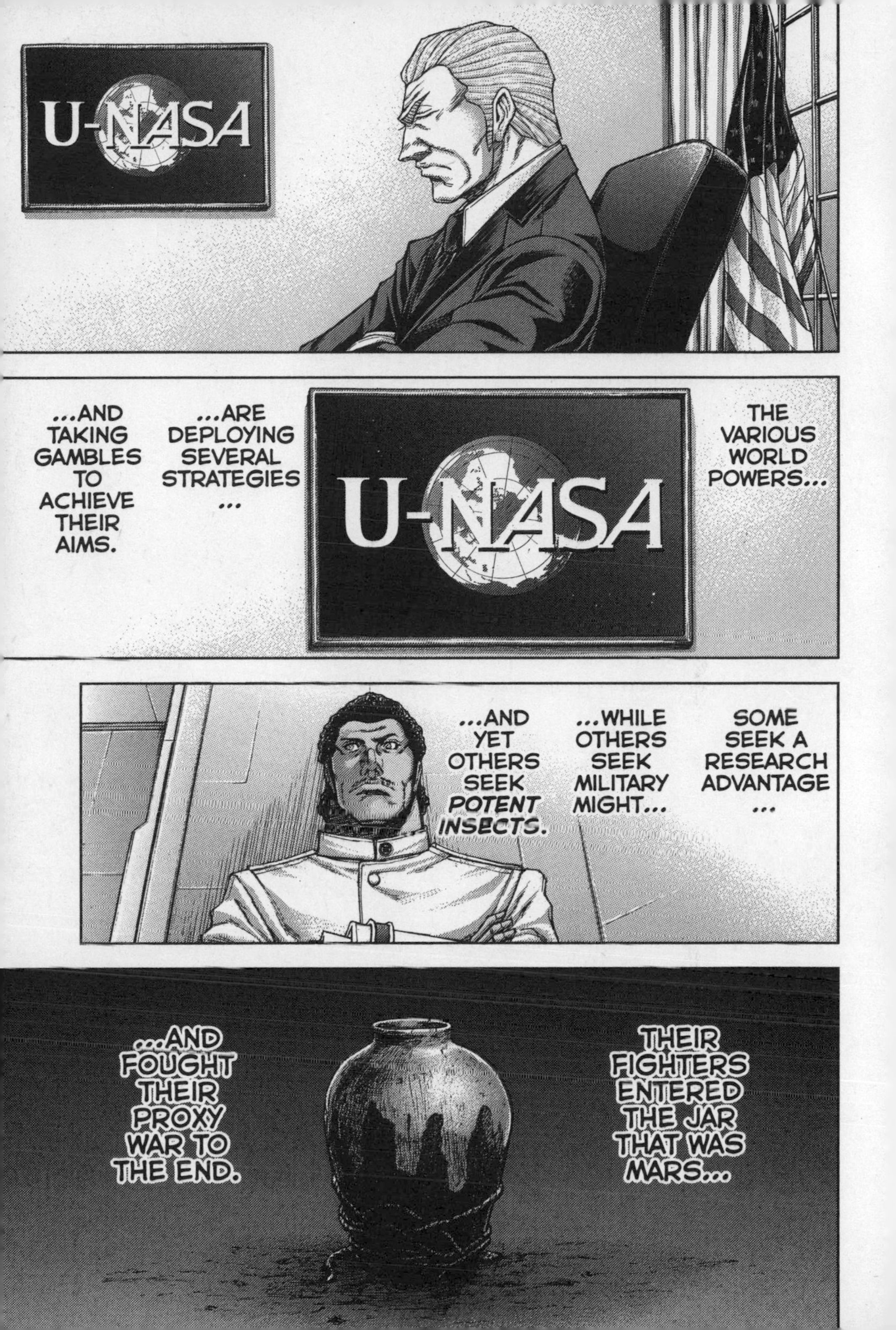
U-NASA
THE VARIOUS WORLD POWERS...
...ARE DEPLOYING SEVERAL STRATEGIES ...
...AND TAKING GAMBLES TO ACHIEVE THEIR AIMS.
U-NASA
SOME SEEK A RESEARCH ADVANTAGE ...
...WHILE OTHERS SEEK MILITARY MIGHT...
...AND YET OTHERS SEEK *POTENT INSECTS*.
THEIR FIGHTERS ENTERED THE JAR THAT WAS MARS...
...AND FOUGHT THEIR PROXY WAR TO THE END.

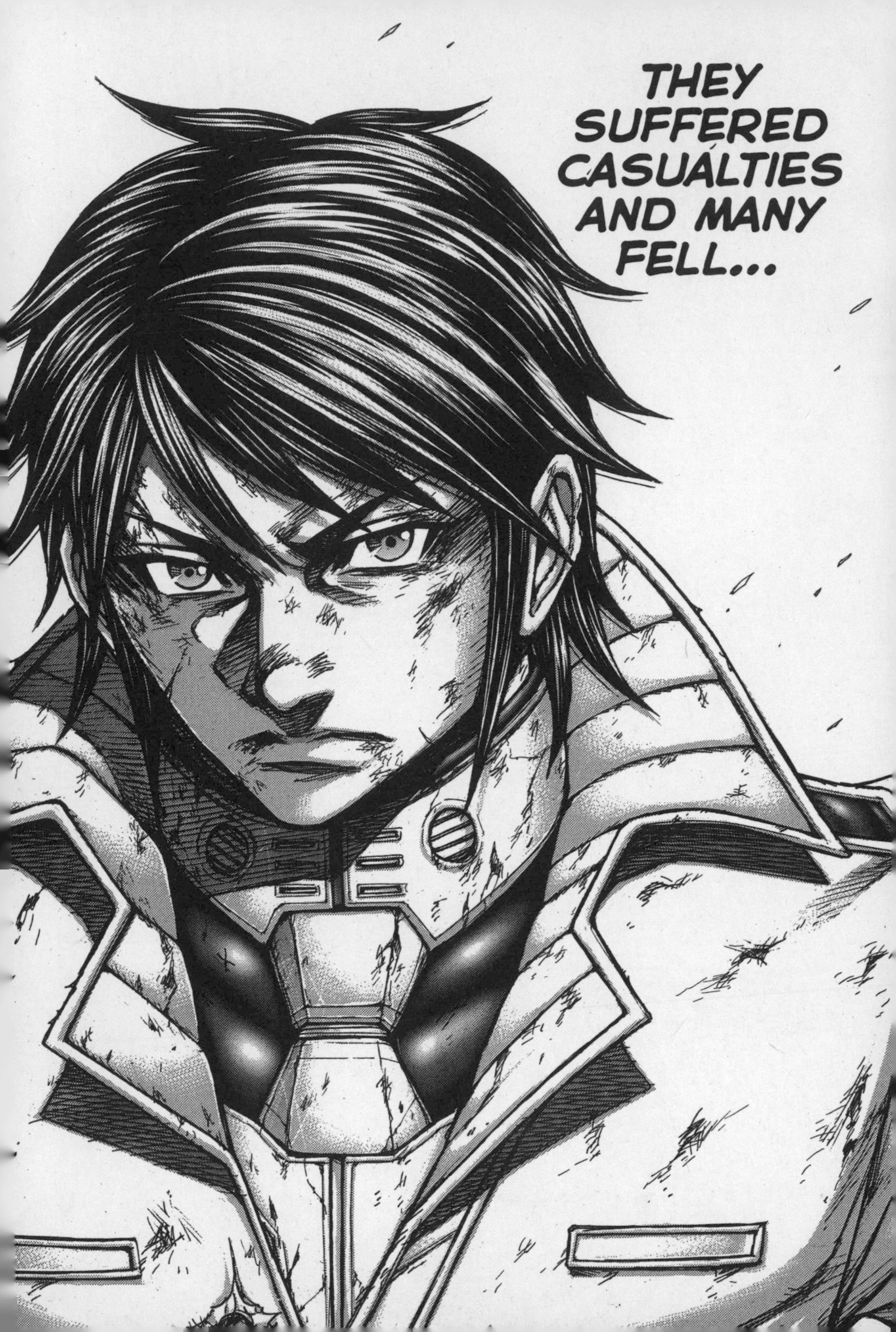
THEY SUFFERED CASUALTIES AND MANY FELL...

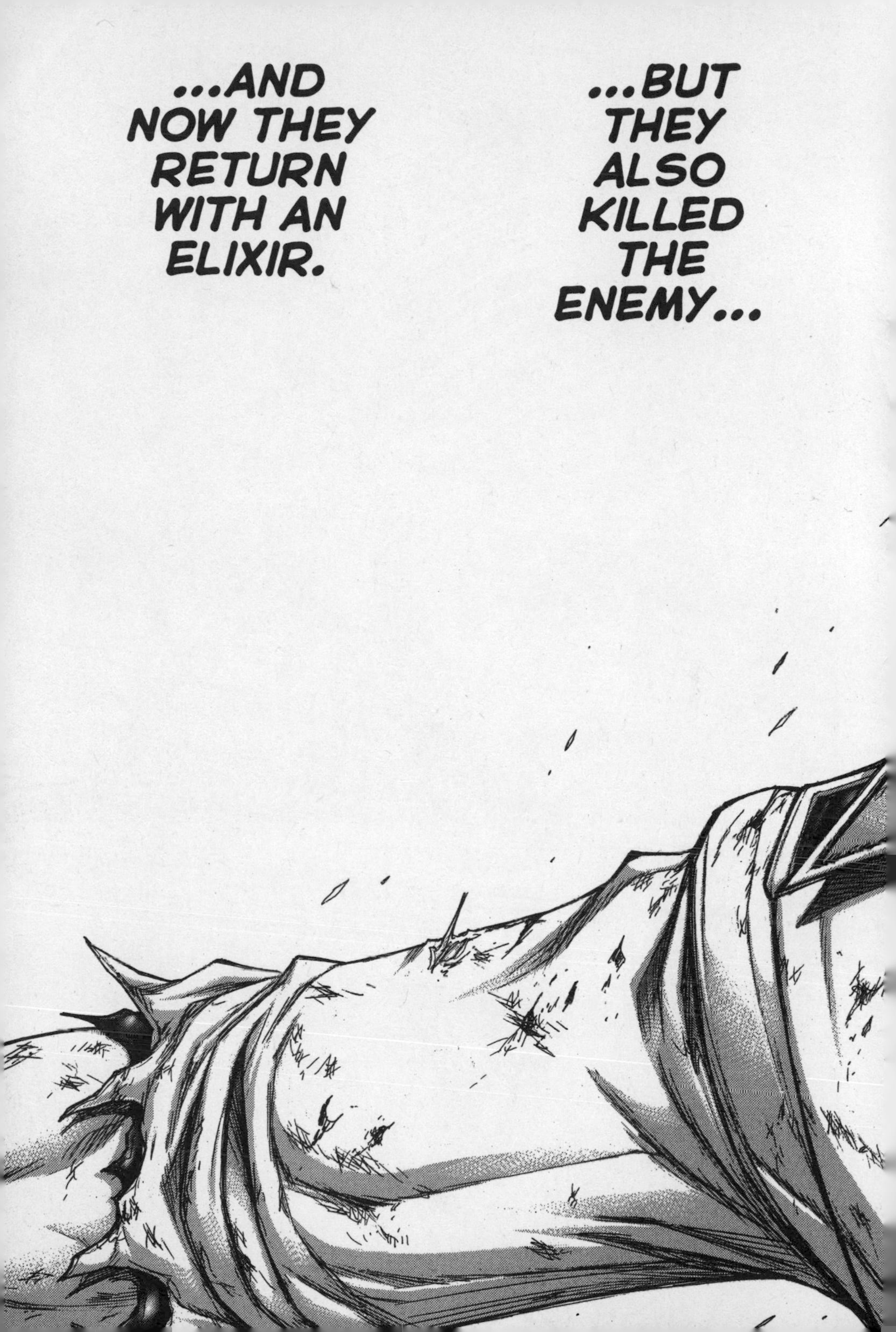
...BUT THEY ALSO KILLED THE ENEMY...
...AND NOW THEY RETURN WITH AN ELIXIR.

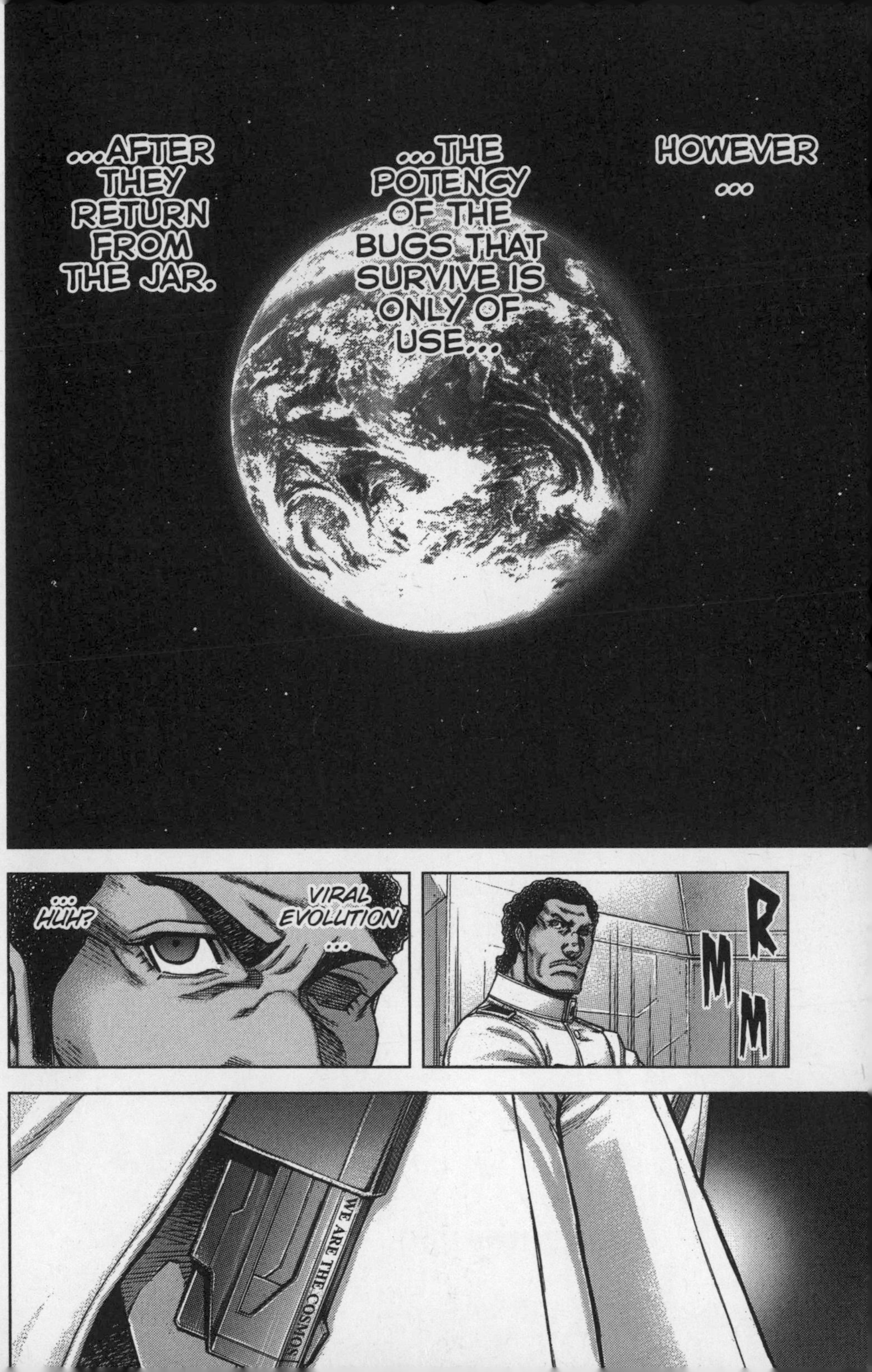
HOWEVER ...
...THE POTENCY OF THE BUGS THAT SURVIVE IS ONLY OF USE...
...AFTER THEY RETURN FROM THE JAR.
RMM
VIRAL EVOLUTION ...
... HUH?
WE ARE THE COSMOS

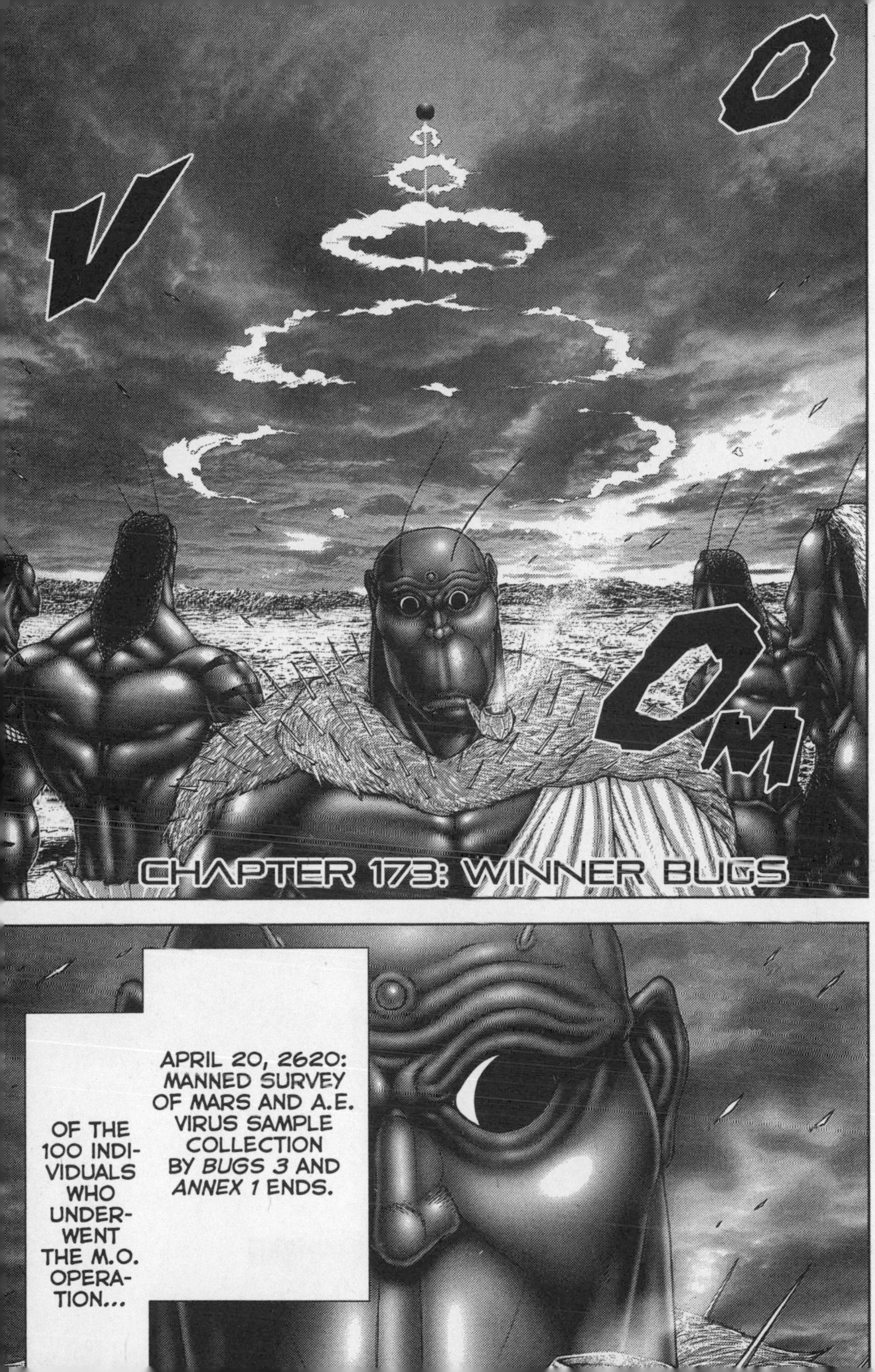
VOOM
CHAPTER 173: WINNER BUGS
APRIL 20, 2620: MANNED SURVEY OF MARS AND A.E. VIRUS SAMPLE COLLECTION BY *BUGS 3* AND *ANNEX 1* ENDS.
OF THE 100 INDIVIDUALS WHO UNDERWENT THE M.O. OPERATION...

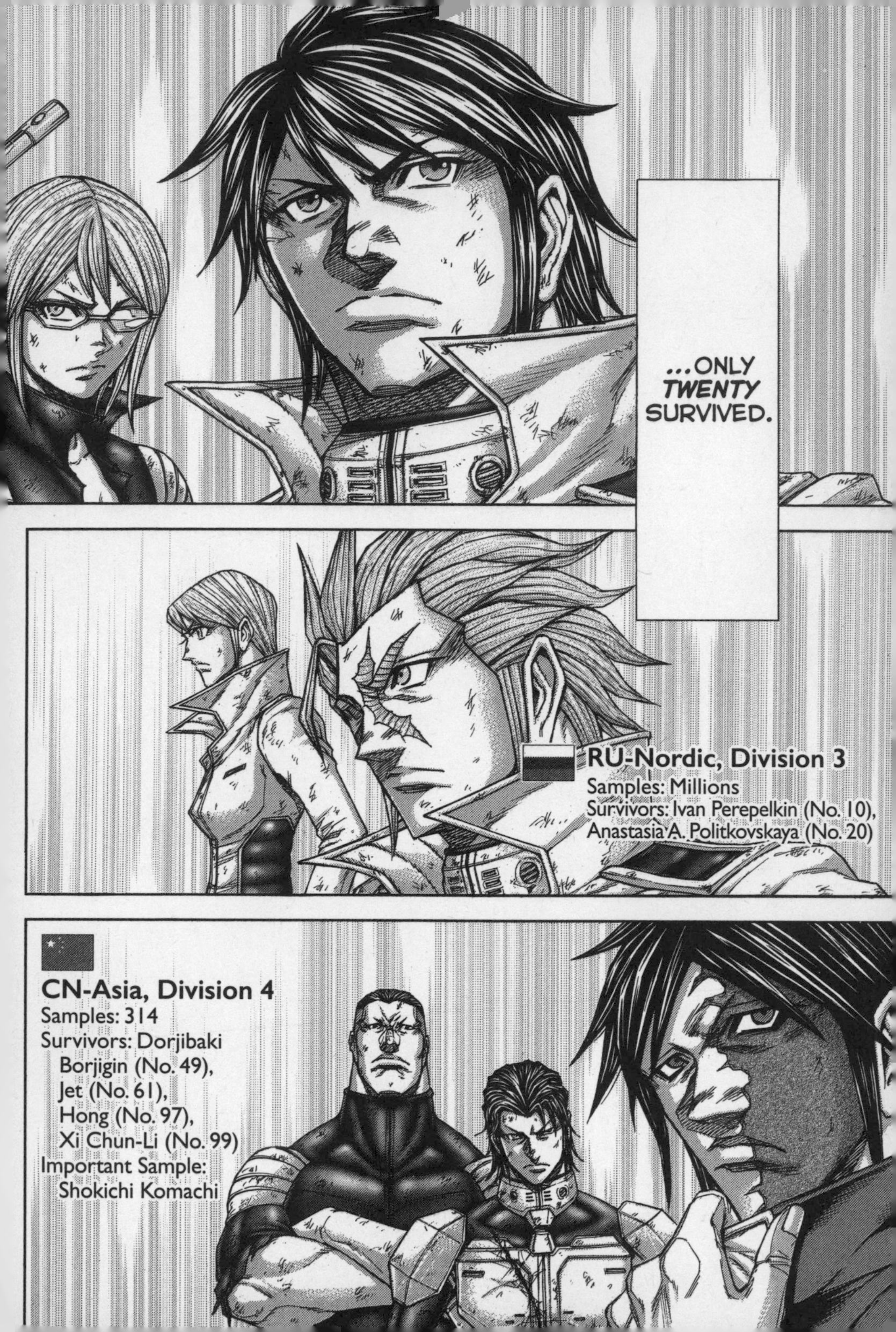
...ONLY TWENTY SURVIVED.
RU-Nordic, Division 3
Samples: Millions
Survivors: Ivan Perepelkin (No. 10), Anastasia A. Politkovskaya (No. 20)
CN-Asia, Division 4
Samples: 314
Survivors: Dorjibaki Borjigin (No. 49), Jet (No. 61), Hong (No. 97), Xi Chun-Li (No. 99)
Important Sample: Shokichi Komachi

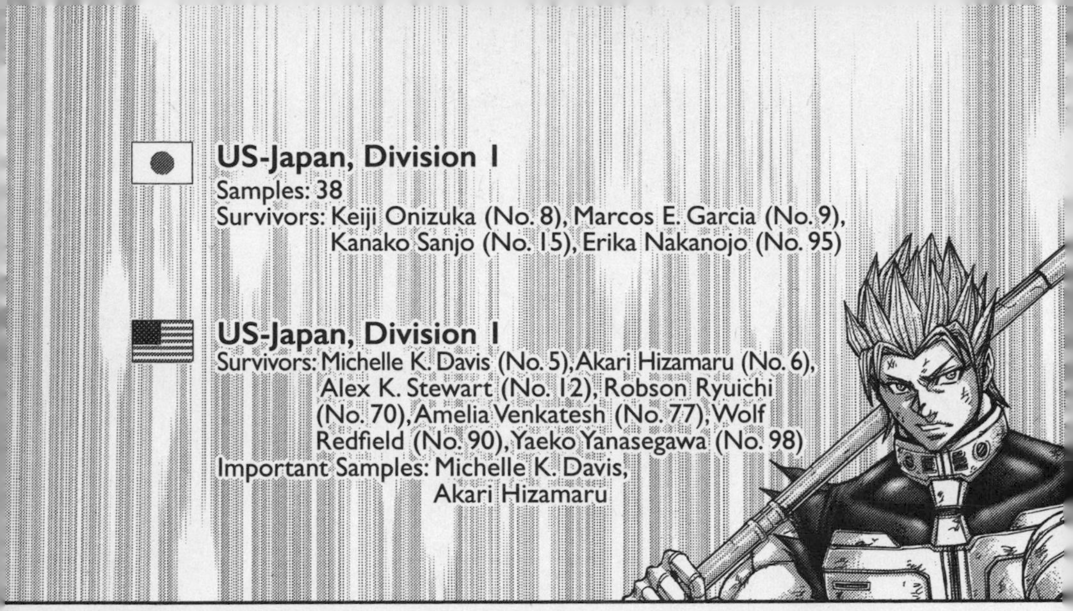
US-Japan, Division 1
Samples: 38
Survivors: Keiji Onizuka (No. 8), Marcos E. Garcia (No. 9), Kanako Sanjo (No. 15), Erika Nakanojo (No. 95)
US-Japan, Division 1
Survivors: Michelle K. Davis (No. 5), Akari Hizamaru (No. 6), Alex K. Stewart (No. 12), Robson Ryuichi (No. 70), Amelia Venkatesh (No. 77), Wolf Redfield (No. 90), Yaeko Yanasegawa (No. 98)
Important Samples: Michelle K. Davis, Akari Hizamaru

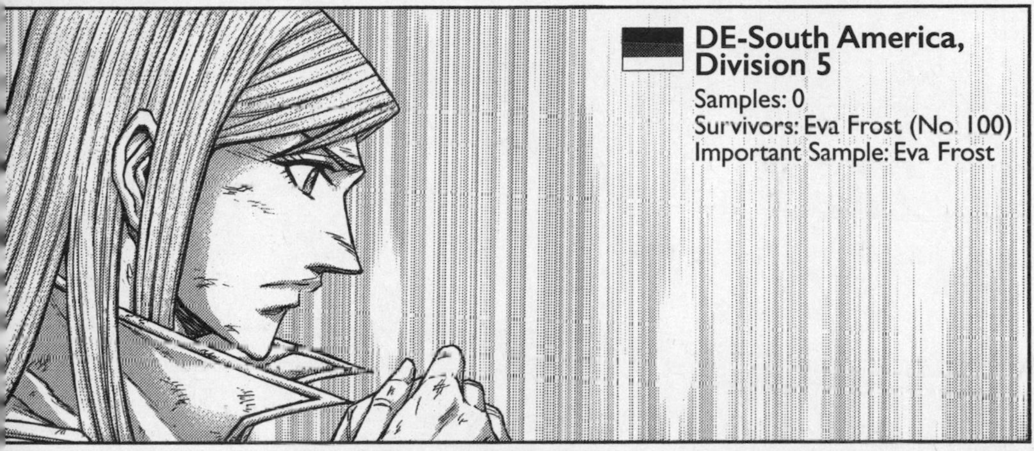
DE-South America, Division 5
Samples: 0
Survivors: Eva Frost (No. 100)
Important Sample: Eva Frost

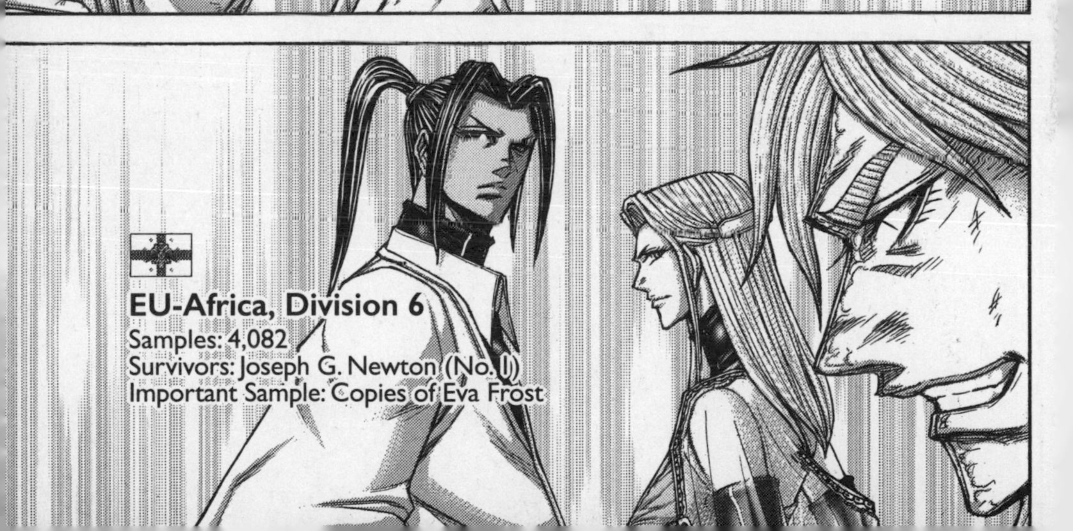
EU-Africa, Division 6
Samples: 4,082
Survivors: Joseph G. Newton (No. 1)
Important Sample: Copies of Eva Frost

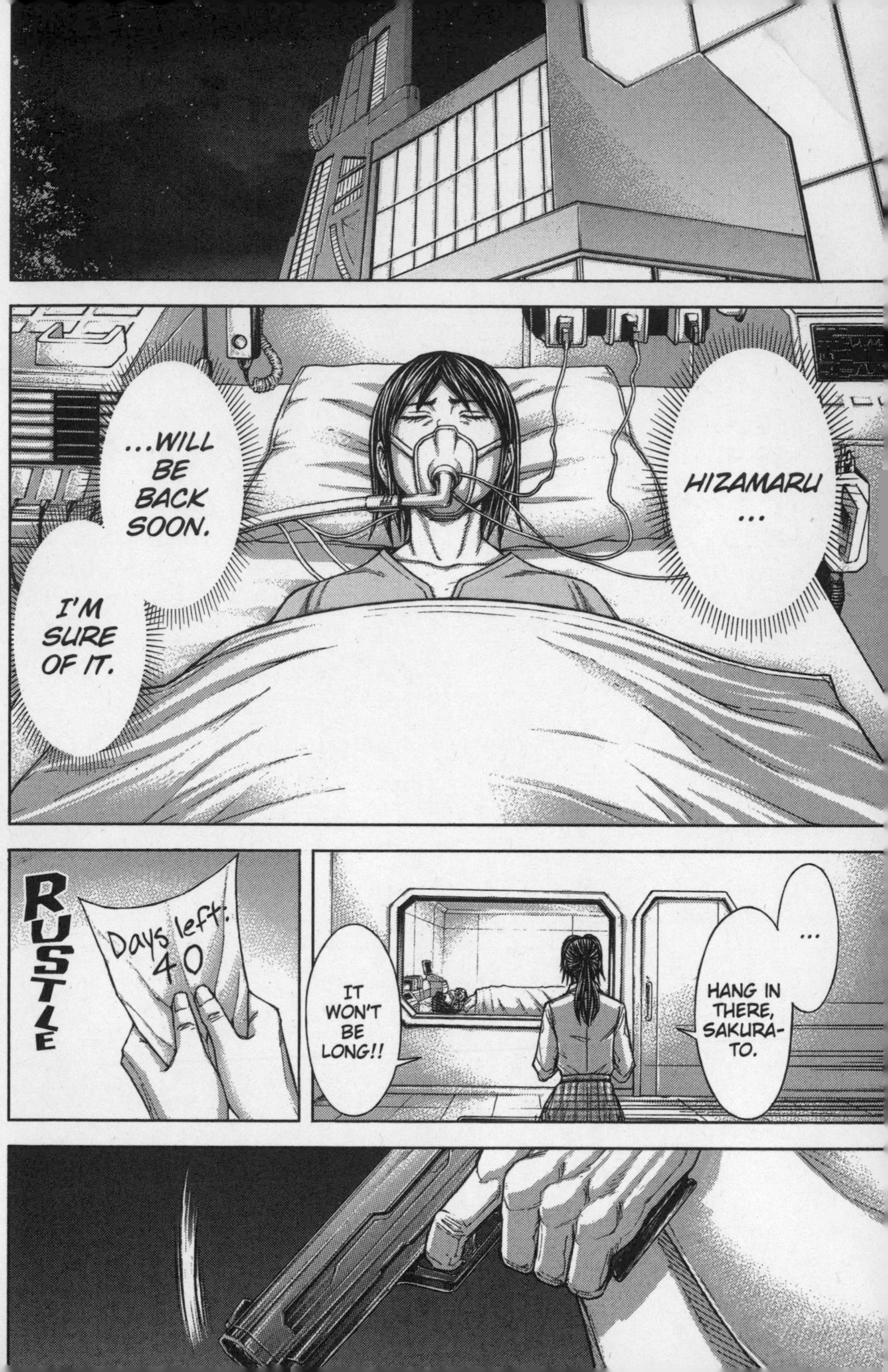
HIZAMARU ...
...WILL BE BACK SOON.
I'M SURE OF IT.
...
HANG IN THERE, SAKURA-TO.
IT WON'T BE LONG!!
RUSTLE
Days left: 40

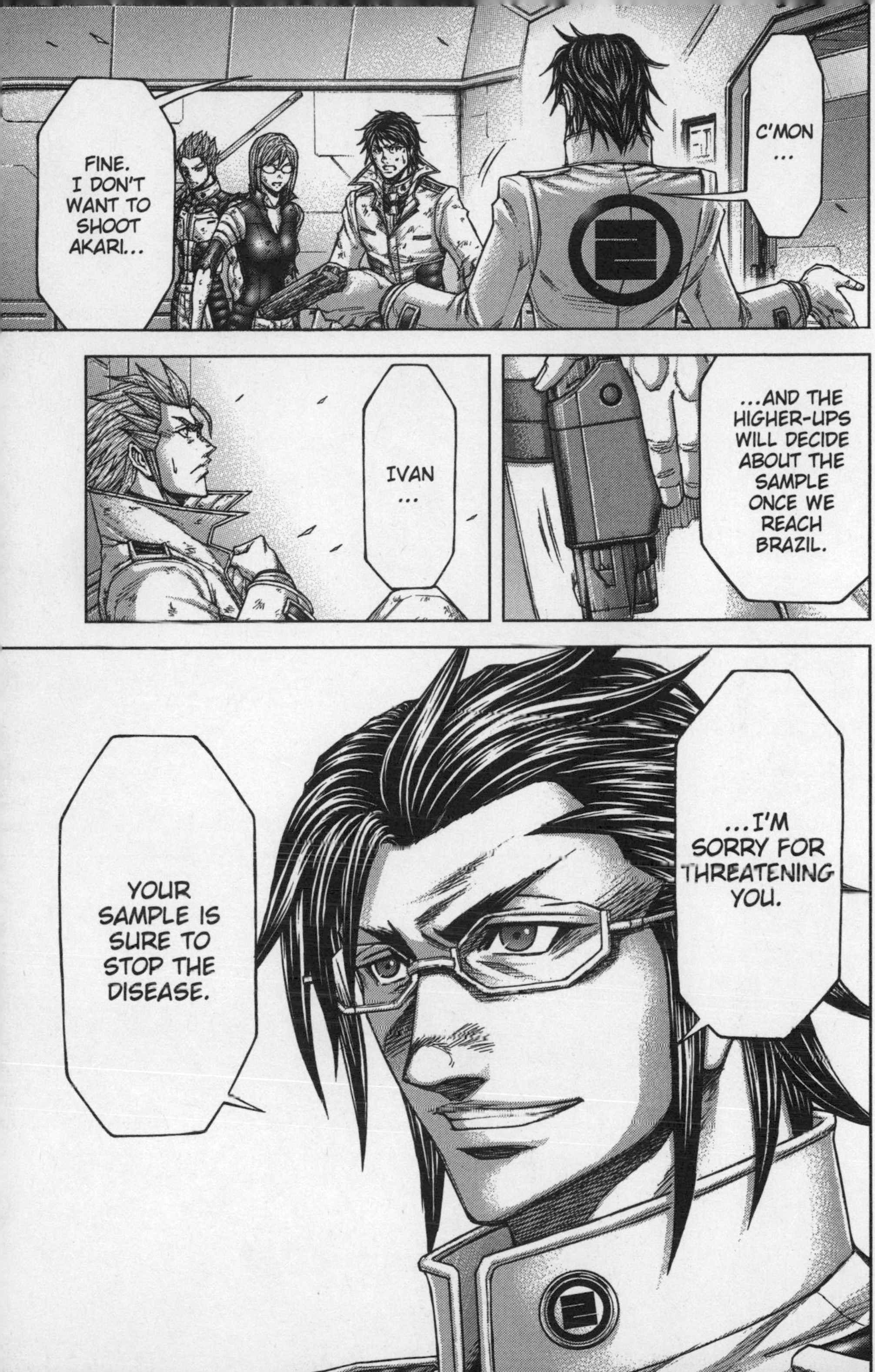
C'MON ...
FINE. I DON'T WANT TO SHOOT AKARI...
...AND THE HIGHER-UPS WILL DECIDE ABOUT THE SAMPLE ONCE WE REACH BRAZIL.
IVAN ...
...I'M SORRY FOR THREATENING YOU.
YOUR SAMPLE IS SURE TO STOP THE DISEASE.

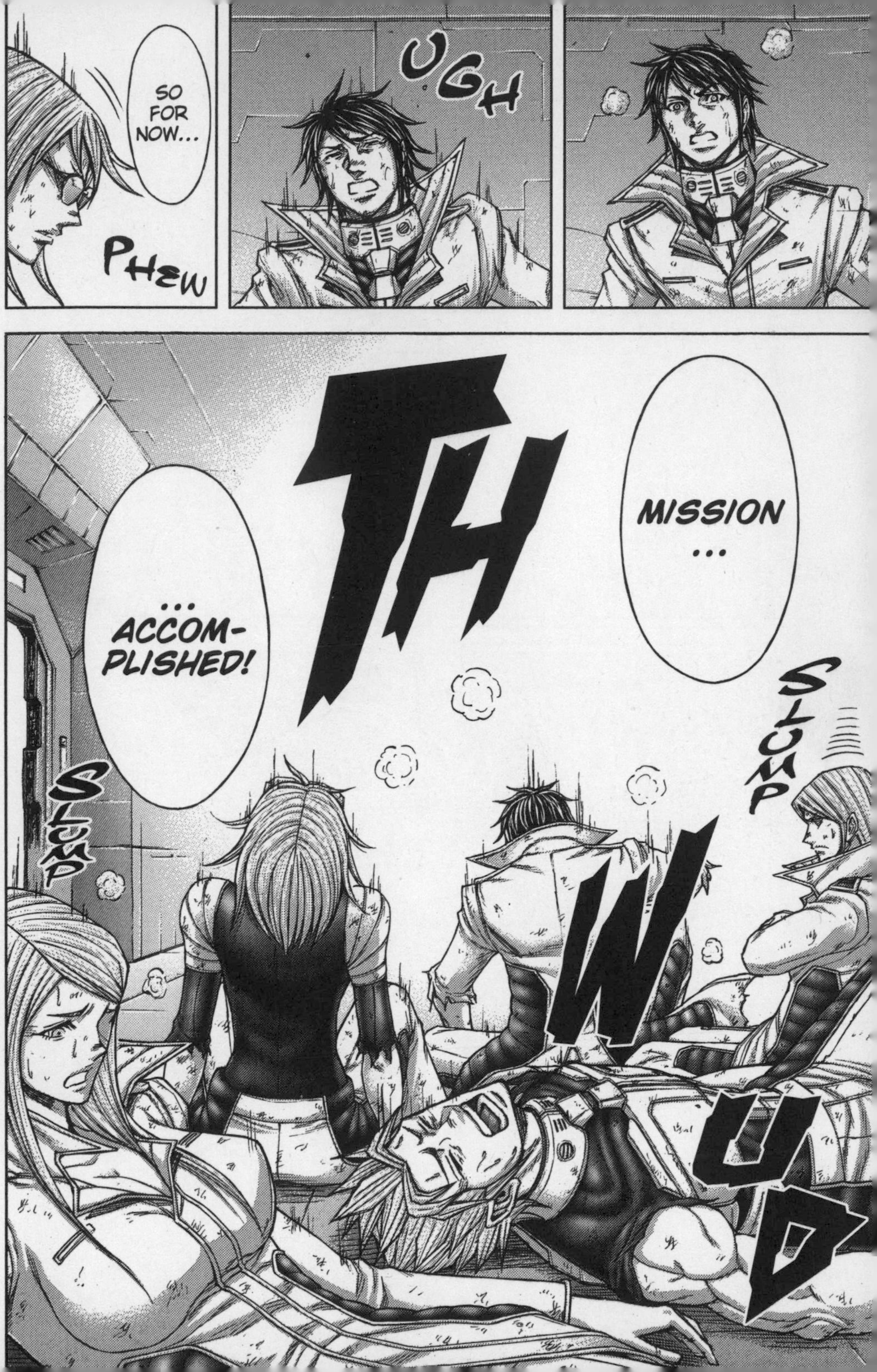
UGH
SO FOR NOW...
PHEW
MISSION ...
SLUMP
... ACCOM-PLISHED!
THWUD
SLUMP

...TO HEAR ABOUT...

I WAS SORRY...

AKARI...

...YURIKO.

...

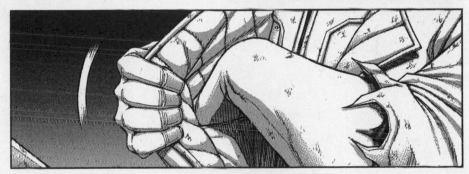

YURIKO

...

...

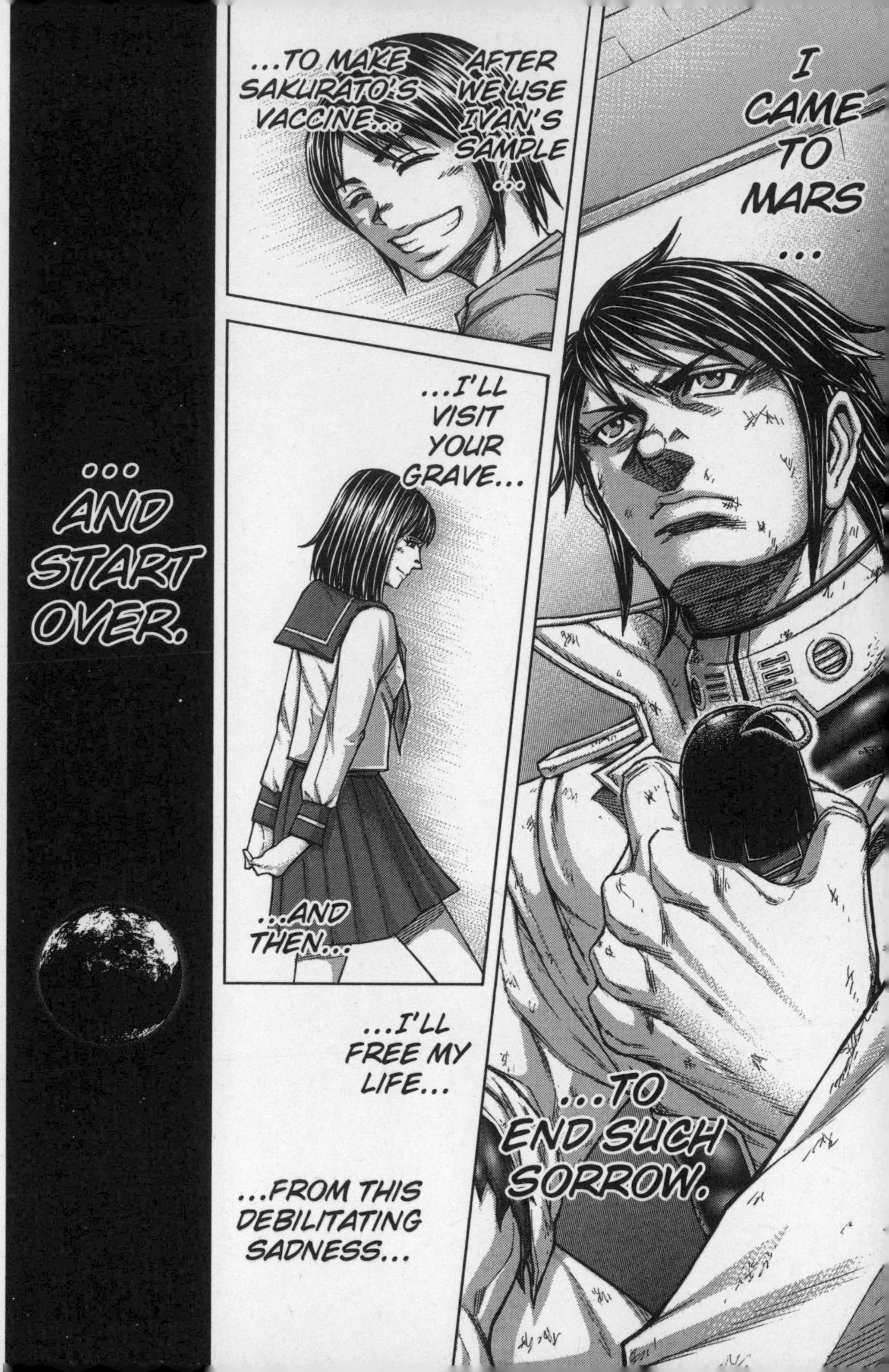
I CAME TO MARS...
...TO END SUCH SORROW.
AFTER WE USE IVAN'S SAMPLE...
...TO MAKE SAKURATO'S VACCINE...
...I'LL VISIT YOUR GRAVE...
...AND THEN...
...I'LL FREE MY LIFE...
...FROM THIS DEBILITATING SADNESS...
...AND START OVER.

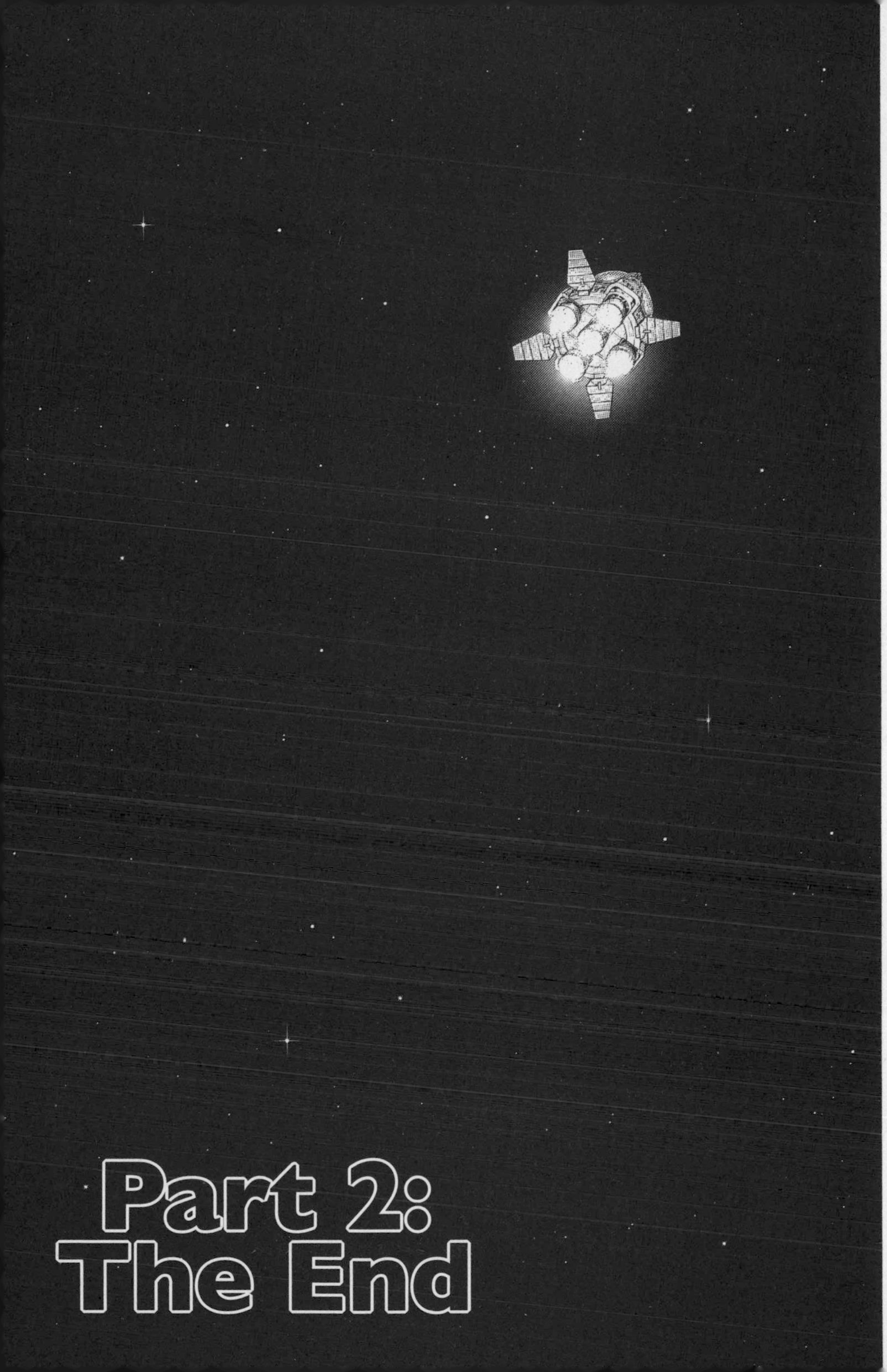
Part 2:
The End

TERRAFORMARS

STORY BY
YU SASUGA

ART BY
KENICHI TACHIBANA

MAIN STAFF
TAKAYUKI TASAKA
MASANORI DOI
KAZUKI KAWABATA
KOTA SANNOMIYA
YU SATO

EDITOR
MASATO SHINDO
(WEEKLY YOUNG JUMP)

REFERENCE

May R. Berenbaum
"The Earwig's Tail: A Modern Bestiary of
Multi-legged Legends"
(2009)

Frank Ryan
"Virolution"
(2009)

Dougal Dixon, John Adams
"The Future is Wild: A Natural History of the
Future"
(2002)

Michael J. Sandel
"The Case Against Perfection: Ethics in the Age of
Genetic Engineering"
(2009)

Konrad Lorenz
"Das Sogenannte Böse - Zur Naturgeschichte der
Aggression"
(1979)

Robin Baker
"Sperm Wars: The Evolutionary Logic of
Love and Lust"
(1997)

Helen Fisher
"Why We Love: The Nature and Chemistry of
Romantic Love"
(2004)

Rachel Herz
"That's Disgusting: Unraveling the Mysteries of
Repulsion"
(2012)

Ken Ellingwood
"Hard Line: Life and Death on the US-Mexico
Border"
(2005)

Lester Grau and Michael Gress
"The Red Army's Do-it-Yourself, Nazi-Bashing
Guerrilla Warfare Manual:
The Partizan's Handbook, Updated and Revised Edition, 1943"
(2011)

Chris Crudelli (translation: Yol" Kawanari, Furu Komu)
Martial Arts and Fighting Skills from
Around the World
(2010)

Richard Fortey
"Fossils: The History of Life"
(2009)

M. et al. Panoff
"L'Ethnologie et Son Owbre"
(1968)

Robert Temple
"The Sirius Mystery: New Scientific Evidence of
Alien Contact 5,000 Years Ago"
(1998)

SPECIAL THANKS

Munetoshi Maruyama
(The Kyushu University Museum)

Kosuke Fujishima
(Researcher at ELSI, Tokyo Institute of Technology and NASA Ames Research Center)

http://youngjump.jp/terraformars/
TERRA FORMARS, 2016

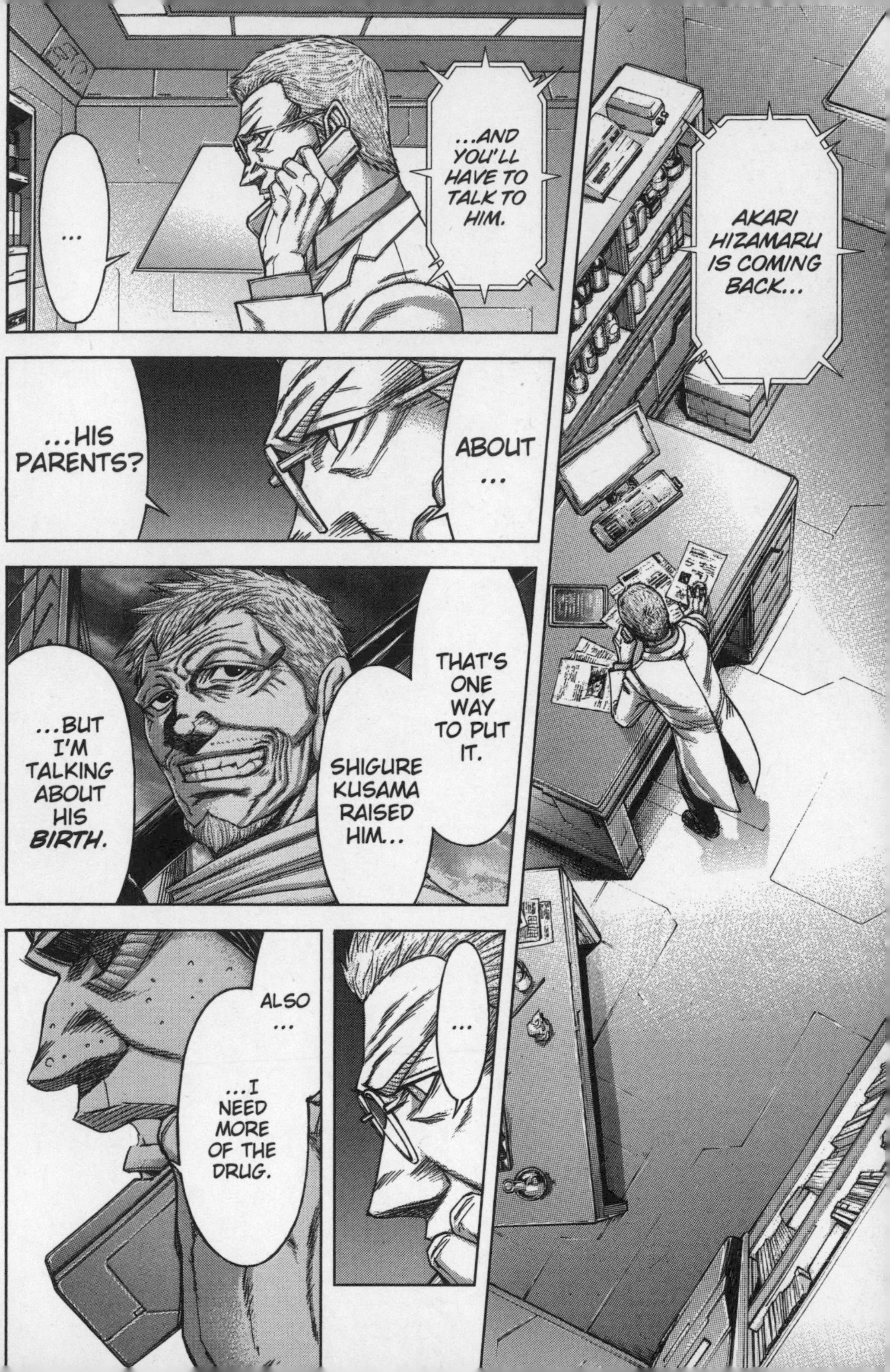
AKARI HIZAMARU IS COMING BACK...
...AND YOU'LL HAVE TO TALK TO HIM.
...
ABOUT ...
...HIS PARENTS?
THAT'S ONE WAY TO PUT IT.
SHIGURE KUSAMA RAISED HIM...
...BUT I'M TALKING ABOUT HIS *BIRTH*.
...
ALSO ...
...I NEED MORE OF THE DRUG.

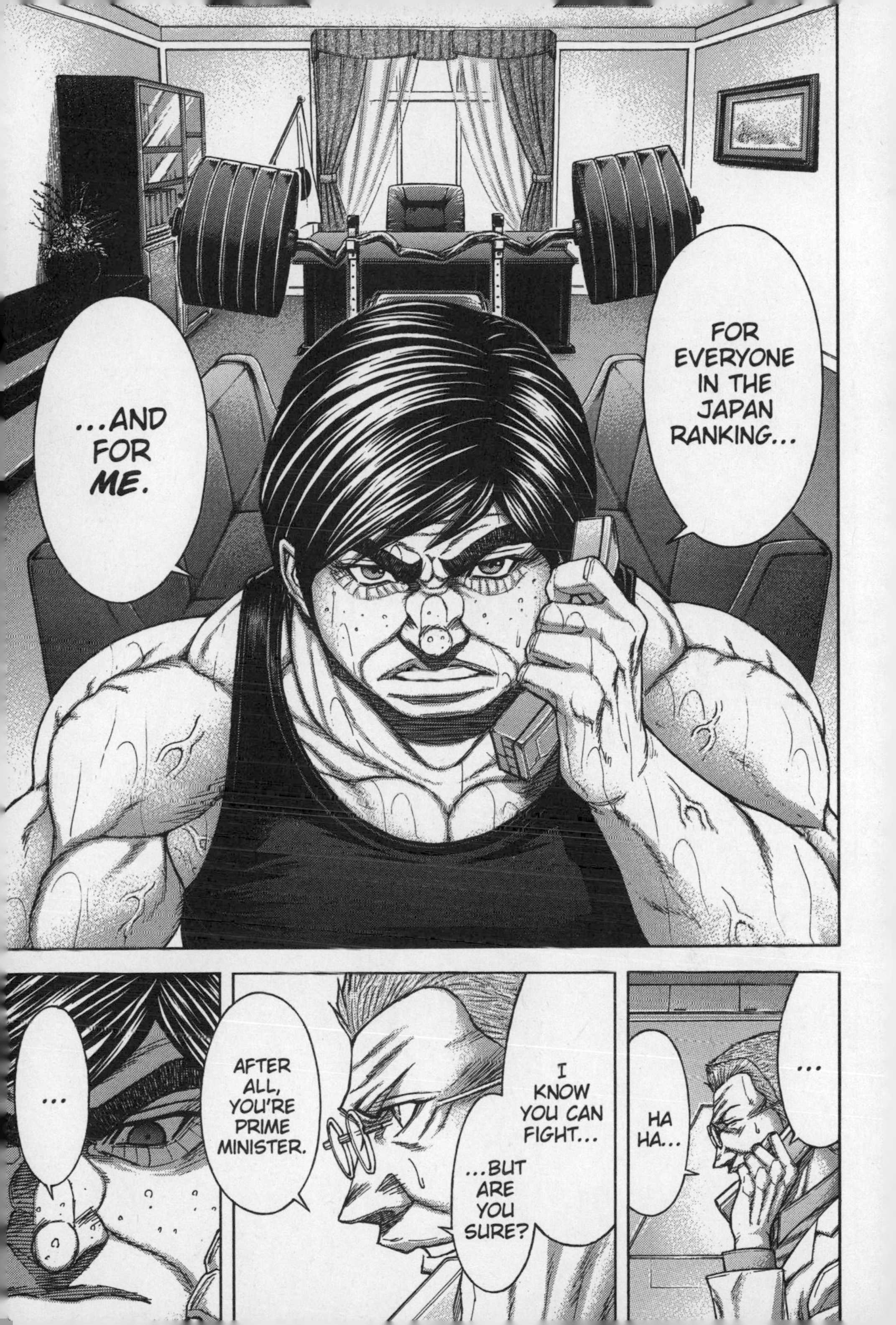
FOR EVERYONE IN THE JAPAN RANKING...
...AND FOR ME.
...
HA HA...
I KNOW YOU CAN FIGHT...
...BUT ARE YOU SURE?
AFTER ALL, YOU'RE PRIME MINISTER.
...

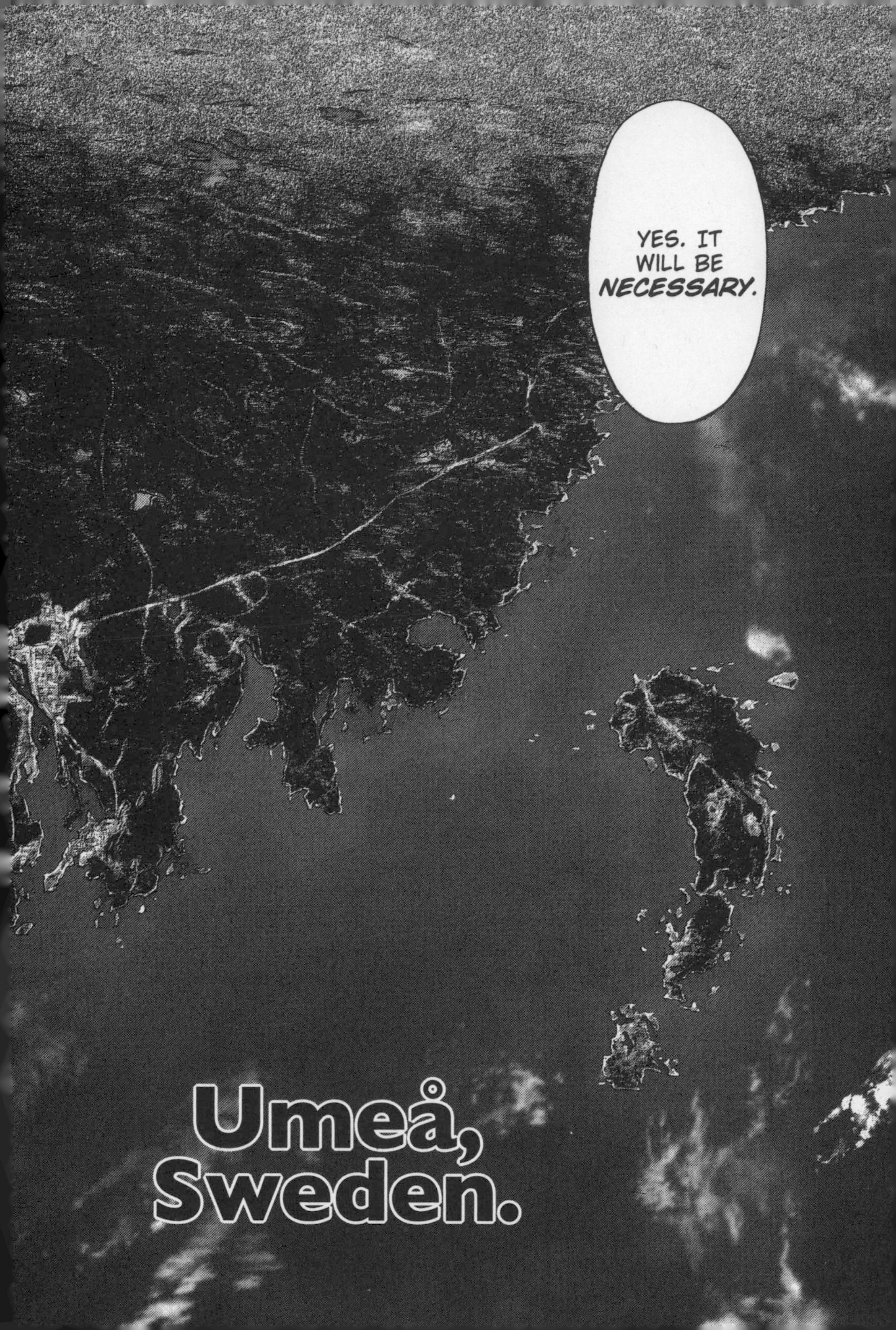
YES. IT WILL BE NECESSARY.
Umeå, Sweden.

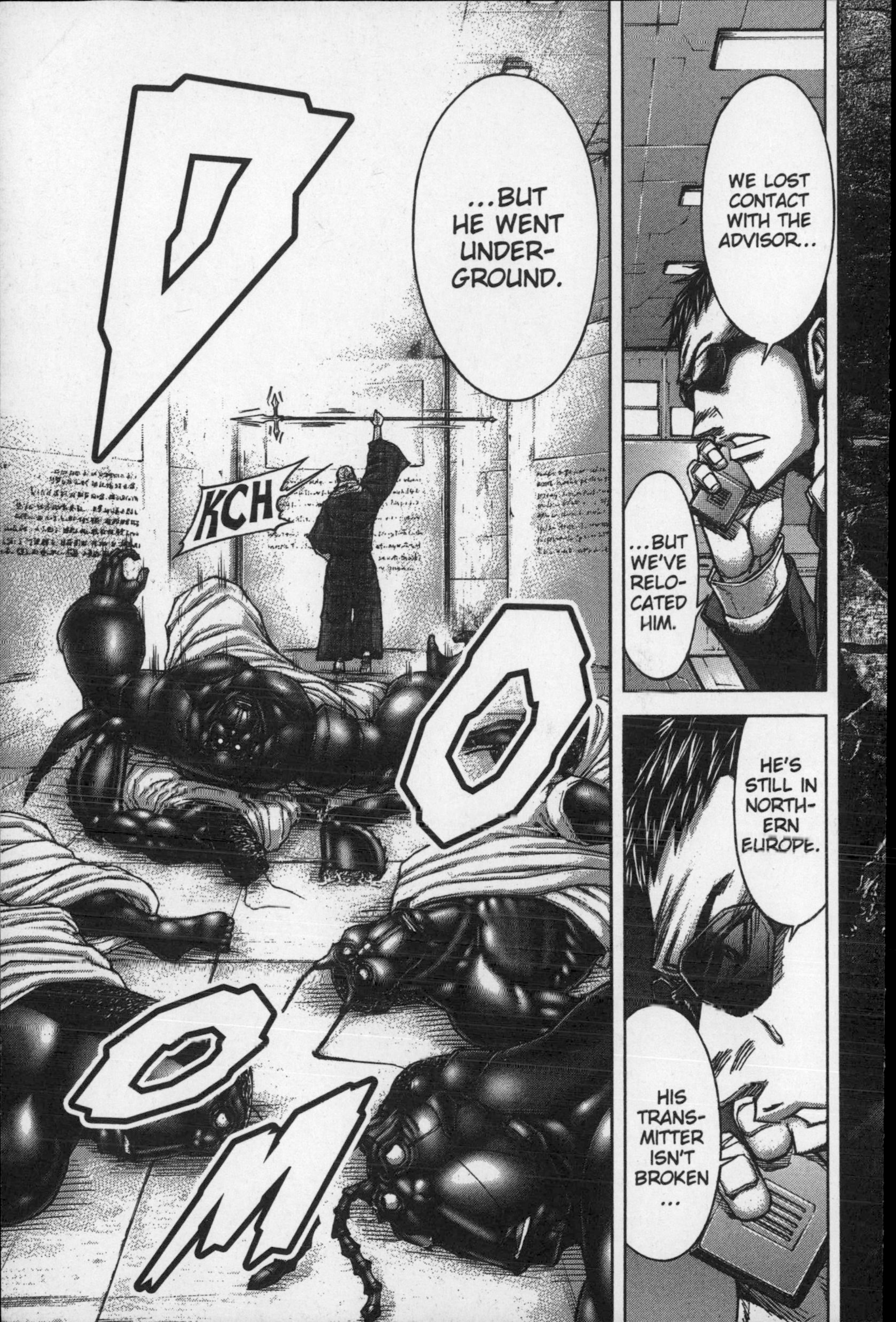
WE LOST CONTACT WITH THE ADVISOR...
...BUT WE'VE RELOCATED HIM.
HE'S STILL IN NORTHERN EUROPE.
HIS TRANSMITTER ISN'T BROKEN...
...BUT HE WENT UNDERGROUND.
KCH
DOOM

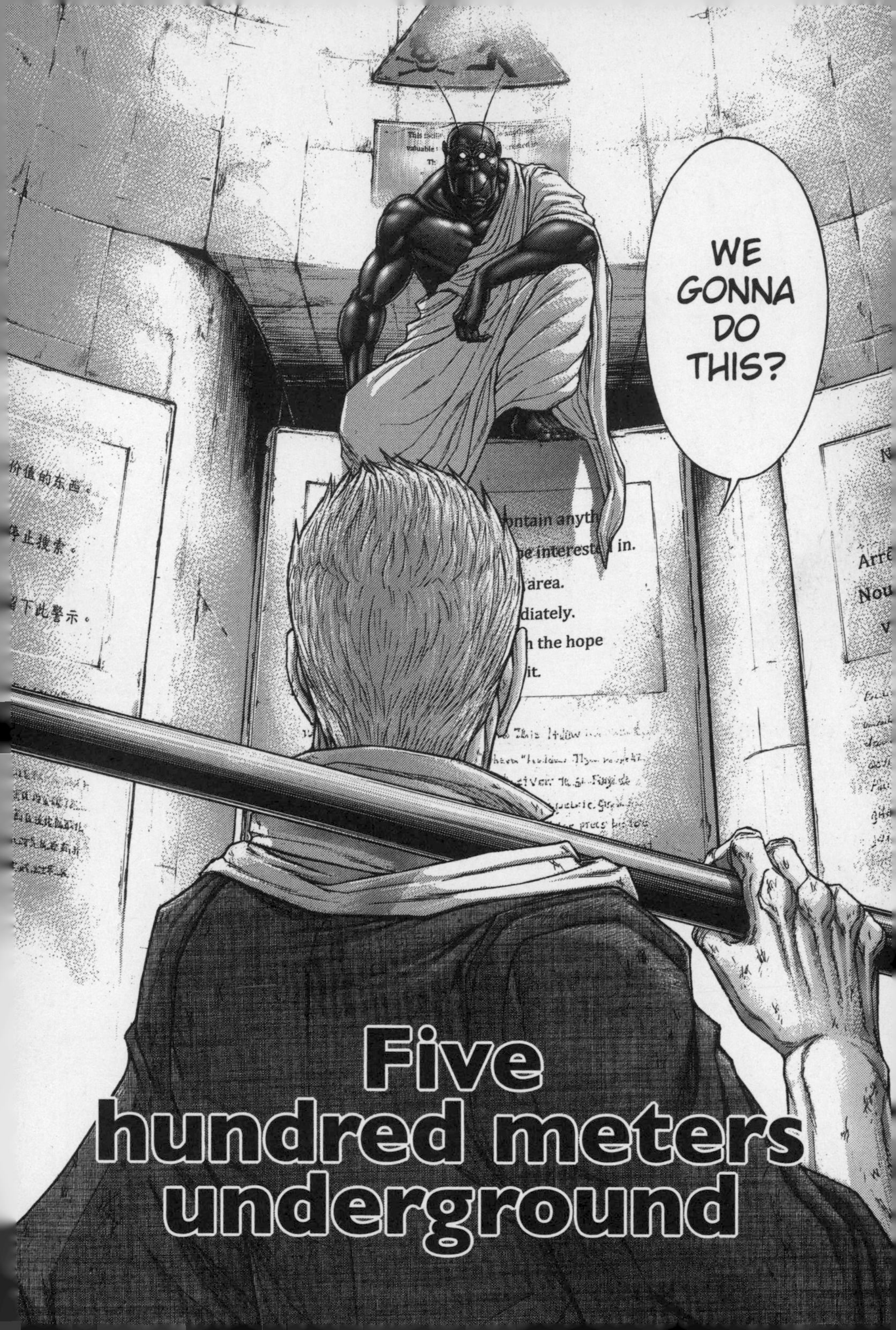
WE GONNA DO THIS?
Five hundred meters underground

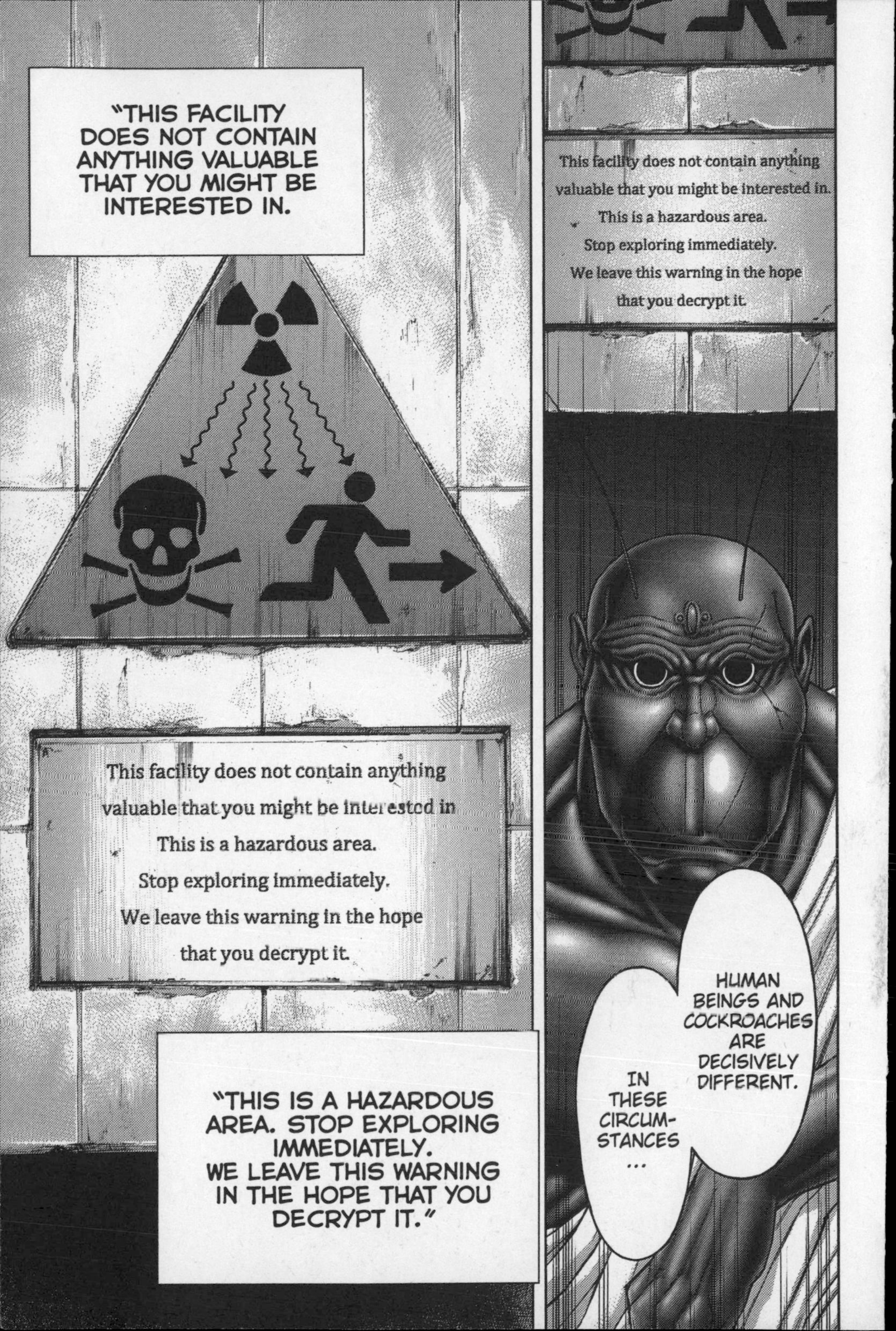
This facility does not contain anything valuable that you might be interested in. This is a hazardous area. Stop exploring immediately. We leave this warning in the hope that you decrypt it.
HUMAN BEINGS AND COCKROACHES ARE DECISIVELY DIFFERENT.
IN THESE CIRCUM-STANCES ...
"THIS FACILITY DOES NOT CONTAIN ANYTHING VALUABLE THAT YOU MIGHT BE INTERESTED IN.
This facility does not contain anything valuable that you might be interested in This is a hazardous area. Stop exploring immediately. We leave this warning in the hope that you decrypt it.
"THIS IS A HAZARDOUS AREA. STOP EXPLORING IMMEDIATELY. WE LEAVE THIS WARNING IN THE HOPE THAT YOU DECRYPT IT."

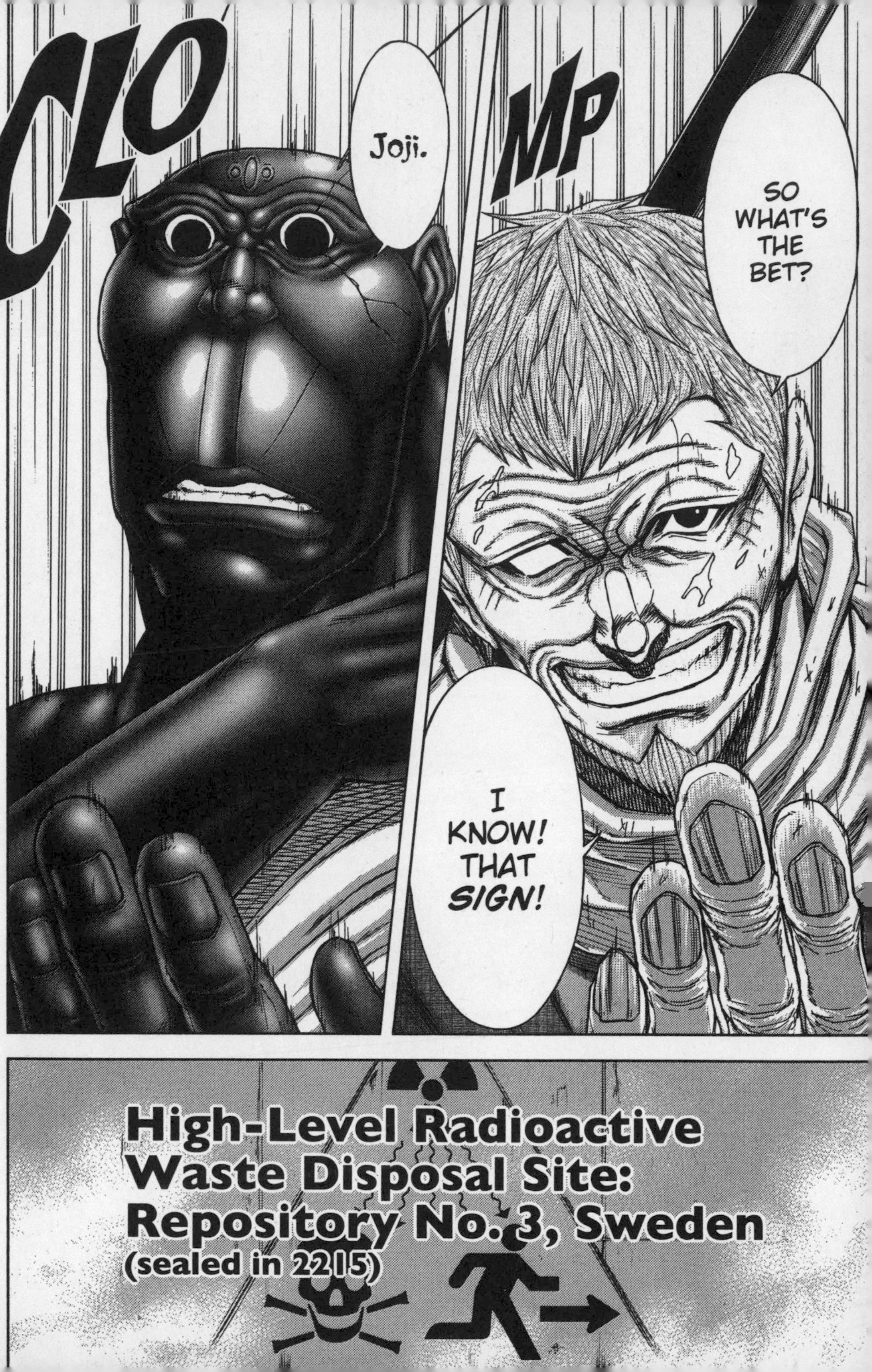
CLOMP
SO WHAT'S THE BET?
I KNOW! THAT *SIGN*!
Joji.
High-Level Radioactive Waste Disposal Site: Repository No. 3, Sweden
(sealed in 2215)

RMM
RMM
RMM
...
VIRAL EVOLUTION...
VIRAL EVOLUTION IS WHEN A VIRUS SPREADS AND ONLY ORGANISMS WITH MUTATED GENES SURVIVE.
BUT DOES THAT EXPLAIN ...
...THE A.E. VIRUS AND THE TERRAFORMARS?
IS ...
... THEORY 2...
... CORRECT?
CONGRATULATIONS ON YOUR RELEASE ...
...BUT COME BACK FOR CHECKUPS!
OKAY, DOCTOR.
THAT'S THE BOY?
YES.
HE'S TRULY A MIRACLE.

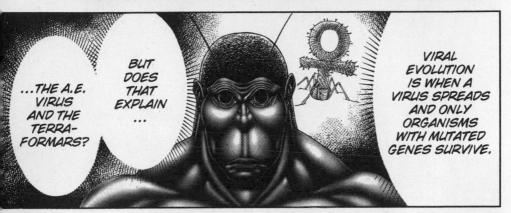

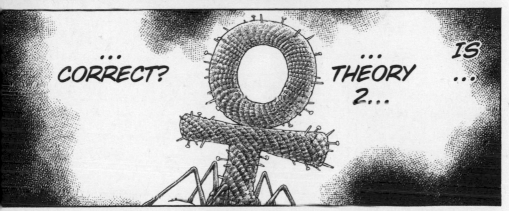

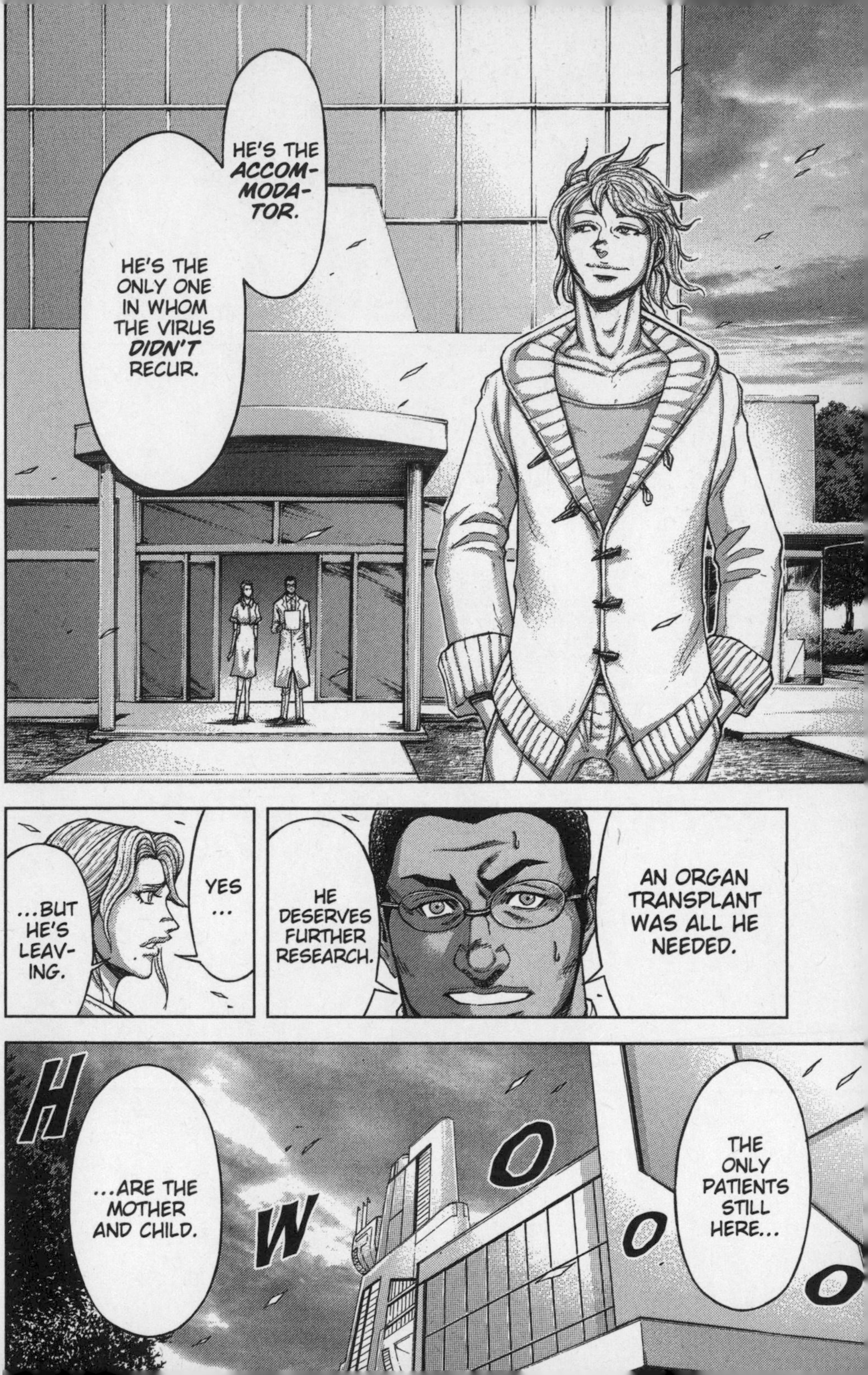

HE'S THE *ACCOMMODATOR.*
HE'S THE ONLY ONE IN WHOM THE VIRUS *DIDN'T* RECUR.
AN ORGAN TRANSPLANT WAS ALL HE NEEDED.
HE DESERVES FURTHER RESEARCH.
YES...
...BUT HE'S LEAVING.
THE ONLY PATIENTS STILL HERE...
WHOOOO
...ARE THE MOTHER AND CHILD.

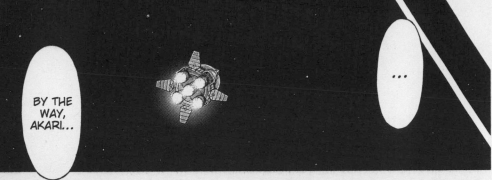

BY THE WAY, AKARI...

...

...

...YOUR FIRST TIME TOO?

WAS THAT...

HUH?

F-FIRST TIME?

HM?

OH, UM...

...

TO DO WHAT?

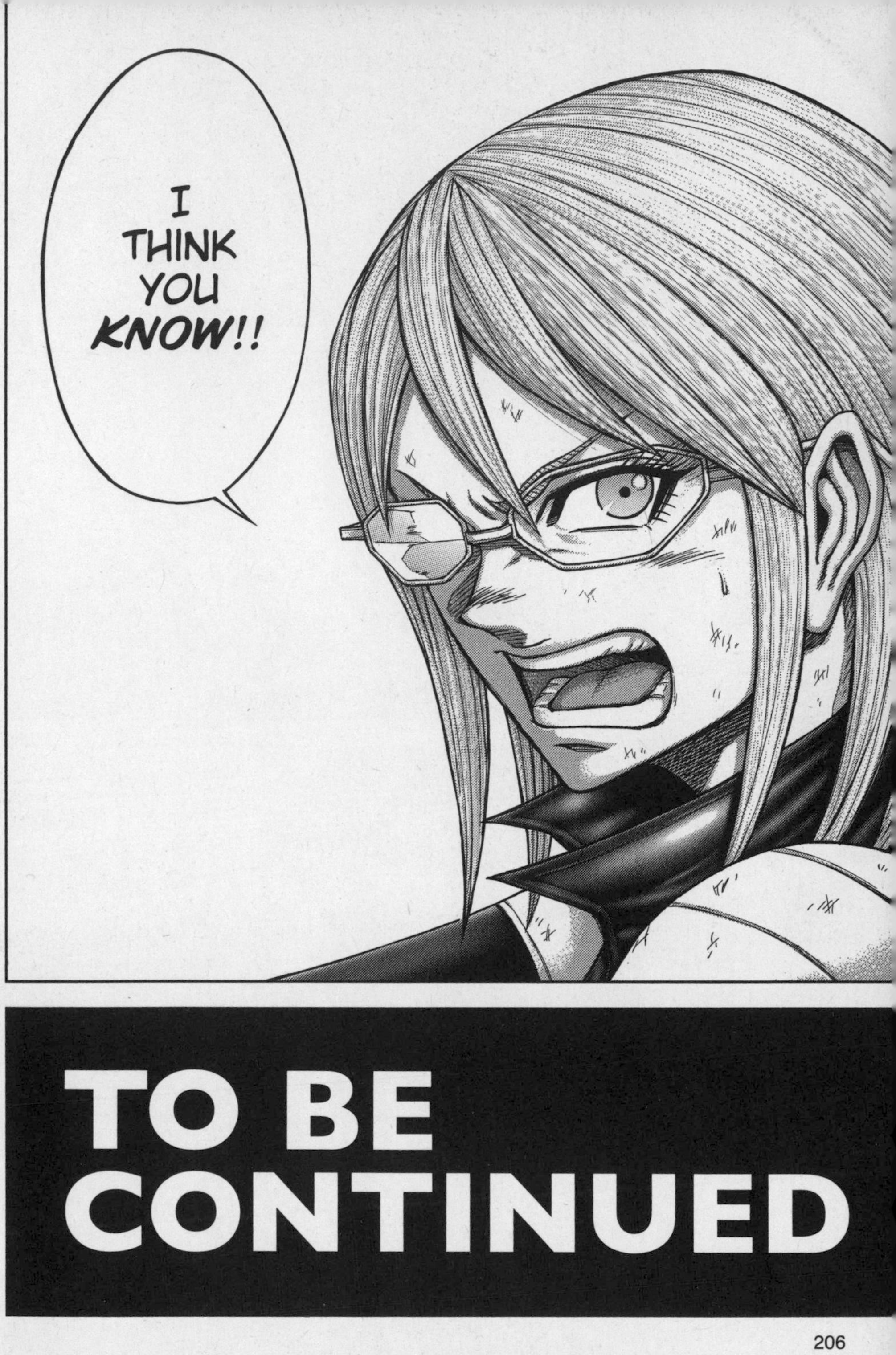
I THINK YOU KNOW!!

TO BE CONTINUED

TERRA FORMARS

Terra Formars Character Review

BIRTH OF a SUPERBAND!

We've got six pages to fill!

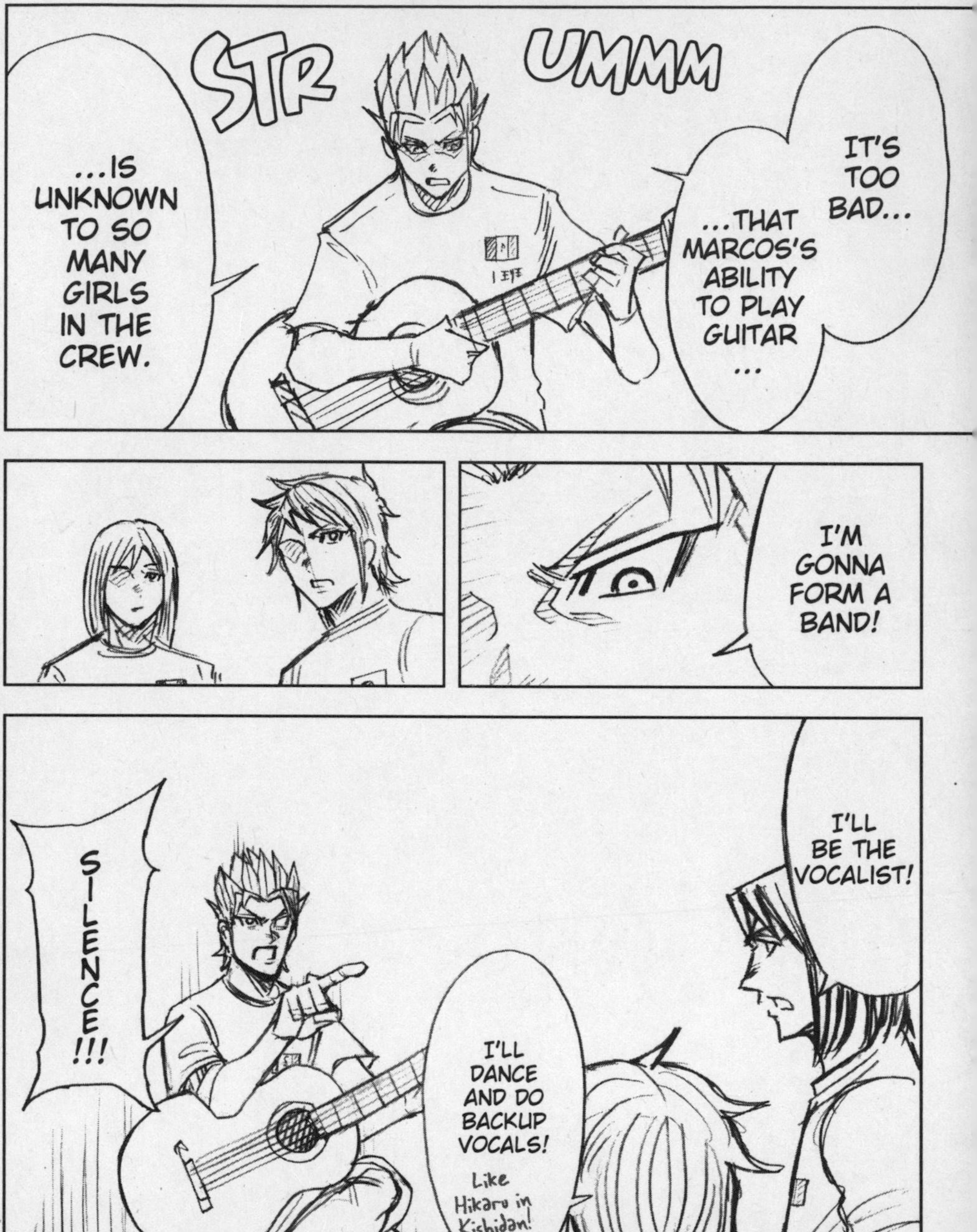

IT'S TOO BAD...
...THAT MARCOS'S ABILITY TO PLAY GUITAR ...
STRUMMM
...IS UNKNOWN TO SO MANY GIRLS IN THE CREW.
I'M GONNA FORM A BAND!
I'LL BE THE VOCALIST!
I'LL DANCE AND DO BACKUP VOCALS!
Like Hikaru in Kishidan!
SILENCE!!!

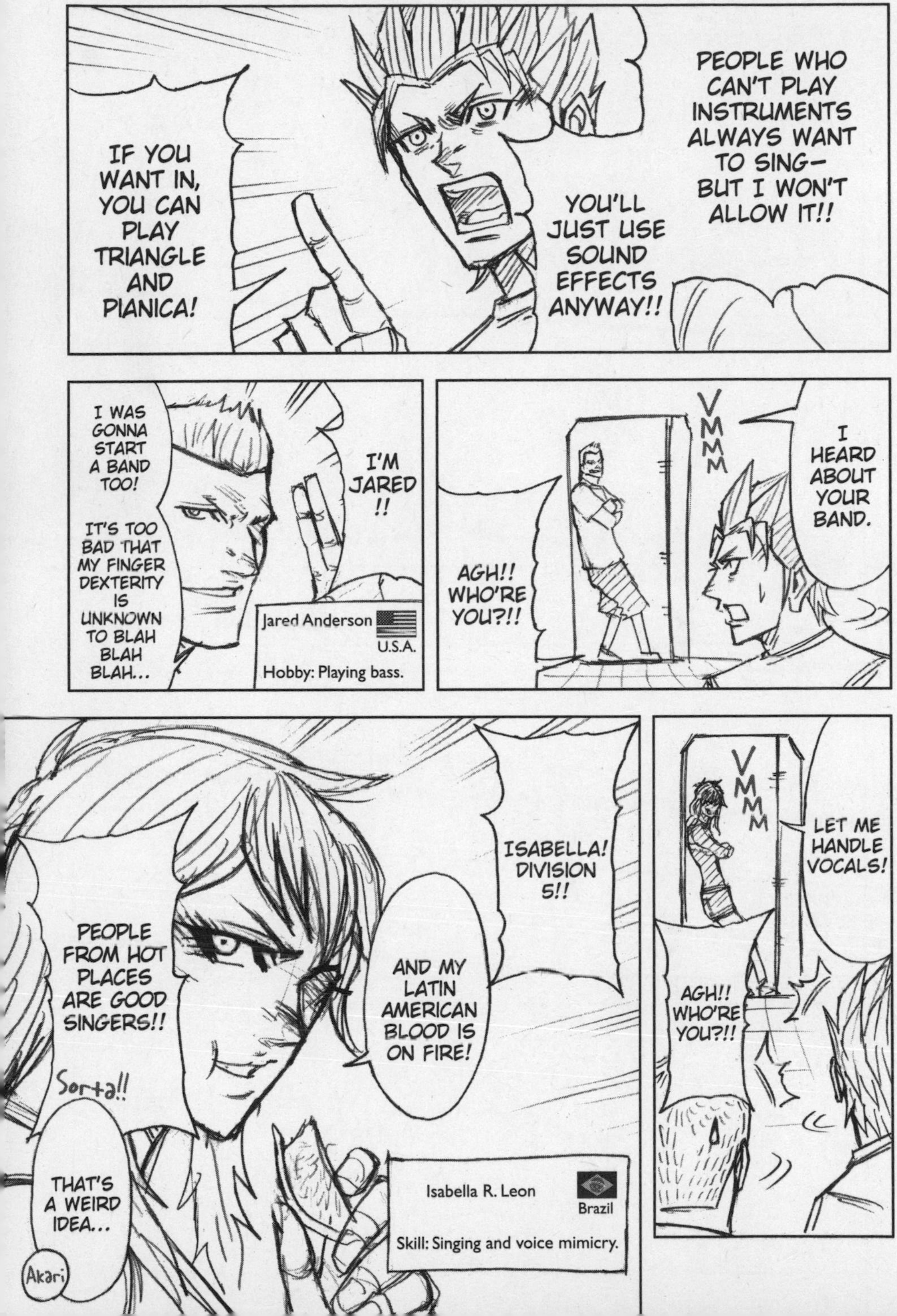

PEOPLE WHO CAN'T PLAY INSTRUMENTS ALWAYS WANT TO SING— BUT I WON'T ALLOW IT!!
YOU'LL JUST USE SOUND EFFECTS ANYWAY!!
IF YOU WANT IN, YOU CAN PLAY TRIANGLE AND PIANICA!
I HEARD ABOUT YOUR BAND.
VMMM
AGH!! WHO'RE YOU?!!
I'M JARED!!
I WAS GONNA START A BAND TOO!
IT'S TOO BAD THAT MY FINGER DEXTERITY IS UNKNOWN TO BLAH BLAH BLAH...
Jared Anderson
U.S.A.
Hobby: Playing bass.
LET ME HANDLE VOCALS!
VMMM
AGH!! WHO'RE YOU?!!
ISABELLA! DIVISION 5!!
AND MY LATIN AMERICAN BLOOD IS ON FIRE!
PEOPLE FROM HOT PLACES ARE GOOD SINGERS!!
Isabella R. Leon
Brazil
Skill: Singing and voice mimicry.
Sorta!!
THAT'S A WEIRD IDEA...
Akari

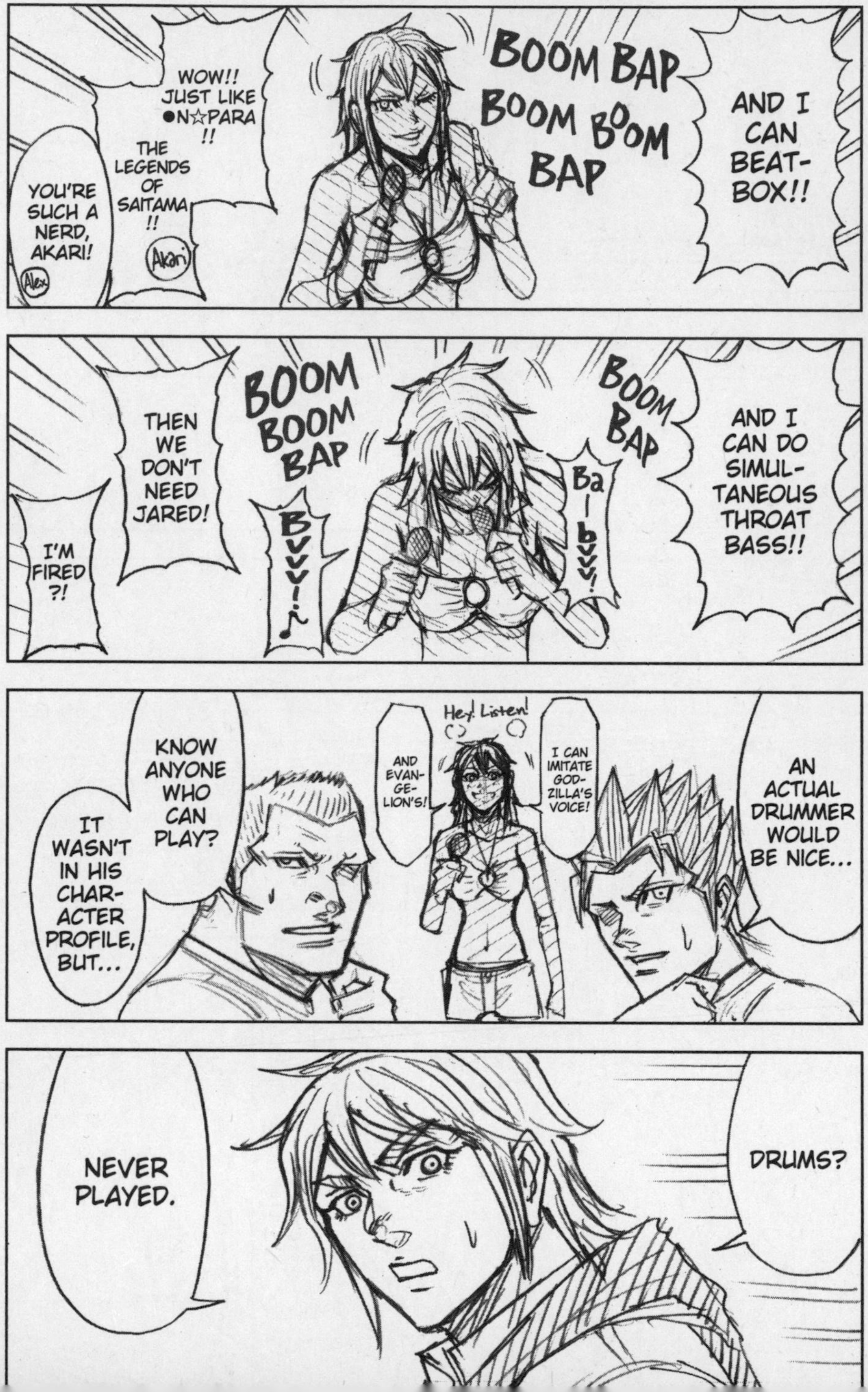
AND I CAN BEAT-BOX!!
BOOM BAP BOOM BOOM BAP
WOW!! JUST LIKE ●N☆PARA !!
THE LEGENDS OF SAITAMA !!
Akari
YOU'RE SUCH A NERD, AKARI!
Alex
AND I CAN DO SIMUL-TANEOUS THROAT BASS!!
BOOM BAP
Ba-bvvv!
BOOM BOOM BAP
Bvvv!♪
THEN WE DON'T NEED JARED!
I'M FIRED?!
AN ACTUAL DRUMMER WOULD BE NICE...
I CAN IMITATE GOD-ZILLA'S VOICE!
Hey! Listen!
AND EVAN-GE-LION'S!
KNOW ANYONE WHO CAN PLAY?
IT WASN'T IN HIS CHAR-ACTER PROFILE, BUT...
DRUMS?
NEVER PLAYED.

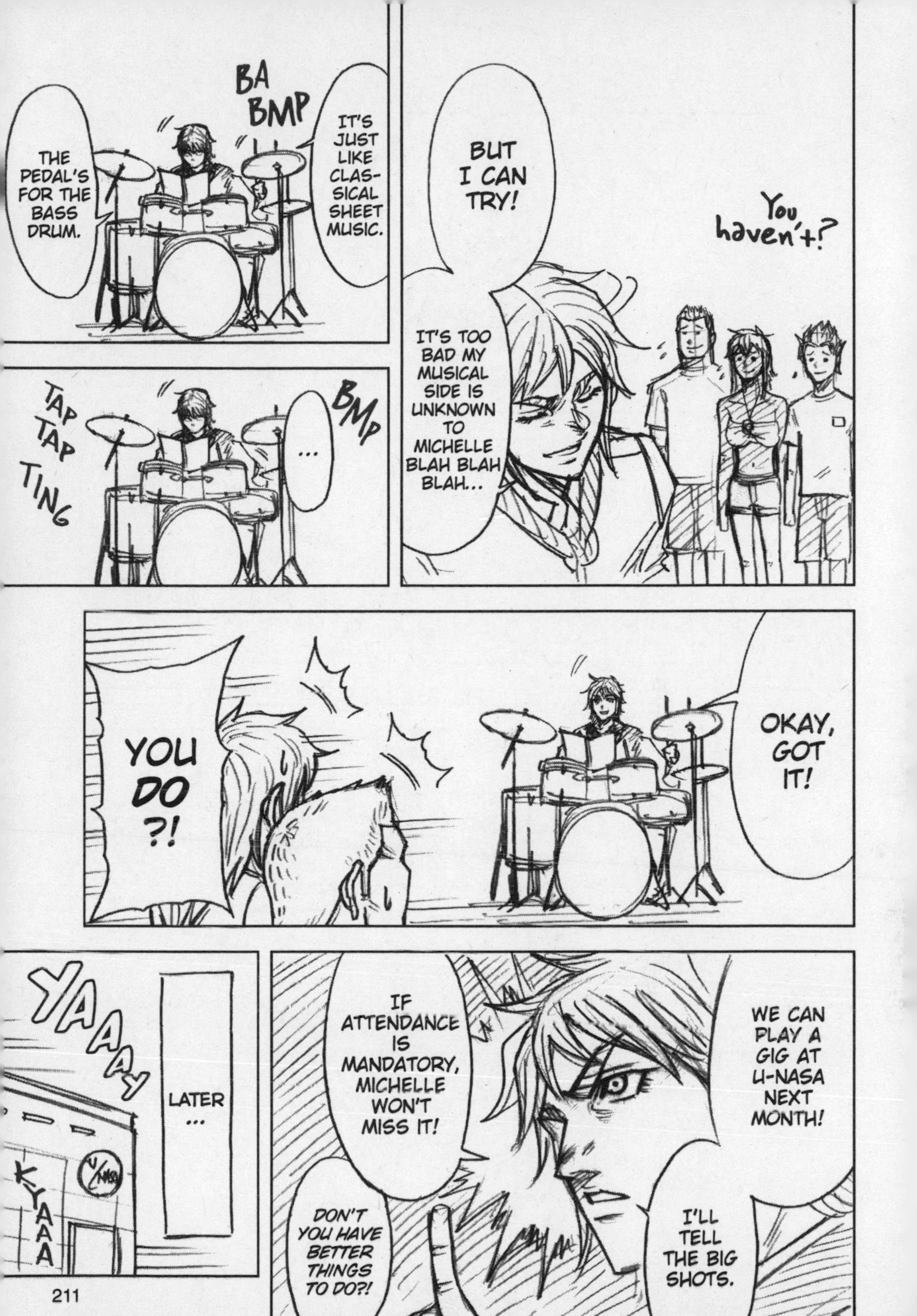
You haven't?
BUT I CAN TRY!
IT'S TOO BAD MY MUSICAL SIDE IS UNKNOWN TO MICHELLE BLAH BLAH BLAH...
BA BMP
IT'S JUST LIKE CLAS-SICAL SHEET MUSIC.
THE PEDAL'S FOR THE BASS DRUM.
BMP
...
TAP TAP TING
OKAY, GOT IT!
YOU DO ?!
WE CAN PLAY A GIG AT U-NASA NEXT MONTH!
IF ATTENDANCE IS MANDATORY, MICHELLE WON'T MISS IT!
I'LL TELL THE BIG SHOTS.
DON'T YOU HAVE BETTER THINGS TO DO?!
YAAAAY
LATER...
KYAAAA

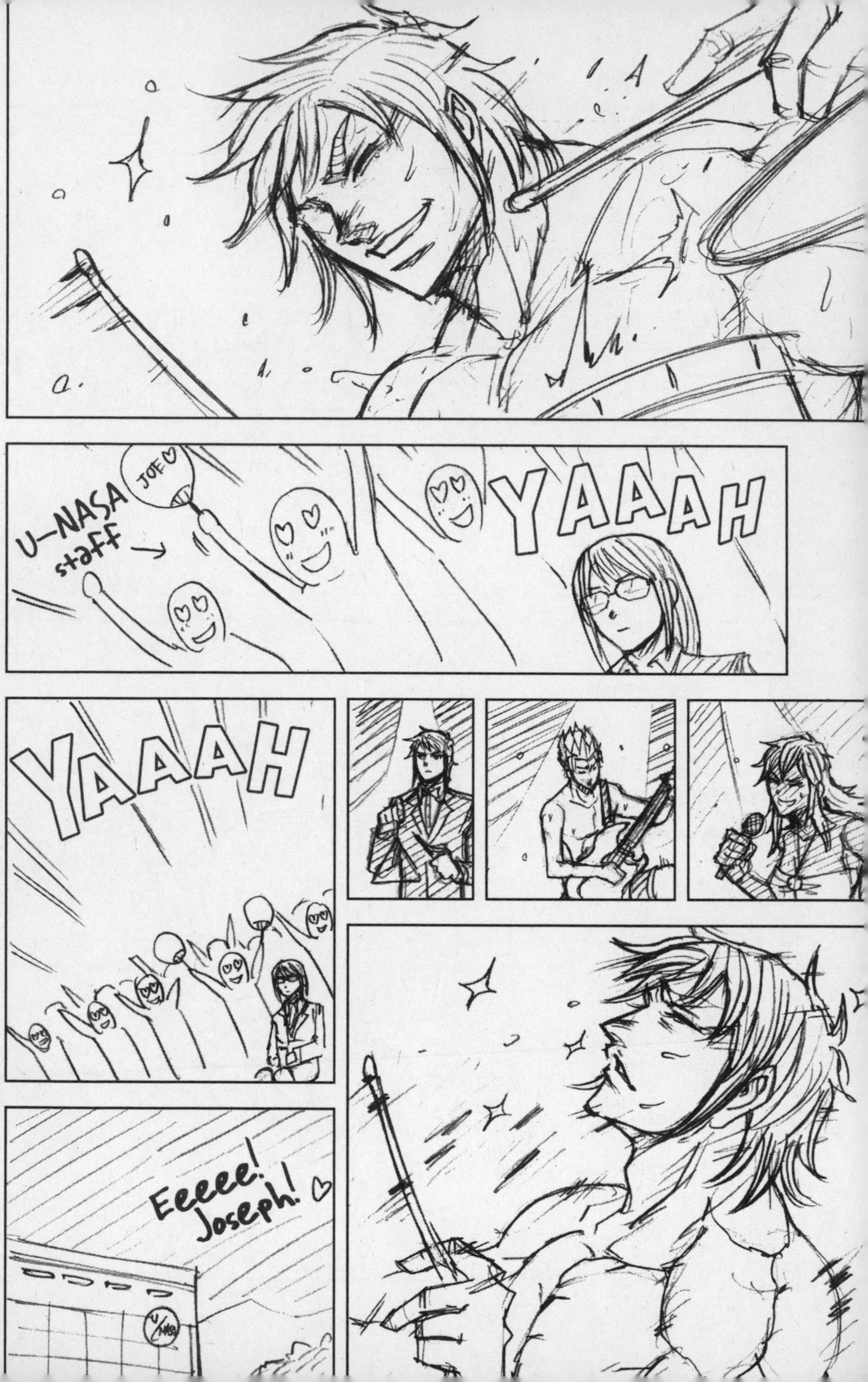
YAAAH
JOE♡
U-NASA staff
YAAAH
Eeeee! Joseph! ♡

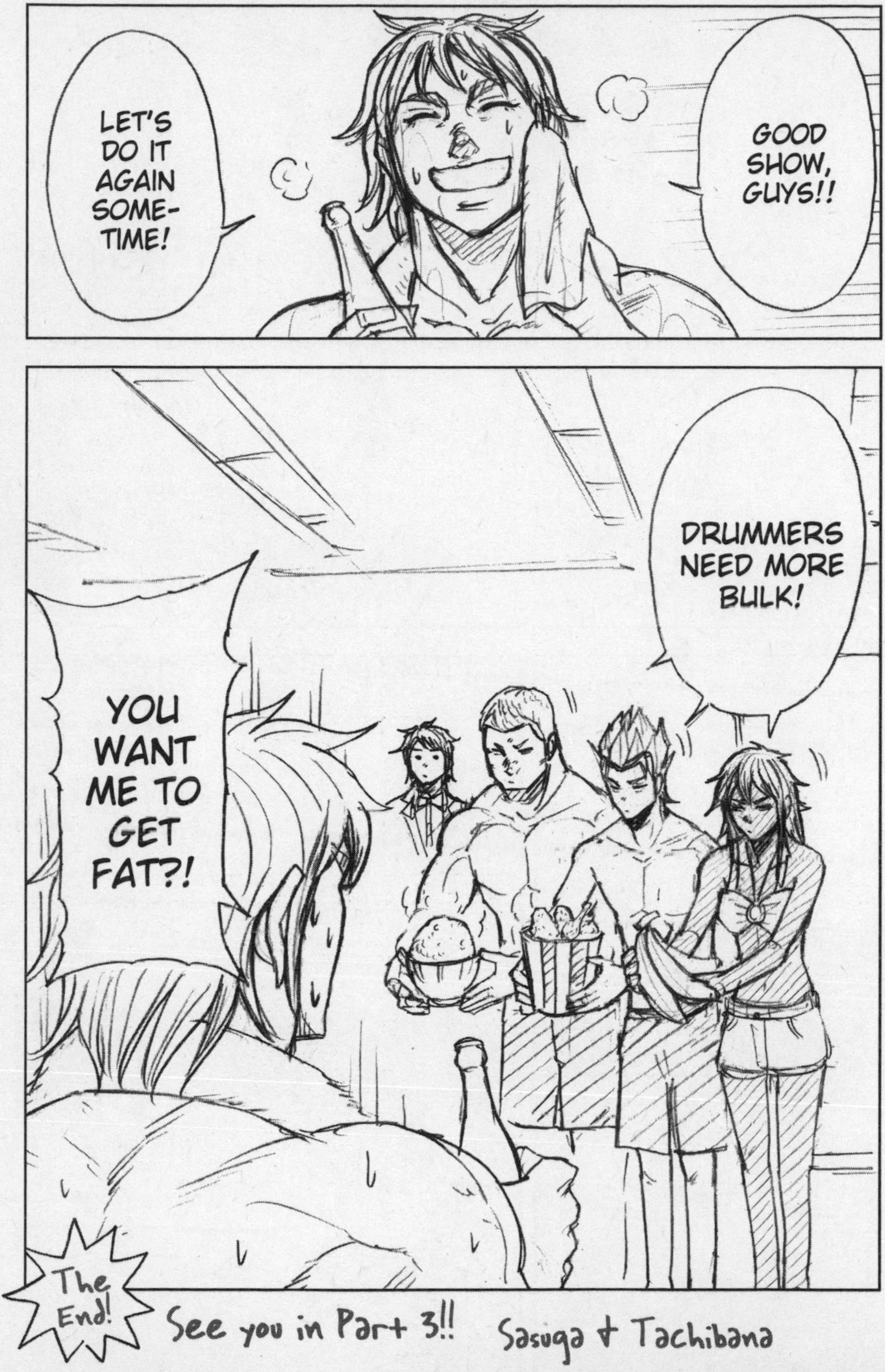
GOOD SHOW, GUYS!!
LET'S DO IT AGAIN SOME-TIME!
DRUMMERS NEED MORE BULK!
YOU WANT ME TO GET FAT?!

The End!

See you in Part 3!! Sasuga + Tachibana

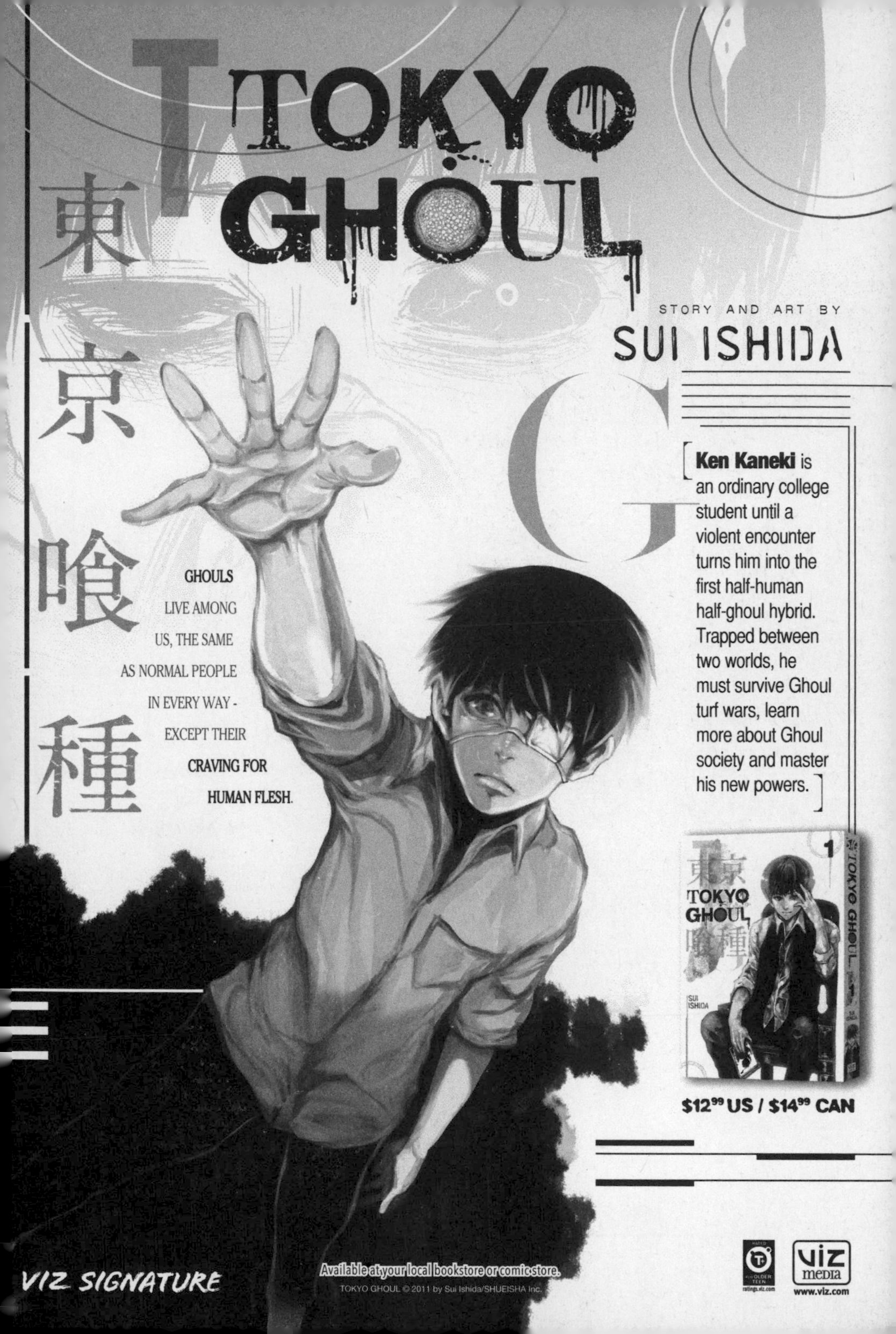
TOKYO GHOUL
東京喰種
STORY AND ART BY
SUI ISHIDA
GHOULS LIVE AMONG US, THE SAME AS NORMAL PEOPLE IN EVERY WAY - EXCEPT THEIR CRAVING FOR HUMAN FLESH.
Ken Kaneki is an ordinary college student until a violent encounter turns him into the first half-human half-ghoul hybrid. Trapped between two worlds, he must survive Ghoul turf wars, learn more about Ghoul society and master his new powers.
$12.99 US / $14.99 CAN
VIZ SIGNATURE
Available at your local bookstore or comic store.
TOKYO GHOUL © 2011 by Sui Ishida/SHUEISHA Inc.
viz media
www.viz.com

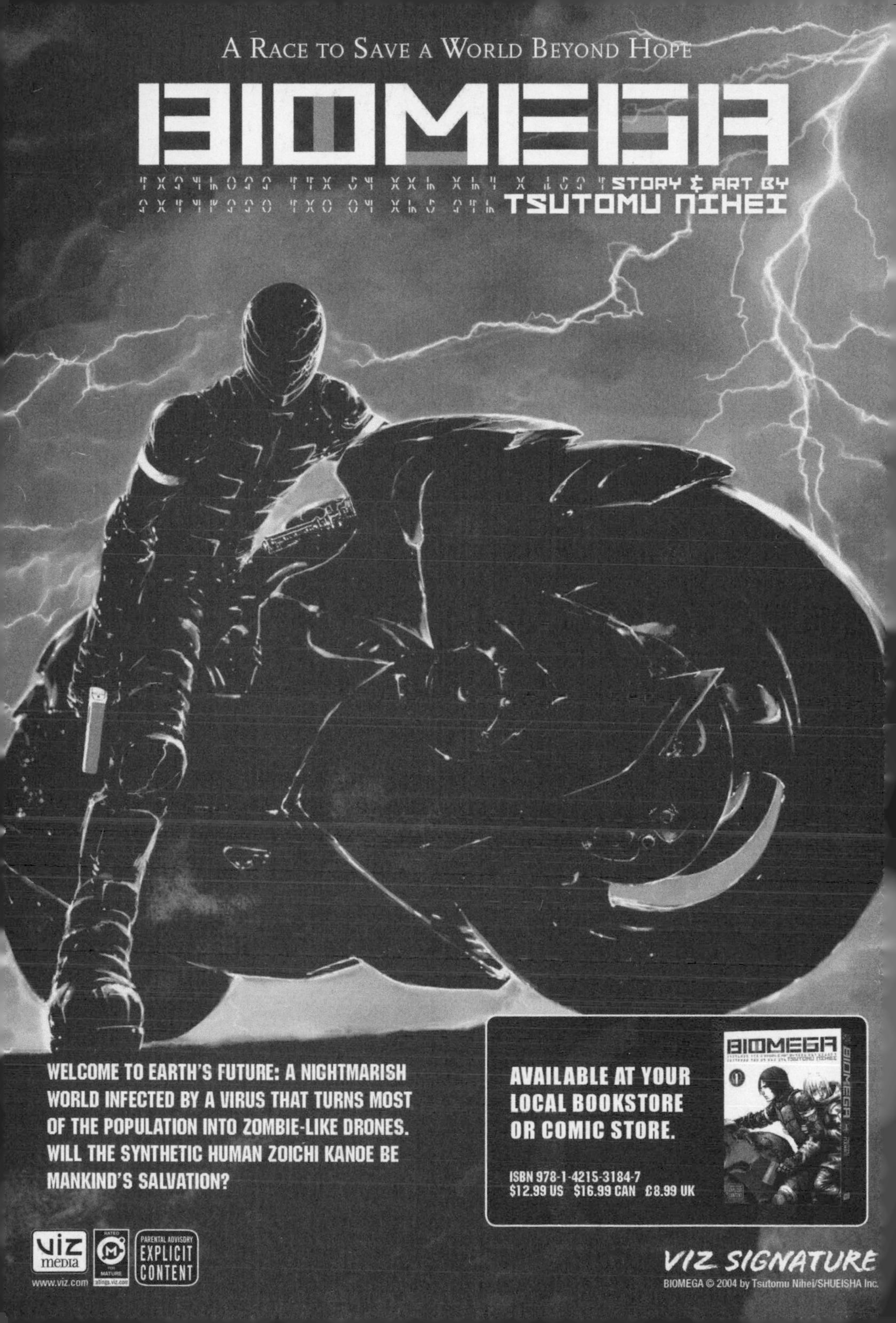
A RACE TO SAVE A WORLD BEYOND HOPE
BIOMEGA
STORY & ART BY
TSUTOMU NIHEI
WELCOME TO EARTH'S FUTURE: A NIGHTMARISH WORLD INFECTED BY A VIRUS THAT TURNS MOST OF THE POPULATION INTO ZOMBIE-LIKE DRONES. WILL THE SYNTHETIC HUMAN ZOICHI KANOE BE MANKIND'S SALVATION?
AVAILABLE AT YOUR LOCAL BOOKSTORE OR COMIC STORE.
ISBN 978-1-4215-3184-7
$12.99 US $16.99 CAN £8.99 UK
viz media
www.viz.com
RATED M FOR MATURE
ratings.viz.com
PARENTAL ADVISORY EXPLICIT CONTENT
VIZ SIGNATURE
BIOMEGA © 2004 by Tsutomu Nihei/SHUEISHA Inc.

TERRA FORMARS
Volume 17
VIZ Signature Edition

Story by YU SASUGA
Art by KENICHI TACHIBANA

TERRA FORMARS © 2011 by Ken-ichi Tachibana, Yu Sasuga/SHUEISHA Inc.
All rights reserved.
First published in Japan in 2011 by SHUEISHA Inc., Tokyo.
English translation rights arranged by SHUEISHA Inc.

Translation & English Adaptation/John Werry
Touch-up Art & Lettering/Annaliese Christman
Design/Izumi Evers
Editor/Mike Montesa

The stories, characters and incidents mentioned in this publication are
entirely fictional.

Printed in the U.S.A.

Published by VIZ Media, LLC
P.O. Box 77010
San Francisco, CA 94107

10 9 8 7 6 5 4 3 2 1
First printing, March 2017